OPEN ACCESS E-RESOURCES IN LIBRARY AND INFORMATION SCIENCE

Open Access E-resources in Library and Information Science

By

KAUSHAL CHAUHAN
R. K. MAHAPATRA

Ess Ess Publications
New Delhi

Open Access E-resources in Library and Information Science

ISBN: 978-81-7000-702-9

₹ 1550/-

First Published 2013

Published by:
Ess Ess Publications
4837/24, Ansari Road,
Darya Ganj,
New Delhi-110 002.
INDIA
Phones: 23260807, 41563444
Fax: 41563334
E-mail: info@essessreference.com
www.essessreference.com

Cover Design by *Patch Creative Unit*

Printed and bound in India at Salasar Imaging Systems.

Dedicated to

GOD

Param Pita Parmatma Shiv

Contents

Preface

Recent years have witnessed increasing role of Open Access E-Resources in every subject including Library and Information Science. The web has become popular publishing media because of technological advances. Evaluating information encourages one to think critically about the reliability, validity, accuracy, and authority of information sources. There has been a rapid urge of the user community to get more and more Information Online. Academic libraries facing shrinking budgets are trying to acquire quality Information Resources in the most efficient and effective means possible. This coupled with the positive attitudes. Academic libraries in India are in a transition period due to the economic environment and increase in price of electronic and print journals. Free Electronic Resources are also playing an important role in facilitating access. The users are aware of free electronic Information Sources and also the Internet. Most of them used these sources in support of their study and teaching. They are adept at using these sources, Even though a majority of the academic community uses electronic information sources for their academic related work. Now a day publishing industry is switching over from print media to electronic media. Most of the publishers offer their journals in electronic form. In the situation where both electronic and print versions are available, the users preferred to have both the versions equally and preferred to read.

The author has planned the entire work descriptions through five chapters. The first chapter Introduction deals with the background Electronic Publishing, Characteristics of free E-Resources, Advantages of free E-Resources, Types of free E-Resources. The second chapter presents the table of Structure of Open Access E-resources in LIS. Third chapter deals with Characteristics of E-Resources. Chapter Four presents the table of various Parameters covered by Open Access E-Resources.

Finally, Chapter Five provides Description of Open Access E-Resources. At the end of the book a detailed Bibliography has been cited Web References, books and other written materials consulted by the author in completion of book has been cited as a detailed Bibliography followed by glossary of the terms used often in the thesis. Besides that the researcher has also enclosed in the some of the list of E-Resources, in the appendices to avoid confusion by the users.

The aim of the book is to determine the overall structure and to examine whether Open Access E-Resources are available according to the accepted standards parameters and guidelines, as well as to discover the user interfaces of the systems.

In this modern digital era the E-Resources provide a new way to think about our user. Now day uses of E-Resources are not at the anticipated level due to lack of awareness about Open Access E-Resources and ineffective channels of communication. The book can be utilized by the students, teachers, researchers, scholars, philosophers and all other user Community to fulfill their information needs and can be useful for information scientists studying or working with portal-based retrieval of E-Journals, and also for the designers and developers of future online interactive IR systems.

List of Abbreviations/ Acronyms

ALHRT	American Library History Round Table
APAIS	Australian public affairs information service
APAIS	Australian Public Affairs Information Service, Info. Science Abstracts
ASIS&T	American Society for Information Science and Technology
CEPIE	China Education Publications Import & Export Corporation
CEPS	Chinese Electronic Periodicals Service
CINDOC	Centro de Information Documentation Científica
CNI	Coalition of network Information
CNRI	Corporation for National Research Initiatives
ECONIS	Economics Information System
EJISDC	The Electronic Journal of Information Systems in Developing Countries
ETAI	Electronic Transactions on Artificial
IASLIC	Indian Association Special Libraries and Information Centers

ICAAP	International Consortium for the Advancement of Academic Publication
ICAAP	International Consortium for the Advancement of academic Publication
ITAL	Information Technology and Libraries
JANET	Joint Academic Network
JISC	Joint Information Systems Committee (JISC)
JISC	Joint Information Systems Committee
LISTA	Library, Information Science & Technology Abstract
LITA	Library and Information Technology Association
LLIS	Library, information science & Technology Abstract
NISS	National Information Services
NSF	Corporation for National Research Initiatives
SPARC	Scholarly Publishing & Academic Resource coalition
SPI	Singapore Periodicals Index
SSL	Secure Sockets Layer
THCI	Taiwan Humanities Citation Index

1

Evaluation of Open Access Online E-Resources in LIS

1.1. INTRODUCTION

Open Access Online Information Sources can be access on internet without paying any subscription charges to the publishers and users do not need to have any membership in the organization. Users can access and download required information available on these sources in their computers and can use for their academic and research purpose. Since emergence of the web in 1990s, there has been a continuous increase in the volume of open access e-resources. These resources have provided a scope for researchers and authors in various subjects, Library and Information Science is no exception to this. Libraries have witnessed that Print medium are increasingly giving way to the electronic form of material. Use of Information Technology has marked a tremendous impact over the all functions and services catered by the traditional library and information professionals. Information sources in a given discipline are referred to as "Literature" that included all definitive sources of information. WWW is the best alternative medium to search for scholarly literature and to use web resources to support their research productivity. Recent past have witnessed a considerable growth in digital information resources like the traditional library system is transforming itself into hybrid information system having a mix of digital and traditional paper resources. The hi-tech development in science and technology coupled with information technology has led to the drastic change in the library and information product and services. The user community is becoming more familiar with the new medium over time and has started to actively bid for alternative forms of access. Technology improvement in the communication network paired with the decreasing cost of hardware, create greater incentives for innovation. Several traditional Journals are now being publishes both on the web and in print. Online subscription of E-Resources is becoming very popular now a day. Many of libraries are going on for such subscription.

Journals: The first International journal was "Le Journal des Scavans" 1665 and First Indian journal "Asiatic Researches" 1788. The initial peer reviewed journals were the philosophical transaction of royal society and Le Journal des Scavans both published in 1665. The coming of the 19th century saw an explosion in the number of journals produced, due to increased specialization and diversification of academic research and also evolution of means of mass publishing. This massive increase in output meant that the societies found it more and more difficult to keep up. Although there had been some commercial publishers around before (Elsevier Scientific Publishing) was publishing engineering journals as far back as 1884. It was Gutenberg's invention of printing press in the 15th century was a great leap towards information dissemination, and then the invention of World Wide Web is equally a great leap towards electronic scholarly communication. The arrival of electronic publishing is the fourth revolution in the means of production of knowledge after spoken language, written language, and the printing press. Although information in electronic format was created with the advent of the computer in the 1950s, by 1960s, Commercial publishers had occupied a major part of the market, The first prototype e-journal was during 1990 to 1995, mainly dominated by non-profit making groups who were exploited the technology of their own sake.

Internet: The Internet is one of the most important and complex innovations in human history, the largest and most complete tool for information exchange ever made available to the global population. Recognizing the value of connecting computer centers for all kinds of readers, the university community created it's on Internet work in 1981. The growth of the Internet is exponential and the addition of more computer networks and computers is happening at a rapid speed. Since more people gaining access to the Internet, It is becoming more and more useful by providing additional information and resources, which are interconnected to each other for the purpose of sharing information. It offers a variety of services for the users of the whole globe, Hence it is referred to as Global Network.

Over the last few years, Internet has revolutionized the ways by which librarians can provide information sources and services to their users. The use of Internet in the libraries is rapidly increasing and is changing the traditional functions and services of the libraries as well as role of the librarians. Internet is being used as an efficient medium for accessing storing and disseminating of information worldwide and access to various useful paid as well as free information sources and services such as online databases, library catalogue, publisher catalogue, electronic journals, online encyclopedia, online dictionaries, e-books, e-conference, virtual libraries, websites of organization, etc. With the advent of Computer, Networking, Internet, it is possible to access information sources form anywhere at any time. Many digital libraries, publishers and organizations provide access to their online information sources and are available on other networks due to developments in ICT. Authors and publishers are also much in favor of making available their articles online for free, because studies have shown that online accessibility of article have dramatically increased their citation, increasing the journal's impact factor and the author's prestige.

World Wide Web: WWW has propelled sufficiently high growth rate in usage of E-Resources. The WWW or w3 or simply the web is one of the most popular facilities for the user on the network. Various software programs known as web browsers are used to seek these documents and display them on the user's local computer. These documents may reside on diffident locations. HTML documents of web pages may contain many different forms of information. These documents are available in various web pages and web sites and they are accessed through links provided by hypertext documents. In this way, the WWW is by far the most heavily used application on the Internet. It is many things to its millions of users. WWW is a network of more than 20,000 networks linking more than 4 million computers and over 30 million users and in nearly 160 countries, they are located at universities, scientific research establishments, institutions, and commercial organizations. The resources can be accessed by a library and can be made available to users. One can increase the user libraries by providing valuable information of the library holdings through Internet. Therefore, each and every library should be attached with Internet.

1.2. ELECTRONIC RESOURCECS

An "electronic resource" is defined as any work encoded and made available for access through the use of a computer. It includes both online data and electronic data in physical formats (e.g., CD-ROM). To avoid confusion with these terms as used in the copyright process, online will refer to intangible works; physical to a tangible work. The term "acquire" refers to any electronic resource, online or physical, which the Library receives through its various, typical acquisitions processes, or which the Library provides access to through official contractual, licensed, or other agreements; any of these electronic resources may or may not be owned by or housed at the Library. "Collect" refers to electronic resources owned by the Library and selected for the permanent collection, including works created by the Library. It may also include works stored elsewhere for which the Library has permanent ownership rights. "Link" refers to pointers from the Library's internet resources or bibliographic records to the Library and non-Library electronic resources, created and maintained by Library staff for a variety of purposes; "link" is not an act of acquiring, and electronic resources linked do not necessarily constitute an acquisition by the Library. There has been a continuous increase in the value of scholarly resources in electronic form such as e-books, e-journals, e-database, e-thesis and dissertations, e-prints of research papers and the like. Electronic publishing become more than a novelty. E-Resources are now emerging as vital somas of information for all recent and nascent thought and ideas coming in to existence in whatever area of research. Whole books and periodicals have started appearing in digitized forms i.e. on CD Disk and others. Internet and www have provided a platform to display these resources globally.

E-Resources can be any E-Journal, E-Zine, E-Newsletter, E-Books, E-Database E-Thesis and Dissertations. Internet information resources can be defined as resources in digital format that provide information or indicator to the information and are accessible over the Internet. Online availability of information enables the user to get relevant information and acquaint with latest development taking place in their respected fields. Electronic journals is a digital periodical dedicated to publishing on the Internet, articles, essays, and analysis that have been read and commented upon initially by a select group of editors and reviewers, to meet a certain standard of excellence for a given discipline addressed by the journal itself. Electronic Journals are full text or abstracts of journals articles available electronically on the Internet or CD-ROMs (Vakauskas). E-Journals are nothing but, Electronic Versions of printed journals that can be viewed online via any PC connected to the Internet.

1.2.1. Purpose of E-Resources

1. Main purpose of electronic resources is providing current information.
2. Update information is necessary for research work.
3. Through electronic resources users are able to access latest information.
4. Save the time of user and staff
5. Solve the space problem in library
6. Easy to use and disseminate

1.2.2. Need of E-Resources

Electronic resources have great potential and bright future to attract users. It combines all the benefits of the multimedia, digital coding and Internet. It enable user to carry everywhere and can be read on all types of computers including handled device.

1. E- Resources can be downloaded instantly.
2. Users can read an e- resource any time
3. Due to portability, E-Resources can be taken any where on portable computer.
4. Font size can be changed suitably;
5. E- resources provide facility to hold and turn pages easily
6. Physically disabled users can hear audible E- resources
7. In buying E- resources, the overhead charges like shipping, postal, handling are totally ruled out
8. Some E- resources are interactive
9. E- Resources have background music and animations.
10. E- resources do not require bindery and repair
11. E- resources save human resources for shelving and rectification
12. User can not misplace e- books

1.2.3. Features of E-Resources

1. Text can be searched, except when represented in the form of images;
2. Hundreds or thousands may be carried together on one device. Approximately 500 average e-books can be stored on one CD;
3. Type size and type face may be adjusted
4. E- Resources can be used with text-to-speech software;
5. Distributed at low cost;
6. Distributed instantly, allowing readers to begin reading at once, without the need to visit a bookstore.
7. No risk of damage, vandalism, etc. on the pages

1.2.4. Benefits of E-Resources

Accessibility and Availability: Rapid advances in ICT have resulted in researchers being able to access information resources from all over the world.

Cost Effective: The cost of electronic journals is decreased because of eradication of paper, printing, postage etc. as compared to printed journals. The tough competition among the publishers; entry of new publishers in the field; availability of E-Journals in public domain; emergence of digital libraries; consortia arrangements of the libraries at local, regional, national and even international level, the electronic journals are cost effective.

Better Storage and Retrieval: Digitally available information has eradicated the problems like- binding, shelving, storage, maintenance etc. and gives opportunity for better retrieval.

Time saving: The time is saved in terms of digitally submission of research work to the publishers, the same is sent for peer review, selected rejected or return to authors for necessary amendments in electronic form and finally by providing the electronic access to the libraries.

Excellent Searching Techniques: The user can search the information by using and, or, not, between, up to, after etc.

phrases. The publishers provide hyperlinks to connect the related work.

Multi-user Access: This is a wonderful gift of electronic publication that by subscribing the electronic journals, books databases etc. many users can access the same material at the same time from different places connected through intranet/ internet.

Self-Publishing: Electronic publication made it possible for the individuals to publish their own work by exploring the World Wide Web. The individual can sought the suggestions from experts in the field and can distribute the publication to his friends and colleagues just Free of cost. Web presents an attractive mode for electronic publishing. People having the knowledge of hypertext markup language (html) can contribute in publishing research material on web. Now scientists make use of Electronic Publishing to communicate their research work with the colleagues, experts, coauthor, collaborator, editors, publishers and other professionals.

Use of Multimedia Technology: It is the beauty of Electronic Publishing that the text material may be provided with audio and visual support for making the text more presentable and effective. It is possible with the help of multimedia technology. The use of multimedia technology in electronic publishing leads to better information quality and better utilization of information resources.

1.2.5. Characteristics of E-Resources

- Potentially huge
- Unorganized
- Comprehensive of everything
- Do not require Physical Space
- Feasibility in Full content search ability
- Constraints that are in physical libraries are barred in E-Resources Time
- Space and Cost constraints are not a problem in Search strategies

- Hyperlinks lead the users quickly to the required information sources
- Easy in archiving the content
- E-Resources need not place like printed documents
- They may be accessed at very low price
- Any revision and correction can easily be done in them
- More than one person can read e-documents at the same time
- The man anywhere can get his required information from e-documents

1.2.6. Advantages of E-Resources

- Searching of e-resource is more easy and speedy then traditional resource.
- Users can quickly build a bibliography, which they use.
- To access the same topic having various ways to get it and can get cross references for further search
- Publishers frequently update E-Resources, so everyone can get up to date information.
- Mainly E-Resources can use from remote access.
- More than one user can use it simultaneously.
- Collections of E-Resources save physical storage space of the library.
- Do not require physical processing for E-Resources like printed document that is a vast task and time consuming.
- It is easy to download, Copy, Save and Print or send by e-mail.
- User can search by different search engines to get more and more information.

Moreover Open Access E-Resources have numerous advantage such as Portability, Instant Access, Search ability, Annotation, Linking, and Multimedia Long term preservation of the material, Multiple titles in single book, Online Dictionary, Link to other sites, Old titles cannot go out-of print, Readers can add several chapters from several books, Update text books minimal cost, Low publishing cost, Low distribution cost, Paper saving, Physical Space saving.

1.2.7. Types of Free E-Resources

- E-Databases
- E-Books
- E-Magazines
- Newsletters and Other E-Resources
- E-Thesis and Dissertation
- Electronic News Papers
- E-Reference books
- CD-ROM
- E-Journals

1.3. OPEN ACCESS ONLINE E-RESOURCES:

"Digitized material offered freely and openly to educate students and independent learners to use and reuse for teaching, learning and research the best thing about the future is that it comes only one day at a time."

Term coined in 2002 in UNESCO Forum on impact of Open Courseware for Higher Education in Developing countries. The selection of Open access E-Resources as part of collection developments is activity practiced by many libraries. With the introduction and popularity of Internet, most of the commercial, govt., educational and research organizations/bodies/institutions have developed their own websites and provide latest and useful information including publications. Therefore these websites can be useful for researchers who always require the latest information. Some electronic journals are only online journals, some are online versions of printed journals and some consist of online equivalent of print journals. An increase number of journals are now available as online open access journals, requiring no subscription and offering free full text article and reviews to all. The resources of library, which is available, Free of cost in electronic form or digital form called Free E-Resources. E-Resources are defined as those electronic information resources and service that users can access freely electronically via a computer network from inside library and or outside library. Now we have the emergence of publications over the electronic networks following the invention of the World Wide Web. The open Access Movement is becoming the order of the day. A number of Free E-Resources archive has thrown a challenge to the publishing industry. Electronic resources are publicly available free of charge with a Free browsing simply open the search engine. Open any link and you will get the required Information, If you want to save this link just copy the link and save it in ms word document and make its hyperlinks. This is more beneficial for the persons who need Information and can afford subscribe of paid journals.

1.4. E-JOURNALS

E-Journals are Electronic versions of printed journals that can be viewed online via any PC connected to the Internet. Information Technology has made it possible to access online many of the research journals. Now a day E-Journals become a major information resource for each and every discipline. E-Journals play a vital role for scientific research and development. E-Journals may be defined as any journal, available over the Internet in electronic format. These are accessed through Gopher, FTP, Telnet and e-mail or discussion list. It was until the early 1960s that the first Database suitable for searching was developed. MEDLARS were the first on demand computer based information retrieval service. In 1971, MEDLINE, the online version of MEDLARS, was the first major online dial-up database search service. In the following year, DIALOG offered first public online commercial online database. The technology of the 1980's namely CD-ROM technologies help a lot in electronic publishing. The E-Journals are otherwise called "Virtual Journal". The Virtual Journals are the focus of attention because of the rising cost of conventional pricing coupled with the failing price of electronic equipments and the vast capabilities of the emerging technologies. The introduction of the CD-ROM for the electronic resource began to have a major impact on selection practice in library. The purchase of these equipments as a part of cost of the information product was not always easy. Only one person could use CD- ROM Databases at a time, a major drawback, specially their high cost. Alternate was to purchase the needed database on magnetic tape and mount it on local computer system which could provide simultaneous access to many users. This however was very expensive solution and one that most libraries could not afford. Gradually hardware and software solutions were found that allowed several users to access the same CD-ROM database simultaneously. Some libraries even found ways to provide access to CD-ROM products to sites outside of the library.

Internet based electronic journals started to appear in the beginning of 1990. Publishers were also becoming too experiment with different approaches to publishing journals electronically. By 1993, there were more than 3,000 titles available in E-format. The commercial publishers joined in around 1996 and are now dominant, mainly with direct electronic copies of their print journals. These Journals were mostly delivered as an attachment to e-mail while their back issues were mounted on anonymous ftp sites and users were required to download them from these ftp sites. The Libraries and Information Centers made these E-Resources accessible through their gopher sites with the advent of www technology. Electronic journals are also known as E-Journals, Electronic Serials and scholarly journals or intellectual magazines that can be accessed via Electronic Transmission. In practice, this means that they are usually published on the web, in a specialized form of electronic document, for purpose of providing materials for academic research and are formatted approximately like journal article in traditional printed journals. Being in electronic form, articles usually contain metadata that can be entered in to specialized databases, such as DOAJ, as well as the databases and search engines for the academic discipline concerned.

Electronic journal is a serial, produced, published and distributed in electronic media. They don't require time-consuming printing and mailing process. Many publishers offer free access to their online journals. Generally they are full text delivery systems and differ from conventional bibliographic databases online. All the activities of publishing from the initial stages of paper submission to publishing and distribution including accessing are performed using electronic media. Electronic journal saves considerable time and effort on the part of authors, users and publishers. E-Journals involves the process of writing editing referring and distribution of information electronically through telecommunication networks where the information is stored digitally and made accessible through network.

Three types of electronic journals are available:

Online E-Journal: These types of E-Journals are available through online hosts such as DIALOG etc. These are basically the online versions of the print journals

CD E-Journal's ROM E-Journals are usually full text of individual or collected journals in a variety of subjects. These are full text journals published and distributed on CD-ROM media periodically

Network E-Journal: Network based e-journal is based on mailing software or client/server computer applications includes www and gopher. First generation of e-journal is ASCII text files and either HTML or www to disseminate specially formatted files. These are networked electronic journals published and distributed via the Internet.

1.4.1. Advantages of Electronic Journals

Speed: Articles can be put on the Web as soon as they are ready, without having to wait may be months for a space in a journal issue. This all means that the information is much more

up-to-date than can be achieved.

Easily searchable : Search ability is one of the core advantages of a digital format. Hitchcock et al. (1998) argue that the easier it is to find research, the fewer duplicated experiments there will be, resulting in less wasted time. However, Missingham (1999) raises the problem of information overload, with information easier to find, there will be much more to read and keep up-to-date with.

Interactive : Articles can be read, commented on by the journal's readers, and amended much more quickly than can be done with print. The ease with which e-mail can be sent, or forms filled in means that there can be much greater **feedback** through the Web.

Accessible : Several people can read an issue at once and also different layers of access can be given to different people with little extra effort.

Links : Links are the mainstay of the hypertext format, and should be exploited. Not only can papers link to those they have cited, but with a bit of effort, they can be linked to those that cite them.

Added value : There are various advantages of Web to add value, for example by using animation, virtual reality and interactive mathematical charts and also a large amount of supporting data can be linked to from the article if the reader wanted to look more deeply into the results.

Inexpensive : There are 100% saving in Open Access E-Resources over print costs.

Flexibility : E-Journals being able to evolve quickly as they are not tied to a format, printer or distribution network.

E-Magazines : An online magazine is a magazine that is delivered in an electronic form. An online magazine may be online-only, or may be the online version. E-Zine means electronic magazine and it is also called web- Zine. The articles that are stored of a file server may be distributed or accessed via a computer network.

Newsletters and Other E-Resources : Newsletters are provided to give you direct access to the information in which you are most interested and Other E-Resources includes Bulletins, Reviews etc.

2

Structure of Open Access Online E-Resources in Library and Information Science

Table 4

	Title/URL	Authority/ Publisher/ Editor/ Country	Scope/ Coverage/ Purpose	Searching/ accessibility / Network-ability/ Browse-bility	For mat	Treatment/ Accuracy/ Objectivity	Arrange ment	Archiving/ Periodicity	Special Features/ Index
1	African Journal of Information &	Faculty of Science,	Computing, electronic	Simple click on Issue	Pdf	Material on all aspects of the	Arranged Volume	Vol. 1, 1 (2005)-	It is indexed,

	Communication Technology http://epress.lib.uts.edu.au/journals/index.php/ajict/index	Technology and Engineering La Trobe University Kingsbury Drive, Bundoora Victoria Australia	communications and information technology systems.	Title.		design, implementation, use and management of computer and communication.	wise.	V. 6 (1) 2011 V. 7, 1, 2013 is not open access	Peer Reviewed and Provides Personalize features
2	Agricultural Libraries Information Notes http://webharvest.gov/peth04/20041023101316/http://www.nal.usda.gov/NewAlin/	National Agricultural Library	Library Science	Simple click on Issue Title.	html	Almost all the aspects of Library and Information science.	Arranged by Volume and Number.	V-20, 1-12, 1994- v. 23, 1-12, 1997	
3	ALAN Review http://scholar.lib.vt.edu/ejournals/ALAN/	DLA, Virginia Tech, Virginia, US	YA literature and its teaching, interviews with authors, reports on publishing	Simple click on Issue Title.	Pdf & Html	Made up of teachers, authors, librarians, publishers, teacher-educators and their	Arranged by Year	Vol. 21, 2, Winter 1994-v. 38, 1, Fall 2010	Prior to Vol. 31, 1 Fall 2003, issues were only

			trends, current research			students, and others who are particularly interested in the area of young adult literature Focus on Manuscript, Library connections etc			available in HTML format.
4	Alki: The Washington Library Association Journal http://www.wla.org/alki/	Washington Library Association, Washington	Library Science, Information Science, Information Management	Simple click on issue title. Internal search engine has been given	pdf	Purpose is to communicate philosophical and substantive analyses of current and enduring issues for and about Washington libraries, personnel and advocates and to facilitate the exchange of research, opinion and information.	Arranged by Volume, Number & Year.	Vol.13, 2-3, July 1997-v. 28, 3. July 2012	Issue indexing has been done. Some issue is not opening full text.
5	American Archivist http://archivists.	Society of American Archivists	Provides a forum for discussion of trends and issues	Simple click on Issue Title.	Pdf	Peer-reviewed research articles, case studies, in-	Arranged by Volume	Vol. 1, 1-4, 1938-V.75, 1-2, 2012	Quarterly journal available

	metapress.com/home/main.mpx		in archival theory and practice, and presents current research			depth perspectives, and international scene papers address a wide variety of topics, such as digitization and digital preservation, electronic records, selection and appraisal, description and cataloging, reference and public services, preservation.	and Number.		with alerts
6	Annals of Library & Information Studies http://nopr.niscair.res.in/	NISCAIR, New Delhi India	Emphasis on analytical study of Indian Journals	Simple click on Issue Title. Internal search is given.	Pdf	Includes Knowledge management, Research Aptitudes, bibliography, citation indexes etc.	Arranged Volume-wise	Vol. 49, 2002-V. 57 2010	Available Quarterly in NISCAIR repository
7	Australian Journal of	University of the Sunshine	A forum for and about library	Simple click on Issue	E-Text	Include research articles, conference	Arranged Volume	Vol.1, 1-2, 1994-v.17, 3,	Author and Title

	Information Systems http://dl.acs.org.au/index.php/ajis/about	Coast, Australia	support staff issues.	Title.	and html	information, development activities, work procedures, resource sharing, opinions	wise.	2012	indexing has been done. AJIS is an international quality, peer reviewed journal
8	Australian Academic and Research Libraries http://www.alia.org.au/publishing/aarl/index.html	Australian Library and Information Association, Australia	High quality contributions to the global Information Systems (IS) discipline with an emphasis on theory and practice on the Australian context	Simple click on Issue Title.	Pdf	IS theory development and application, information and knowledge, formal representations of the world, the interaction of people, organizations and information technologies; the analysis, design and deployment of information systems; the	Arranged by Year and Volume	Vol. 32, 1-4, 2001-v. 41, 1-4, 2010. (42, 2012 & 43 2013 is not open access)	Abstracted or indexed in *Australian education index, Australian library and information science abstracts, APAIS, Information science abstracts, Library and*

						impacts of information systems on individuals, organizations and society			*information science abstracts*, and *Library literature*. Peer-refereed.
9	Australian Library Journal http://alia.org.au/publishing/alj/	Australian Library and Information Association, Australia	Contains a wide coverage of Australian library issues ranging from ongoing research to day-to-day news from the workplace.	Simple click on Issue Title	html	Acknowledged flagship publication and an appropriate vehicle for publishers, suppliers and services wishing to reach the decision-makers.	Arranged Volume and year wise.	Vol. 48, Nov, Aug May, Feb. 1999-v. 59, (1-4) Feb., May, Aug, Nov. 2010.	Quarterly, 2011 and 2012 are available in print to subscribers only
10	B Sides http://ir.uiowa.edu/bsides/	University of Iowa, School of Library and Information Science, United States	Including writing, images, posters, presentation slides, audio recordings, and videos.	Simple click on Issue Title & Internal search engine	Pdf	Provides a space for current students and alumni to converse about their work and contribute to the scholarly literature of Library and Information	Arranged in Spring, Fall, Summer, Winter	2010-2013	ISSN-2155-6687 and Peer Reviewed

						Science.			
11	Chinese Librarianship: An International Electronic Journal http://www.iclc.us/cliej/	Publishes in various electronic channels, United States	Facilitating information exchange among librarians and information professionals worldwide and focuses on both practical and theoretical aspects of the Chinese librarianship.	Simple click on Issue Title on Author, Title, and Web index	E-Text	Publishes research findings, theoretical explorations, and case studies by librarians, information scientists, library school faculty and students of Chinese heritage, as well as by librarians and information professionals of other nationalities on issues related to serving patrons with Chinese materials and major development of the Chinese librarianship.	Author, title and web Indexing have been done and arranged Issue number-wise.	No.1June 1996-No.36 Dec. 2013 Half Yearly	Peer reviewed and Indexed in Ebsco's Library, Information Science & Technology Abstracts (LISTA), Wislon's Library and Information Science Index (LISI), CSA's Library and Information Science Abstracts (LISA);

									Listed in Ulrich's and Cabell's
12	Christian Library Journal http://www.christianlibraryj.org/pdf/index.htm	Nancy L. Hesch Christian Library Services	Covers all subjects from picture books for little ones through in depth nonfiction for adults, fiction and other literature for all ages.	Simple click on Issue Title	Pdf	Cover all nonfiction subjects, as well as fiction, picture books, fairy and folk tales, and poetry and drama. Build library collection in the Christian school, international school, home school, or church using the core collection	Arranged Volume-wise.	Oct. 1995- Oct/Dec 2010. v. XVI, No 1-2, 2012,	Provides personalize features
13	Cites & Insights: Crawford at Large http://citesandinsights.info/citoc.htm	Author, editor, and publisher is Walt Crawford and sponsored by YBP Library Services	A Web-based journal of libraries, policy, technology, and media.	Simple click on Issue Title	E-Text	Walt Crawford's commentary and annotated citations of selected articles on library and computer related issues.	Articles are arranged Volume wise.	Vol.6, Jan - Dec 2006- v.13, April 2013	Current plan: At least 12 issues each year

14	Code4Lib Journal http://journal.code4lib.org/	Code4Lib, Editor: Carol Bean, North County Regional Library, Country: United States	Foster community and share information among those interested in the intersection of libraries, technology, and the future.	Simple click on Issue Title. Internal search engine have given.	E-Text	Helps Libraries in computer technology, using computers and the Internet to offer unprecedented access to information and library resources. C4LJ aims to help engender collective understanding and the necessary support for improving library technology and digital services.	Arranged Issue wise.	Issue 1, 2007-Issue 19, 2013	
15	Colby Quarterly (formerly: Colby Library Quarterly) http://digitalcommons.colby.edu/cq/	Powered by the press	A forum both for publicizing Colby's rare books and manuscripts and for literary discussion.	Simple click on Issue Title	Pdf	Published lists and descriptions of books and manuscripts recently acquired by the Special Collections department of the	Arranged by Volume and Number.	Vol.32, 3-4, 1996 v. 39, 1-4, 2003	The Quarterly, then named the Colby Library Quarterly published

						Colby College Library. Articles included examinations of and excerpts from collections of manuscript correspondence.			from 1943 to 2003
16	Collaborative Librarianship http://www.collaborativelibrarianship.org/index.html	Regis University	Library cooperation, Sharing, International collaboration, professional, consortium	Simple click on Issue Title	Pdf	Improving access to and delivery of information resources. Developing a system of sustainable ongoing resources. Enhancing human resource development. Considering what is good for Colorado.	Arranged by Vol & N.	Vol.1, 1-4, 2009- v43, 4, 2012	Link to collaborative Librarianship News has been given.
17	College and Research Libraries	American Library Association, Chicago	Library Science, Information Science, Information	Simple click on Issue Title.	Pdf	Latest trends and practices affecting academic and research libraries	Arranged Issue-wise.	Vol. 1, (1), 1939-v. 74, 1, Nov 2013	Vol.69, 6 not open access.

	http://crl.acrl.org/		Management			and official news magazine			
18	Communications in Information Literacy http://www.comminfolit.org/index.php/cil/issue/archive	University of Oklahoma.	Dedicated to advancing knowledge, theory, and research in information literacy.	Simple click on Issue Title	Pdf	An independent, professional, refereed electronic journal dedicated to advancing knowledge, theory, and research in information literacy. Committed to the principles of information literacy as set forth by the Association of College and Research Libraries and to the principles of open access for academic research	Arranged Volume-wise and Information for Author, Librarian and Readers has been given.	Vol.1, 1-2, 2007-v.6, 2, 2012	Available in OJS. and indexed in Directory of Open Access Journals, EBSCO (Library, Information Science & Technology Abstracts), Elsevier Science (SCOPUS), Google Scholar, H.W. Wilson (Library

									Literature & Information Science Full Text), Proquest (Library Science)
19	Computer and Information Science http://journal.ccsenet.org/index.php/cis/index	Canadian Center of Science	Focus on computer, information science, e-business, internet, electronic	Simple click on Issue Title and Internal search engine with search tips has been given.	Pdf	Publishes research papers in the fields of computer, information science, e-business, and internet, electronic and relevant subjects.	Arranged Volume wise.	Vol.1, 1-4, 2008-v. 6, 2, 2013	Peer Reviewed and Indexed in DOAJ, PKP, J-Gate, LOCKSS etc.
20	Coordinates: Online Journal of the Map and Geography Round Table of the American Library	The Map and Geography Round Table (MAGERT) of the American Library Association	Series A focus on Original, peer-reviewed articles. Series B focuses on Essays, project reports, technical notes,	Simple click on Issue Title	Html & Pdf	Articles are on a wide range of subjects relating to maps and GIS. Target audience is primarily users and curators of maps	Arranged Issue-wise.	Series A: N. 1-9 28 May 2005- March 2010 and Series B: N.1 Jan 2005- No 9, 20 Aug	Irregular and indexed in The Directory of Open Access

	Association. Series A and B http://www.sunysb.edu/libmap/coordinates.htm	produce and publish; Editor is David Y. Allen, United States	republished articlesand other materials of interest to the cartographic community. Series B Focus on			and articles include map and GIS librarianship, history of cartography, map cataloging and bibliography, map reading and interpretation, new developments in online mapping, and other subjects of interest to a broad spectrum of cartographically literate readers.		2009	Journals
21	Current Cites http://lists.webjunction.org/currentcites/	Hosted by the Community at WebJunction. org. Editor:Roy Tennant, USA	Covers Library Science, Information Science, and Information Management, Information Technology.	Simple click on Issue Title. Internal search engine has been given.	E-Text	Covers the bibliography of selected articles, books and digital documents in both print and digital forms on Information Technology issue.	Arranged Volume-wise	Vol1, 1990- v. 24, 1-2, March 2013	Information resulting issue of 8-12 annotated citations of current literature is emailed to a

									mailing list and is available as an RSS feed.
22	Current Issues in Education http://cie.asu.edu/index.php	Arizona State University	Devoted to advancing scholarly thoughts in the field of education.	Simple click on Issue Title	Html	Articles promote educational dialogue, research, practice, and policy. Strive to develop and deepen a sense of scholarship within our academic community and end the privilege to add additional articles as special topics and current events warrant extra attention to timely educational issues.	Arranged Volume and year wise.	Vol. 1, 10, 1998-v. 16, 1, 2013	Publish approximately three Issues per year and peer reviewed
23	Cybermetrics : International Journal of	Cybermetrics Lab of the National	Library and information science,	Simple click on Issue Title	Html & Pdf	Devoted to the description and analysis of the	Arranged by volume	Vol. 1, 1 1997-v. 14,1, 2010	Cybermetrics is an Internation

	Scientometrics, Informetrics and Bibliometrics http://www.cindoc.csic.es/cybermetrics/	Research Council (CSIC), Madrid (Spain)	scientrometrics, bibliometrics, infometrics, Internet			Internet as scholarly communication tool. It is a public service for the world community of researchers in the metrics of scientific communication.			al Peer-reviewed Journal published since 1997 in English and distributed free-of-charge in the World Wide Web.
24	Data Science Journal http://www.jstage.jst.go.jp/browse/dsj	International Council for Science; Editor-in-Chief: Dr. John Rumble, Jr.Editorial Specialist: Diane Smith.	Data systems, Physical Sciences, Engineering, the Geosciences and the Biosciences, along with Agriculture and the Medical Science.	Simple click on Issue Title	Pdf	Scientific and engineering data and focus on Data Management and delivery issue rather than contents of specific databases. The Journal Publishes papers about data and the data systems and publish papers about methods data	Arranged by volume	Vol.1, 2002-v. 12, 2013	UNESCO provides financial contributions to this Journal and Peer reviewed electronic publication with papers appearing

						compilation or analysis.			throughout the year.
25	DESIDOC Journal of Library & Information Science http://publications.drdo.gov.in/ojs/index.php/djlit/index	DESIDOC and DRDO	It endeveavours to bring recent developments in Information technology	Simple click on Issue Title	Pdf	Recent development applicable to Library and information science, to the notice of Librarians, Documentation, Information professional, students and others interested in the field.	Arranged by Issue, Author and Title.	Vol. 26,1-6, 2006-v. 33,1, 2013	Bi-monthly and indexed in LISA.
26	Digital Document Quarterly http://home.pacbell.net/hgladney/ddqstart.htm	H.M. Gladney, HMG Consulting	Treats with books, newspapers, scholarly papers, scientific tables, legal briefs, medical charts, engineering designs, and government and business records,	Simple click on Issue Title	E-Text	For intelligent readers who can think about technical policy, but who have neither time nor inclination to study digital engineering and provides filtering to identify important	Arranged by volume	Vol.1,1-3, 2002 -v. 9, 1, 2009	Treats quality for digital documents. Quality is meaningful only with respect to what clients and

			the carriers for many kinds of information.			articles, synopses comprehensible by non-technical readers, and opinions on the content. Deal with long-range preservation of digital information and emphasizes background without which later topics might be difficult to understand or appear ill founded.			customers want.
27	DIGITHUM: The Humanities in Digital Age http://www.uoc.edu/digithum/7/eng/numeros.html	Fundació per la Universitat Oberta de Catalunya (FUOC)	Designed for academics, professionals and students from the various fields relating to the humanities and social sciences, digital culture, information	Simple click on Issue Title and Internal search engine has been given.	Pdf	Focus on the knowledge society, ICT, teaching and the dissemination of the humanities and social sciences. Academic community and amongst its readers.	Arranged in Issue-wise	Issue n. 1, 1999-Issue N. 7, 2005	Peer Reviewed and annual publication that comes out in May.

			society, ICT						
28	EBIB Electronic Information Bulletin for librarians http://ebib.info/ biuletyn/	Stowarzyszenie Bibliotekarzy Polskich Komisja Wydawnictw; Bulletin Editor-in-Chief Bożena Bednarek-Michalska, Poland	Focus on Librarianship, information, and library technologies.	Simple click on Issue Title	E-Text and Rtf	Includes essays, reports, announcements, letters, discussions/polemics, and agenda.	Arranged in Year-wise and materials are published in the following departments Research, theory, views, Interviews, Law, Conference reports and others.	Selected full text No.10, Dec 2000-No.3, April 2008. Fulltext 2002 Special issue for the Frankfurt book fair 2000. (Abstract 1999-2010)	Selected Full text, full text 2002 and Special 2000 is available for browsing. Links for Polish libraries, OPAC catalogues via Internet, international library services, foreign OPAC catalogues, national and virtual

									libraries, journals, books, publishers, and various library organizations
29	EDUCAUSE Quarterly http://www.educause.edu/eq	Mission is to advance higher education by promoting the intelligent use of information technology	EDUCAUSE Quarterly is an online, peer-reviewed, practitioner's journal about managing and using information resources in higher education.	Simple click on Issue Title and Internal search engine has been given.	Pdf & Html	Publishes materials that relate to planning, developing, managing, using, and evaluating information resources in higher education. Information resources encompass technology, services, and information.	Arranged Volume wise.	Vol.23, 1-4, 2000-V.34, 1-4, 2011	Applied filters have been given to make search easier like Author, Tags, Year published, Publication, Organization, Content Type, Document

									type.
30	E-JASL: The Electronic Journal of Academic and Special Librarianship http://southernlibrarianship.icaap.org/	International Consortium for the Advancement of Academic Publication (ICAAP) Country: Canada	Covers all aspects of academic and special librarianship without regard to region or country	Simple click on Issue Title	Html	Independent, professional, refereed electronic journal dedicated first and foremost to advancing knowledge and research in the areas of academic and special librarianship	Arranged Volume wise.	Vol. 1, 1996- v.10,1-3, Winter 2009 Three issues in year Spring, Summer, Winter	1996-2000 was known as "Journal of southern academic and special librarianship". Spring, Summer, Winter and Listed in the DOAJ and Indexed in LISA.
31	Electronic Journal of Africana Bibliography http://ir.uiowa.edu/ejab/all_issues.html	University of Iowa; United states	Bibliographies	Simple click on Issue Title and Internal search engine has been given.	Pdf	Coverage includes any aspect of Africa, its peoples, their homes, cities, towns, districts, states, countries, regions, including	Arranged volume wise	Vol.1, 1997- V. 13, 2012	ISSN:1092-9576 and Refereed

						social, economic sustainable development, creative literature, the arts, and the Diaspora.			
32	Electronic Journal of Health Informatics http://www.ejhi.net/ojs/index.php/ejhi	Central Queensland University, Australia	Advancement of Health Informatics and information technology in healthcare.	Simple click on Issue Title and Internal search engine has been given.	Pdf	Provide health care workers with a readily accessible, electronic vehicle for sharing information about research, knowledge, experiences, perceptions and wisdom with colleagues involved in all facets of health informatics and health information technology.	Information for readers, authors and librarians is available and arranged Volume wise.	Vol.1, 1, 2006-v.7,2, 2012	Author, Title and Issue Indexing has been given. Uses a single-blind peer-review process.
33	Electronic Journal of	Academic Conferences	Includes on topics relevant to the	Simple click on Issue	Pdf	Contributes to the development of	Arranged Volume	Vol. 1, 1, Sep 2003-v.	Bi-annually and blind-

	Knowledge Management http://www.ejkm.com/	International Limited, United Kingdom	study, implementation and management of knowledge management.	Title and Internal search engine is given.		both theory and practice in the field of knowledge management and accepts academically robust papers, topical articles and case studies that contribute to the area of research in, and practice of knowledge management	wise	10, 3, March 2012	refereed by members of the editorial board or other suitably qualified readers.
34	Electronic Journal on Information Systems in Developing Countries http://www.ejisdc.org/ojs2/index.php/ejisdc	Department of Information Systems, City University of Hong Kong,	Foremost international forum for practitioners, teachers, researchers and policy makers	Simple click on Issue Title	Pdf	Forum for practitioners, teachers, researchers and policy makers to share their knowledge and experience in the design, development, implementation,	Arranged Volume and Year-wise	V.1, 2000- V. 55, 2012	Information for reader, librarians, and authors has been given

						management and evaluation of information systems and technologies in developing countries.			
35	Electronic Transactions on Artificial Intelligence http://www.ida.liu.se/ext/etai/	Linkoping University Electronic Press	Artificial Intelligence, Knowledge Representation, Intelligent User Interface	Simple click on Issue Title	Pdf	Radically new approach to reviewing procedures, communication between peers, information services within a research community, and even to the very concept of scientific publication.	Arranged Volume wise.	Vol. 1, 1-3, 4, 1997-v.5, 2001	Annual and can be reached at http://www.etaij.org/ and at http://www.etai.info/. The. Info URL may eventually replace the one under .Org
36	European Journal of e-Practice http://www.epracticejournal.eu/	ePractice.eu, Spain	e-Transformation	Simple click on Issue Title and Internal	Pdf	Promote the diffusion and exchange of good practice in e-	Arranged Issue-wise.	No. 1 Nov. 2007- No. 18 Oct 2012	Peer reviewed and Issue indexing

				search engine has been given.		Government, e-Health and e-Inclusion. Types of material are articles, case studies and interviews.			has been given.
37	Evidence Based Library and Information Practice http://ejournals.library.ualberta.ca/index.php/EBLIP/index	University of Alberta. Editor-in-Chief:Lindsay Glynn, Canada	EBLIP focus on Evidence-based librarianship, evidence-based practice.	Simple click on Issue Title and Internal search engine has been given.	Pdf	It provides a forum for librarians and other information professionals to discover research that may contribute to decision-making in professional practice and publishes original research and commentary on the topic of evidence based library and information practice	Arranged Year, Volume and Number-wise. Information for Reader, librarians, Author has been given.	Vol. 1, 1-4, 2006-v.7, 4, 2012	Peer Reviewed and Quarterly. Author Title and Issue index have been given.
38	Firstmonday http://firstmonday.org/	University of Illinois, Chief Editor:Edward	Solely devoted to the Internet.	Simple click on Issue Title	Pdf & Html	Publishes original research papers about the Internet	Arranged volume and issue	Vol. 10, 5-12 Dec 2005-v. 18, 3-4,	Published 1114 papers in

		Valauskas, Chicago				and related technologies.	wise. Information is categories for Authors, Librarians and Readers. Author and Title Index have been given.	March 2013	148 issues; written by 1428 different authors. Indexed in CCSA, CA, INSPEC, ISTA, LISA, PAIS, and other services etc.
39	Health Information and Libraries Journal http://www3.interscience.wiley.com/journal/120118368/grouphome/home.html	Wiley Inter Science	Library and Information science	Simple click on Issue Title	Pdf & Html	Provides practitioners, researchers, and students in library and health professions an international and interdisciplinary forum and encourage	Arranged by Issue and Year	Vol. 1-4, 1984-v.30, 1, March 2013	Abstract has been given separately. All are not Free Access, Some Required Password,

						discussion and to disseminate developments at the frontiers of information management and libraries, communicating practices that are evidence based both in managing information and in supporting health care.			till 2007 Free Access.
40	High Energy Physics Libraries Webzine http://library.web.cern.ch/library/Webzine/index.shtml	HEPLW Team	Purchasing, cataloguing, preservation, ILL, quality control, user surveys & education, copyright, E-Journals & management, reference services, grey	Simple click on Issue Title	Html	Devoted to high-energy physics libraries, aim to help you in your daily activities by discussing experience in the delivery of services to users. Some of the problems we confront are unique	Arranged Issue wise	Issue 1 Mach 2000-Issue 13 Oct 2006	

			literature management.			to our field; others are of a more general nature. We are interested in knowing about effective and useful solutions to problems (and the problems), based on your experience in the following areas.			
41	Human IT: Journal for Information Technology Studies as a Human Science http://etjanst.hb.se/bhs/ith//info-eng.htm	Högskolan i Borås Country: Sweden	Bringing forth new research and discussion about digital media as communicative, aesthetic, and ludic instruments	Simple click on Issue Title	Pdf	Closely aligned with the new field of research, which is alternatively referred to as humanities computing, social informatics, or informatics humanistic.	Arranging volume wise.	Vol. 1, 1-4, 1997- v.12, 2, 2013	Decided in 2003 to henceforth use volumes not limited to a calendar year.
42	IFLA Journal http://www.ifla.org/V/iflaj/index.h	Royal Library (the national library of the	Library Science, Information Science,	Simple click on Issue Title	Pdf	Provides information about authoritative	Arranging volume wise.	Vol. 19,1-4, 1993- v. 28, 1-6, 2002	Vol. 27 (2002) and Vol. 28

	tm	Netherlands) for IFLA headquarters. Editor: J. Stephen Parker.	Information Management			coverage and analysis of (a) the activities of IFLA and its various constituent bodies and members.(b) Completed, ongoing and proposed policies, plans related to the development of library.			(2003) Indexed.
43	Informatica Economica Journal http://revistaie.ase.ro/index.html	Inforec Association, Published with the support of Ministry of Education, Research and Youth, Romania	Economic informatics, information society, information systems, IT	Simple click on Issue Title	Pdf	Focusing on Economic informatics, information society, information systems, and information technology.	Arranging volume wise.	Vol. 2, 1-4, 1998-v. 16, 4, 2012	Founded by faculty of Cybernetics, Statistics and Economic Informatics Academy of Economic Studies, Bucharest.

									Listed in the DOAJ.
44	Information for Social Change **http://libr.org/isc/journal.html**	Publication of the organization, "Information for Social Change".	Focuses on issues of censorship, freedom and ethics amongst library and information workers.	Simple click on Issue Title	Pdf	Focuses on freedom of information and censorship; promote alternatives to mainstream. Provide a forum for the exchange of radical views, debate ethics and freedom of library and information work.	Arranging volume wise.	N. 1, Winter 1994-N. 31, Summer 2012	Journal Information for Social Change published twice a year Summer and Winter.
45	Information Research: An International Electronic Journal http://informationr.net/ir/	Professor T.D. Wilson, Support by Lund University Libraries, Sweden, United Kingdom	Library and information science	Internal search engine has been given. Articles can get by simple click on particular article.	E-Text	Open access, international, peer-reviewed, scholarly journal, dedicated to making accessible the results of research across a wide range of information-related disciplines.	Arranged volume wise. Author index and subject index has been given	Vol.1, 1-3, 1995-1996-v.17, 1-4, 2012	Indexed by Google Scholar, INSPEC: Engineering Village, Library Information Science & Technolog

									y Abstracts, LISA. It is also indexed for ISI's Web of Knowledge
46	Information Scotland: The Journal of the Chartered Institute of Library and Information Professionals in Scotland http://www.slainte.org.uk/publications/serials/infoscot/vol1(1)/vol1(1)contents.html	Chartered Institute of Library and Information Professionals, Scotland.	Tips to get to grips, Cables and connections, National Research base	Simple click on Issue Title	XHTML	Offers open access to the journal's articles in electronic form and acts as an archive of this content.	Content delivered in the online edition of Information Scotland has been designed following the World Wide Web Consortium's	Vol. 1 (1-6) February 2003-v. 7(1-3) June 2009	A current news and events calendar is available from SLAINTE.

							guidance on accessibility.		
47	Information Technologies and International Development http://itidjournal.org/itid	University of Southern California, USA	Focuses on the intersection of information and communication technologies (ICTs)	Simple click on Issue Title, Author and Issue. Internal search engine with search tips has been given.	Pdf	It is a peer-reviewed, international, multidisciplinary quarterly designed for researchers and practitioners from the engineering and social sciences, technologists, policy makers, and development specialists.	Articles are arranged Volume wise.	V.1, 1-2, 2003-V 9, 1, 2013	This peer-reviewed, international, multidisciplinary quarterly journal indexed in EBSCO Host, Proquest etc. and It is Ranked 1 ICTuD Journal in the New York Study. ISBN is 1544-

									7529.
48	Information Technology and Disabilities http://people.rit.edu/easi/itd.htm	E A S I: Equal Access to Software and Information Country: United States	Information technology, disabilities, education	Simple click on Issue Title	E-Text	Covering Information technology, disabilities, education.	Arranged Volume-wise.	Vol. 1 Jan 1994-v.11, 2005 and v. 12, 1, June 2008	Peer Reviewed and accessible IT Through Podcasts, Webinars and Online Courses
49	Information Technology and Libraries http://www.ala.org/ala/mgrps/divs/lita/ital/italinformation.cfm	Informing Science Institute Country: United States	Web programming online, Africans studies, Information and technology.	Simple click on Issue Title	Pdf	Distance learning course in web programming discovers, Africans studies, teaching courses relating to the history of Africa and the history of genocide, discusses some of the particular challenges that his field presents.	Articles are arranged Volume wise.	Available V.20, No 1-4, 2011 – v.29, No 1-3, 2010 But freely available from V. 23, No. 1-4 -V. 29, No1, 2010	Tutorial Materials: 1. Case writing: the three little pigs A,B,and c. 2. Case writing checklist.

50	Informing Faculty: An International Journal of Higher Education Discussion Cases http://informingfaculty.org/	Informing Science Institute, United States	Library and information science, journalism, informing science	Simple click on Issue Title	Pdf	The academically peer refereed journal Informing Science endeavors to provide an understanding of the complexities in informing clientele. Fields from information systems, library science, journalism in all its forms to education all contribute to this science.	Arranged volume wise.	Vol.1, 2006 only	Indexed in Cabell, Computer Science Index, Communication Abstracts, EBSCO and others.
51	Informing Science The International Journal of an Emerging Transdiscipline http://inform.nu/	Library and Information Technology Association (LITA), a division of the American Library Association.	Information Technology and Libraries publishes material related to all aspects of libraries and information technology,	Information can be browse by simple click. Internal search engine has been given	Pdf and Html	Including digital libraries, metadata, authorization and authentication, electronic journals and electronic publishing, telecommunications, distributed systems	Arranged by Year and Volume	Vol.1 1998- v.1. 16, 2013	Refereed and published quarterly

		Association.				and networks, computer security and intellectual property rights, technical standards, geographic information systems, desktop applications, online catalogs and bibliographic systems, optical information systems, software engineering, etc.			
52	Inter-Actions: UCLA Journal of Education and Information Studies http://repositories.cdlib.org/gseis/interactions/	e-Scholarship initiative of the California Digital Library	Promotion of interdisciplinary and critical scholarship and provides an outlet for emerging scholars in the fields of education and information studies.	Simple click on Issue Title	Pdf	Focus on legal theory, literary criticism, design, and technology studies exercises a profound impact on educational, information studies research, sociology, curriculum, policy,	Arranged Volume wise.	Vol. 1, 1-2, 2004-v. 9, 1, 2013	Peer Reviewed and published twice yearly with funding provided by the UCLA

						psychological studies, systems design, information literacy, and digital preservation			Graduate Students Association and the UCLA Graduate School of Education & Information Studies.
53	Interdisciplinary Journal of E-Learning and Learning Objects http://ijklo.org/	Informing Science Institute, United States	E-Learning and Learning Objects, Knowledge, learning objects, e-learning.	Simple click on Issue Title	Pdf	Provide readers around the world with the widest possible coverage of developments in E-Learning and Learning Objects and Publishes high quality articles on theory, practice, innovation, and research that cover all aspects of E-learning and	Articles are arranged volume wise.	Vol. 1, 2005-v. 7, 2011	Blind Peer refereed by three or more peers.

						Learning Objects.			
54	Interdisciplinary Journal of Information, Knowledge, and Management http://www.ijikm.org/	Informing Science Institute, United States	Information technology, information management, knowledge management, organizational learning	Simple click on Issue Title	Pdf	Includes Information, Knowledge, and Management, Organizational learning etc.	Arranged volume wise.	Vol. 1, 2006- v. 7, 2012	Blind refereed by three or more peers.
55	International Journal of Communication http://ijoc.org/ojs/index.php/ijoc/about/editorialPolicies#focusAndScope	International Journal of Communication (IJoC), Los Angeles, CA	Open and welcoming to contributions from the many disciplines and approaches that meet at the crossroads that is communication study.	Simple click on Issue Title	Pdf	A forum for scholars when they address the wider audiences of our many sub-fields and specialties, rather than the location for the narrower conversations more appropriately conducted within more specialized journals and major focus on Communication.	Arranged volume wise	V.1, 2007- V.7 2013	Online, multi-media, academic journal that adheres to the highest standards of peer review and engages established and emerging

									scholars from anywhere in the world.
56	International Journal of Communication Networks and Information Security http://www.ijcnis.org/index.php/ijcnis	Institute of Information Technology, Kohat University of Science and Technology, Pakistan	Focusing on theories, methods, and applications in networks and information security.	Simple click on Issue Title. Internal search engine with search tips.	Pdf	Provides a challenging forum for researchers, industrial professionals, engineers, managers, and policy makers working in the field to contribute and disseminate innovative new work on networks and information security.	Articles are arranged Volume wise.	V.1 No 1-3, 2009- v. 4, No. 3, 2012	Peer reviewed, International and Indexed in DOAJ, Inspec, Proquest etc. It is Peer Review and Referred journal
57	International Journal of Computer and Information	Published by World Academy of Science,	Focusing on theories, methods and applications in Computer and	Simple click on Issue Title	Pdf	IJCISE covers all areas of Computer and Information Science and	Articles are arranged Volume	Vol.1. No 1-8, 2007-v. 6, 2012	IJCISE is a scholarly open access,

	Engineering http://www.waset.org/journals/ijcie/	Engineering and Technology	Information Science and Engineering.			Engineering, publishing refereed original research articles and technical notes	and then Number wise.		peer-reviewed, interdisciplinary, quarterly and fully refereed journal.
58	International Journal of Computer Science and Information Technology http://airccse.org/journal/ijcsit.html	Academy & Industry Research Collaboration Center	The mission of this journal is to publish original contributions in its field in order to propagate knowledge amongst its readers and to be a reference publication.	Simple click on Issue Title	Pdf	Devoted to fields of Computer Science and Information Systems.	Arranged volume wise	V. 1, 1-2 2009- v. 5, 1-6 2013	Peer-reviewed scientific journal published in electronic form as well as print form.
59	International Journal of Digital Curation http://www.ijdc.net/./ijdc/issue/c	The Digital Curation Centre Country: United	Digital curation, digital preservation, digital access	Simple click on Vol. & Title, Internal search	Pdf	Devoted to papers, articles and news items on curation of digital objects and related issues.	Arranged Volume wise. Information for	V,1 ,1, 2006-v.7, 2, 2012	Issues and Author Index has been given.

	urrent	Kingdom		engine			Author, Reader and Librarians has been given.		
60	International Journal of Doctoral Studies (IJDS) http://ijds.org/	Informing Science Institute, United States	Focus on informing science, information systems, information technology, information science, information security, IT education	Simple click on Issue Title. Internal search engine has been given.	Pdf	Facilitation of knowledge enhancement related to doctoral studies in areas such as (but not limited to): informing science, information systems, information technology, information science, decision science, information security, and IT education.	Arranged Volume wise.	Vol. 1, 2006- v. 8, 2013	Blind Peer Reviewed, listed in Cabell's Directory of Publishing Opportunities: in Educational Curriculum, Methods, & in Educational Psy.Admin., EBSCO,

									DOAJ.
61	International Journal of Legal Information http://scholarship.law.cornell.edu/ijli/vol33/iss1/	Published by Cornell Law Library	Focus on Legal Issues	Information can be browse by simple click. Internal search engine has been given.	Pdf	Behaviour Economic Issues, Islamic Governance, Commercial Issues etc.	Arranged volume wise	Vol. 33, No.1, Spring 2005-v. 38, No. 2, Spring 2010	It has columns for Book reviews and International calendars.
62	International Journal of Library and Information Science http://www.academicjournals.org/ijlis/index.htm	Academic Journals, Victoria Island, Lagos	Manuscripts	Information can be browse by simple click and Internal search engine has been given	Pdf	Papers cover manuscripts that meet the general criteria of significance and scientific excellence.	Arranged volume wise	V.1, No. 1-6, 2009-V. 5, No 2, 2013	Peer reviewed and open access.
63	International Journal of Managing Public Sector Information and Communication Technologies	Academy & Industry Research Collaboration Center	Contribute new results in regards to the use of information and communication technologies (ICT) in the public	Simple click on Issue Title	Pdf	Topics of interest include, Electronic records, Information preservation, Management, Security, RFID, Privacy, Open	Arranged Year, Volume and then by No.	V.1, 1- 2, Dec 2010- V.3, No2 Dec 2012	ISBN are 0976 - 9773 (Online) ; 2230 - 7958 (Print)

	http://airccse.org/journal/mpict/ijmpict.html		sector around the world.			source, Knowledge Management, Internet, Infrastructure. Provides a platform to disseminate new ideas and new research, advance theories, and propagate best practices in the management of ICT in public sector organizations			(Print)
64	International Journal of Multimedia and Its Applications http://airccse.org/journal/ijma_index.html	Academy & Industry Research Collaboration Center	Technical and practical aspects of Multimedia & its applications	Simple click on Issue Title. Internal search engine has been given.	Pdf	Bring together researchers and practitioners from academia and industry to focus on understanding recent developments this arena, and establishing new collaborations in	Arranged volume wise and Information for Author, Librarian and Readers has been given.	V.1, 1, 2009-v.5,1, 2013	Indexed in Inspec, Google Scholar, Open Jgate, Scirus etc.

						these areas.			
65	International Journal of Special Libraries http://forge.fh-potsdam.de/~IFLA/INSPEL/intro.htm	Fachhochschule Potsdam, Germany	Members of the IFLA Division of Special Libraries. It focus on Library Science, Science, Technology	Simple click on Issue Title.	Pdf	Promotes and coordinates the work of particular relevance to the specific types of libraries or library activities in its Standing Committees for Art Libraries, Map Libraries, Government Libraries, Science and Technology Libraries and Social Science Libraries.	Arranged Volume wise.	Vol.27, 1-4, 1993-v. 36, 1-4, 2002 Discontinued now	c/o Stefan Bernhardt Fachbereich Archiv, Bibliothek, Documentation Friedrich-Ebert-Straße, Potsdam
66	International Review of Information Ethics http://www.i-r-i-e.net/	International Center for Information Ethics, Germany	Cyberethics, computer ethics, library and information science	Simple click on Issue Title.	Pdf	Focusing on the ethical impacts of information technology on human practices and thinking, social interaction, other	Arranged Volume wise.	Vol. 1 ,1-2 June & Oct 2004-v.18, Dec 2012	Author index has been given.

						areas of science and research and the society itself.			
67	International Review of Research in Open and Distance Learning http://www.irrodl.org/index.php/irrodl	Athabasca University	Theory, and best practice in open and distance learning worldwide	Simple click on Issue Title. Internal search engine has been given.	Pdf and Html	Aims to disseminate research, theory, and best practice in open and distance learning worldwide.	Arranged Volume and year wise. Information for author, librarian and Readers has been given.	Vol. 5, 1-3, 2004-v. 14, 1, 2013	Author, Issue and Title indexing has been given. Peer reviewed and refereed.
68	Internet Writing Journal http://www.internetwritingjournal.com/	Writers Write, Inc.	Writers and Book Lovers	Simple click on Issue Title.	Html	The Online Magazine for Writers and Book Lovers	Arranged by issue and Year.	August 1997-Dec-Jan 2007	
69	Interpersonal Computing and Technology Journal	Association for Educational Communications and	Computer Mediated Communication,	Simple click on Issue Title.	E-Text	Focus is on computer-mediated communication, and the pedagogical	Arranging by issue, author.	Vol.1, 1,1993-v. 5, 1-2, 1997	Scholarly, peer-reviewed journal

	http://www.helsinki.fi/science/optek/#byissue	Technology				issues surrounding the use of computers and technology in educational settings.	author.		and Published quarterly
70	Issues in Informing Science and Information Technology http://iisit.org/	Informing Science Institute, United States	Encourage the sharing of knowledge and collaboration among the wide variety of fields that use information technology to inform clients.	Simple click on Issue Title.	Pdf	Includes Communications, Communicating Meaning, Community and Society, Computer Science, Data Communications, Distance Education, E-Commerce, Education, Government, Health Care, Medicine, History, Information Science & Library.	Arranged Volume wise.	Vol. 1, 2004 - v. 9, 2012	Provide insight into how best to inform clients using information technology and cover research in IT Education, such as Curriculum and Techniques for teaching IT.

71	Issues in Science and Technology Librarianship http://www.library.ucsb.edu/istl/ Or http://www.istl.org/	Association of College and Research Libraries, United States	Science, Library Science, Information Science, Information Technology, Technology	Simple click on Issue Title.	E-Text	Serves as a vehicle for science-tech librarians to share details of successful programs, materials for the delivery of information services, background information and opinions on topics of current interest, and to publish research and bibliographies on issues in science and technology libraries.	Arranged volume wise. Information for author has been given.	Dec 1991-71 Fall 2012	Author index has been given. Published quarterly Summer, Winter, Fall, Spring.
72	IT&Society http://www.itandsociety.org/index.html	SIQSS, Stanford University	Scientific analysis of the social impact of information technology on society, with special emphasis on quantitative	Simple click on Issue Title.	Html	Includes the community of scholars interested in the social impact of new technologies, as well as policy makers, media analysts, computer	Arranged issue and year wise.	V.1, 1-7, 2004	Issue indexing has been given. Currently suspended

			survey analysis.			professionals and interested members of the general public.			
73	ITALICS: Innovations in Teaching and Learning in Information and Computer Sciences http://www.ics.heacademy.ac.uk/italics/	Higher education academy	Archival Studies, Library Science, Information Studies	Simple click on Issue Title.	Pdf	Highlight current issues in learning and teaching Information and Computer Sciences at the Higher Education (HE) level including, For academics within the Information and Computer Sciences communities	Arranged by issue.	Vol. 4, 1-3, 2005-v. 10, 3, 2011	Rigorous reviewed by appropriate specialists.
74	JEP: The Journal of Electronic Publishing http://www.journalofelectronicpublishing.org/	Scholarly Publishing Office (SPO), University of Michigan University Library, Editor: Judith Axler	Forum for research and discussion about contemporary publishing practices, and the impact of those practices upon	Simple click on Volume and Internal search engine.	E-Text	Provides archive of works covering current trends and issues in electronic publishing. The articles present innovative ideas, best practices, and	Arranged by issue.	Vol.1, 1-2, 1995-v. 15, 1-3, 2012	Author and Title Indexing. Readers are publishers, scholars, librarians,

		Turner.	users.			leading-edge thinking about all aspects of publishing, authorship, and readership.			journalists, students, technologists, attorneys, retailers, and others
75	JLIS.it Italian Journal of Library and Information Science http://leo.cilea.it/index.php/jlis/article/view/4539/4416	University of Florence	Library and Information science	Simple click on Issue Title	Pdf	Contribute in Library and Information Science, aims to valorize Italian research	Arranged volume wise	Vol.1, No. 1-2, 2010- V.4 No.1, 2013	Peer-reviewed electronic open access format, academic journal of international scope.
76	Journal of Artificial Intelligence Research http://www.jair.org/	AI Access Foundation, Inc.	Artificial Intelligence, Computer Science, Computer Engineering	Simple click on Issue Title. Internal search engine.	Pdf	Provides all areas of artificial intelligence (AI), publishing refereed research articles, survey articles, and technical notes.	Arranged volume wise.	Vol.1, (August 1993- June 1994) - Vol. 46, Jan 2013.	Biannual and Author, papers, title, abstract search has

									been given.
77	Journal of Digital Information http://jodi.ecs.soton.ac.uk/r or http://journals.tdl.org/jodi	Texas Digital Library,United States	Information Management, Information Science, Information Technology	Simple click on Issue Title. Internal search engine for searching has been given.	Html	Covers the topic of information management, information science and information technology, digital libraries, hypermedia systems, hypertext criticism, and information discovery.	Arranged by Issue, author, Title, and theme	Vol. 1, 1-2, 1997-v. 13, 1, 2012	Issue, author, title, theme index has been given.
78	Journal of East Asian Libraries http://www.lib.byu.edu/dlib/spc/jeal/	Council on East Asian Libraries and the Association for Asian Studies, Inc.	Asian Libraries	Simple click on Issue Title.	Pdf	Focus on Asian Libraries perspectives.	Arranged by No.	V.1, No1, 1963- No. 156, No.1 Feb 2013	
79	Journal of Educational Media & Library	Tamkang University Press, Taiwan	Library science, information science,	Simple click on Issue Title.	Pdf	Cover all the aspects of Library science, information science,	Arranged Volume wise.	Vol. 28, 1-4, 1991-1990- v. 50, 2,	Scopus, LISTA, DOAJ,

	Sciences http://joemls.tku .edu.tw/index_e. htm	Press, Taiwan	information technology, publishing, book trade	Title.		and information technology.	wise.	2012	H.W. Wilson Database, LLIS, LISA, PAIS, Ulrich's, Chinese ERIC, THCI, and CEPS index it.
80	Journal of e-Literacy http://www.jelit. org/index.html	University of Glasgow, United Kingdom	Illiteracy	Simple click on Issue Title. Internal search engine is given	Pdf	Discuses on topics relevant to JeLit themes involving a theoretical, comparative, overview or critical element. Case Studies, Research Reports, Reviews.	Arranged Volume wise.	Vol. 1, 1, 2004-v.2, 1-2, 2005	
81	Journal of Health Informatics in Developing Countries http://www.jhidc	University of Otago, New Zealand. Information is given for	Covers Information science, medicine, health care.	Simple click on Issue Title. Internal search	Pdf	Share and promote academic knowledge in the field and to encourage writers	Arranged Volume wise.	Vol.1,1, 2007-v.7,1, 2013	Author, Title and Issue index has been given.

	.org/index.php/jhidc	author, Reader, Librarians.		engines given		from developing countries to contribute their writings, health Librarianship			
82	Journal of Information Architecture http://journalofia.org/archives/	REG-iA, the Research & Education Group in IA. Sponsored by the Information Architecture Institute & by Copenhagen Business School.	Facilitate the systematic development of the scientific body of knowledge in the field of information architecture.	Simple click on Issue Title. Internal search engine has been given.	Pdf	Research and sharing of good ideas and case studies that are useful to the field's researchers, practitioners, students, and all other interested parties and focus information architecture research and development in all types of shared information environments, such as for example social networks, web sites, intranets,	Arranged volume wise	V.1, 1 spring 2009- V.3, 1 spring 2011	Indexed and Peer-reviewed scholarly Journal. Published twice in Year

						mobile and Rich Internet Applications			
83	Journal of Information Law and **Technology** http://www2.warwick.ac.uk/fac/soc/law/elj/jilt/ **or European** Journal of Law and Technology http://ejlt.org//issue/archive	Universities of Warwick and Strathclyde, United Kingdom.	Covers a wide range of topics relating to IT Law and IT applications in law	Simple click on Issue Title.	Pdf	Contains a diversity of materials including peer reviewed and non-refereed articles, commentaries, work in progress articles, book and IT reviews, and conference reports and papers, as well as information papers, news and UK and global conferences.	Arranged Issue wise.	Issue 1-3, 1996- Vol.4, 1, 2013 (v .Starts from 2010)	Issue indexing has been done.
84	Journal of Information Literacy http://ojs.lboro.ac.uk/ojs/index.php/JIL/index	Chartered Institute of Library and Information Professionals, United Kingdom	Investigate Information Literacy.	Simple click on Issue Title. Internal search engine	Pdf	Investigate and to make generalized observations on how Information Literacy impacts on organizations, systems and the	Arranged Volume wise and Information is given for author,	Vol. 1, N. 1-3, 2007-Vol. 6, N.2, 2012	Author, Issue and Title index has been given.

						individual.	Reader, Librarians.		
85	Journal of Information Technology Education (JITE: Research) http://www.informingscience.us/icarus/journals/jiteresearch/publications	Informing Science Institute Country: United States	Endeavors to improve IT Education around the world	Simple click on Issue Title. Internal search engine has been given.	Pdf	Improve IT education around the world by publishing high quality articles on best practices and other topics of use. Types of articles, including primary, action, and secondary research, provide.	Arranged Volume wise.	Vol.1, 2002- v. 12, 2012	Annual and Listed in Applied Math and Science Education Repository (AMSER), Cabell's
86	Journal of Information, Information Technology, and Organizations http://jiito.org/	Informing Science Institute, California, United States	Information systems research	Simple click on Issue Title	Pdf	JIITO covers a specialized area of information systems research indicated in its title. It focused on empirical studies. Conceptual articles are published just exceptionally.	Articles are arranged Volume wise.	Vol.1, 2006- v. 8, 2013 (Annual)	All submissions are blind refereed by three or more peers.

87	Journal of Internet Cataloguing http://www.internetcataloging.com/home.html	Published by Haworth, Binghamton, NY	Focus on the Internet Cataloguing	Simple click on Volume and then on particular title.	Html	It basically focuses on the cataloguing of Internet E-Resources.	List of all the issues have been given in one page. Which can be Browse	Vol-1, No1, 1997-v. 5, No1, 2001	
88	Journal of Knowledge Management Practice http://www.tlainc.com/boutjkmp.htm	Free Press Journals	Knowledge Management	Simple click on Issue Title	Html	Devoted to collecting serious research about knowledge management and its practical applications. Authors are invited to read the notes for contributors, and are encouraged to contribute.	Articles are arranged issue and year wise.	Vol. 1. 1998-99-Vol.13 N. 4, Dec 2012	Issue indexing has been done JKMP is published in 2006 and onward in Quarterly Issues.
89	Journal of Library	Published by	Disseminate	Simple click	Pdf	Original research,	Informati	V.1 No 1-2,	The

	Innovation http://www.libraryinnovation.org/about/contact	Western New York Library Resources Council, 4455 Genesee St., PO Box 400, Buffalo, New York 14225-0400	research and information on innovative practice in libraries of all types.	on Issue Title. Internal search engine has been given.		reports on innovative practices, literature reviews, case .studies, and book, conference and product reviews. The Journal also welcomes provocative essays that will stimulate thought on the current and future role of libraries in an Internet Age.	on is arranged volume wise	2010- V3 No 2, 2012	Journal of Library Innovation (JOLI) is a peer reviewed open access journal
90	Journal of Medical Internet Research http://www.jmir.org/	Published by Gunther Eysenbach Country: Canada	Focus on Medicine, Internet.	Simple click on Issue Title. Internal search engine with search tips	Html	Covers health informatics and all aspects of research, information and communication in the healthcare field using Internet and Intranet-related technologies; which is nowadays called	Articles are arranged Volume wise. Author and title search category has been	Vol. 1, 1-2, -supplement 1, 1999-v. 12, 2, 2013	Indexed in MEDLINE and numerous other databases, and full-text articles are permanent

						"eHealth"	given.		ly archived in PubMed Central. The new JMIR Impact Factor released in June 2008 is now 3.0!
91	Journal of Philippine Librarianship http://journals.upd.edu.ph/index.php/jpl/issue/current	University of the Philippine	All aspects of Library and information science	Simple click on Issue Title	Pdf	Includes librarianship, health librarianship, information system, archival studies, children and young adult library services, emerging technology and services, information storage, retrieval, collection management, cataloging, classification,	Arrange by year	Vol. 27, 1-2, 2010- v.31, 1, 2011	ISBN: 0022-359x

						indexing, abstracting, thesaurus construction, reference, access, reader services, preservation and conservation of collections etc.			
92	Journal of Research and Practice in Information Technology http://ws.acs.org.au/jrpit/JRPIT_Volumes.html	Australian Computer Society Inc.	Includes all aspects of Information Technology deemed to be of interest to part of the readership	Simple click on Issue Title. Internal search engine has been given.	Pdf	Including, but not limited to: Computer Science; Information Systems; Computer Systems and Information Engineering; Software Engineering.	Arranged volume wise and Information for Author, Librarian and Readers has been given.	Vol. 35, 1-4, 2003-v. 43, 1-3, 2011	Indexed by Applied Mechanics Reviews, Applied Mechanics Reviews, Compumath Citation Index etc.
93	Journal of Staff Development http://learningforward.org/public	National Staff Development Council	Restructuring, the role of principals, program planning, ensures results	Simple click on Issue Title.	Pdf	Focuses on issues of leadership and learning relevant to all educators	Arranged issue wise.	Vol. 13, N. 3, summer 1992-v. 34. N. 1, 2013	Issue indexing has been done. All

	ations/jsd#.UUQ guzcynUc		with students, and follow-up strategies.			involved in professional learning. Articles are written primarily by practitioners who bring a real world to the challenges of school improvement and organizational change.			articles are not open access.
94	Journal of Technology Studies http://scholar.lib.vt.edu/ejournals/JOTS/	DLA University libraries	Technology education, student development	Simple click on Issue Title.	Pdf	Provides current trends on Technology education, student development etc.	Arranged by issue and Year.	Vol. XXII, 2, Summer /Fall 1996- v. XXXVIII, 2, Fall 2012	
95	Journal of the American Medical Informatics Association http://www.pubmedcentral.nih.gov/tocrender.fcgi	American Medical Informatics Association	Preservation, IT, Communication	Simple click on Issue Title.	Pdf and Html	Focus on mainly Decision making, Health communication, IT, Preservation.	Arranged by issue and Year.	Vol 1, 1-6 1994- v. 19, 3, March 2012	

	?action=archive& journal=76								
96	Journal of the Association for History and Computing http://quod.lib.umich.edu/j/jahc/browse.html	Sponsored by the American Association for History and Computing	Promote and develop interest in the use of computers in all types of historical study at every level, in both teaching and research	Simple click on Issue Title. Internal search engine has been given.	E-Text	Define useful standards to maximize the utility of computers in historical studies and intended for a general audience of teachers, students, and researchers interested in the application of computers in historical studies.	Arranged by issue and Year.	Vol.1, 1-6, 1994- v.13, 1, May 2010	Index by Subject, Author, Articles, Columns, Editorials, Reviews, Books Reviewed by Title, Books Reviewed by Author, Software Reviewed.
97	Journal of the European Association for Health Information and Libraries http://www.eahil	Medical Library-Univ. of Cambridge, Cambridge	Uniting and motivating librarians and information officers working in medical and health science	Simple click on Issue Title. Internal search engine has been given.	Pdf	Encourages professional development, improves cooperation and enables exchanges of experience	Arranged volume wise	Vol.1, 1-4, 2005-v.9, 4, 2013	

	.net/journal/		libraries in Europe.			amongst its members.			
98	Journal of the Medical Library association http://www.ncbi.nlm.nih.gov/pmc/journals/93/	PubMed. And from 2002 Medical Library Association, United States	Covers health sciences, librarianship, education, and information technology	Simple click on the Volume. Internal search engine is available	Pdf	Contribute to the education of health sciences librarians, role of the medical librarian and help to broaden the profession's skill set and has been on continuing work to foster a research mentality among JMLA readers.	Arranged Volume wise at home page.	Vol1, 1898 - v.101 1, 2013	Archive includes: J Med Libr Assoc: Vols. 90 to 96; 2002 to 2008, Med Library Hist J: Vols. 1 to 5; 1903 to 1907 Bull Assoc Med Libr: Vol. 1; 1902 Med Lib: Vols. 1 to 5; 1898 to 1902
99	Journal of Virtual	TDL electronic	Pedagogy,	Simple click	Pdf	Includes limitations	Articles	Vol. 1, N. 1-	Published

	Worlds Research http://www.jvwresearch.org/index.html	Press, Hosted by the JVWR Editorial Team.	Education and Innovation in Virtual Worlds	on Issue Title.		and advantages of educational practices, Development and use of instructional tools, Evaluation and assessment, Innovations in educational assessment methods, Interdisciplinary curriculum and instruction, Educational and research ethics in virtual world.	are arranged Volume wise.	3, 2008-Vol. 3, N.2, 2010	peer reviewed research papers. Indexed in EBSCO
100	LASIE: Library Automated Systems Information Exchange http://search.informit.com.au/browseJournalTitle;	RMIT University	Automation	Simple click on Issue Title.	Pdf	Includes mainly Library automation and Information Exchange platform.	Arranged by volume and then Number.	Vol. 17, 1-6, 1986-v. 33, 1, 2002	

	res=E-LIBRARY;issn=0047-3774								
101	Law Library Journal http://www.aallnet.org/products/pub_journal.asp	American Association of Law Libraries	Scholarly articles on law, legal materials, and librarianship are the mainstay of the Journal.	Simple click on Issue Title.	Pdf	Practice-oriented articles, proceedings of the business sessions of the Annual Meeting, and annual reports of committees, special interest sections, representatives, and chapters are also included.	Arranged by Year, Volume and then Number	Vol.92, 1 (Winter 2000)-v.105, 1 (Winter 2013)	The Law Library Journal is available on Lexis-Nexis®, WESTLAW, H.W. Wilson and Hein Online.
102	Learned Publishing http://www.ingentaconnect.com/content/alpsp/lp	Association of Learned and Professional Society Publishers	Scholarly Publishing	Simple click on Issue Title.	Pdf	Learned Publishing is the journal of the Association of Learned and Professional Society Publishers, published in collaboration with the Society for	Arranged by Volume.	Vol.1, 10, 1997-v.26, 1, 2013	Published quarterly in January/April/July/October.

						Scholarly Publishing.			
103	LIBER Quarterly Journal of European Research Libraries http://liber.library.uu.nl/index.html	Association of Learned and Professional Society Publishers	Represents Interests, needs improvement, standardization of European research libraries.	Simple click on Issue Title. Internal search engine with search tips has been given	E-text and Pdf	Aim is to assist research libraries in Europe to support a functional network across national boundaries in order to ensure the preservation of the European cultural heritage, to improve access to collections in European research libraries, and to provide more efficient information services in Europe	Arranged Volume wise.	Vol. 12, 2002-v. 20, 3/4 2013	
104	Library & Information Research: Research into Practice for Information & Library Services	CILIP Library & Information Research Group, United Kingdom	Library and Information science	Simple click on Issue Title. Internal search engine with search tips	Pdf	Focus on research for LIS community; reporting of research; reflective and evidence-based practice etc.	Arranged Volume wise. Information is given for author,	Vol. 31, 97, 2007-v. 36, 113, 2012	Issue, Author and title indexing has been given. Publishes

	http://www.lirgjournal.org.uk/lir/ojs/index.php/lir			has been given.			Reader, Librarians.		both refereed and non-refereed submissions.
105	Library Journal http://www.libraryjournal.com	Cahners Business Information, Editor Ron Shank, Editor in chief: Francine Fialkoff.	Library Field	Simple click on Issue Title. Internal search engine have been given.	E-Text	Single-most comprehensive publication for librarians, with groundbreaking features and analytical news reports covering technology, management, policy, and other professional concerns.	Arranged Issue-wise	Issue 1-20 Jan-Dec, 2002-Issue 1-16 March 2013; Free subscription is also available.	Over 100,000 library directors, administrators, and staff in public, academic, and special libraries read LJ. Its hefty review sections evaluate nearly 7000 books

									annually.
106	Library Philosophy and Practice http://www.webpages.uidaho.edu/~mbolin/lpp.htm	University of Nebraska, Lincoln libraries, United States	Library practice and the philosophy and theory	Simple click on !ssue Title.	Pdf	Include explorations of current, past, and emerging theories of librarianship and library practice, as well as reports of successful, innovative, or experimental library procedures, methods, or projects in all areas of librarianship, set in the context of applied research.	Arranged Volume wise	Annual Vol. Dec. 2007-Annual v. June 2012	Issue, Author and title indexing has been given.LPP is indexed in LISTA, DOAJ, Library Literature & Information Science, and SCOPUS.
107	Library Resources & Technical Services (LRTS) http://alcts.metapress.com/home/main.mpx	Association for Library Collections & Technical Services, A division of the American	Communicate thoughtful reflection on practice as well as research including collections, Preservation,	Simple click on Issue Title.	Pdf	LRTS supports the theoretical, intellectual, practical, and scholarly aspects of the profession of collection	Arranged Volume wise at home page.	Full text from Vol. 40, 1-4, 1996-v. 55, 1-4, 2011 Toc and abstract available till	2008: 0.698 Journal Citation Reports® 2009, published

		Library Association	acquisition, Serials, Cataloguing and classification.			management and development, acquisitions, cataloging and classification, preservation and reformatting, serials by publishing articles and book reviews. It is primary communication tool of all librarians, information professionals, and educators.		v. 57, 1, 2013	by Thomson Scientific.
108	Library Student Journal http://www.librarystudentjournal.org/index.php/lsj/index	University at Buffalo, United States	Library, information science	Simple click on Issue Title. Internal search engine with search tips has been given.	Pdf and Html	Focus on education, training, career paths, future trends and advance discussion of LIS topics.	Arranged Volume wise and divided into four sections: Articles, Essay, Editorials - opinion	2006-2012	Issue, Author and title indexing has been given.

							pieces of any length, Reviews.		
109	LIBRES: Library and Information Science Research Electronic Journal http://libres.curtin.edu.au/	Curtin University of Technology, Australia	Library Science, Information Science	Simple click on Issue Title.	Pdf	Devoted to new research in Library and Information Science.	Arranged volume wise.	Vol. 6, 1-2 July 1996- V.22,2 March 2012 (bi-annual)	Bi-annual and distributed through a list server, and an ftp site. ISA, LISA, EBSCO, and SPI index it.
110	LIBRI: International Journal of Libraries and Information Services http://www.librijournal.org/	K. G. Saur Verlag, München, Germany	Original articles on all aspects of libraries and information services.	Simple click on Issue Title.	Pdf	Examine historical and Current perspective of LIS, analyze the role of information in cultural, organizational, national and international	Arranged Number wise.	Vol. 49, 1-4, 1999- v. 59, 1, 2009	Abstracted or indexed in SSCI, Research Alert, Social & Behavioral Sciences, LISA,

						developments, and report on current trends in LIS.			Information Science Abstracts, Library Literature.
111	Malaysian Journal of Library & Information Science http://ejum.fsktm.um.edu.my/VolumeListing.aspx?JournalID=3	Faculty of Computer Science & Information Technology, University of Malaya.	Higher learning institutions or research and development	Simple click on Issue Title.	Pdf	Provides scholarly journal management system for university, higher learning institutions or research and development centers.	Arranged by volume.	Vol.1, 1-2, 1996-v. 18, 1, 2013	Author Index has been given
112	MC Journal: The Journal of Academic Media Librarianship http://wings.buffalo.edu/publications/mcjrnl/	The AV Review.	Academic media librarianship.	Simple click on Issue Title. Internal search is given	Pdf	Focus on practical and scholarly information concerning	Arranged Volume wise.	Vol. 1, 1-2, 1993-v.8, 2, 2002	
113	MELA Notes: The Journal of the Middle East	Middle East Librarians Association	Focus mainly on middle east librarianship.	Simple click on Issue Title.	Pdf	Discuss mainly university and schools of middle	Arranged by Number.	N. 64, Spring 1997- N. 82, 2009 & N. 1,	MELA NOTES is published

	Librarians Association http://www.mela.us/MELANotes/MELANotesIntro.html	Association	librarianship.	Title.		east.	Number.	1973	twice a year, in spring and fall.
114	Mississippi Libraries http://www.misslib.org/index.php/publications/mississippi-libraries/mississippi-libraries/	Mississippi Library Association.	Library and Librarianship	Simple click on Issue Title.	Pdf	Professional leadership for the development, promotion, and improvement of library and information services and the profession of librarianship in order to enhance learning and ensure access to information for all.	Articles are arranged Volume wise.	V.64, No. 1 2000- V. 75, No 3, 2012	It is indexed in Library Literature.
115	MLA Forum http://www.mlaforum.org/	Michigan Library Association, United States	Library education, information science	Simple click on Issue Title.	E-Text	Focuses on all the aspect of Library and education.	Articles are arranged Volume wise	Vol. 1, Issue1-2, 2002-v. 7, 2009	It is indexed in Library Literature & LISA. In

									Jan. 2008, It began publishing a single annual volume. Prior to 2008.
116	Multimedia Information and Technology Journal (MmIT) http://www.cilip.org.uk/get-involved/special-interest-groups/multimedia/journal/pages/default.aspx	Chartered Institute of Library and Information Professionals	Information and Technology	Simple click on Issue Title.	Pdf	Includes mainly database, Research and Technology in the field of library and Information Science.	Arranged by volume and then Number.	Vol. 30, 1-4, 2004-v.37, 1, August 2011	Vol. 38 is not open access
117	New Knowledge Environments http://journals.uvic.ca/index.php/INKE	University of Victoria	New Knowledge	Simple click on Issue Title. Internal search	Pdf	Focus on the implementation of new knowledge in environment, Virtual library , Designing	Information is arranged volume wise	Vol.1, 1, 2009	

				engine has been given.		interface etc			
118	North Carolina Libraries http://www.ncl.ecu.edu/index.php/NCL	North Carolina Library Association, United States	Libraries, librarianship, media centers, academic libraries	Simple click on Issue Title.	Pdf	Focus on Libraries, librarianship, media centers, and academic libraries.	Arranged Volume wise	Vol. 47, 1, 1989-v. 70, 1-2, 2012	All the volumes are indexed.
119	Northwestern Journal of Technology and Intellectual Property http://www.law.northwestern.edu/journals/njtip/issues.htm	Northwestern University School of Law	Intellectual property and the intersection of law and technology, copyright, trademark, patents, the Internet, media, telecommunications, health care, antitrust, e-discovery, and trial and litigation technology.	Simple click on Issue Title.	Pdf	Dedicated to the analysis of the burgeoning body of academic, business, newsworthy and legal issues regarding the rapidly increasing and shifting field of intellectual property and technology law. Provides insightful and timely perspectives on intellectual property and technology law, an important area in	Arranged Volume wise	V. 8, Issue 2 2010- V. 11, Issue 2 2013	It is among the top ranked intellectual property and technology journals in the country.

						the academic, legal and business communities.			
120	NPO Journal/NPO E-Journal http://www.bl.uk/blpac/publicationsjournals.html	Preceded by the NPO Journal	Preservation of library and archive collections.	Simple click on Issue Title.	E-Text	Believe that preservation is everyone's responsibility. By working together and sharing knowledge and experience users, volunteers and staff working with library and archive collections can embed a culture which ensures that the way collections are managed and used contributes to their long-term accessibility.	Arranged by Year and then Number.	No. 1, Feb. 1998- No. 13, Nov 2003 & No.1 May 2004- No.5 March 2007	Proceeded by Library Conservation News (1983-1997).
121	Partnership: The Canadian Journal	The Partnership,	Librarians, information	Simple click on Issue	Pdf and	Feature articles on theory & research	Arranged Volume	Vol. 1, 1, 2006-v. 7 2,	Published twice a

	of Library and Information Practice and Research http://journal.lib.uoguelph.ca/index.php/perj/index	Canada	professionals, library workers, library and information studies	Title. Internal search engine with search tips has been given.	Html	and on innovations in practice are in-depth, peer-reviewed articles. Other types of articles include viewpoints, conference presentations, profiles, news & announcements, professional development and reviews	wise. Information is given for author, Reader, Librarians	2012	year. It is Peer reviewed and Indexed Journal
122	Progressive Librarian http://libr.org/pl/	Progressive Librarians Guild	Critical perspectives in Librarianship.	Simple click on Issue Title.	E-Text	Forum for critical perspectives in Librarianship, featuring articles, book reviews, bibliographies, reports and documents that explore progressive perspectives on librarianship and	Arranged Volume wise.	N.1, 1990-N.32, 2009 TOC access till **Issue no. 38-39, spring 2012**	Issue 1, 1990 and Issue 38-39, 2011-2012 is not open access.

						information issues.			
123	RBM Journal of Rare Books , Manuscripts, and Cultural Heritage http://rbm.acrl.org/content/2/2	American Library Association	Books and Manuscripts	Simple click on Issue Title.	Pdf	Discuss about Books, Manuals, and Manuscripts.	arranged by Year and then Number	March & Sept 1986- March & Sept 1990. Vol.1, 1-2, March & Sept 2000- v.13, 2, 2012	From 1991-1999 issues are not available
124	Research Management Review http://www.ncura.edu/content/news/rmr/archive.php	National Council of University Research Administrators	LIS and Research	Simple click on Issue Title.	Pdf	Serves its members and advances the field of research administration through education and professional development programs, the sharing of knowledge and experience, and by fostering a professional, collegial, and respected	Arranged by Volume and year	Vol.1, N1, Spring 1987- v.17 N.1 Fall/Winter 2009	

						community.			
125	Scandinavian Public Library Quarterly http://www.splq.info/	Scandinavian Public Library Quarterly	Concerned with the broad range of issues affecting the administration of research, Research Management Review provides a forum for the dissemination of knowledge about the study and Practice of the profession of research administration.	Simple click on Issue Title. Internal search engine has been given.	E-Text	Converge is about networking, about establishing good and highly relevant content on the Internet, about bridging the virtual and the real library, about outstanding library architecture, about information policies in some of the strongest democracies in the world.	Arranged by year.	Vol. 35, 2002- v. 45, 4, 2012	
126	School libraries in Canada (SLIC): A Journal of the Canadian	Canadian Association for School Libraries.	Development and maintenance of excellence in Canada's school	Simple click on Issue Title.	Pdf	Promotes articles of interest on a broad range of topics from collaboration with	Arranged volume wise	Vol. 18 N02, 1998-v. 30 No. 1, 2012	Founded Vol.1 in 1980.

	Association for School Libraries http://www.clatoolbox.ca/casl/slic/links.html		libraries, media centres, and school library personnel.			the classroom teacher to information technology/literacy skills needed to prepare students for life-long learning.			
127	School Library Journal Online http://www.schoollibraryjournal.com/	Reed Business Information, a division of Reed Elsevier Inc.	School Libraries	Simple click on Issue Title.	E-Text	Includes Features current news about school libraries and librarians.	Arranged Volume wise.	Issue 1,3,5,7,9,11, 1996-Issue 1, 2013	Issue indexing has been done.
128	School Library Research http://www.ala.org/aasl/slr	American Association of School Librarians, United States	Library and information science, school libraries	Simple click on Issue Title.	Html	Explore topics as varied as science and history, geography and the arts. Latest issue offers you lots of concrete ways to incorporate the best new books and media into your lesson plans. It's imperative that	Arranged by Issue.	Vol.1, 1998-v.16, 2013	It is the successor to *School Library Media Research* (ISSN: 1523-4320) and *School Library Media*

						quality materials, especially those that address neglected subjects, find their way into your libraries and classrooms			*Quarterly Online*. It is ranked by Deans of Library and Information Science as a respected research journal. See College and Research Libraries July 2005
129	Simile: Studies in Media and Information Literacy Education http://utpjournals.metapress.com/content/120764	University of Toronto Press	Bibliographic instruction and information and media literacy.	Simple click on Issue Title.	Pdf	Publishing research that advances knowledge about media and information literacy and explore the ways in which social and cultural	Arranged Volume wise.	Vol.1,1-4, 2001-v. 1, 1-2, 2009	Abstracting and Indexing in Academic Search Premier CBCA Education

	/					environments impact media production and the methods that could be used to teach the skills needed to "read" these environments			CEPIEC, EBSCO. Vol. 2,1-4, 2002-v. 8, 1and3, 2008 are not open access.
130	South African Journal of Information Management http://www.sajim.co.za/index.php/sajim/issue/current	University of Johannesburg, South Africa	Information management theory, information management technologies, knowledge management, competitive intelligence, education, business	Simple click on Issue Title.	Html	Presents original research (i.e. not previously published), novel synthesis, or judicious review of current theory, method, policy, or practice in the fields mentioned below. Article submission, review and publication are accomplished entirely electronically.	Arranged Volume wise.	Vol.1, No.1-4, 1999-v.15, 1, 2013.	Peer reviewed and Published four times a year in numbered issues.

131	Special Libraries http://www.sla.org/content/shop/speclibs.cfm#1910	Special Library Association (SLA)	Focus on all the aspects of special Libraries	Simple click on Issue Title.	Pdf	Offers a wide array of professional development opportunities, including the industry's best online education programs, designed to sharpen professional skills throughout your career.	Arranged Volume wise.	Vol. 1, 1910-v. 87, 1996	1910-1929 (Volumes 1 to 20) 1930-1949 (Volumes 21 to 40) 1950-1969 (Volumes 41 to 60) 1970-1980 (Volumes 61 to 71) 1981-1996 (Volumes 72 to 87)
132	Studies in Bibliography http://etext.lib.virginia.edu/bsuva/sb	The bibliographical society of the university of Virginia	It enhance ongoing bibliographical work and encouraging new	Simple click on Issue Title.	E-Text	Contain an extraordinary number of fundamental articles of permanent	Arranged volume wise	Vol. 1, 1948-49-v. 55, 2002	

	/sb	Virginia	developments in the field			interest			
133	Technological Librarianship: An Online Journal of the American Theological Library Association http://journal.atla.com/ojs/index.php/theolib/index	American Theological Library Association	Publishes essays, columns, critical reviews, bibliographic essays all aspects of professional librarianship	Simple click on Issue Title. Internal search engine has been given.	Html	Includes professional librarians in colleges, universities, and theological seminaries and others with an interest in theological librarianship in those settings, Professional development of theological librarians, and to contribute to and enrich the profession of theological librarianship.	Arranged volume wise and Information for Author, Librarian and Readers has been given.	Vol.1, 1-2, 2008-v.6, 1, 2013	Indexed
134	Technology	Library and	Information	Simple click	Pdf	Provides reviews of	Arranged	Vol. 1, 1-3,	

	Electronic Reviews (TER) http://www.ala.org/lita/publications/archive/ter	Information Technology Association (ALA), United States	Technology	on Issue Title. Internal search engine has been given.		and pointers to resources, both print and electronic. Resources include books, articles, serials, discussion lists, software, training materials, and bibliographies.	Volume wise.	1994- v. 14, 2, 2007	
135	Texas library journal http://www.txla.org/TLJ	Texas Library Association	Cover all the aspects of library science	Simple click on Issue Title.	Pdf	Focus on Academic library, Leadership, Principles, Intellectual freedom, librarians etc.	Arranged volume wise	Vol. 84, 1-4, 2008-v. 88,1-4, 2012	Four Issues Spring, Summar, Fall, Winter.
136	The Bone folder: An outgrowth of the Book Arts Web http://www.philobiblon.com/bonefolder/	The Book Arts Web - Peter D., Syracuse University Library, Syracuse, NY, United States	Bookbinding & the book arts bookbinding, decorative techniques, education, exhibition reviews, tips & tricks, or book	Simple click on Issue Title.	Pdf	Established and emerging authorities on a variety of book arts topics including hand bookbinding, teaching, business practice, the history of the book, the	Arranged Volume wise at home page.	Vol. 1, 1, Fall 2004-v. 8, 1, 2012	Listed in DOAJ and is archived as part of the New York University Library's contributio

			reviews.			book as art, general tips & tricks, exhibitions, how-to technical articles, and reviews.			n to LOCKSS (Lots of Copies Keep Stuff Safe)
137	The Idaho Librarian: A Publication of the Idaho Library Association http://www.idaholibraries.org/idlibrarian/index.php/idaho-librarian/index	Idaho Library Association	Articles and information relevant to libraries and librarianship in Idaho	Simple click on Issue Title. Internal Search engine for searching has been given.	Pdf and Html	Publishes articles and information relevant to libraries and librarianship in Idaho, though topics need not be unique to the state. Idaho-related articles written by authors not located in Idaho and not members of the Idaho Library Association are within the scope of the journal.	Arranged Volume wise. Information is given for author, Reader, Librarians.	Vol. 59,1-2, 2009-v.61, 1, 2011	Indexed and peer reviewed.
138	The International Journal of Database	Academy & Industry Research	Database management systems & its	Simple click on Title and Issue.	Pdf	Topics of interest include, but are not limited to, the	Arranged Volume wise.	Vol.1,1, 2009-v.5, 1, 2013	Indexed in Open Jgate,

	Management Systems http://airccse.org/journal/ijdms/ijdms.html	Collaboration Center	applications	Internal search engine is given.		following Digital Libraries, Knowledge Acquisition, discovery & Management, Metadata Management, Knowledge Processing.			EBSCO, Inspac, Google etc.
139	The International Journal of Managing Information Technology http://airccse.org/journal/ijmit/ijmit.html	Academy & Industry Research Collaboration Center	Contribute New results in all areas of the strategic application of information technology (IT) in organizations.	Simple click on Issue Title. Internal search engine is given.	Pdf	Focuses on innovative ideas and best practices in using IT to advance organizations for-profit, non-profit,	Arranged Volume wise.	Vol. 1, 2009-v.5, 1, 2013	Indexed in Google, EBSCO, Pub Zone, PKP, Scirus etc.
140	The Journal of the Rutgers University Library http://jrul.libraries.rutgers.edu/index.php/jrul/index	Rutgers University Country: United States	History of libraries, history of books, New Jersey history	Simple click on title. Internal search engine with search tips	Pdf	Articles based on the holdings of the Rutgers University Libraries, and in the areas of New Jersey history, Rutgersensia,	Arranged Volume wise. Information is given for author,	Vol. 1, No. 1, 1937-v. 65, 2012	Fully reviewed & Issue, Author and title indexing has been

						bibliography, and the history of libraries, books and printing.	Reader, Librarians.		given.
141	The Public Access Computer Systems Review http://epress.lib.uh.edu/pr/pacsrev.html#history	University of Houston Libraries, Editor in Chief :Charles W. Bailey, Jr.	End user computer systems	Simple click on Issue Title. Internal search is given	Html	An electronic journal about end-user computer systems in libraries. Initially, published scholarly papers (Communications section), columns, and reviews.	Arranged Volume wise.	Vol.1, 1-3 1990-v.9 No.1, 1998	
142	Urban Library Journal http://lacuny.cuny.edu/ulj/	City University of New York Country: United States	Urban academic libraries, librarianship	Simple click on Issue Title.	Pdf and Html	All aspects of urban libraries and librarianship, welcomes articles dealing with academic, research, public, school, and special libraries in an urban setting, public higher education, urban	Articles are arranged Volume wise.	Vol. 9, 2, summer 1995-v.18, 1 Spring 2012	Refereed

						studies, multiculturalism, library and educational services to immigrants, preservation etc.			
143	Virginia Libraries http://scholar.lib.vt.edu/ejournals/VALib/	Virginia Library Association, United States	Promote, and improve library and information services and the profession of librarianship.	Simple click on Issue Title.	Pdf and Html	Vehicle for members to exchange information, ideas, and solutions to mutual problems in professional articles on current topics in the library and information field in order to advance literacy and learning and to ensure access to information in the Commonwealth of Virginia.	Arranged Volume wise.	Vol. 42, 1, 1996- v. 58, 4, 2012.	Vol. 30: 1984 - v. 41: 1995 tables of contents only
144	Webology http://www.webology.ir/	University of Tehran, Iran	Devoted to the field of the World Wide Web	Simple click on Issue Title.	E-text	The World Wide Web: Web: information	Arranged Volume wise.	Vol. 1, 1-2, 2004-v.9, 1-2, 2012	Peer Reviewed and

			Periodicals, Web science Periodicals, Information science Periodicals, and Library science Periodicals.			retrieval; Web crawling and indexing; Web cataloging; Web searching; Search engines and directories; Search behavior; Metadata etc. Library and Information Science: Information retrieval systems; Indexing; Abstracting; Information and communication technology; Information Evaluation.	Information is divided in two parts The world wide web and Library and information science.		Indexed by LISA, Scopus. The Informed Librarian Online, The Index of Information Systems Journals, DOAJ, EBSCO, Ulrich, Web Citation Index, World Cat etc.
145	World Libraries http://www.worlib.org/	Dominican University Graduate School of Library and	Focusing on libraries and socio economic development.	Simple click on Issue Title.	E-text	Dedicated to librarians and libraries in regions without associations or agencies to	Arranged Volume wise.	Vol. 1, 1, 1990-v.20, 1, 2012	Formerly known as Third World Libraries.

		Information Science				encourage scholarly communication and professional development. World Libraries is simply dedicated to the international nature of librarianship, promoting communication and relationships both professionally and personally.			Peer Reviewed and Published twice in Year

E-MAGAZINES

	Title/URL	Authority/ Publisher/ Editor/ Country	Scope/ Coverage/ Purpose	Searching/accessibility/ Networkability/Browsebility	Format	Treatment/ Accuracy/ Objectivity	Arrangement	Archiving/ Periodicity	Special Features/ Index

1	AALL Spectrum http://www.aallnet.org/main-menu/Publications/spectrum	American Association of Law Libraries	For members of the American Association of Law Libraries.	Simple click on Issue Title.	Pdf	Topics of real interest to law librarians, as well as news about the American Association of Law Libraries - Chapters, Committees, Special Interest Sections, etc.	Arranged by volume and Issue.	Vol.1,.9-10, 1997-v.17, July, 2013	
2	Access http://www.aardvarknet.info/access/number46/index.cfm	iGroup, England	Library Science, Web	Simple click on Issue Title.	Pdf	Aspects of Library and Information science.	Arranged by No.	No-36, March 2001-No-79, Dec 2011	
3	American Libraries http://americanlibrariesmagazine.org/	American Library Association.	Covers library science issues.	Simple click on Issue Title.	E-text	Open to any individual or organization interested in library service and library and information science.	Arranged Volume wise.	Jan/Feb 2008-March/April 2013	From 2003 to the present is available online free through library. published 10 times a

									year
4	Ariadne http://www.ariadne.ac.uk/	UKOLN (UK Office for Library Networking), funded by MLA, the Museums, Libraries and Archives Council.	Covers current digital library initiatives, technological, information service developments and information networking issues, Information Management.	Simple click on Issue Title. Has Internal search engine to search.	E-text	Targeted principally at information science professionals in academia, and also to interested lay people both in and beyond the Higher Education community. It concentrated originally on reporting in depth to the information community at large on progress and developments within the UK Electronic Libraries Programme (eLib)	Arranged by Issue. The articles of every issue has been divided in to three parts Main article, at the Event, News and Reviews	Issue 1, Jan 1996- Issue 70, Nov 2012	Published in January, April, July and October.

5	Book business http://www.bookbusinessmag.com/	North American Publishing Company	Books Information, News & Trends, Digital Directions, Internet	Simple click on Issue Title.	Html	Includes Digital rights management, Everything regarding books.	Information is arranged by Year. Information is arranged in five parts Cover Story, Features, Editor's Note, Columns and departments.	June 2006-Nov 2012	Monthly sometime irregular

6	Book Links http://www.ala.org/ala/aboutala/offices/publishing/booklinks/archiveonline/archive_of_online_articles.cfm	American Library Association	Focus on Connecting Books, Libraries, and Classrooms is a magazine designed for teachers, librarians, library media specialists, booksellers, parents, and other adults interested in connecting children with books.	Simple click on Issue Title. Internal search has been given for searching.	Html and Pdf	Response to curriculum role of the school library media center, the increased programming in public libraries, and the heavy reliance of child-care centers on children's literature, Book Links publishes bibliographies, essays linking books on a similar theme, retrospective reviews, and other features targeted at those educating young people.	Articles are arranged Volume and year wise.	Vol. 8, May 1999-v. 18, 1-5, July 2009.	Helping librarians, teachers, and parents connect children with high qualified books.

7	CHOICE http://www.ala.org/ala/mgrps/divs/acrl/publications/choice/previousissues/previousissues.cfm	Association of College & Research Libraries	Choice reaches almost every undergraduate college and university library in the United States.	Simple click on Issue Title.	Html	More than 35,000 academic librarians, faculty, and key decision makers rely on the reviews in Choice magazine and Choice Reviews Online for collection development and scholarly research.	Arranged by Year, Volume and then Number	Vol. 47, 5 Jan 2009-v. 50, 7, March 2013	Provides Trial access for two months or more time .
8	Computer in Libraries http://www.infotoday.com/cilmag/default.shtml	Information Today Inc,USA	Computer in Libraries is a monthly magazine that provides complete coverage of the news and issues in the rapidly evolving field of library information technology.	Simple click on Issue Title.	Pdf	Focusing on the practical application of technology in community, school, academic, and special libraries, includes discussions of the impact of emerging computer technologies on library systems and services, and on the	Arranged Volume wise.	Vol. 20, 1-10, 2000- v. 24, 1-8, 2004	VOL. 25, 2005- Vol. 33, 2013 is not open access.

						library community itself.			
9	Cultivate Interactive http://www.cultivate-int.org/index-2.html	UKLON	Disseminate information on digital cultural heritage	Simple click on Issue Title.	E-Text	Including articles on the ARCHEOGUIDE, the CIDOC Conceptual Reference Model, LIBECON, MESMUSES, Open Heritage.	Arranged Issue wise	Issue1, July 2000-Issue 9, Feb 2003	Funded under the European Commission's Digital heritage and Cultural Content (DIGICULT) programme.

10	D-Lib Magazine http://www.dlib.org/dlib/september08/09contents.html	Corporation for National Research Initiatives (CNRI), Currently supported by the D-Lib Alliance, Editor: Bonita Wilson	Focus on digital library research and development, including but not limited to new technologies, applications, and contextual social and economic issues.	Simple click on Issue Title. Search engine ht://Dig for searching.	E-text	The primary goal is timely and efficient information exchange for the digital library community. Articles and the shorter pieces are solicited or selected from among unsolicited submissions.	Arranged Issue wise	Vol.1, Issue1, 1995-v. 19, Number 1/2, Jan/Feb 2013	The Defense Advanced Research Project Agency (DARPA) on behalf of the Digital Libraries and the National Science Foundation (NSF) sponsors it. Published six times a year.

11	E-Content http://www.ecmag.net/	Online, A division of Information Today, Inc.	Emerging digital content trends, strategies, and resources that will help readers navigate the content maze and find a clear path to profits and improved business processes.	Simple click on Issue Title.	E-text	Delivers essential research, reporting, news, and analysis of content related issues. It is essential reading for executives and professionals involved in content creation, management, acquisition, organization, and distribution in both commercial and enterprise environments.	Arranged Year wise.	May 2002-Jan/Feb 2013	Publishes ten issues in a year.
12	EDUCAUSE Review http://www.educause.edu/	D. Teddy Diggs.	higher education IT community	Simple click on Issue Title. It has its own search engine	E-Text	Takes a broad look at current developments and trends in information technology, how they may affect the	Arranged volume wise.	Vol. 35, 1-6, 2000-v. 48, 1, Jan/Feb 2013	

						college/university as an institution, and what these mean for higher education and society.			
13	Ex Libris http://marylaine.com/exlibris/	Marylaine Block	Librarians and information junkies.	Simple click on Issue Title.	E-text	Focus on Computers, Information, It is a free promotional part of business, workshops for librarians and made presentations at several conferences.	Arranged Issue wise.	March 2002-April 2008	Past issue indexing has been done.
14	Exploit Interactive http://www.exploit-lib.org/	UKOLN with the support of the DBI and the British	Promote the results of EU library projects and Market of library and information systems	Simple click on Issue Title.	Html	Promote awareness, disseminate and exploit reusable project applications and results.	Arranged Issue wise.	Issue1, May 1999-Issue7, Oct 2000	

15	inCite http://alia.org.au/publishing/incite/archive.html	Australian Library and Information Association	New and emerging technologies	Simple click on Issue Title.	Html	Focus on Research and Education, Special Libraries, IFLA/Engagement	Arranged by Year, Volume and then Month	Vol.17, Jan-Dec.1996-v. 32, Jan-Dec 2011	V. 33 & 34, 2012/2013 is not open access
16	Information Today http://www.infotoday.com/IT/nov08/index.shtml	Information Today Inc,USA	Designed to meet the needs of the information professional.	Simple click on Issue Title.	Pdf and html	Coverage News and Trends in the information industry. Accurate, timely news articles inform the reader of the people, products, services, and events that impact the industry, while hard-hitting, topical articles explain significant developments in the field.	Arranged Volume and then Number wise.	Vol. 17, 1-10, 2000-V. 21, No.1/11, 2004	V. 22-28, 2005-2013 is not open access.

17	Knowledge Management World http://www.kmworld.com/index.cfm	Information Today, Inc	Knowledge management, Content Management, Document Management	Simple click on Issue Title.	E-text	Km world provide actionable Information through real world case studies, advice from key practitioners and best practice advice from market leaders.	Arranged issue and Volume wise.	Vol.7 Issue 1-13, 1998- v. 22 Issue 3, 2013	Issue indexing has been done.
18	Library Juice http://libr.org/juice/	Edited and published by Rory Litwin.	Electronic zine for librarians, library and information science students, and other interested people.	Simple click on Issue Title.	E-Text	Included discussions, commentary, announcements, humor, web links and news affecting the library world.	Arranged Issue wise.	Vol.1, 1998- V.8, 2005	Ceased
19	Link-Up http://www.infotoday.com/linkup/default.shtml	Incorporated into ITI's flagship publication	Digital Issues and ew special section of IT packed	Simple click on Issue Title.	Pdf	Includes featuring articles, reviews,	Arranged by date.	10/1/2002- 3/15/2013	All articles are not freely available.

20	Online http://www.infotoday.com/online/default.shtml	Information Today Inc, USA	Providing articles, product reviews, case studies, and evaluations about selecting, using, and managing electronic resources.	Simple click on Issue Title.	E-text	Provides articles, product reviews, case studies, evaluation, and informed opinion about selecting, using, and managing electronic information products, plus industry and professional information about online database systems, CD-ROM, and the Internet.	Arranged Volume wise.	Vol. 24, 1 Jan- 6 Dec, 2000-V. 28, No. 1-5, 2004 Volume 29-36, 2005-2012 is not open access.	Published six times in a year.

21	Provenance http://www.provenance.ca/about-provenance/index.html	Managing editor: Guy Robertson.	Newest columnist-journalist and arctic stories	Simple click on Issue Title. Internal search engine has been given.	E-text	Travel articles in Provenance came around the time of the International Conference of the Special Libraries Association of America, meeting in Seattle, Washington. literature covering the implementation of Western designed information systems in developing countries	Arranged by year.	Vol. 1,1 December, 1995-v. 11,2009	Maintain www.netpac.com developers of "findable" search engine web sites ©2002, 2003, 2004, 2005, 2006 2007 Vancouver , Canada.
22	Research Information http://www.researchinformation.info/	Europa Science Ltd	Library and Information science	Simple click on Issue Title.	E-Text	Focus on E-books, Digital, Lis Management etc	Arranged by Volume and Year	May-June 2004-Dec/Jan 2013	

23	Searcher: The Magazine for Database Professionals http://www.infotoday.com/searcher/default.asp	Information Today Inc, USA	Experienced, knowledgeable searchers and combines evaluations of data content with discussions of delivery media	Simple click on Issue Title.	E-text	Includes evaluated online news, searching tips and techniques; reviews of search aid software and database documentation, revealing interviews with leaders and entrepreneurs of the industry, and trenchant editorials.	Arranged Volume wise.	Issues 2000-Issues 2004. Current Issue Vol. 20 Dec (11) 2012	2005-2012 issues are not open access.

24	The Bulletin of the American Society for Information Science and Technology http://www.asis.org/bulletin.html	American Society for Information Science and Technology (ASIS&T) and its editor is Irene Travis, United States	Developments and issues affecting the field, pragmatic management reports, opinion, and news of people and events in the info. Science community.	Simple click on Issue Title.	Html and Pdf	Vehicle for sharing news and information regarding developments in the field of information science and technology, including political developments, dealt with such areas as information architecture, technology developments in libraries, indexing languages, information seeking behavior.	Arranged by year.	Vol. 21, 2-6, 1995-v. 39, 3, Feb/March 2013	Bi-monthly

25	The Marginal http://www.gslis.mcgill.ca/marginal/	McGill Library & Information Studies Student Association, MLISSA	Library, archives and knowledge management	Simple click on Issue Title.	E-Text	The aim is to be a place to publish experiences; not only do we publish articles related to the LIS field, but also those related to other aspects of the lives of library, archives and knowledge management students.	Arranged Number wise.	Volume 4, 3-4, 1997-v. 16, 2, Winter 2009	Issue Indexing has been done.
26	Virginia Tech Magazine http://www.vtmagazine.vt.edu/	Virginia Polytechnic Institute and State University, Blacksburg, Virginia	Alumni Association News	Simple click on Issue Title.	Html	Includes employees, students, or applicants for admission or employment on the basis of race, color, disability, age, veteran status, national origin, religion, or political	Information is arrange by year	Winteter/Summer 1996-Vol.33, 2, Winter 2011	ISSN: 0274-9904 and quarterly (fall, winter, spring, and summer)

NEWSLETTERS

	Title/URL	Authority/ Publisher/ Editor/ Country	Scope/ Coverage/ Purpose	Searching/accessibility/ Networkability/ Browsebility	Format	Treatment/Accuracy / Objectivity	Arrangement	Archiving /Periodicity	Special Features/Index
1	ABAA Newsletter http://hq.abaa.org/books/antiquarian/abaapages/newsletter	Publications Committee of The Antiquarian Booksellers	Library Science	Simple click on Issue Title.	Pdf	Covers Association of America for members of the organization, libraries and institutions, the antiquarian book community at large and the general public.	Arranged by Issue.	Fall 1989- Issue 9 Fall 2011	ISSN:1070-7000X and quarterly

2	Abbey Newsletter http://cool.conservation-us.org/byorg/abbey/an/	Abbey Publications Inc, New York	Library and Information Science	Simple click on Issue Title. Internal search has been given for searching.	E-text	Focuses on all the aspects of Library and Information Science including digital library and computers in libraries etc.	Arranged Volume wise.	Vol. 1, 1978- v. 26, No.1-6, 2002	Author and Title Indexing have been done.
3	Against the grain http://www.against-the-grain.com/d/TOC	Edited by Katina Strauch	Gives news about libraries, publishers, book jobbers, and subscription agents.	Simple click on Issue Title.	Pdf, E-text, Html	Key to the latest news about libraries, publishers, book jobbers, and subscription agents. It is a unique collection of reports on the issues, literature, and people that impact the world of books and journals.	Arranged Volume wise.	Vol. 1, 1, March 1989 and v. 12, 1-6, 2000-v.21, 1-2, 2009	All are articles are not open access. Publish Six Times in Year

4	ALAWON: The ALA Washington Office Electronic Newsline http://www.ala.org/ala/aboutala/offices/wo/washnews/archivea/archive.cfm	ALA Washington Office	Library and Information Science	Simple click on Issue Title.	Pdf	Keeping library advocates up to date on major legislative issues in the Nation's Capital.	Arranged by Volume and Number.	2009-2011	ALAWON stands for ALA Washington Office News line. It's a free, irregular e-mail publication
5	ALCTS Network News http://bubl.ac.uk/archive/journals/alctsnn/	Published by Association for Library Collections and Technical Services	An electronic publication of the Association for Library Collections and Technical Services.	Simple click on Issue Title.	E-Text	Carries diversity in libraries to another level and also includes the involvement the members of the community being served. Focus on re-tooling Technical Services staff for the future; changing old habits and concepts.	Arranged Volume wise.	Vol. 6 , N.20, 1994-v. 19, N. 1-6, 2000	Fortnightly, Volume 15 Number 14 1998 Not Published

6	ARL: A bimonthly newsletter for library issues and action http://www.arl.org/resources/pubs/br/index.shtml	ARL	Report on current issues of interest to academic and research library administrators, staff, library education.	Simple click on Issue Title.	Html and Pdf	Working tool prepared to assist member leaders to understand, discuss, and engage how the Association deploys its resources.	Arranged by Year	Issues 178-183 1995- Issues 256-261, 2008	Bimonthly and Links to Membership Meetings, E-News for ARL Directors. This also can't be loaded locally for home use
7	Biblia's Warrior Librarian Weekly http://warriorlibrarian.com/ARCHIVE/00archives.html	Created and maintained by A B Credaro	Library and information science	Simple click on Issue Title.	E-text	Includes Pokes fun at the people who use libraries and the funnier ones who work in them.	Arranged Volume wise.	Issue 95, Sept 2001- Issue 261, Dec 2008	Library humor index has been done.
8	Biblio-Tech Review http://www.ringgold.com/biblio-tech/si_pd.cfm?pid=2	Biblio Tech Ltd	News, Analysis and Comments	Simple click on Issue Title. Internal search is given	E-Text	Includes latest news updates from the library automation industry	Arranged year wise.	Jan-Dec 1999- Jan-Dec 2000 Brief articles are available	Year wise indexing has been done.

								till 2013	
9	Business and Finance Division Bulletin http://bf.sla.org/resources/the-bulletin/	Special Libraries Association (SLA).	Communicated with the members of the Business & Finance Division of the Special Libraries Association.	Simple click on Issue Title.	Pdf	Conveys information about Division and member activities. It also has developed a reputation for publishing informative and practical articles on the many topics that are of interest to a specially skilled and influential, worldwide readers	Arranged Volume wise.	No. 120, Spring 2002 -No 149, Fall 2012	Peer-Reviewed and Published in Spring, Fall, and winter. Complete issues available for 2002. Selected articles available 2003.
10	Cataloging and Classification Quarterly http://bubl.ac.uk/archive/journals/cacq/	BUBL Information Service, Andersonian Library, Strathclyde University, Scotland	Library and information science.	Simple click on Issue Title.	E-Text	Topics include her research interests in subject and descriptive cataloging, development of information science and its relationship to librarianship.	Arranged Volume wise.	Vol. 18 N. 1-2, 1993-v. 29, N. 1-4, 2000	Issue indexing has been done.

11	CIT Infobits http://serials.infomotions.com/infobits/	Sponsorship by the UNC-Chapel Hill ITS Teaching and Learning division.	Electronic service of the University of North Carolina at Chapel Hill ITS Teaching and Learning division.	Simple click on Issue Title.	E-text	Academic Outreach Consultant monitors and selects from a number of information and instructional technology sources that come to her attention and provides brief notes for electronic dissemination to educators	Arranged by year.	1993-2002	Began in 1993 by the UNC-Chapel Hill Institute for Academic Technology, titled IAT Infobits. From July 1998 changed to CIT Infobits.
12	Conserline http://www.loc.gov/acq/conser/consrlin.html	Library of Congress	News of the CONSER Program and information of interest to the serials cataloging community.	Simple click on Issue Title.	Html	Includes news and recent events about the program.	Arranged by Year	N. 1-3, 1994-No 29 Fall 2007	
13	Free Pint http://www.freepint.com/	Free Pint limited	Global network of people who find, use, manage and share work-related	Simple click on Issue Title.	Html	Publishes a family of resources to help information workers be more effective, raise the value of	Arranged by year.	Issue 1-4, 1997-March, Issue 371,	

			information			information in their organisations and contribute to success.		2013	
14	Information today and Tomorrow http://www.dsir.gov.in/pubs/itt/index.htm	NISSAT	Information on new tools and techniques	Simple click on Issue Title.	Html	Contents include information on new tools and techniques, events concluded and announcements, interesting Internet sites, new database products and services.	Arranged by year.	Vol. 8, 1-4, 1989- v. 21, 1-4, 2002	Quarterly with a change in the title, Information Today & Tomorrow, the quarterly periodical is distributed free to 5000 individuals and institutions
15	**Internet on a Disk http://www.samizdat.com/ioad.html**	Richard Seltzer.	Newsletter to share Richard Seltzer insights and opinions free with all	Simple click on Issue Title.	E-Text	Newsletter of electronic texts and Internet trends.	Arranged by Issue	1 Feb 1994 - 72 Dec 2011	

16	Internet Resources Newsletter http://www.hw.ac.uk/libwww/irn/irn.html	Edited and published by Heriot-Watt University Library staff.	Academics, students, engineers, scientists and social scientists.	Simple click on Issue Title.	E-text	Internet-related Material, new and notable sites, lots of interesting blogs and RSS, including engineering, science, and Social science.	Arranged by Issue.	Issue 1, Oct 1994-Issue 178 Dec 2009. Now ceased.	
17	LC Cataloging Newsline http://www.loc.gov/catdir/lccn/	Library of Congress	Cataloging Directorate	Simple click on Issue Title.	Pdf	Includes Bibliographic Access Directorate of the Library of Congress.	Arranged by volume and then Number.	Vol.1, No. 1-8, 1993-v. 16, No. 1-4, 2008	
18	MLS: Marketing Library Services http://www.infotoday.com/MLS/default.shtml	Information Today Inc, USA	Marketing information geared specifically towards librarians.	Simple click on Issue Title.	E-Text	All types of libraries with specific ideas for marketing, Suggestions for planning programs, making money, increasing business, and proving your value to your administrator.	Arranged Volume wise.	Jan-Dec 1998-Jan/Feb 2013	Published six times in a year.

19	NLM Technical Bulletin http://www.nlm.nih.gov/pubs/techbull/current_issue.html	U.S. National Library of Medicine. It is created by MEDLARS Management Section, NLM.	General Surgery, Primary Health Care, Pulmonary Medicine, Statistics as Topic, Technology, Disaster Medicine, Nanotechnology	Simple click on Issue Title.	Html and Pdf	Broad Medical Subject Headings are covered.	Arranged by year.	Issue 1, 1969-March/April 2013	HTML format (January-February 1997 - present). PDF format (May 1969 - November-December 1997)
20	RLG DigiNews http://www.oclc.org/programs/publications/newsletters/diginews.htm	Staff in the Department of Research, Cornell University Library, & OCLC	RLG DigiNews focuses on digitization and digital preservation.	Simple click on Issue Title. Internal search engine is given	Pdf	Indispensable reports on evolving practices and technology for digitizing materials and digital preservation of research collections, as well as in-depth coverage of notable projects in the field	Arranged by Issue	Vol. 1, 1, April 15, 1997-v.11, 1, April 15, 2007	Indispensable for its articles on evolving practices and technology, events, new projects and publications.

21	Serials E-News http://www.ringgold.com/UKSG/si_pd.cfm	UK Serials Group	Web Service, Current Issues and Developments	Simple click on Issue Title.	E-text	Associated web service provides up-to-the-minute news of current issues and developments within the global serials industry.	Arranged by Issue	No.33, March 2003- No.291, 8 March 2013	ISSN: 1476-0576 and published every two weeks exclusively for UKSG members and subscribers.
22	SPARC Open Access Newsletter or Free Online Scholarship Newsletter http://www.earlham.edu/~peters/fos/index.htm	Written by Peter Suber	Many OA initiatives focus on taxpayer-funded research.	Simple click on Issue Title.	Html	Covers Research topics especially taxpayer-funded research.	Articles are arranged by Issue.	28 March 2001-2 Issue 167, March 2013	Monthly Issues No. starts form 2003 (63-167)

23	Sprouts: Working Papers on Information Systems http://sprouts.aisnet.org/home.html	Sprouts Alliance, Netherlands	Information : Technology, environments, infrastructures, socio-technical design, management information systems	Simple click on Issue Title.	Pdf	Provides a fast-turnaround outlet for authentic and original research and work-in-progress carried out by scholars of the information systems field and members of AIS. Devoted to research about the ways in which information is generated and	Arranged by Year	2000-2013	Year, Subject, Tag and organization have done indexing.
24	The Wired Librarian's Newsletter http://www.wiredlibrarian.com/wln/wlnfront.htm	Micro Libraries	Advice on the implementation of microcomputers in libraries.	Simple click on Issue Title.	E-text	Unbiased source for news and ideas regarding the implementation of microcomputers in libraries	Arranged Year wise.	1983-1985	

Summary Table : Distribution of 195 Evaluated E-Resources

S.N	E-Resources	No.
1	E-Journals	145
2	E-Magazines	26
3	E-Newsletters	24

Fig. 4. Number of Evaluated free E-Resources E-Journals, e-magazine and E-Newsletters in library and information science Chart shows that maximum E-Resources are E-Journal 75%, E-Magazines 13 %, and E-Newsletters 12%.

3

CHARACTERISTICS OF OPEN ACCESS E-RESOURCES

3.1 ARCHIVING OF OPEN ACCESS E-RESOURCES IN LIS

E-Journals

URL	ARCHIVE	Year Free Full text
Special Libraries http://www.sla.org/content/shop/speclibs.cfm#1910	V. 1, 1910-V. 87, 1996	1910-1996
The Journal of the Rutgers University Library http://jrul.libraries.rutgers.edu/index.php/jrul/index	Vol. 1, No. 1, 1937-v. 65, 2012	1937-2012

American Archivist http://archivists.metapress.com/home/main.mpx	Vol. 1, 1-4, 1938-V.75, 1-2, 2012	1938-2012
College and Research Libraries http://crl.acrl.org/	V. 1, N. 1, 1939-V. 74, N. 1, Nov 2013	1939-2013
Studies in Bibliography http://etext.lib.virginia.edu/bsuva/sb	V.1, 1948-49,-V. 55, 2002	1948-2002
Journal of East Asian Libraries http://www.lib.byu.edu/dlib/spc/jeal/	V.1, No1, 1963- No. 156, No.1 Feb 2013	1963-2013
Health Information and Libraries Journal http://www3.interscience.wiley.com/journal/120118368/grouphome/home.html	Vol. 1-4, 1984-v.30, 1, March 2013	1984-2013
LASIE: Library Automated Systems Information Exchange http://search.informit.com.au/browseJournalTitle;res=E-LIBRARY;issn=0047-3774	V. 17, No 1-6, 1986-V. 33, No1, 2002	1986-2002
RBM Journal of Rare Books , Manuscripts, and Cultural Heritage http://rbm.acrl.org/content/2/2	March & Sept 1986- March & Sept 1990. Vol.1, 1-2, March & Sept 2000- v.13, 2, 2012	1986-2012
Research Management Review http://www.ncura.edu/content/news/rmr/archive.php	Vol.1, N1, Spring 1987- v.17 N.1 Fall/Winter 2009	1987-2009
North Carolina Libraries http://www.ncl.ecu.edu/index.php/NCL	Vol. 47, 1, 1989-v. 70, 1-2, 2012	1989-2012

The Public Access Computer Systems Review http://epress.lib.uh.edu/pr/pacsrev.html#history	V.1-No. 1-3 1990-V.9 No.1, 1998	1990-1998
Progressive Librarian http://libr.org/pl/	N.1, 1990-N.32, 2009 TOC access till Issue no. 38-39, spring 2012	1990-2009
Journal of Educational Media & Library Sciences http://joemls.tku.edu.tw/index_e.htm	Vol. 28, 1-4, 1991-1990-v. 50, 2, 2012	1990-2012
World Libraries http://www.worlib.org/	Vol. 1, 1, 1990-v.20, 1, 2012	1990-2012
Current Cites http://lists.webjunction.org/currentcites/	Vol1, 1990-v. 24, 1-2, March 2013	1990-2013
Issues in Science and Technology Librarianship http://www.library.ucsb.edu/istl/ Or http://www.istl.org/	Dec 1991- 71 Fall 2012	1991-2012
Journal of Staff Development http://learningforward.org/publications/jsd#.UUQguzcynUc	Vol. 13, N. 3, summer 1992-v. 34. N. 1, 2013	1992-2013
Interpersonal Computing and Technology Journal http://www.helsinki.fi/science/optek/#byissue	V.1, N.1,1993-V. 5, N1-.2, 1997	1993-1997
IFLA Journal http://www.ifla.org/V/iflaj/index.htm	V. 19, N.1-4, 1993- V. 28, No 1-6, 2002	1993-2002

International Journal of Special Libraries http://forge.fh-potsdam.de/~IFLA/INSPEL/intro.htm	V.27, N. 1-4, 1993-V. 36, N.1-4, 2002 Discontinued now	1993-2002
MC Journal: The Journal of Academic Media Librarianship http://wings.buffalo.edu/publications/mcjrnl/	V. 1, N1-2, 1993-V. 8, N. 2, 2002	1993-2002
Australian Journal of Information Systems http://dl.acs.org.au/index.php/ajis/about	Vol.1, 1-2, 1994-v.17, 3, 2012	1993-2012
Agricultural Libraries Information Notes http://webharvest.gov/peth04/20041023101316/http://www.nal.usda.gov/NewAlin/	V-20, No1-12, 1994- V-23, No 1-12, 1997	1994-1997
Technology Electronic Reviews (TER) http://www.ala.org/lita/publications/archive/ter	V. 1, N. 1-3, 1994- V. 14, N.2, 2007	1994-2007
ALAN Review http://scholar.lib.vt.edu/ejournals/ALAN/	Vol. 21, 2, Winter 1994-v. 38, 1, Fall 2010	1994-2010
Information for Social Change http://libr.org/isc/journal.html	N. 1, Winter 1994-N. 31, Summer 2012	1994-2012
Journal of the American Medical Informatics Association http://www.pubmedcentral.nih.gov/tocrender.fcgi?action=archive&journal=76	Vol 1, 1-6 1994- v. 19, 3, March 2012	1994-2012
Journal of Artificial Intelligence Research http://www.jair.org/	Vol.1, (August 1993- June 1994) - Vol. 46, Jan 2013	1994-2013

Information Research: An International Electronic Journal http://informationr.net/ir/	V.1, N. 1-3, 1995-1996-V. 16, N. 1, 2011	1995-2011
Christian Library Journal http://www.christianlibraryj.org/pdf/index.htm	Oct. 1995- Oct/Dec 2010. v. XVI, No 1-2, 2012,	1995-2012
JEP: The Journal of Electronic Publishing http://www.journalofelectronicpublishing.org/	Vol.1, 1-2, 1995-v. 15, 1-3, 2012	1995-2012
Urban Library Journal http://lacuny.cuny.edu/ulj/	Vol. 9, 2, summer 1995-v.18, 1 Spring 2012	1995-2012
Colby Quarterly (formerly: Colby Library Quarterly) http://digitalcommons.colby.edu/	V.32, no. 3-4-, 1996- v. 39 no 1-4, 2003	1996-2003
E-JASL: The Electronic Journal of Academic and Special Librarianship http://southernlibrarianship.icaap.org/	V. 1, 1996-V.10 N.1-3, Winter 2009 (Three issues in year Spring, Summer, Winter)	1996-2009
Chinese Librarianship: An International Electronic Journal http://www.iclc.us/cliej/	N.1 June 1996-N.36 Dec. 2013 Half Yearly	1996-2010
Journal of Information Law and Technology http://www2.warwick.ac.uk/fac/soc/law/elj/jilt/ or European Journal of Law and Technology http://ejlt.org//issue/archive	Issue1-3, 1996- V.1 No. 3, 2010 (V. Starts from 2010)	1996-2010

Library Resources & Technical Services (LRTS) http://alcts.metapress.com/home/main.mpx	Full text from Vol. 40, 1-4, 1996-v. 55, 1-4, 2011 Toc and abstract available till v. 57, 1, 2013	1996-2011
Journal of Technology Studies http://scholar.lib.vt.edu/ejournals/JOTS/	Vol. XXII, 2, Summer /Fall 1996- v. XXXVIII, 2, Fall 2012	1996-2012
LIBRES: Library and Information Science Research Electronic Journal http://libres.curtin.edu.au/	Vol. 6, 1-2 July 1996-V.22,2 March 2012 (bi-annual)	1996-2012
Virginia Libraries http://scholar.lib.vt.edu/ejournals/VALib/	Vol. 42, 1, 1996- v. 58, 4, 2012. (V. 30: 1984 - V. 41: 1995 tables of contents only)	1996-2012
Malaysian Journal of Library & Information Sciencehttp://ejum.fsktm.um.edu.my/V.Listing.aspx?JournalID=3	Vol.1, 1-2, 1996-v. 18, 1, 2013	1996-2013
School Library Journal Online http://www.schoollibraryjournal.com/	Issue 1,3,5,7,9,11, 1996-Issue 1, 2013	1996-2013
Electronic Transactions on Artificial Intelligence http://www.ida.liu.se/ext/etai/	V. 1, N. 1-3, 4, 1997-V.5, 2001	1997-2001

Journal of Internet Cataloguing http://www.internetcataloging.com/home.html	V.-1, No1, 1997-V. 5, No1, 2001	1997-2001
Internet Writing Journal http://www.internetwritingjournal.com/	August 1997-Dec-Jan 2007	1997-2007
Electronic Journal of Africana Bibliography http://ir.uiowa.edu/ejab/all_issues.html	Vol.1, 1997-V. 13, 2012	1997-2009
MELA Notes: The Journal of the Middle East Librarians Association http://www.mela.us/MELANotes/MELANotesIntro.html	Number 64 (Spring 1997)-number 82 (2009) and no. 1-(1973)	1997-2009
Cybermetrics : International Journal of Scientometrics, Informatics and Bibliometrics http://www.cindoc.csic.es/cybermetrics/	V. 1, Issue -1, 1997-V. 14, Issue1, 2010	1997-2010
Alki: The Washington Library Association Journal http://www.wla.org/alki/	Vol.13, 2-3, July 1997-v. 28, 3. July 2012	1997-2012
Journal of Digital Information http://jodi.ecs.soton.ac.uk/r or http://journals.tdl.org/jodi	V.1, No1-2, 1997-V. 12 No 1, 2012	1997-2012
Human IT: Journal for Information Technology Studies as a Human Science http://etjanst.hb.se/bhs/ith//info-eng.htm	Vol. 1, 1-4, 1997- v.12, 2, 2013	1997-2013
Learned Publishing http://www.ingentaconnect.com/content/alpsp/lp	Vol.1, 10, 1997-v.26, 1, 2013	1997-2013

NPO Journal/NPO E-Journal http://www.bl.uk/blpac/publicationsjournals.html	No. 1, Feb. 1998- No. 13, Nov 2003 & No.1 May 2004- No.5 March 2007	1998-2007
Journal of the Association for History and Computing http://quod.lib.umich.edu/j/jahc/browse.html	V. 1, N. 1, June 1998- V.13, N.1, May 2010	1998-2010
Informatica Economica Journal http://revistaie.ase.ro/index.html	Vol. 2, 1-4, 1998-v. 16, 4, 2012 (V.1 and V.2(2) are not open access)	1998-2012
Journal of Knowledge Management Practice http://www.tlainc.com/boutjkmp.htm	Vol. 1. 1998-99-Vol.13 N. 4, Dec 2012	1998-2012
School libraries in Canada (SLIC): A Journal of the Canadian Association for School Libraries http://www.clatoolbox.ca/casl/slic/links.html	Vol. 18 N02, 1998-v. 30 No. 1, 2012	1998-2012
Current Issues in Education http://cie.asu.edu/index.php	Vol. 1, 10, 1998-v. 16, 1, 2013	1998-2013
Informing Science The International Journal of an Emerging Transdiscipline http://inform.nu/	Vol.1 1998-v.1. 16, 2013	1998-2013
School Library Research http://www.ala.org/aasl/slr	Vol.1, 1998-v.16, 2013	1998-2013
DIGITHUM: The Humanities in Digital Age http://www.uoc.edu/digithum/7/eng/numeros.html	Issue n. 1, 1999-Issue N. 7, 2005	1999-2005

LIBRI: International Journal of Libraries and Information Services http://www.librijournal.org/	V. 49, N.1-4, 1999- V. 59, N.1, 2009	1999-2009
Australian Library Journal http://alia.org.au/publishing/alj/	Vol. 48, Nov, Aug May, Feb. 1999-v. 59, (1-4) Feb., May, Aug, Nov. 2010. 2011 and 2012 are available in print to subscribers only	1999-2010
Journal of Medical Internet Research http://www.jmir.org/	Vol. 1, 1-2, - supplement1, 1999-v. 12, 2, 2013	1999-2013
High Energy Physics Libraries Webzine http://library.web.cern.ch/library/Webzine/index.shtml	Issue 1 Mach 2000-Issue 13 oct 2006	2000-2006
EBIB Electronic Information Bulletin for librarians http://ebib.info/biuletyn/	Selected fulltext No.10, Dec 2000- No.3, April2008. Fulltext 2002 Special issue for the Frankfurt book fair 2000. (Abstract 1999-2010)	2000-2008
EDUCAUSE Quarterly http://www.educause.edu/eq	V.23, 1-4, 2000-V.34, 1-4, 2011	2000-2011
Electronic Journal on Information Systems in Developing Countries http://www.ejisdc.org/ojs2/index.php/ejisdc	V.1, 2000- V. 55, 2012	2000-2012

Mississippi Libraries http://www.misslib.org/index.php/publications/mississippi-libraries/	V.64, No. 1 2000- V. 75, No 3, 2012	2000-2012
Law Library Journal http://www.aallnet.org/products/pub_journal.asp	Vol.92, 1 (Winter 2000)-v.105, 1 (Winter 2013)	2000-2013
Simile: Studies in Media and Information Literacy Education http://utpjournals.metapress.com/content/120764/	V.1 Issue1-4, 2001-V. 1, N. 1-2, 2009	2001-2009
Australian Academic and Research Libraries http://www.alia.org.au/publishing/aarl/index.html	Vol. 32, 1-4, 2001-v. 41, 1-4, 2010. (42, 2012 & 43 2013 is not open access)	2001-2010
Digital Document Quarterly http://home.pacbell.net/hgladney/ddqstart.htm	V.1 N.1-3, 2002 - V. 9- No 1, 2009	2002-2009
MLA Forum http://www.mlaforum.org/	V. 1, Issue1-2, 2002-V. 7, 2009	2002-2009
Library Journal http://www.libraryjournal.com	Issue 1-20 Jan-Dec, 2002-Issue 1-17, Jan 2011	2002-2011
Annals of Library & Information Studies http://nopr.niscair.res.in/	Vol. 49, 2002-V. 59, 2012	2002-2012
Journal of Information Technology Education (JITE: Research) http://www.informingscience.us/icarus/journals/jiteresearch/publications	Vol.1, 2002-v. 12, 2012	2002-2012

Scandinavian Public Library Quarterly http://www.splq.info/	Vol. 35, 2002- v. 45, 4, 2012	2002-2012
Data Science Journal http://www.jstage.jst.go.jp/browse/dsj	Vol.1, 2002-v. 12, 2013	2002-2013
Journal of the Medical Library association http://www.ncbi.nlm.nih.gov/pmc/journals/93/	Vol1, 1898 - v.101 1, 2013	2002-2013
LIBER Quarterly Journal of European Research Libraries http://liber.library.uu.nl/index.html	Vol.1, 10, 1997-v.26, 1, 2013	2002-2013
Information Scotland: The Journal of the Chartered Institute of Library and Information Professionals in Scotland http://www.slainte.org.uk/publications/serials/infoscot/V.1(1)/V.1(1)contents.html	V. 1 (1-6) February 2003-V.7(1-3) June 2009	2003-2009
Journal of Research and Practice in Information Technology http://ws.acs.org.au/jrpit/JRPIT_Volumes.html	Vol. 35, 1-4, 2003-v. 43, 1-3, 2011	2003-2011
Electronic Journal of Knowledge Management http://www.ejkm.com/	Vol. 1, 1, Sep 2003-v. 10, 3, March 2012	2003-2012
Information Technologies and International Development http://itidjournal.org/itid	V.1, 1-2, 2003-V 9, 1, 2013	2003-2013
IT&Society http://www.itandsociety.org/index.html	V.1, No.1-7, 2004 (Currently suspended)	2004-2004

Journal of e-Literacy http://www.jelit.org/index.html	V. 1, Issue 1, 2004-V.2, Issue1-2, 2005 (One item of 2003 is also available)	2004-2005
Multimedia Information and Technology Journal (MmIT) http://www.cilip.org.uk/get-inV.ved/special-interest-groups/multimedia/journal/pages/default.aspx	Vol. 30, 1-4, 2004-v.37, 1, August 2011 (38 is not open access)	2004-2011
International Review of Information Ethics http://www.i-r-i-e.net/	Vol. 1 ,1-2 June & Oct 2004-v.18, Dec 2012	2004-2012
Issues in Informing Science and Information Technology http://iisit.org/	Vol. 1, 2004 - v. 9, 2012	2004-2012
The Bonefolder: An outgrowth of the Book Arts Web http://www.philobiblon.com/bonefolder/	Vol. 1, 1, Fall 2004-v. 8, 1, 2012	2004-2012
Webology http://www.webology.ir/	Vol. 1, 1-2, 2004-v.9, 1-2, 2012	2004-2012
Inter-Actions: UCLA Journal of Education and Information Studies http://repositories.cdlib.org/gseis/interactions/	Vol. 1, 1-2, 2004-v. 9, 1, 2013	2004-2013
International Review of Research in Open and Distance Learning http://www.irrodl.org/index.php/irrodl	Vol. 5, 1-3, 2004-v. 14, 1, 2013	2004-2013

South African Journal of Information Management http://www.sajim.co.za/index.php/sajim/issue/current	Vol.1, No.1-4, 1999-v.15, 1, 2013.	2004-2013
Information Technology and Disabilities http://people.rit.edu/easi/itd.htm	V. 1 Jan 1994-V. 11, 2005 and V. 12, No. 1, June 2008	2005-2008
Coordinates: Online Journal of the Map and Geography Round Table of the American Library Association. Series A and B http://www.sunysb.edu/libmap/coordinates.htm	Series A: N. 1-9 28 May 2005-March 2010 and Series B: N.1 Jan 2005- No 9, 20 Aug 2009	2005-2010
International Journal of Legal Information http://scholarship.law.cornell.edu/ijli/V.33/iss1/	V. 33, No.1,Spring 2005-V. 38, No. 1, Spring 2010	2005-2010
African Journal of Information & Communication Technology http://epress.lib.uts.edu.au/journals/index.php/ajict/index/	Vol. 1, 1 (2005)- V. 6 (1) 2011 V. 7, 1, 2013is not open access	2005-2011
Interdisciplinary Journal of E-Learning and Learning Objects http://ijklo.org/	V. 1, 2005-V. 7, 2011	2005-2011
ITALICS: Innovations in Teaching and Learning in Information and Computer Sciences http://www.ics.heacademy.ac.uk/italics/	Vol. 4, 1-3, 2005-v. 10, 3, 2011	2005-2011
Firstmonday http://firstmonday.org/	Vol. 10, 5-12 Dec 2005-v. 18, 3-4, March 2013	2005-2013

Journal of the European Association for Health Information and Libraries http://www.eahil.net/journal/	Vol.1, 1-4, 2005-v.9, 4, 2013	2005-2013
Informing Faculty: An International Journal of Higher Education Discussion Cases http://informingfaculty.org/	Only V.1, 2006	2006-2006
Electronic Journal of Health Informatics http://www.ejhi.net/ojs/index.php/ejhi	Vol.1, 1, 2006-v.7,2, 2012	2006-2012
Evidence Based Library and Information Practice http://ejournals.library.ualberta.ca/index.php/EBLIP/index	Vol. 1, 1-4, 2006-v.7, 4, 2012	2006-2012
Interdisciplinary Journal of Information, Knowledge, and Management http://www.ijikm.org/	Vol. 1, 2006-v. 7, 2012	2006-2012
Library Student Journal http://www.librarystudentjournal.org/index.php/lsj/index	2006-2012	2006-2012
Partnership: The Canadian Journal of Library and Information Practice and Research http://journal.lib.uoguelph.ca/index.php/perj/index	Vol. 1, 1, 2006-v. 7 2, 2012	2006-2012
Cites & Insights: Crawford at Large http://citesandinsights.info/citoc.htm	Vol.6, Jan -Dec 2006-v.13, April 2013	2006-2013
DESIDOC Journal of Library & Information Science http://publications.drdo.gov.in/ojs/index.php/djlit/index	Vol. 26,1-6, 2006-v. 33,1, 2013	2006-2013

International Journal of Digital Curation http://www.ijdc.net/./ijdc/issue/current	V,1 ,1, 2006-v.7, 2, 2012	2006-2013
International Journal of Doctoral Studies (IJDS) http://ijds.org/	Vol. 33, No.1, Spring 2005-v. 38, No. 2, Spring 2010	2006-2013
Journal of Information, Information Technology, and Organizations http://jiito.org/	Vol.1, 2006-v. 8, 2013 (Annual)	2006-2013
Communications in Information Literacy http://www.comminfolit.org/index.php/cil/issue/archive	Vol.1, 1-2, 2007-v.6, 2, 2012	2007-2012
European Journal of ePractice http://www.epracticejournal.eu/	No. 1 Nov. 2007- No. 18 Oct 2012	2007-2012
International Journal of Computer and Information Engineering http://www.waset.org/journals/ijcie/	Vol.1. No 1-8, 2007-v. 6, 2012	2007-2012
Journal of Information Literacy http://ojs.lboro.ac.uk/ojs/index.php/JIL/index	Vol. 1, N. 1-3, 2007-Vol. 6, N.2, 2012	2007-2012
Library & Information Research: Research into Practice for Information & Library Services http://www.lirgjournal.org.uk/lir/ojs/index.php/lir	Vol. 31, 97, 2007-v. 36, 113, 2012	2007-2012
Library Philosophy and Practice http://www.webpages.uidaho.edu/~mbolin/lpp.htm	Annual Vol. Dec. 2007-Annual v. June 2012	2007-2012

International Journal of Communication http://ijoc.org/ojs/index.php/ijoc/about/editorialPolicies#focusAndScope	V.1, 2007- V.7 2013	2007-2013
Journal of Health Informatics in Developing Countries http://www.jhidc.org/index.php/jhidc	Vol.1,1, 2007-v.7,1, 2013	2007-2013
Code4Lib Journal http://journal.code4lib.org/	Issue 1, 2007-Issue 19, 2013	2007-2013
Journal of Virtual Worlds Research http://www.jvwresearch.org/index.html	V. 1, N. 1-3, 2008-V. 3, N.2, 2010	2008-2010
Texas library journal http://www.txla.org/TLJ	Vol. 84, 1-4, 2008-v. 88,1-4, 2012	2008-2012
Computer and Information Science http://journal.ccsenet.org/index.php/cis/index	Vol.1, 1-4, 2008-v. 6, 2, 2013	2008-2013
Technological Librarianship: An Online Journal of the American Theological Library Association http://journal.atla.com/ojs/index.php/theolib/index	Vol.1, 1-2, 2008-v.6, 1, 2013	2008-2013
New Knowledge Environments http://journals.uvic.ca/index.php/INKE	V.1, No. 1, 2009	2009
Journal of Information Architecture http://journalofia.org/archives/	V.1, 1 spring 2009- V.3, 1 spring 2011	2009-2011
The Idaho Librarian: A Publication of the Idaho Library Association http://www.idaholibraries.org/idlibrarian/index.php/idaho-librarian/index	Vol. 59,1-2, 2009-v.61, 1, 2011	2009-2011

Collaborative Librarianship http://www.collaborativelibrarianship.org/index.html	Vol.1, 1-4, 2009- v43, 4, 2012	2009-2012
International Journal of Communication Networks and Information Security http://www.ijcnis.org/index.php/ijcnis	V.1 No 1-3, 2009- v. 4, No. 3, 2012	2009-2012
International Journal of Computer Science and Information Technology http://airccse.org/journal/ijcsit.html	V. 1, 1-2 2009- v. 5, 1- 6 2013	2009-2013
International Journal of Library and Information Science http://www.academicjournals.org/ijlis/index.htm	V.1, No. 1-6, 2009-V. 5, No 2, 2013	2009-2013
International Journal of Multimedia and Its Applications http://airccse.org/journal/ijma_index.html	V.1, 1, 2009- v.5,1, 2013	2009-2013
The International Journal of Database Management Systems http://airccse.org/journal/ijdms/ijdms.html	Vol.1,1, 2009-v.5, 1, 2013	2009-2013
The International Journal of Managing Information Technology http://airccse.org/journal/ijmit/ijmit.html	Vol. 1, 2009- v.5, 1, 2013	2009-2013
Information Technology and Libraries http://www.ala.org/ala/mgrps/divs/lita/ital/italinformation.cfm	Available V.20, No 1-4, 2001 – V.29, No 1-3, 2010 But freely available from V. 23, No. 1-4 -V. 29, No1, 2010	2010-2010
Journal of Philippine Librarianship	Vol. 27, 1-2, 2010- v.31, 1,	2010-2011

http://journals.upd.edu.ph/index.php/jpl/issue/current	2011	
International Journal of Managing Public Sector Information and Communication Technologies http://airccse.org/journal/mpict/ijmpict.html	V.1, 1- 2, Dec 2010-V.3, No2 Dec 2012	2010-2012
Journal of Library Innovation http://www.libraryinnovation.org/about/contact	V.1 No 1-2, 2010- V3 No 2, 2012	2010-2012
B Sides http://ir.uiowa.edu/bsides/	2010-2013	2010-2013
JLIS.it Italian Journal of Library and Information Science http://leo.cilea.it/index.php/jlis/article/view/4539/4416	Vol.1, No. 1-2, 2010- V.4 No.1, 2013	2010-2013
Northwestern Journal of Technology and Intellectual Property http://www.law.northwestern.edu/journals/njtip/issues.htm	V. 8, Issue 2 2010- V. 11, Issue 2 2013	2010-2013

E-Magazines

Provenance http://www.provenance.ca/about-provenance/index.html	V. 1 - No. 1 December, 1995-V. 11,2009	1995-2009
D-Lib Magazine http://www.dlib.org/dlib/september08/09contents.html	Vol.1, Issue1, 1995-v. 19, Number 1/2, Jan/Feb 2013	1995-2013

The Bulletin of the American Society for Information Science and Technology http://www.asis.org/bulletin.html	Vol. 21, 2-6, 1995-v. 39, 3, Feb/March 2013	1995-2013
Virginia Tech Magazine http://www.vtmagazine.vt.edu/	Summer 1996- V.31 No2, Winter 2009	1996-2009
inCite http://alia.org.au/publishing/incite/archive.html	Vol.17, Jan-Dec.1996-v. 32, Jan-Dec 2011	1996-2011
Ariadne http://www.ariadne.ac.uk/	Issue 1, Jan 1996- Issue 70, Nov 2012	1996-2012
The Marginal http://www.gslis.mcgill.ca/marginal/	Volume 4, 3-4, 1997-v. 16, 2, Winter 2009	1997-2009
AALL Spectrum http://www.aallnet.org/main-menu/Publications/spectrum	Vol.1,.9-10, 1997-v.17, July, 2013	1997-2013
Library Juice http://libr.org/juice/	V.1, 1998-V.8, 2005	1998-2005
Knowledge Management World http://www.kmworld.com/index.cfm	Vol.7 Issue 1-13, 1998-v. 22 Issue 3, 2013	1998-2013
Exploit Interactive http://www.exploit-lib.org/	Issue1, May 1999-Issue7, Oct 2000	1999-2000

Book Links http://www.ala.org/ala/aboutala/offices/publishing/booklinks/archiveonline/archive_of_online_articles.cfm	V. 8, May 1999-V. 18, N.1-5, July 2009.	1999-2009
Cultivate Interactive http://www.cultivate-int.org/index-2.html	Issue1, July 2000-Issue9, Feb 2003	2000-2003
Computer in Libraries http://www.infotoday.com/cilmag/default.shtml	V. 20, N. 1-10, 2000- V. 24, N.1-8, 2004 (2005-2013 Only some issues are available full text)	2000-2004
Information Today http://www.infotoday.com/IT/nov08/index.shtml	Vol. 17, 1-10, 2000-V. 21, No.1/11, 2004 V. 22-28, 2005- 2013 is not open access.	2000-2004
Online http://www.infotoday.com/online/default.shtml	Vol. 24, 1 Jan- 6 Dec, 2000-V. 28, No. 1-5, 2004 Volume 29- 36, 2005-2012 is not open access.	2000-2004
Searcher: The Magazine for Database Professionals http://www.infotoday.com/searcher/default.asp	Issues 2000-Issues 2004. Current Issue Vol. 20 Dec (11) 2012	2000-2004
EDUCAUSE Review http://www.educause.edu/	Vol. 35, 1-6, 2000-v. 48, 1,	2000-2013

	Jan/Feb 2013	
Access http://www.aardvarknet.info/access/number46/index.cfm	No-36, March 2001- No-79, Dec 2011	2001-2011
Ex Libris http://marylaine.com/exlibris/	March 2002- April 2008	2002-2008
E-Content http://www.ecmag.net/	May 2002-Jan/Feb 2013	2002-2013
Link-Up http://www.infotoday.com/linkup/default.shtml	10/1/2002-3/15/2013	2002-2013
Research Information http://www.researchinformation.info/	May-June 2004- Dec/Jan 2013	2004-2013
Book business http://www.bookbusinessmag.com/	June 2006-Nov 2012	2006-2012
American Libraries http://americanlibrariesmagazine.org/	Jan/Feb 2008- March/April 2013	2008-2013
CHOICE http://www.ala.org/ala/mgrps/divs/acrl/publications/choice/previousissues/previousissues.cfm	Vol. 47, 5 Jan 2009-v. 50, 7, March 2013	2009-2013

E-Newsletters

NLM Technical Bulletin http://www.nlm.nih.gov/pubs/techbull/current_issue.html	Issue 1, 1969-March/April 2013	1970-2013
Abbey Newsletter http://cool.conservation-us.org/byorg/abbey/an/	V. 1, N. 1-4, 7, 15, 1978- V26, No.1-6, 2002	1978-2002
The Wired Librarian's Newsletter http://www.wiredlibrarian.com/wln/wlnfront.htm	1983-1985	1983-1985
Information today and Tomorrow http://www.dsir.gov.in/pubs/itt/index.htm	V. 8, Issue 1-4, 1989-V. 21, Issue 1-4, 2002	1989-2002
ABAA Newsletter http://hq.abaa.org/books/antiquarian/abaapages/newsletter	Fall 1989- Issue 9 Fall 2011	1989-2011
Cataloging and Classification Quarterly http://bubl.ac.uk/archive/journals/cacq/	V. 18 N. 1-2, 1993-V. 29, N. 1-4, 2000	1993-2000
CIT Infobits http://serials.infomotions.com/infobits/	1993- 2002	1993-2002
LC Cataloging Newsline http://www.loc.gov/catdir/lccn/	V.1, No. 1-8, 1993-V. 16, No. 1-4, 2008	1993-2008
ALCTS Network News http://bubl.ac.uk/archive/journals/alctsnn/	Vol. 6 , N.20, 1994-v. 19, N. 1-6, 2000	1994-2000
Conserline http://www.loc.gov/acq/conser/consrlin.html	N. 1-3, 1994-No 29 Fall 2007	1994-2007

Internet on a Disk http://www.samizdat.com/ioad.html	#1 Feb 1994-- # 71 August 2009	1994-2009
Internet Resources Newsletter http://www.hw.ac.uk/libwww/irn/irn.html	Issue 1, October 1994- Issue 178 Dec 2009. This pub. Has now ceased.	1994-2009
ARL: A bimonthly newsletter for library issues and action http://www.arl.org/resources/pubs/br/index.shtml	Issues 178-183 1995- Issues 256-261, 2008	1995-2008
RLG DigiNews http://www.oclc.org/programs/publications/newsletters/diginews.htm	V. 1, N.1, April 15, 1997-V.11, N.1, April 15, 2007	1997-2007
Free Pint http://www.freepint.com/	Issue 1-4, 1997- March, Issue 371, 2013	1997-2013
MLS: Marketing Library Services http://www.infotoday.com/MLS/default.shtml	Jan-Dec 1998-March/April 2011	1998-2011
Biblio-Tech Review http://www.ringgold.com/biblio-tech/si_pd.cfm?pid=2	Jan-Dec 1999-Jan-Dec 2000 Brief articles are available till 2013	1999-2000
Against the grain http://www.against-the-grain.com/d/TOC	Vol. 1, 1, March 1989 and v. 12, 1-6, 2000-v.21, 1-2, 2009	2000-2009
Sprouts: Working Papers on Information Systems http://sprouts.aisnet.org/home.html	2000- 2013	2000-2013
Biblia's Warrior Librarian Weekly http://warriorlibrarian.com/ARCHIVE/00archives.html	Issue 95, Sept 2001-Issue 261, Dec 2008	2001-2008

SPARC Open Access Newsletter or Free Online Scholarship Newsletter http://www.earlham.edu/~peters/fos/index.htm	28 March 2001-2 Issue 167, March 2013	2001-2013
Business and Finance Division Bulletin http://bf.sla.org/resources/the-bulletin/	No. 120, Spring 2002 -No 149, Fall 2012	2002-2012
Serials E-News http://www.ringgold.com/UKSG/si_pd.cfm	No.33, March 2003-No.291, 8 March 2013	2003-2013
ALAWON. The ALA Washington Office Electronic Newsline http://www.ala.org/ala/aboutala/offices/wo/washnews/archivea/archive.cfm	2009-2011	2009-2011

Table shows that all E-Resources have Archiving Features i.e. 195 (100%). Found that Archives of 195 Open Access E-Resources starts form 1910 to 2013. The trend growth of E-Resources is increasing day by day.

Summary Table: Distribution of E-Resources by Growth

S.N	Growth of E-Resources	No of E-Resources	Percentage
1	1910-1980	9	4.00%
2	1981-1990	13	13.00%
3	1991-2000	84	43.00%
4	2001-2010	89	46.00%
	Total	**195**	**100.00%**

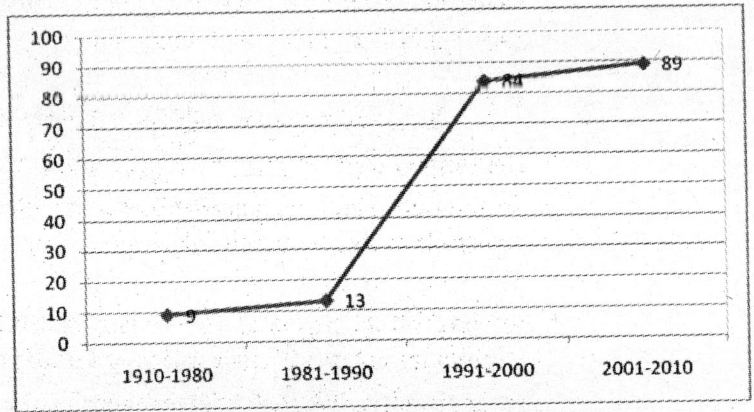

Fig: Trend Line of Growth of E-Resources

Chart shows that Open Access E-Resources are increasing, from 1910-1980 (70 Years) growth of E-Resources was 4% (9), From 1981-1990 (10 Years) the growth of E-Resources was 13% (13), From 1991-2000 (10 Years) the growth of Open Access E-Resources was 43% (84), and from 2001-2010 (10 Years) the growth of Open Access E-Resources is 46% (89).

3.2 SUBJECT COVERAGE OF OPEN ACCESS E-RESOURCES

		Coverage	
SL. No.	Title/URL	Complete	Partial
1	College and Research Libraries http://crl.acrl.org/	Y	
2	African Journal of Information & Communication Technology http://epress.lib.uts.edu.au/ojs/index.php/ajict/	Y	
3	Agricultural Libraries Information Notes http://webharvest.gov/peth04/20041023101316/http://www.nal.usda.gov/NewAlin/	Y	
4	Alki: The Washington Library Association Journal http://www.wla.org/alki/	Y	
5	American Archivist http://archivists.metapress.com/home/main.mpx	Y	
6	Australian Library Journal http://alia.org.au/publishing/alj/	Y	
7	Chinese Librarianship: An International Electronic Journal http://www.iclc.us/cliej/	Y	
8	Christian Library Journal http://www.christianlibraryj.org/pdf/index.htm	Y	
9	Collaborative Librarianship http://www.collaborativelibrarianship.org/index.html	Y	
10	Communications in Information Literacy http://www.comminfolit.org/index.php/cil/issue/archive	Y	
11	Current Cites http://lists.webjunction.org/currentcites/	Y	

12	Cybermetrics : International Journal of Scientometrics, Informetrics and Bibliometrics http://www.cindoc.csic.es/cybermetrics/	Y	
13	DESIDOC Journal of Library & Information Science http://publications.drdo.gov.in/ojs/index.php/djlit/index	Y	
14	EBIB Electronic Information Bulletin for librarians http://ebib.info/biuletyn/	Y	
15	E-JASL: The Electronic Journal of Academic and Special Librarianship http://southernlibrarianship.icaap.org/	Y	
16	Evidence Based Library and Information Practice http://ejournals.library.ualberta.ca/index.php/EBLIP/index	Y	
17	Health Information and Libraries Journal http://www3.interscience.wiley.com/journal/120118368/grouphome/home.html	Y	
18	High Energy Physics Libraries Webzine http://library.web.cern.ch/library/Webzine/index.shtml	Y	
19	IFLA Journal http://www.ifla.org/V/iflaj/index.htm	Y	
20	Information for Social Change http://libr.org/isc/journal.html	Y	
21	Information Research: An International Electronic Journal http://informationr.net/ir/	Y	
22	Informing Faculty: An International Journal of Higher Education Discussion Cases http://informingfaculty.org/	Y	
23	Informing Science The International Journal of an Emerging Transdiscipline http://inform.nu/	Y	
24	International Journal of Special Libraries http://forge.fh-potsdam.de/~IFLA/INSPEL/intro.htm	Y	

25	Issues in Science and Technology Librarianship http://www.library.ucsb.edu/istl/ Or http://www.istl.org/	Y	
26	JLIS.it Italian Journal of Library and Information Science http://leo.cilea.it/index.php/jlis/article/view/4539/4416	Y	
27	Journal of Educational Media & Library Sciences http://joemls.tku.edu.tw/index_e.htm	Y	
28	Journal of Library Innovation http://www.libraryinnovation.org/about/contact	Y	
29	Journal of Philippine Librarianship http://journals.upd.edu.ph/index.php/jpl/issue/current	Y	
30	Journal of the Medical Library association http://www.ncbi.nlm.nih.gov/pmc/journals/93/	Y	
31	Library & Information Research: Research into Practice for Information & Library Services **http://www.lirg.org.uk/lir/ojs/index.php/lir**	Y	
32	Library Journal **http://www.libraryjournal.com**	Y	
33	Library Philosophy and Practice http://www.webpages.uidaho.edu/~mbolin/lpp.htm	Y	
34	Library Resources & Technical Services (LRTS) **http://www.ala.org/ala/mgrps/divs/alcts/resources/lrts/index.cfm**	Y	
35	Library Student Journal **http://www.librarystudentjournal.org/index.php/lsj/index**	Y	
36	LIBRES: Library and Information Science Research Electronic Journal http://libres.curtin.edu.au/	Y	
37	LIBRI: International Journal of Libraries and Information Services http://www.librijournal.org/	Y	
38	Malaysian Journal of Library & Information Sciencehttp://ejum.fsktm.um.edu.my/VolumeListing.aspx?JournalID=3	Y	

39	MC Journal: The Journal of Academic Media Librarianship http://wings.buffalo.edu/publications/mcjrnl/	Y	
40	MELA Notes: The Journal of the Middle East Librarians Association http://www.mela.us/MELANotes/MELANotesIntro.html	Y	
41	Mississippi Libraries http://www.misslib.org/index.php/publications/mississippi-libraries/	Y	
42	MLA Forum http://www.mlaforum.org/	Y	
43	North Carolina Libraries http://www.ncl.ecu.edu/index.php/NCL	Y	
44	Partnership: The Canadian Journal of Library and Information Practice and Research http://journal.lib.uoguelph.ca/index.php/perj/index	Y	
45	Progressive Librarian http://libr.org/pl/	Y	
46	Technological Librarianship: An Online Journal of the American Theological Library Association http://journal.atla.com/ojs/index.php/theolib/index	Y	
47	Texas library journal http://www.txla.org/TLJ	Y	
48	Code4Lib Journal http://journal.code4lib.org/	Y	
49	The Idaho Librarian: A Publication of the Idaho Library Association http://www.idaholibraries.org/idlibrarian/index.php/idaho-librarian/index	Y	
50	Urban Library Journal http://lacuny.cuny.edu/ulj/	Y	
51	Virginia Libraries http://scholar.lib.vt.edu/ejournals/VALib/	Y	
52	World Libraries http://www.worlib.org/	Y	
53	ALAN Review http://scholar.lib.vt.edu/ejournals/ALAN/	N	Y

54	Annals of Library & Information Studies http://nopr.niscair.res.in/	N	Y
55	Australian Journal of Information Systems http://dl.acs.org.au/index.php/ajis/about	N	Y
56	Australian Academic and Research Libraries http://www.alia.org.au/publishing/aarl/index.html	N	Y
57	B Sides http://ir.uiowa.edu/bsides/	N	Y
58	Cites & Insights: Crawford at Large http://citesandinsights.info/citoc.htm	N	Y
59	Colby Quarterly (formerly: Colby Library Quarterly) http://digitalcommons.colby.edu/	N	Y
60	Computer and Information Science http://journal.ccsenet.org/index.php/cis/index	N	Y
61	Coordinates: Online Journal of the Map and Geography Round Table of the American Library Association. Series A and B http://www.sunysb.edu/libmap/coordinates.htm	N	Y
62	Current Issues in Education http://cie.asu.edu/index.php	N	Y
63	Data Science Journal http://www.jstage.jst.go.jp/browse/dsj	N	Y
64	Digital Document Quarterly http://home.pacbell.net/hgladney/ddqstart.htm	N	Y
65	DIGITHUM: The Humanities in Digital Age http://www.uoc.edu/digithum/7/eng/numeros.html	N	Y
66	EDUCAUSE Quarterly http://www.educause.edu/eq	N	Y
67	Electronic Journal of Africana Bibliography http://ir.uiowa.edu/ejab/all_issues.html	N	Y
68	Electronic Journal of Health Informatics http://www.ejhi.net/ojs/index.php/ejhi	N	Y
69	Electronic Journal of Knowledge Management http://www.ejkm.com/	N	Y
70	Electronic Journal on Information Systems in Developing Countries	N	Y

	http://www.ejisdc.org/ojs2/index.php/ejisdc		
71	Electronic Transactions on Artificial Intelligence http://www.ida.liu.se/ext/etai/	N	Y
72	European Journal of ePractice http://www.epracticejournal.eu/	N	Y
73	Firstmonday http://firstmonday.org/	N	Y
74	Human IT: Journal for Information Technology Studies as a Human Sciencehttp://etjanst.hb.se/bhs/ith//info-eng.htm	N	Y
75	Informatica Economica Journal http://revistaie.ase.ro/index.html	N	Y
76	Information Scotland: The Journal of the Chartered Institute of Library and Information Professionals in Scotland http://www.slainte.org.uk/publications/serials/infoscot/vol1(1)/vol1(1)contents.html	N	Y
77	Information Technologies and International Development http://itidjournal.org/itid	N	Y
78	Information Technology and Disabilities http://people.rit.edu/easi/itd.htm	N	Y
79	Information Technology and Libraries http://www.ala.org/ala/mgrps/divs/lita/ital/italinformation.cfm	N	Y
80	Inter-Actions: UCLA Journal of Education and Information Studies http://repositories.cdlib.org/gseis/interactions/	N	Y
81	Interdisciplinary Journal of E-Learning and Learning Objects http://ijklo.org/	N	Y
82	Interdisciplinary Journal of Information, Knowledge, and Management http://www.ijikm.org/	N	Y
83	International Journal of Communication http://ijoc.org/ojs/index.php/ijoc/about/editorialPolicies#focusAndScope	N	Y

84	International Journal of Communication Networks and Information Security http://www.ijcnis.org/index.php/ijcnis	N	Y
85	International Journal of Computer and Information Engineering http://www.waset.org/journals/ijcie/	N	Y
86	International Journal of Computer Science and Information Technology http://airccse.org/journal/ijcsit.html	N	Y
87	International Journal of Digital Curation http://www.ijdc.net/./ijdc/issue/current	N	Y
88	International Journal of Doctoral Studies (IJDS) http://ijds.org/	N	Y
89	International Journal of Legal Information http://scholarship.law.cornell.edu/ijli/vol33/iss1/	N	Y
90	International Journal of Library and Information Science http://www.academicjournals.org/ijlis/index.htm	N	Y
91	International Journal of Managing Public Sector Information and Communication Technologies http://airccse.org/journal/mpict/ijmpict.html	N	Y
92	International Journal of Multimedia and Its Applications http://airccse.org/journal/ijma_index.html	N	Y
93	International Review of Information Ethics http://www.i-r-i-e.net/	N	Y
94	International Review of Research in Open and Distance Learning http://www.irrodl.org/index.php/irrodl	N	Y
95	Internet Writing Journal http://www.internetwritingjournal.com/	N	Y
96	Interpersonal Computing and Technology Journal http://www.helsinki.fi/science/optek/#byissue	N	Y

97	Issues in Informing Science and Information Technology http://iisit.org/	N	Y
98	IT&Society http://www.itandsociety.org/index.html	N	Y
99	ITALICS: Innovations in Teaching and Learning in Information and Computer Sciences http://www.ics.heacademy.ac.uk/italics/	N	Y
100	JEP: The Journal of Electronic Publishing http://www.journalofelectronicpublishing.org/	N	Y
101	Journal of Artificial Intelligence Research http://www.jair.org/	N	Y
102	Journal of Digital Information http://jodi.ecs.soton.ac.uk/r or http://journals.tdl.org/jodi	N	Y
103	Journal of East Asian Libraries http://www.lib.byu.edu/dlib/spc/jeal/	N	Y
104	Journal of eLiteracy http://www.jelit.org/index.html	N	Y
105	Journal of Health Informatics in Developing Countries http://www.jhidc.org/index.php/jhidc	N	Y
106	Journal of Information Architecture http://journalofia.org/archives/	N	Y
107	Journal of Information Law and Technology http://www2.warwick.ac.uk/fac/soc/law/elj/jilt/ or European Journal of Law and Technology http://ejlt.org//issue/archive	N	Y
108	Journal of Information Literacy (JIL) **http://www.informationliteracy.org.uk/JIL.aspx**	N	Y
109	Journal of Information Technology Education (JITE: Research) http://www.informingscience.us/icarus/journals/jiteresearch/publications	N	Y
110	Journal of Information, Information Technology, and Organizations http://jiito.org/	N	Y
111	Journal of Internet Cataloguing **http://www.internetcataloging.com/home.html**	N	Y
112	Journal of Knowledge Management Practice http://www.tlainc.com/boutjkmp.htm	N	Y

113	Journal of Medical Internet Research http://www.jmir.org/	N	Y
114	Journal of Research and Practice in Information Technology http://acs.org.au/jrpit/index.html	N	Y
115	Journal of Staff Development http://learningforward.org/publications/jsd#.UUQguzcynUc	N	Y
116	Journal of Technology Studies http://scholar.lib.vt.edu/ejournals/JOTS/	N	Y
117	Journal of the American Medical Informatics Association http://www.pubmedcentral.nih.gov/tocrender.fcgi?action=archive&journal=76	N	Y
118	Journal of the Association for History and Computing http://quod.lib.umich.edu/j/jahc/browse.html	N	Y
119	Journal of the European Association for Health Information and Libraries http://www.eahil.net/journal/	N	Y
120	Journal of Virtual Worlds Research http://www.jvwresearch.org/index.html	N	Y
121	LASIE: Library Automated Systems Information Exchange http://search.informit.com.au/browseJournalTitle;res=E-LIBRARY;issn=0047-3774	N	Y
122	Law Library Journal http://www.aallnet.org/products/pub_journal.asp	N	Y
123	Learned Publishing http://www.ingentaconnect.com/content/alpsp/lp	N	Y
124	LIBER Quarterly Journal of European Research Libraries http://liber.library.uu.nl/index.html	N	Y
125	Multimedia Information and Technology Journal (MmIT) http://www.cilip.org.uk/get-involved/special-interest-groups/multimedia/journal/pages/default.aspx	N	Y
126	New Knowledge Environments http://journals.uvic.ca/index.php/INKE	N	Y

127	Northwestern Journal of Technology and Intellectual Property http://www.law.northwestern.edu/journals/njtip/issues.htm	N	Y
128	NPO Journal/NPO E-Journal http://www.bl.uk/blpac/publicationsjournals.html	N	Y
129	RBM Journal of Rare Books , Manuscripts, and Cultural Heritage http://rbm.acrl.org/content/2/2	N	Y
130	Research Management Review http://www.ncura.edu/content/news/rmr/archive.php	N	Y
131	Scandinavian Public Library Quarterly http://www.splq.info/	N	Y
132	School libraries in Canada (SLIC): A Journal of the Canadian Association for School Libraries http://www.clatcolbox.ca/casl/slic/links.html	N	Y
133	School Library Journal Online http://www.schoollibraryjournal.com/	N	Y
134	School Library Research http://www.ala.org/aasl/slr	N	Y
135	Simile: Studies in Media and Information Literacy Education http://utpjournals.metapress.com/content/120764/	N	Y
136	South African Journal of Information Management http://www.sajim.co.za/index.php/sajim/issue/current	N	Y
137	Special Libraries http://www.sla.org/content/shop/speclibs.cfm#1910	N	Y
138	Studies in Bibliography http://etext.lib.virginia.edu/bsuva/sb	N	Y
139	Technology Electronic Reviews (TER) http://www.ala.org/lita/publications/archive/ter	N	Y
140	The Bonefolder: An outgrowth of the Book Arts Web http://www.philobiblon.com/bonefolder/	N	Y

141	The International Journal of Database Management Systems http://airccse.org/journal/ijdms/ijdms.html	N	Y
142	The International Journal of Managing Information Technology http://airccse.org/journal/ijmit/ijmit.html	N	Y
143	The Journal of the Rutgers University Library http://jrul.libraries.rutgers.edu/index.php/jrul/index	N	Y
144	The Public Access Computer Systems Review http://epress.lib.uh.edu/pr/pacsrev.html#history	N	Y
145	Webology http://www.webology.ir/	N	Y

E-Magazines

1	Library Juice http://libr.org/juice/	Y	
2	American Libraries http://americanlibrariesmagazine.org/	Y	
3	Ariadne http://www.ariadne.ac.uk/	Y	
4	Computer in Libraries http://www.infotoday.com/cilmag/default.shtml	Y	
5	D-Lib Magazine http://www.dlib.org/dlib/september08/09contents.html	Y	
6	The Marginal http://www.gslis.mcgill.ca/marginal/	Y	
7	AALL Spectrum http://www.aallnet.org/main-menu/Publications/spectrum	N	Y
8	Access http://www.aardvarknet.info/access/number46/index.cfm	N	Y
9	Book business http://www.bookbusinessmag.com/	N	Y

10	Book Links http://www ala.org/ala/aboutala/offices/publishing/booklinks/archiveonline/ archive_of_online_articles.cfm	N	Y
11	CHOICE http://www.ala.org/ala/mgrps/divs/acrl/publications/choice/previousissues/previousissues.cfm	N	Y
12	Cultivate Interactive http://www.cultivate-int.org/index-2.html	N	Y
13	E-Content http://www.ecmag.net/	N	Y
14	EDUCAUSE Review http://www.educause.edu/	N	Y
15	Ex Libris http://marylaine.com/exlibris/	N	Y
16	Exploit Interactive http://www.exploit-lib.org/	N	Y
17	inCite http://alia.org.au/publishing/incite/archive.html	N	Y
18	Information Today http //www.infotoday.com/IT/nov08/index.shtml	N	Y
19	Knowledge Management World http://www.kmworld.com/index.cfm	N	Y
20	Online http://www.infotoday.com/online/default.shtml	N	Y
21	Provenance http://www.provenance.ca/about-provenance/index.html	N	Y
22	Research Information http://www.researchinformation.info/	N	Y
23	Searcher: The Magazine for Database Professionals http://www.infotoday.com/searcher/default.asp	N	Y
24	The Bulletin of the American Society for Information Science and Technology http://www.asis.org/bulletin.html	N	Y

25	Virginia Tech Magazine http://www.vtmagazine.vt.edu/	N	Y
26	Link-Up http://www.infotoday.com/linkup/default.shtml	N	Y

E-Newsletters and Others

1	ABAA Newsletter http://hq.abaa.org/books/antiquarian/abaapages/newsletter	Y	
2	Abbey Newsletter http://cool.conservation-us.org/byorg/abbey/an/	Y	
3	Against the grain http://www.against-the-grain.com/d/TOC	Y	
4	ALAWON. The ALA Washington Office Electronic Newsline http://www.ala.org/ala/aboutala/offices/wo/washnews/archivea/archive.cfm	Y	
5	ARL: A bimonthly newsletter for library issues and action http://www.arl.org/resources/pubs/br/index.shtml	Y	
6	Biblia's Warrior Librarian Weekly http://warriorlibrarian.com/ARCHIVE/00archives.html	Y	
7	Business and Finance Division Bulletin http://bf.sla.org/resources/the-bulletin/	Y	
8	MLS: Marketing Library Services http://www.infotoday.com/MLS/default.shtml	Y	
9	The Wired Librarian's Newsletter http://www.wiredlibrarian.com/wln/wlnfront.htm	Y	
10	ALCTS Network News http://bubl.ac.uk/archive/journals/alctsnn/	N	Y
11	Biblio-Tech Review http://www.ringgold.com/biblio-tech/si_pd.cfm?pid=2	N	Y
12	Cataloging and Classification Quarterly http://bubl.ac.uk/archive/journals/cacq/	N	Y

13	CIT Infobits http://serials.infomotions.com/infobits/	N	Y
14	Conserline http://www.loc.gov/acq/conser/consrlin.html	N	Y
15	Free Pint http://www.freepint.com/	N	Y
16	Information today and Tomorrow http://www.dsir.gov.in/pubs/itt/index.htm	N	Y
17	Internet on a Disk http://www.samizdat.com/ioad.html	N	Y
18	Internet Resources Newsletter http://www.hw.ac.uk/libwww/irn/irn.html	N	Y
19	LC Cataloging Newsline http://www.loc.gov/catdir/lccn/	N	Y
20	NLM Technical Bulletin http://www.nlm.nih.gov/pubs/techbull/current_issue.html	N	Y
21	RLG DigiNews http://www.oclc.org/programs/publications/newsletters/diginews.htm	N	Y
22	Serials E-News http://www.ringgold.com/UKSG/si_pd.cfm	N	Y
23	SPARC Open Access Newsletter or Free Online Scholarship Newsletter http://www.earlham.edu/~peters/fos/index.htm	N	Y
24	Sprouts: Working Papers on Information Systems http://sprouts.aisnet.org/home.html	N	Y

Table shows out of 195 E-Resources the complete subject coverage 67 and Partial Subject Coverage 128 (75%). Although all the E-resources have partial subject coverage but these 128 (75%) E-Resources have only Partial Subject Coverage not complete Subject Coverage.

Summary Table: Distribution of E-resources by Complete Subject Coverage

Sl.No.	E-Resources		No
1	Complete Subject Coverage E-Journals	20%	52
2	Complete Subject Coverage E-Magazines	2%	6
3	Complete Subject Coverage E-Newsletters	3%	9
4	Complete Subject Coverage	25%	67
5	Partial Subject Coverage	75%	128

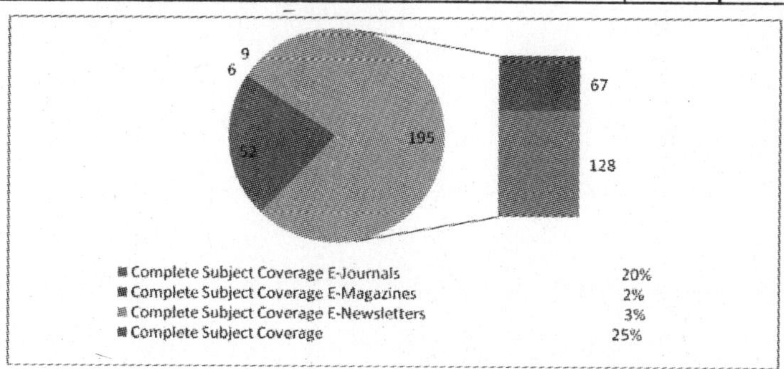

Fig. : E-Resources by Complete Subject Coverage

The chart shows that out of total 195 open Access E-Resources 128 (75%) E- Resources have Partial and 67 (25%) E-Resources have completed Subject Coverage of Library Science. It is found that Complete Subject coverage E-Resources are 52 (36%) E-Journals out of total 145 E-Journals, E-Magazines 6 (23%) out of total 26 E-Magazines, and 9 (37%) E-Newsletters out of total 24 E-Newsletters have Complete Subject Coverage.

3.3. E-RESOURCES HAVING CURRENT TRENDS

SL. No.	E-Journals	Current Trends
1	College and Research Libraries http://crl.acrl.org/	Provides articles on the latest trends and practices affecting academic and research libraries and serves as the official newsmagazine and publication of record of ACRL.
2	African Journal of Information & Communication Technology http://epress.lib.uts.edu.au/ojs/index.php/ajict/	Material on all current aspects of the design, implementation, use and management of computer and communication.
3	ALAN Review http://scholar.lib.vt.edu/ejournals/ALAN/	Contains current articles on YA literature and its teaching, interviews with authors, reports on publishing trends, current research on YA literature, a section of reviews of new books, and ALAN membership news.
4	Annals of Library & Information Studies http://nopr.niscair.res.in/	Includes Knowledge management, Research Aptitudes, bibliography, citation indexes etc.
5	Australian Journal of Information Systems http://dl.acs.org.au/index.php/ajis/about	It include research articles, conference information, development activities, work procedures, resource sharing, opinions, etc.

6	Australian Academic and Research Libraries http://www.alia.org.au/publishing/aarl/index.html	Includes the Technical and Further Education in research libraries of all types and all aspects of librarianship past and present, pure and applied bibliography, publishing, information science and related subjects.
7	B Sides http://ir.uiowa.edu/bsides/	Current students and alumni to converse and contribute to the scholarly literature of Library and Information Science.
8	Chinese Librarianship: An International Electronic Journal http://www.iclc.us/cliej/	Publishes current research findings, theoretical explorations, and case studies by librarians, information scientists, library school faculty and students of Chinese heritage, as well as by librarians and information professionals of other nationalities on issues related to serving patrons with Chinese materials and major development of the Chinese librarianship.
9	Christian Library Journal http://www.christianlibraryj.org/pdf/index.htm	Cover all nonfiction subjects, as well as fiction, picture books, fairy and folk tales, and poetry and drama. Build library collection in the Christian school, international school, home school, or church using the core collection
10	Collaborative Librarianship http://www.collaborativelibrarianship.org/index.html	Providing current trends in LIS. Published materials appear from time to time on library cooperation and partnerships.

11	Communications in Information Literacy http://www.comm nfolit.org/index.php/cil/issue/archive	Dedicated to advancing knowledge, theory, and research in information literacy. CIL is committed to the principles of information literacy as set forth by the Association of College and Research Libraries. CIL is also committed to the principles of open access for academic research.
12	Computer and Information Science http://journal.ccsenet.org/index.php/cis/index	The journal publishes research papers in the fields of computer, information science, e-business, and internet, electronic and relevant subjects.
13	Coordinates: Online Journal of the Map and Geography Round Table of the American Library Association. Series A and B http://www.sunysb.edu/libmap/coordinates.htm	Series A focus on Original, peer-reviewed articles. Series b focuses on Essays, project reports, technical notes, republished articles, and other materials of interest to the cartographic community. Series B Focus on
14	Current Cites http://lists.webjunction.org/currentcites/	Provides Current in Library and Information Science.
15	Current Issues in Education http://cie.asu.edu/index.php	Promote educational dialogue, research, practice, and policy. We also strive to develop and deepen a sense of scholarship within our academic community. Articles published in Current Issues in Education (CIE) are peer reviewed by the journal's ad-hoc reviewers.

16	Cybermetrics : International Journal of Scientometrics, Informetrics and Bibliometrics http://www.cindoc.csic.es/cybermetrics/	Devoted to the description and analysis of the Internet as scholarly communication tool. Cybermetrics is a public service for the world community of researchers in the metrics of scientific communication.
17	Data Science Journal http://www.jstage.jst.go.jp/browse/dsj	Publishes papers about data and the data systems. It may publish papers about methods data compilation or analysis.
18	DESIDOC Journal of Library & Information Science http://publications.drdo.gov.in/ojs/index.php/djlit/index	Endeveavours to bring recent developments in Information technology as applicable to Library and information science, to the notice of Librarians, Documentation, Information professional, students and others interested in the field.
19	EDUCAUSE Quarterly http://www.educause.edu/eq	EDUCAUSE Quarterly is an online, peer-reviewed, practitioner's journal about managing and using information resources in higher education.
20	E-JASL: The Electronic Journal of Academic and Special Librarianship http://southernlibrarianship.icaap.org/	Dedicated first and foremost to advancing knowledge and research in the areas of academic and special librarianship.

21	Electronic Journal of Africana Bibliography http://ir.uiowa.edu/ejab/all_issues.html	Coverage includes any aspect of Africa, its peoples, their homes, cities, towns, districts, states, countries, regions, including social, economic sustainable development, creative literature, the arts, and the Diaspora.
22	Electronic Journal of Health Informatics http://www.ejhi.net/ojs/index.php/ejhi	Provides practitioners, researchers, and students in library and health professions an international and interdisciplinary forum. Its objectives are to encourage discussion and to disseminate developments at the frontiers of information management and libraries. A major focus is communicating practices that are evidence based both in managing information and in supporting health care.
23	Electronic Journal on Information Systems in Developing Countries http://www.ejisdc.org/ojs2/index.php/ejisdc	Forum for practitioners, teachers, researchers and policy makers to share their knowledge and experience in the design, development, implementation, management and evaluation of information systems and technologies in developing countries.

24	European Journal of ePractice http://www.epracticejournal.eu/	The publication promotes the diffusion and exchange of good practice in eGovernment, eHealth and eInstitution. The following types of material are published in the journal: articles, case studies and interviews.
25	Evidence Based Library and Information Practice http://ejournals.library.ualberta.ca/index.php/EBLIP/index	Provides forum for librarians and other information professionals to discover research that may contribute to decision-making in professional practice. EBLIP publishes original research and commentary on the topic of evidence based library and information practice
26	Firstmonday http://firstmonday.org/	First Monday publishes original research papers about the Internet and related technologies.
27	Health Information and Libraries Journal http://www3.interscience.wiley.com/journal/120118368/grouphome/home.html	Provides Interdisciplinary interest to practitioners, researchers, and students in the library and health sectors. Its objectives include promoting debate about new health information developments with an emphasis on communicating evidence-based information both in the management and support of healthcare services.
28	Human IT: Journal for Information Technology Studies as a Human Sciencehttp://etjanst.hb.se/bhs/ith//info-eng.htm	Closely aligned with the new field of research, which is alternatively referred to as humanities computing, social informatics, or informatica

		umanistica.
29	Informatica Economica Journal http://revistaie.ase.ro/index.html	Provides current trends on Research and Youth focusing on Economic informatics, information society, information systems, and information technology.
30	Information for Social Change http://libr.org/isc/journal.html	Focuses on freedom of information and censorship; promote alternatives to mainstream. Provide a forum for the exchange of radical views, debate ethics and freedom of library and information work.
31	Information Research: An International Electronic Journal http://informationr.net/ir/	Information Research is an open access, international, peer-reviewed, scholarly journal, dedicated to making accessible the results of research across a wide range of information-related disciplines.
32	Information Scotland: The Journal of the Chartered Institute of Library and Information Professionals in Scotland http://www.slainte.org.uk/publications/serials/infoscot/vol1(1)/vol1(1)contents.html	Offers open access to the current journal's articles in electronic form and acts as an archive of this content.
33	Information Technologies and International Development http://itidjournal.org/itid	It is a peer-reviewed, international, multidisciplinary quarterly designed for researchers and practitioners from the engineering and social sciences, technologists,

		policy makers, and development specialists.
34	Informing Science The International Journal of an Emerging Transdiscipline http://inform.nu/	The academically peer refereed journal Informing Science endeavors to provide an understanding of the complexities in informing clientele. Fields from information systems, library science, and journalism in all its forms to education all contribute to this science.
35	Inter-Actions: UCLA Journal of Education and Information Studies http://repositories.cdlib.org/gseis/interactions/	It focus on legal theory, literary criticism, design, and technology studies exercises a profound impact on educational, information studies research, sociology, curriculum, policy, psychological studies, systems design, information literacy, and digital preservation
36	Interdisciplinary Journal of E-Learning and Learning Objects http://ijklo.org/	Provide readers around the world with the widest possible coverage of developments in E-Learning and Learning Objects. IJELLO is an interdisciplinary forum that publishes high quality articles on theory, practice, innovation, and research that cover all aspects of E-learning and Learning Objects.
37	Interdisciplinary Journal of Information, Knowledge, and Management http://www.ijikm.org/	Interdisciplinary Journal of Information, Knowledge, and Management is an academically peer reviewed journal.

38	International Journal of Communication http://ijoc.org/ojs/index.php/ijoc/about/editorialPolicies#focusAndScope	Address the wider audiences of our many sub-fields and specialties, rather than the location for the narrower conversations more appropriately conducted within more specialized journals
39	International Journal of Communication Networks and Information Security http://www.ijcnis.org/index.php/ijcnis	Provides a challenging forum for researchers, industrial professionals, engineers, managers, and policy makers working in the field to contribute and disseminate innovative new work on networks and information security.
40	International Journal of Computer and Information Engineering http://www.waset.org/journals/ijcie/	Covers all current areas of Computer and Information Science and Engineering, publishing refereed original research articles and technical notes
41	International Journal of Computer Science and Information Technology http://airccse.org/journal/ijcsit.html	Devoted to fields of Computer Science and Information Systems.
42	International Journal of Digital Curation http://www.ijdc.net/./ijdc/issue/current	Devoted to papers, articles and news items on curation of digital objects and related issues. The journal is published in electronic form, two times a year.
43	International Journal of Doctoral Studies (IJDS) http://ijds.org/	Includes current trends on informing science, information systems, information technology, information science, decision science, information security, and IT education.

44	International Journal of Legal Information http://scholarship.law.cornell.edu/ijli/vol33/iss1/	Focus on legal Issues such as Behaviors Economic Issues, Islamic Governance, Commercial Issues etc.
45	International Journal of Library and Information Science http://www.academicjournals.org/ijlis/index.htm	The Journal welcomes the submission of manuscripts that meet the general criteria of significance and scientific excellence.
46	International Journal of Managing Public Sector Information and Communication Technologies http://airccse.org/journal/mpict/ijmpict.html	Provides a platform to disseminate new ideas and new research, advance theories, and propagate best practices in the management of ICT in public sector organizations at the international, national, state/provincial and local levels.
47	International Journal of Multimedia and Its Applications http://airccse.org/journal/ijma_index.html	Publishes articles which contribute new results in all areas of the Multimedia & its applications. The journal focuses on all technical and practical current aspects of Multimedia and its applications.
48	International Review of Information Ethics http://www.i-r-i-e.net/	Disseminate research, theory, and best practice in open and distance learning worldwide.
49	International Review of Research in Open and Distance Learning http://www.irrodl.org/index.php/irrodl	Disseminate current research, theory, and best practice in open and distance learning worldwide.

50	Issues in Informing Science and Information Technology http://iisit.org/	Includes Communications, Communicating Meaning, Community and Society, Computer Science, Data Communications, Distance Education, E-Commerce, Education, Government, Health Care, Medicine, History, Information Science & Library, Journalism, Justice and Law, Mathematics, Philosophical Issues, Psychology, Public Policy, Sociology, Technology, Working Together.
51	Issues in Science and Technology Librarianship http://www.library.ucsb.edu/istl/ Or http://www.istl.org/	Publishes substantive current material of interest to science and technology librarians. It serves as a vehicle for science-tech librarians to share details of successful programs, materials for the delivery of information services, background information and opinions on topics of current interest, and to publish research and bibliographies on issues in science and technology libraries.
52	IT&Society http://www.itandsociety.org/index.html	Includes the community of scholars interested in the social impact of new technologies, as well as policy makers, media analysts, computer professionals and interested members of the general public.

53	JEP: The Journal of Electronic Publishing http://www.journalofelectronicpublishing.org/	Provides archive of works covering current trends and issues in electronic publishing. The articles present innovative ideas, best practices, and leading-edge thinking about all aspects of publishing, authorship, and readership.
54	JLIS.it Italian Journal of Library and Information Science http://leo.cilea.it/index.php/jlis/article/view/4539/4416	Contributions in LIS, Library and Information Science, are welcome.
55	Journal of Artificial Intelligence Research http://www.jair.org/	Provides all areas of artificial intelligence (AI), publishing refereed research articles, survey articles, and technical notes.
56	Journal of Digital Information http://jodi.ecs.soton.ac.uk/r or http://journals.tdl.org/jodi	Covers the topic of information management, information science and information technology, digital libraries, hypermedia systems, hypertext criticism, and information discovery.
57	Journal of East Asian Libraries http://www.lib.byu.edu/dlib/spc/jeal/	It basically focuses on Asian Libraries perspectives.
58	Journal of Educational Media & Library Sciences http://joemls.tku.edu.tw/index_e.htm	Cover current issues on all the aspects of Library science, information science, and information technology.
59	Journal of Health Informatics in Developing Countries http://www.jhidc.org/index.php/jhidc	Share and promote current academic knowledge in the field. One of its aims is also to encourage writers from developing countries to contribute

		their writings.
60	Journal of Information Architecture http://journalofia.org/archives/	Facilitate the systematic development of current scientific body of knowledge in the field of information architecture.
61	Journal of Information Law and Technology http://www2.warwick.ac.uk/fac/soc/law/elj/jilt/ or European Journal of Law and Technology http://ejlt.org//issue/archive	Contains a diversity of current materials including peer reviewed and non-refereed articles, commentaries, work in progress articles, book and IT reviews, and conference reports and papers, as well as information papers, news and UK and global conferences.
62	Journal of Information Literacy http://ojs.lboro.ac.uk/ojs/index.php/JIL/index	Investigate and make generalized observations on how current Information Literacy impacts on organizations, systems and the individual.
63	Journal of Information Technology Education (JITE: Research) http://www.informingscience.us/icarus/journals/jiteresearch/publications	Improve IT education around the world by publishing high quality articles on best practices and other topics of use. Types of articles, including primary, action, and secondary research, provide.
64	Journal of Information, Information Technology, and Organizations http://jiito.org/	JIITO covers a specialized area of information systems research indicated in its title. It focused on empirical studies. Conceptual articles are published just exceptionally.

65	Journal of Knowledge Management Practice http://www.tlainc.com/boutjkmp.htm	Devoted to collecting serious research about knowledge management and its practical applications. Authors are invited to read the notes for contributors, and are encouraged to contribute.
66	Journal of Library Innovation http://www.libraryinnovation.org/about/contact	Publishes original research, reports on innovative practices, literature reviews, case .studies, and book, conference and product reviews. The Journal also welcomes provocative essays that will stimulate thought on the current and future role of libraries in an Internet Age.
67	Journal of Medical Internet Research http://www.jmir.org/	Covers health informatics and all aspects of latest research, information and communication in the healthcare field using Internet and Intranet-related technologies; which is nowadays called "eHealth"
68	Journal of Philippine Librarianship http://journals.upd.edu.ph/index.php/jpl/issue/current	All fields in the area of library and information science
69	Journal of Research and Practice in Information Technology http://ws.acs.org.au/jrpit/JRPIT_Volumes.html	Including current trends, but not limited to: Computer Science; Information Systems; Computer Systems and Information Engineering; Software Engineering.

70	Journal of Staff Development http://learningforward.org/publications/jsd#.UUQguzcynUc	Professional magazine on leading and learning published quarterly. Focuses on issues of leadership and learning relevant to all educators involved in professional learning. Articles are written primarily by practitioners who bring a real world to the challenges of school improvement and organizational change.
71	Journal of Technology Studies http://scholar.lib.vt.edu/ejournals/JOTS/	Provides current trends on Technology education, student development etc.
72	Journal of the American Medical Informatics Association http://www.pubmedcentral.nih.gov/tocrender.fcgi?action=archive&journal=76	JAMIA focus on mainly Decision making, Health communication, IT, Preservation.
73	Journal of the Association for History and Computing http://quod.lib.umich.edu/j/jahc/browse.html	Goal of journal is to help define useful standards to maximize the utility of computers in historical studies. The Journal is intended for a general audience of teachers, students, and researchers interested in the application of computers in historical studies.
74	Journal of the European Association for Health Information and Libraries http://www.eahil.net/journal/	EAHIL encourages professional development, improves cooperation and enables exchanges of experience amongst its members.

75	Journal of Virtual Worlds Research http://www.jvwresearch.org/index.html	Topics of interest include: Limitations and advantages of educational practices, Development and use of instructional tools, Evaluation and assessment, Innovations in educational assessment methods, Interdisciplinary curriculum and instruction, Educational and research ethics in virtual world.
76	Law Library Journal http://www.aallnet.org/products/pub_journal.asp	Practice-oriented articles, proceedings of the business sessions of the Annual Meeting, and annual reports of committees, special interest sections, representatives, and chapters are also included.
77	Learned Publishing http://www.ingentaconnect.com/content/alpsp/lp	Learned Publishing is the journal of the Association of Learned and Professional Society Publishers, published in collaboration with the Society for Scholarly Publishing.
78	LIBER Quarterly Journal of European Research Libraries http://liber.library.uu.nl/index.html	The overall aim is to assist research libraries in Europe to support a functional network across national boundaries in order to ensure the preservation of the European cultural heritage, to improve access to collections in European research libraries, and to provide more efficient information services in Europe

79	Library & Information Research: Research into Practice for Information & Library Services http://www.lirgjournal.org.uk/lir/ojs/index.php/lir	This peer review journal focus on research for LIS community; reporting of research; reflective and evidence-based practice etc.
80	Library Journal http://www.libraryjournal.com	LJ is the single-most comprehensive publication for librarians, with groundbreaking features and analytical news reports covering technology, management, policy, and other professional concerns.
81	Library Philosophy and Practice http://www.webpages.uidaho.edu/~mbolin/lpp.htm	It include explorations of current, past, and emerging theories of librarianship and library practice, as well as reports of successful, innovative, or experimental library procedures, methods, or projects in all areas of librarianship, set in the context of applied research.
82	Library Student Journal http://www.librarystudentjournal.org/index.php/lsj/index	This Peer reviewed Journal provides Current Trends on education, training, career paths, future trends and advance discussion of LIS topics.
83	LIBRES: Library and Information Science Research Electronic Journal http://libres.curtin.edu.au/	Devoted to new research in Library and Information Science.
84	LIBRI: International Journal of Libraries and Information Services http://www.librijournal.org/	Publishes original Current articles on all aspects of libraries and information services.

85	Malaysian Journal of Library & Information Sciencehttp://ejum.fsktm.um.edu.my/VolumeListing.aspx?JournalID=3	Provides scholarly journal management system for university, higher learning institutions or research and development centers.
86	MELA Notes: The Journal of the Middle East Librarians Association http://www.mela.us/MELANotes/MELANotesIntro.html	Provides currents information of the Middle East Librarians Association
87	Mississippi Libraries http://www.misslib.org/index.php/publications/mississippi-libraries/	Provide professional leadership for the development, promotion, and improvement of library and information services and the profession of librarianship in order to enhance learning and ensure access to information for all.
88	MLA Forum http://www.mlaforum.org/	Provides current trends on all the aspect of Library and education.
89	Multimedia Information and Technology Journal (MmIT) http://www.cilip.org.uk/get-involved/special-interest-groups/multimedia/journal/pages/default.aspx	Includes mainly database, Research and Technology in the field of library and Information Science.
90	New Knowledge Environments http://journals.uvic.ca/index.php/INKE	Focus on the implementation of Current and New knowledge in environment, Virtual library , Designing interface etc.
91	North Carolina Libraries http://www.ncl.ecu.edu/index.php/NCL	Focus on current issues of Libraries, librarianship, media centers, and academic libraries.

92	Northwestern Journal of Technology and Intellectual Property http://www.law.northwestern.edu/journals/njtip/issues.htm	Addresses subjects relating Current trends on intellectual property and the intersection of law and technology and publishes articles on a variety of topics
93	Partnership: The Canadian Journal of Library and Information Practice and Research http://journal.lib.uoguelph.ca/index.php/perj/index	Feature articles on theory & research and on innovations in practice are in-depth, peer-reviewed articles. Other types of articles include viewpoints, conference presentations, profiles, news& announcements, professional development and reviews
94	RBM Journal of Rare Books , Manuscripts, and Cultural Heritage http://rbm.acrl.org/content/2/2	Discuses about Books, Manuals, Manuscripts.
95	Scandinavian Public Library Quarterly http://www.splq.info/	Converge is about current trends in networking, about establishing good and highly relevant content on the Internet, about bridging the virtual and the real library, about outstanding library architecture, about information policies in some of the strongest democracies in the world.
96	School libraries in Canada (SLIC): A Journal of the Canadian Association for School Libraries http://www.clatoolbox.ca/casl/slic/links.html	Mission is to provide national support for the development and maintenance of excellence in Canada's school libraries, media centers, and school library personnel.

97	School Library Journal Online http://www.schoollibraryjournal.com/	Online version of the print publication includes Features current news about school libraries and librarians. Includes job opportunities.
98	School Library Research http://www.ala.org/aasl/slr	Books and visual media that explore topics as varied as science and history, geography and the arts. latest issue offers you lots of concrete ways to incorporate the best new books and media into your lesson plans. It's imperative that quality materials, especially those that address neglected subjects, find their way into your libraries and classrooms
99	Simile: Studies in Media and Information Literacy Education http://utpjournals.metapress.com/content/120764/	Publishing research that advances knowledge about media and information literacy.
100	South African Journal of Information Management http://www.sajim.co.za/index.php/sajim/issue/current	It presents original research (i.e. not previously published), novel synthesis, or judicious review of current theory, method, policy, or practice in the fields mentioned below. Article submission, review and publication are accomplished entirely electronically.
101	Technological Librarianship: An Online Journal of the American Theological Library Association http://journal.atla.com/ojs/index.php/theolib/index	Foster the professional development of theological librarians, and to contribute to and enrich the profession of theological librarianship.

102	Texas library journal http://www.txla.org/TLJ	Focus on Academic library, Leadership, Principles, Intellectual freedom, librarians etc.
103	The Bonefolder: An outgrowth of the Book Arts Web http://www.philobiblon.com/bonefolder/	The Bonefolder publishes significant articles by established and emerging authorities on a variety of book arts topics. These include hand bookbinding, teaching, business practice, the history of the book, the book as art, general tips & tricks, exhibitions, how-to technical articles, and reviews.
104	Code4Lib Journal http://journal.code4lib.org/	C4LJ helps Libraries in computer technology, using computers and the Internet to offer unprecedented access to information and library resources. C4LJ aims to help engender collective understanding and the necessary support for improving library technology and digital services.
105	The Idaho Librarian: A Publication of the Idaho Library Association http://www.idaholibraries.org/idlibrarian/index.php/idaho-librarian/index	The Idaho Librarian publishes articles and information relevant to libraries and librarianship in Idaho, though topics need not be unique to the state. Idaho-related articles written by authors not located in Idaho and not members of the Idaho Library Association are within the scope of the journal.

106	The International Journal of Database Management Systems http://airccse.org/journal/ijdms/ijdms.html	Current trends in this Journal includes, but are not limited to, the following Digital Libraries, Knowledge Acquisition, discovery & Management , Metadata Management , Knowledge Processing.
107	The International Journal of Managing Information Technology http://airccse.org/journal/ijmit/ijmit.html	The journal focuses on innovative ideas and best practices in using IT to advance organizations – for-profit, non-profit,
108	Urban Library Journal http://lacuny.cuny.edu/ulj/	Journal of research and discussion dealing with all aspects of urban libraries and librarianship, welcomes articles dealing with academic, research, public, school, and special libraries in an urban setting, public higher education, urban studies, multiculturalism, library and educational services to immigrants, preservation of public higher education, and universal access to World Wide Web resources.
109	Virginia Libraries http://scholar.lib.vt.edu/ejournals/VALib/	It is used as a vehicle for members to exchange information, ideas, and solutions to mutual problems in professional articles on current topics in the library and information field in order to advance literacy and learning and to ensure access to information in the Commonwealth of Virginia.

110	Webology http://www.webology.ir/	The World Wide Web: Web: information retrieval; Web crawling and indexing; Web cataloging; Web searching; Search engines and directories; Search behavior; Metadata etc. Library and Information Science: Information retrieval systems; Indexing; Abstracting; Information and communication technology; Information Evaluation.
111	World Libraries http://www.worlib.org/	Dedicated to librarians and libraries in regions without associations or agencies to encourage scholarly communication and professional development. World Libraries is simply dedicated to the international nature of librarianship, promoting communication and relationships both professionally and personally.

E-Magazines

1	AALL Spectrum http://www.aallnet.org/main-menu/Publications/spectrum	AALL Spectrum publishes substantive, well-written articles on topics of real interest to law librarians, as well as news about the American Association of Law Libraries - Chapters, Committees, Special Interest Sections, etc.
2	Access http://www.aardvarknet.info/access/number46/index.cfm	It covers almost all the aspects of Library and Information science.

3	American Libraries http://americanlibrariesmagazine.org/	It is open to any individual or organization interested in library service and library and information science. American Libraries is published 10 times a year.
4	Ariadne http://www.ariadne.ac.uk/	It covers current digital library initiatives, technological, information service developments and information networking issues, Information Management.
5	Book business http://www.bookbusinessmag.com/	It provides current trends on Number of titles published, Digital rights management, Everything regarding books.
6	Book Links http://www.ala.org/ala/aboutala/offices/publishing/booklinks/archiveonline/archive_of_online_articles.cfm	Provides Curriculum role of the school library media center, the increased programming in public libraries, and the heavy reliance of child-care centers on children's literature, Book Links publishes bibliographies, essays linking books on a similar theme, retrospective reviews, and other features targeted at those educating young people.
7	CHOICE http://www.ala.org/ala/mgrps/divs/acrl/publications/choice/previousissues/previousissues.cfm	Latest trends on academic librarians, faculty, and key decision makers rely on the reviews in Choice magazine and Choice Reviews Online for collection development and scholarly research.

8	Computer in Libraries http://www.infotoday.com/cilmag/default.shtml	Focusing on the practical application of technology in community, school, academic, and special libraries. CIL include discussions of the impact of emerging computer technologies on library systems and services, and on the library community itself.
9	D-Lib Magazine http://www.dlib.org/dlib/september08/09contents.html	The primary goal of the magazine is timely and efficient information exchange for the digital library community. To meet this goal, both the articles and the shorter pieces are solicited or selected from among unsolicited submissions.
10	E-Content http://www.ecmag.net/	Delivers essential research, reporting, news, and analysis of content related issues. It is essential reading for executives and professionals involved in content creation, management, acquisition, organization, and distribution in both commercial and enterprise environments.
11	EDUCAUSE Review http://www.educause.edu/	The magazine takes a broad look at current developments and trends in information technology, how they may affect the college/university as an institution, and what these mean for higher education and society.
12	inCite http://alia.org.au/publishing/incite/archive.html	It focus on Research and Education, Special Libraries, IFLA/Engagement etc.

13	Information Today http://www.infotoday.com/IT/nov08/index.shtml	Delivers total coverage of late-breaking news and long-term trends in the information industry. Accurate, timely news articles inform the reader of the people, products, services, and events that impact the industry, while hard-hitting, topical articles explain significant developments in the field.
14	Knowledge Management World http://www.kmworld.com/index.cfm	Km world provide actionable Information through real world case studies, advice from key practitioners and best practice advice from market leaders.
15	Link-Up http://www.infotoday.com/linkup/default.shtml	Link Up provides current trends on a new special section of IT packed with news you can us.
16	Online http://www.infotoday.com/online/default.shtml	ONLINE is written for information professionals and provides articles, product reviews, case studies, evaluation, and informed opinion about selecting, using, and managing electronic information products, plus industry and professional information about online database systems, CD-ROM, and the Internet.

17	Provenance http://www.provenance.ca/about-provenance/index.html	Travel articles in Provenance came around the time of the International Conference of the Special Libraries Association of America, meeting in Seattle, Washington. literature covering the implementation of Western designed information systems in developing countries
18	Research Information http://www.researchinformation.info/	Focus on E-books, Digital, LIS Management etc.
19	Searcher: The Magazine for Database Professionals http://www.infotoday.com/searcher/default.asp	Searcher includes evaluated online news, searching tips and techniques; reviews of search aid software and database documentation, revealing interviews with leaders and entrepreneurs of the industry, and trenchant editorials.
20	The Bulletin of the American Society for Information Science and Technology http://www.asis.org/bulletin.html	It is ASIS&T's primary means of maintaining regular contact with its membership regarding ASIS&T activities. This e-magazine is also a vehicle for sharing news and information regarding developments in the field of information science and technology, including political developments

21	The Marginal http://www.gslis.mcgill.ca/marginal/	Publish latest experiences; not only do we publish articles related to the LIS field, but also those related to other aspects of the lives of library, archives and knowledge management students.
22	Virginia Tech Magazine http://www.vtmagazine.vt.edu/	does not discriminate against employees, students, or applicants for admission or employment on the basis of race, color, sex, sexual orientation, disability, age, veteran status, national origin, religion, or political affiliation

Newsletters and other E-Resources

1	ABAA Newsletter http://hq.abaa.org/books/antiquarian/abaapages/newsletter	Provides latest trends on libraries and institutions, the antiquarian book community at large and the general public.
2	Against the grain http://www.against-the-grain.com/d/TOC	Key to the latest news about libraries, publishers, book jobbers, and subscription agents. It is a unique collection of reports on the issues, literature, and people that impact the world of books and journals.
3	ALAWON. The ALA Washington Office Electronic Newsline http://www.ala.org/ala/aboutala/offices/wo/washnews/archivea/archive.cfm	Keeping library advocates up to date on major legislative issues in the Nation's Capital.

4	Biblio-Tech Review http://www.ringgold.com/biblio-tech/si_pd.cfm?pid=2	It includes latest news updates from the library automation industry
5	Business and Finance Division Bulletin http://bf.sla.org/resources/the-bulletin/	Publishing informative and practical articles on the many topics that are of interest to a specially skilled and influential, worldwide readership
6	Free Pint http://www.freepint.com/	Publishes a family of resources to help information workers be more effective, raise the value of information in their organizations and contribute to success.
7	Internet on a Disk http://www.samizdat.com/ioad.html	Provides current trends on electronic texts and Internet trends.
8	MLS: Marketing Library Services http://www.infotoday.com/MLS/default.shtml	Provide information professionals in all types of libraries with specific ideas for marketing their services. You'll find numerous suggestions for planning programs, making money, increasing business, and proving your value to your administrator.
9	NLM Technical Bulletin http://www.nlm.nih.gov/pubs/techbull/current_issue.html	Broad Medical Subject Headings are covered.
10	RLG DigiNews http://www.oclc.org/programs/publications/newsletters/diginews.htm	Focuses on latest trends on digitization and digital preservation.

11	Serials E-News http://www.ringgold.com/UKSG/si_pd.cfm	Provide up-to-the-minute news of current issues and developments within the global serials industry.
12	Sprouts: Working Papers on Information Systems http://sprouts.aisnet.org/home.html	Provides a fast-turnaround outlet for authentic and original research and work-in-progress carried out by scholars of the information systems field and members of AIS. Sprouts are devoted to research about the ways in which information is generated and used in the prevailing complex socio-technical landscape.

E-Resources containing Current Literature have greater demand, as Academician and Researchers always look for latest development on their specific subject field. It has found that 149 E-Resources are providing Current Trends E-Journals are 111, E-Magazines are 22, and E-Newsletter is 12.

Summary Table: Distribution of E-Resources by Current Trends

Sl. No.	E-Resources by Current Trends	No	Percentage
1	E-Journals	111	76%
2	E-Magazines	22	84%
3	Other E-Resources	12	50%
	Total	**145**	**74%**

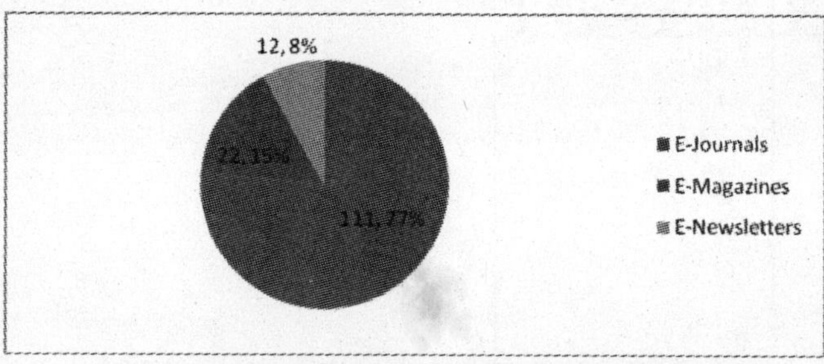

Fig: E-Resources providing Current Trends

This chart shows that out of 195 E-Resources 145 (74%) E-Resources are providing Current trends. Out of total 145 E-Journals 111 (76%), Out of Total 26 E-Magazines 22 (84%), and out of 24 E-Newsletters 12 (50%) are providing Current and latest trends.

3.4. PUBLISHER OF OPEN ACCESS E-RESOURCES IN LIS

Major Electronic Journal Publishers are like JSTOR, Blackwell Publishers, Springer Verlag & Kluwer, American Chemical society etc. There are four possi ble sources of electronic journals can be identified.

Existing publishers;

Intermediaries;

Innovative researchers and scholars; and

University -based electronic publishers.

Existing Publishers: A number of scholarly publishers both commercial and profes sional are experimenting with networking options. In commercial arena, publishers such as Elsevier, John Wiley and Pergamon are implementing projects. Scientific societies, like the American Chemical Society, the American mathematical Society and the Ameri can Psychological Association , are pursuing development of electronic journals. Paral lel electronic versions on -line and on CD - ROM - to several standard paper versions are now becoming widely available. In addition to bringing out electronic versions of cu rrent paper issues, several publishers are also experimenting with converting back files into electronic form, generally in collabo ration with universities or libraries.

Intermediaries: A number of intermediary organizations have negotiated copyright agr eements with publishers and are able to deliver their output to customers. These include indexing and abstractin g services, library consortia subscription agents and so on. Among them is the Institute for Scientific Information, American Chemical Society, the Colorado Alliance of Research Libraries (CARL) which Provides document delivery as an extension of it uncovered table of contents database service, Faxon Company, a major paper journal subscription agency . They are involved in some kind of e1ectronic p ublishing .

Innovative Research and Scholars: These are editors of publications like:

Electronic Journ al of communication (University of Windsor);

Journal of the International academy of hospitality research (Virginia Tech);

Journal of Reproductive Tech nology, (Joyce Sigaloff and Embryonic, Inc.);

New horizons in adult education (Syracuse University, Kellogg Project);

Postmodern Culture (North Carolina State);

Psyoloquy (Princeton/Rutgers/ APA); and

Public-Access Computer Systems Review (University of Houston Libraries).

University based Electronic Publishers: It has been estimated that universities publish at most 15 percent of their faculty's output. This includes dis cussion papers and periodicals emanating from individual academic departments as w ell as formalized university outlets like university presses and publications offices. Many librarians and other members of the university community in conversations express networked publishing about academics regaining control and distribution of its own intellectual output.

PUBLISHERS OF EVALUATED OPEN ACCESS E-RESOURCES

E-Journals

SL	URL	PUBLISHER
1	Electronic Journal of Knowledge Management http://www.ejkm.com/	Academic Conferences International Limited publishes EJKM.
2	International Journal of Library and Information Science http://www.academicjournals.org/ijlis/index.htm	Academic journals
3	International Journal of Computer Science and Information Technology http://airccse.org/journal/ijcsit.html	Academy & Industry Research Collaboration Center
4	International Journal of Managing Public Sector Information and Communication Technologies http://airccse.org/journal/mpict/ijmpict.html	Academy & Industry Research Collaboration Center
5	International Journal of Multimedia and Its Applications http://airccse.org/journal/ijma_index.html	Academy & Industry Research Collaboration Center
6	The International Journal of Database Management Systems http://airccse.org/journal/ijdms/ijdms.html	Academy & Industry Research Collaboration Center
7	The International Journal of Managing Information Technology http://airccse.org/journal/ijmit/ijmit.html	Academy & Industry Research Collaboration Center
8	Journal of Artificial Intelligence Research http://www.jair.org/	AI Access Foundation, Inc
9	College and Research Libraries http://crl.acrl.org/	ALA

10	Alki: The Washington Library Association Journal http://www.wla.org/alki/	ALA
11	Law Library Journal http://www.aallnet.org/products/pub_journal.asp	ALA
12	Library Resources & Technical Services (LRTS) http://alcts.metapress.com/home/main.mpx	ALA
13	RBM Journal of Rare Books , Manuscripts, and Cultural Heritage http://rbm.acrl.org/content/2/2	ALA
14	School Library Media Research (formerly: School Library Media Quarterly) http://www.ala.org/ala/mgrps/divs/aasl/aaslpubsandjournals/slmrb/aboutsmr/aboutslmr.cfm	ALA
15	Technological Librarianship: An Online Journal of the American Theological Library Association http://journal.atla.com/ojs/index.php/theolib/index	ALA
16	Technology Electronic Reviews (TER) http://www.ala.org/lita/publications/archive/ter	ALA
17	Australian Academic and Research Libraries http://www.alia.org.au/publishing/aarl/index.html	ALIA
18	Journal of the American Medical Informatics Association http://www.pubmedcentral.nih.gov/tocrender.fcgi?action=archive&journal=76	American Association for History and Computing
19	Journal of Technology Studies http://scholar.lib.vt.edu/ejournals/JOTS/	American Medical Informatics Association
20	Interpersonal Computing and Technology Journal http://www.helsinki.fi/science/optek/#byissue	Association for Educational Communications and Technology

21	Issues in Science and Technology Librarianship http://www.library.ucsb.edu/istl/ Or http://www.istl.org/	Association of College and Research Libraries
22	Learned Publishing http://www.ingentaconnect.com/content/alpsp/lp	Association of Learned and Professional Society Publishers
23	LIBER Quarterly Journal of European Research Libraries http://liber.library.uu.nl/index.html	Association of Learned and Professional Society Publishers
24	International Review of Research in Open and Distance Learning http://www.irrodl.org/index.php/irrodl	Athabasca University
25	Journal of Medical Internet Research http://www.jmir.org/	Australian Computer Society Inc.
26	Australian Library Journal http://alia.org.au/publishing/alj/	Australian Library and Information Association
27	The Bonefolder: An outgrowth of the Book Arts Web http://www.philobiblon.com/bonefolder/	Book Arts Web - Peter D. Verheyen: Bookbinder & Conservator / Special Collections Preservation & Digital Access Librarian, Syracuse University Library, Syracuse, NY.
28	Journal of Staff Development http://learningforward.org/publications/jsd#.UUQguzcynUc	Bowling Green State University
29	School libraries in Canada (SLIC): A Journal of the Canadian Association for School Libraries http://www.clatoolbox.ca/casl/slic/links.html	Canadian Association for School Libraries
30	Computer and Information Science http://journal.ccsenet.org/index.php/cis/index	Canadian Center of Science

31	Journal of Information Literacy http://ojs.lboro.ac.uk/ojs/index.php/JIL/index	Cathie Jackson, Managing Editor, JIL, Information Services, Cardiff University
32	Electronic Journal of Health Informatics http://www.ejhi.net/ojs/index.php/ejhi	Central Queensland University
33	Cybermetrics : International Journal of Scientometrics, Informetrics and Bibliometrics http://www.cindoc.csic.es/cybermetrics/	Centro de Informacion y Documentacion Cientifica
34	Multimedia Information and Technology Journal (MmIT) http://www.cilip.org.uk/get-involved/special-interest-groups/multimedia/journal/pages/default.aspx	Chartered Institute of Library and Information Professionals
35	Information Scotland: The Journal of the Chartered Institute of Library and Information Professionals in Scotland http://www.slainte.org.uk/publications/serials/infoscot/vol1(1)/vol1(1)contnts.html	Chartered Institute of Library and Information Professionals in Scotland.
36	The Public Access Computer Systems Review http://epress.lib.uh.edu/pr/pacsrev.html#history	City University of New York
37	Code4Lib Journal http://journal.code4lib.org/	Code4Lib
38	Current Cites http://lists.webjunction.org/currentcites/	Community at WebJunction.org. Editor: Roy Tennant
39	International Journal of Legal Information http://scholarship.law.cornell.edu/ijli/vol33/iss1/	Cornell Law Library
40	Journal of East Asian Libraries http://www.lib.byu.edu/dlib/spc/jeal/	Council on East Asian Libraries and the

		Association for Asian Studies, Inc.
41	LIBRES: Library and Information Science Research Electronic Journal http://libres.curtin.edu.au/	Curtin University of Technology
42	Electronic Journal on Information Systems in Developing Countries http://www.ejisdc.org/ojs2/index.php/ejisdc	Department of Information Systems, City University of Hong Kong,
43	DESIDOC Journal of Library & Information Science http://publications.drdo.gov.in/ojs/index.php/djlit/index	DESIDOC and DRDO. New Delhi
44	International Journal of Computer and Information Engineering http://www.waset.org/journals/ijcie/	Digital Curation Centre
45	World Libraries http://www.worlib.org/	Dominican University Graduate School of Library and Information Science
46	Information Technology and Disabilities http://people.rit.edu/easi/itd.htm	E A S I: Equal Access to Software and Information Country: United States
47	EDUCAUSE Quarterly http://www.educause.edu/eq	EDUCAUSE (a nonprofit association whose mission is to advance higher education by promoting the intelligent use of information technology).
48	European Journal of ePractice http://www.epracticejournal.eu/	ePractice.eu
49	Inter-Actions: UCLA Journal of Education and Information Studies http://repositories.cdlib.org/gseis/interactions/	eScholarship initiative of the California Digital Library,

50	International Journal of Special Libraries http://forge.fh-potsdam.de/~IFLA/INSPEL/intro.htm	Fachhochschule Potsdam c/o Stefan Bernhardt Fachbereich Archiv, Bibliothek
51	Malaysian Journal of Library & Information Sciencehttp://ejum.fsktm.um.edu.my/VolumeListing.aspx?JournalID=3	Faculty of Computer Science & Information Technology, University of Malaya.
52	DIGITHUM: The Humanities in Digital Age http://www.uoc.edu/digithum/7/eng/numeros.html	Fundació per la Universitat Oberta de Catalunya (FUOC)
53	Digital Document Quarterly http://home.pacbell.net/hgladney/ddqstart.htm	H.M. Gladney, HMG Consulting
54	JLIS.it Italian Journal of Library and Information Science http://leo.cilea.it/index.php/jlis/article/view/4539/4416	HAWORTH
55	Journal of Internet Cataloguing http://www.internetcataloging.com/home.html	Haworth, Binghamton, NY
56	High Energy Physics Libraries Webzine http://library.web.cern.ch/library/Webzine/index.shtml	HEPLW Team
57	ITALICS: Innovations in Teaching and Learning in Information and Computer Sciences http://www.ics.heacademy.ac.uk/italics/	Higher education academy
58	Human IT: tidskrift for studier av IT ur ett humanvetenskapligt perspektiv http://etjanst.hb.se/bhs/ith//info-eng.htm	Högskolan i Borås Country: Sweden
59	The Idaho Librarian: A Publication of the Idaho Library Association http://www.idaholibraries.org/idlibrarian/index.php/idaho-librarian/index	Idaho Library Association
60	International Journal of Communication http://ijoc.org/ojs/index.php/ijoc/about/editorialPolicies#focusAndScope	IJoC, Los Angeles, CA

61	Informatica Economica Journal http://revistaie.ase.ro/index.html	Inforec Association.
62	Information Technology and Libraries http://www.ala.org/ala/mgrps/divs/lita/ital/italinformation.cfm	Informing Science Institute
63	Informing Faculty: An International Journal of Higher Education Discussion Cases http://informingfaculty.org/	Informing Science Institute
64	Interdisciplinary Journal of E-Learning and Learning Objects http://ijklo.org/	Informing Science Institute
65	Interdisciplinary Journal of Information, Knowledge, and Management http://www.ijikm.org/	Informing Science Institute
66	International Journal of Doctoral Studies (IJDS) http://ijds.org/	Informing Science Institute
67	Issues in Informing Science and Information Technology http://iisit.org/	Informing Science Institute
68	Journal of Information Technology Education (JITE: Research) http://www.informingscience.us/icarus/journals/jiteresearch/publications	Informing Science Institute
69	Journal of Information, Information Technology, and Organizations http://jiito.org/	Informing Science Institute
70	International Journal of Communication Networks and Information Security http://www.ijcnis.org/index.php/ijcnis	Institute of Information Technology ,Kohat University of Science and Technology, Pakistan
71	International Review of Information Ethics http://www.i-r-i-e.net/	International Center for Information Ethics
72	E-JASL: The Electronic Journal of Academic and Special Librarianship http://southernlibrarianship.icaap.org/	International Consortium for the Advancement of Academic Publication (ICAAP)

73	Data Science Journal http://www.jstage.jst.go.jp/browse/dsj	International Council for Science
74	Chinese Librarianship: An International Electronic Journal http://www.iclc.us/cliej/	Internet Chinese Librarians Club publishes CLIEJ in various electronic channels
75	LIBRI: International Journal of Libraries and Information Services http://www.librijournal.org/	K. G. Saur Verlag, München
76	Library & Information Research: Research into Practice for Information & Library Services http://www.lirgjournal.org.uk/lir/ojs/index.php/lir	Library and Information Research Group.
77	Informing Science The International Journal of an Emerging Transdiscipline http://inform.nu/	Library Association.
78	Electronic Transactions on Artificial Intelligence http://www.ida.liu.se/ext/etai/	Linköping University Electronic Press
79	Current Issues in Education http://cie.asu.edu/index.php	Mary Lou Fulton Teachers College, (College of Education) Arizona State University
80	Journal of the Association for History and Computing http://quod.lib.umich.edu/j/jahc/browse.html	Medical Library-Univ. of Cambridge
81	MLA Forum http://www.mlaforum.org/	Michigan Library Association
82	MELA Notes: The Journal of the Middle East Librarians Association http://www.mela.us/MELANotes/MELANotesIntro.html	Middle East Librarians Association
83	Mississippi Libraries http://www.misslib.org/index.php/publications/mississippi-libraries/	Mississippi Library Association.

84	Christian Library Journal http://www.christianlibraryj.org/pdf/index.htm	Nancy L. Hesch Christian Library Services
85	Agricultural Libraries Information Notes http://webharvest.gov/peth04/20041023101316/http://www.nal.usda.gov/NewAlin/	National Agricultural Library
86	Research Management Review http://www.ncura.edu/content/news/rmr/archive.php	National Council of University Research Administrators
87	Journal of Research and Practice in Information Technology http://ws.acs.org.au/jrpit/JRPIT_Volumes.html	National Staff Development Council
88	ALAN Review http://scholar.lib.vt.edu/ejournals/ALAN/	NCTE
89	Annals of Library & Information Studies http://nopr.niscair.res.in/	NISCAIR, New Delhi India
90	North Carolina Libraries http://www.ncl.ecu.edu/index.php/NCL	North Carolina Library Association
91	Northwestern Journal of Technology and Intellectual Property http://www.law.northwestern.edu/journals/njtip/issues.htm	Northwestern University School of Law
92	Colby Quarterly (formerly: Colby Library Quarterly) http://digitalcommons.colby.edu/	Powered by bepress
93	NPO Journal/NPO E-Journal http://www.bl.uk/blpac/publicationsjournals.html	Preservation Advisory Centre British Library 96 Euston Road London
94	Information Research: An International Electronic Journal http://informationr.net/ir/	Professor T.D. Wilson.
95	Progressive Librarian http://libr.org/pl/	Progressive Librarians Guild

96	Information for Social Change http://libr.org/isc/journal.html	Publication of the organization, "Information for Social Change".
97	Partnership: The Canadian Journal of Library and Information Practice and Research http://journal.lib.uoguelph.ca/index.php/perj/index	Published by practitioner's journal of The Partnership (Open Journal Systems)
98	Journal of the European Association for Health Information and Libraries http://www.eahil.net/journal/	PubMed. And from 2002 Medical Library Association
99	School Library Journal Online http://www.schoollibraryjournal.com/	Reed Business Information, a division of Reed Elsevier Inc.
100	Journal of Information Architecture http://journalofia.org/archives/	REG-iA
101	Collaborative Librarianship http://www.collaborativelibrarianship.org/index.html	Regis University
102	LASIE: Library Automated Systems Information Exchange http://search.informit.com.au/browseJournalTitle;res=E-LIBRARY;issn=0047-3774	RMIT University
103	Library Journal http://www.libraryjournal.com	Ron Shank
104	IFLA Journal http://www.ifla.org/V/iflaj/index.htm	Royal Library (Neatherlands) provides the facilities for IFLA.
105	Journal of the Medical Library association http://www.ncbi.nlm.nih.gov/pmc/journals/93/	Rutgers University Libraries, Available in OJS
106	Scandinavian Public Library Quarterly http://www.splq.info/	Scandinavian Public Library Quarterly

107	JEP: The Journal of Electronic Publishing http://www.journalofelectronicpublishing.org/	Scholarly Publishing Office (SPO), a unit of the University of Michigan University Library
108	IT&Society http://www.itandsociety.org/index.html	SIQSS, Stanford University
109	American Archivist http://archivists.metapress.com/home/main.mpx	Society of American Archivists
110	Special Libraries http://www.sla.org/content/shop/speclibs.cfm#1910	Special Library Association (SLA)
111	EBIB Electronic Information Bulletin for librarians http://ebib.info/biuletyn/	Stowarzyszenie Bibliotekarzy Polskich Komisja Wydawnictw
112	Journal of Educational Media & Library Sciences http://joemls.tku.edu.tw/index_e.htm	Tamkang University Press
113	Journal of Virtual Worlds Research http://www.jvwresearch.org/index.html	TDL electronic Press. Hosted by the JVWR Editorial Team.
114	Journal of Digital Information http://jodi.ecs.soton.ac.uk/r or http://journals.tdl.org/jodi	Texas Digital Library
115	Texas library journal http://www.txla.org/TLJ	Texas Library Association
116	MC Journal: The Journal of Academic Media Librarianship http://wings.buffalo.edu/publications/mcjrnl/	The AV Review.
117	Studies in Bibliography http://etext.lib.virginia.edu/bsuva/sb	The bibliographical society of the university of virginia

118	Coordinates: Online Journal of the Map and Geography Round Table of the American Library Association. Series A and B http://www.sunysb.edu/libmap/coordinates.htm	The Map and Geography Round Table (MAGERT) of the American Library Association produce and publish this publication.
119	International Journal of Digital Curation http://www.ijdc.net/./ijdc/issue/current	UKOLN
120	Journal of Information Law and Technology http://www2.warwick.ac.uk/fac/soc/law/elj/jilt/ or European Journal of Law and Technology http://ejlt.org//issue/archive	Universities of Warwick and Strathclyde in the United Kingdom.
121	Evidence Based Library and Information Practice http://ejournals.library.ualberta.ca/index.php/EBLIP/index	University of Alberta
122	Australian Journal of Information Systems http://dl.acs.org.au/index.php/ajis/about	University of Canberra, Faculty of Communication
123	Journal of eLiteracy http://www.jelit.org/index.html	University of Glasgow
124	The Journal of the Rutgers University Library http://jrul.libraries.rutgers.edu/index.php/jrul/index	University of Houston Libraries
125	Library Student Journal http://www.librarystudentjournal.org/index.php/lsj/index	University of Illinois
126	Firstmonday http://firstmonday.org/	University of Illinois at Chicago University Library
127	Electronic Journal of Africana Bibliography http://ir.uiowa.edu/ejab/all_issues.html	University of Iowa

128	B Sides http://ir.uiowa.edu/bsides/	University of Iowa; School of Library and Information Science
129	South African Journal of Information Management http://www.sajim.co.za/index.php/sajim/issue/current	University of Johannesburg
130	Library Philosophy and Practice http://www.webpages.uidaho.edu/~mbolin/lpp.htm	University of Nebraska, Lincoln libraries
131	Communications in Information Literacy http://www.comminfolit.org/index.php/cil/issue/archive	University of Oklahoma-Tulsa Library
132	Journal of Health Informatics in Developing Countries http://www.jhidc.org/index.php/jhidc	University of Otago
133	Information Technologies and International Development http://itidjournal.org/itid	University of Southern California
134	African Journal of Information & Communication Technology http://epress.lib.uts.edu.au/ojs/index.php/ajict/	University of Technology
135	Webology http://www.webology.ir/	University of Tehran
136	Journal of Philippine Librarianship http://journals.upd.edu.ph/index.php/jpl/issue/current	University of the Phillippine
137	Journal of Library Innovation http://www.libraryinnovation.org/about/contact	University of Toronto
138	Simile: Studies in Media and Information Literacy Education http://utpjournals.metapress.com/content/120764/	University of Toronto Press

139	New Knowledge Environments http://journals.uvic.ca/index.php/INKE	University of Victoria
140	Virginia Libraries http://scholar.lib.vt.edu/ejournals/VALib/	Virginia Library Association
141	Urban Library Journal http://lacuny.cuny.edu/ulj/	Virginia Tech
142	Cites & Insights: Crawford at Large http://citesandinsights.info/citoc.htm	Walt Crawford and sponsored by YBP Library Services
143	Journal of Knowledge Management Practice http://www.tlainc.com/boutjkmp.htm	Western New York Library Resources Council
144	Health Information and Libraries Journal http://www3.interscience.wiley.com/journal/120118368/grouphome/home html	Wiley Inter Science
145	Internet Writing Journal http://www.internetwritingjournal.com/	Writers Write, Inc.

E-Magazines

1	AALL Spectrum http://www.aallnet.org/main-menu/Publications/spectrum	ALA
2	American Libraries http://americanlibrariesmagazine.org/	ALA
3	Book Links http://www.ala.org/ala/aboutala/hqops/publishing/booklinks/index.cfm	ALA
4	CHOICE http://www.ala.org/ala/mgrps/divs/acrl/publications/choice/previousissues previousissues.cfm	ALA

5	The Bulletin of the American Society for Information Science and Technology http://www.asis.org/bulletin.html	American Society for Information Science and Technology (ASIS&T)
6	inCite http://alia.org.au/publishing/incite/archive.html	Australian Library and Information Association
7	D-Lib Magazine http://www.dlib.org/dlib/september08/09contents.html	Corporation for National Research Initiatives (CNRI) produces d-Lib Magazine.
8	EDUCAUSE Review http://www.educause.edu/	D. Teddy Diggs.
9	Research Information http://www.researchinformation.info/	Europa Science Ltd
10	Provenance http://www.provenance.ca/about-provenance/index.html	Guy Robertson.
11	Access http://www.aardvarknet.info/access/number46/index.cfm	iGroup
12	Computer in Libraries http://www.infotoday.com/cilmag/default.shtml	Information Today Inc
13	Information Today http://www.infotoday.com/IT/nov08/index.shtml	Information Today Inc
14	Knowledge Management World http://www.kmworld.com/index.cfm	Information Today Inc
15	Link-Up http://www.infotoday.com/linkup/default.shtml	Information Today Inc
16	Online http://www.infotoday.com/online/default.shtml	Information Today Inc
17	Searcher: The Magazine for Database Professionals http://www.infotoday.com/searcher/default.asp	Information Today Inc
18	E-Content http://www.ecmag.net/	Information Today, Inc.
19	Ex Libris http://marylaine.com/exlibris/	Marylaine Block

20	Book business http://www.bookbusinessmag.com/	North American Publishing Company (NAPCO)
21	Library Juice http://libr.org/juice/	Rory Litwin.
22	The Marginal http://www.gslis.mcgill.ca/marginal/	The McGill Library and Information Studies Student Association, known around the school as MLISSA, publish this e-zine.
23	Ariadne http://www.ariadne.ac.uk/	UKOLN
24	Cultivate Interactive http://www.cultivate-int.org/index-2.html	UKOLN
25	Exploit Interactive http://www.exploit-lib.org/	UKOLN
26	Virginia Tech Magazine http://www.vtmagazine.vt.edu/	Virginia Polytechnic Institute and State University

Newsletters and other E-Resources

1	Biblia's Warrior Librarian Weekly http://warriorlibrarian.com/ARCHIVE/00archives.html	A B Credaro
2	Abbey Newsletter http://cool.conservation-us.org/byorg/abbey/an/	Abbey Publications, Inc
3	ALAWON. The ALA Washington Office Electronic Newsline http://www.ala.org/ala/aboutala/offices/wo/washnews/archivea/archive.cfm	ALA
4	ALCTS Network News http://bubl.ac.uk/archive/journals/alctsnn/	ALA

5	ARL: A bimonthly newsletter for library issues and action http://www.arl.org/resources/pubs/br/index.shtml	ALA
6	Biblio-Tech Review http://www.ringgold.com/biblio-tech/si_pd.cfm?pid=2	Biblio Tech Ltd
7	Cataloging and Classification Quarterly http://bubl.ac.uk/archive/journals/cacq/	BUBL Information Service, Andersonian Library, Strathclyde University.
8	Business and Finance Division Bulletin http://bf.sla.org/resources/the-bulletin/	Business & Finance Division Executive Board
9	RLG DigiNews http://www.oclc.org/programs/publications/newsletters/diginews.htm	Department of Research, Cornell University Library, in consultation with RLG and, later, the RLG Programs unit of OCLC Programs & Research
10	Free Pint http://www.freepint.com/	Free Pint limited
11	Internet Resources Newsletter http://www.hw.ac.uk/libwww/irn/irn.html	Heriot-Watt University Library staff.
12	MLS: Marketing Library Services http://www.infotoday.com/MLS/default.shtml	Information Today Inc
13	Against the grain http://www.against-the-grain.com/d/TOC	Katina Strauch
14	Conserline http://www.loc.gov/acq/conser/consrlin.html	Library of Congress
15	LC Cataloging Newsline http://www.loc.gov/catdir/lccn/	Library of Congress
16	The Wired Librarian's Newsletter http://www.wiredlibrarian.com/wln/wlnfront.htm	Micro Libraries

17	Information today and Tomorrow http://www.dsir.gov.in/pubs/itt/index.htm	NISSAT
18	SPARC Open Access Newsletter or Free Online Scholarship Newsletter http://www.earlham.edu/~peters/fos/index.htm	Peter Suber
19	ABAA Newsletter http://hq.abaa.org/books/antiquarian/abaapages/newsletter	Publications Committee of The Antiquarian Booksellers
20	Internet on a Disk http://www.samizdat.com/ioad.html	Richard Seltzer.
21	Sprouts: Working Papers on Information Systems http://sprouts.aisnet.org/home.html	Sprouts Alliance
22	NLM Technical Bulletin http://www.nlm.nih.gov/pubs/techbull/current_issue.html	U.S. National Library of Medicine.
23	Serials E-News http://www.ringgold.com/UKSG/si_pd.cfm	UK Serials Group
24	CIT Infobits http://serials.infomotions.com/infobits/	UNC-Chapel Hill ITS Teaching and Learning division.

Traditional publisher has not been the only one who has used the publishing services of the Internet Authors who write in trade Journals expect to be paid. While those who publish in esoteric journals do so for reasons other than payment. Four possible sources of Electronic Journals can be identified. Intermediaries; Innovative researchers and scholars; and University-Existing publishers; based electronic publishers. Table shows that total publishers of 200 E-resources are 163 and Maximum E-resources are being published by ALA.

Summary Table: Distribution of Publishers Supporting Free E-Resources

Chartered Institute of Library & Info. Professionals	2
University of Toronto Press	2
UKLON	4
Academy & Industry Research Collaboration Center	5
Informing Science Institute	8
Information Today	8
American Library Association	16
Single Publishers are	150
Total Publishers	**157**

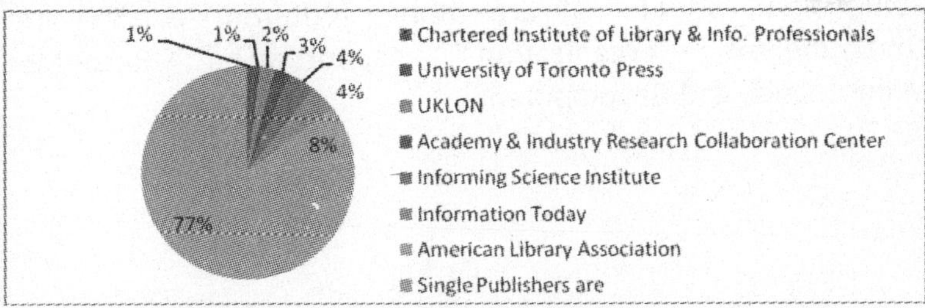

Fig: Publishers Supporting E-Resources Maintenance and Development

Chart Shows that 77% E-Resources are published by Single Publishers, 8% published by ALA, 4% published by Informing science Institute, 4% by Information Today, 3% by academic & Industrial Research Center, 2%by Chartered Institute of Library and information Professional, 2% by UKLON and 1% by University of Toronto Press.

Summary Table: Distribution of Organizations Supporting Free E-Resources

Organization	79
Academic	41
Commercial	36
Others	30
Government	9
Total	195

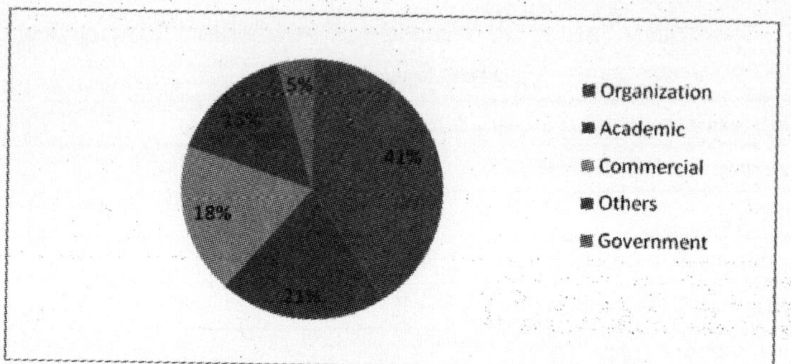

Fig.: Distribution of Organizations Supporting E-Resources Maintenance and Development

This chart shows that maximum 79 (41%) E-Resources are of Organizations. 41 (21%) is Academic, 36 (18%) are Commercial, 30 (15 %) are others (different) 9 (5%) are governmental organization supporting E-Resources Maintenance and Development.

3.5. AUTHORITATIVE RANKING OF E-RESOURCES

E-Journals

SL. No.	URL	Domain
1	ITALICS: Innovations in Teaching and Learning in Information and Computer Sciences http://www.ics.heacademy.ac.uk/italics/	.ac
2	Journal of Information Law and Technology http://www2.warwick.ac.uk/fac/soc/law/elj/jilt/ or European Journal of Law and Technology http://ejlt.org//issue/archive	.ac
3	Evidence Based Library and Information Practice http://ejournals.library.ualberta.ca/index.php/EBLIP/index	.ca
4	New Knowledge Environments http://journals.uvic.ca/index.php/INKE	.ca
5	Partnership: The Canadian Journal of Library and Information Practice and Research http://journal.lib.uoguelph.ca/index.php/perj/index	.ca
6	School libraries in Canada (SLIC): A Journal of the Canadian Association for School Libraries http://www.clatoolbox.ca/casl/slic/links.html	.ca
7	High Energy Physics Libraries Webzine http://library.web.cern.ch/library/Webzine/index.shtml	.ch
8	American Archivist http://archivists.metapress.com/home/main.mpx	.com
9	Electronic Journal of Knowledge Management http://www.ejkm.com/	.com
10	Health Information and Libraries Journal http://www3.interscience.wiley.com/journal/120118368/grouphome/home.html	.com

11	Internet Writing Journal http://www.internetwritingjournal.com/	.com
12	Journal of Internet Cataloguing http://www.internetcataloging.com/home.html	.com
13	Journal of Knowledge Management Practice http://www.tlainc.com/boutjkmp.htm	.com
14	LASIE: Library Automated Systems Information Exchange http://search.informit.com.au/browseJournalTitle;res=E-LIBRARY;issn=0047-3774	.com
15	Learned Publishing http://www.ingentaconnect.com/content/alpsp/lp	.com
16	School Library Journal Online http://www.schoollibraryjournal.com/	.com
17	Simile: Studies in Media and Information Literacy Education http://utpjournals.metapress.com/content/120764/	.com
18	South African Journal of Information Management http://www.sajim.co.za/index.php/sajim/issue/current	.com
19	Technological Librarianship: An Online Journal of the American Theological Library Association http://journal.atla.com/ojs/index.php/theolib/index	.com
20	The Bonefolder: An outgrowth of the Book Arts Web http://www.philobiblon.com/bonefolder/	.com
21	African Journal of Information & Communication Technology http://epress.lib.uts.edu.au/ojs/index.php/ajict/	.edu
22	ALAN Review http://scholar.lib.vt.edu/ejournals/ALAN/	.edu
23	Australian Journal of Information Systems http://dl.acs.org.au/index.php/ajis/about	.edu
24	B Sides http://ir.uiowa.edu/bsides/	.edu
25	Colby Quarterly (formerly: Colby Library Quarterly) http://digitalcommons.colby.edu/	.edu

26	Coordinates: Online Journal of the Map and Geography Round Table of the American Library Association. Series A and B http://www.sunysb.edu/libmap/coordinates.htm	.edu
27	Current Issues in Education http://cie.asu.edu/index.php	.edu
28	DIGITHUM: The Humanities in Digital Age http://www.uoc.edu/digithum/7/eng/numeros.html	.edu
29	EDUCAUSE Quarterly http://www.educause.edu/eq	.edu
30	Electronic Journal of Africana Bibliography http://ir.uiowa.edu/ejab/all_issues.html	.edu
31	European Journal of ePractice http://www.epracticejournal.eu/	.edu
32	Information Technology and Disabilities http://people.rit.edu/easi/itd.htm	.edu
33	International Journal of Communication Networks and Information Security http://www.ijcnis.org/index.php/ijcnis	.edu
34	International Journal of Legal Information http://scholarship.law.cornell.edu/ijli/vol33/iss1/	.edu
35	International Journal of Special Libraries http://forge.fh-potsdam.de/~IFLA/INSPEL/intro.htm	.edu
36	Journal of East Asian Libraries http://www.lib.byu.edu/dlib/spc/jeal/	.edu
37	Journal of Educational Media & Library Sciences http://joemls.tku.edu.tw/index_e.htm	.edu
38	Journal of Philippine Librarianship http://journals.upd.edu.ph/index.php/jpl/issue/current	.edu
39	Journal of Technology Studies http://scholar.lib.vt.edu/ejournals/JOTS/	.edu
40	Journal of the Association for History and Computing http://quod.lib.umich.edu/j/jahc/browse.html	.edu
41	Library Philosophy and Practice http://www.webpages.uidaho.edu/~mbolin/lpp.htm	.edu

42	LIBRES: Library and Information Science Research Electronic Journal http://libres.curtin.edu.au/	.edu
43	Malaysian Journal of Library & Information Sciencehttp://ejum.fsktm.um.edu.my/VolumeListing.aspx?JournalID=3	.edu
44	MC Journal: The Journal of Academic Media Librarianship http://wings.buffalo.edu/publications/mcjrnl/	.edu
45	North Carolina Libraries http://www.ncl.ecu.edu/index.php/NCL	.edu
46	Northwestern Journal of Technology and Intellectual Property http://www.law.northwestern.edu/journals/njtip/issues.htm	.edu
47	Research Management Review http://www.ncura.edu/content/news/rmr/archive.php	.edu
48	Studies in Bibliography http://etext.lib.virginia.edu/bsuva/sb	.edu
49	The Journal of the Rutgers University Library http://jrul.libraries.rutgers.edu/index.php/jrul/index	.edu
50	The Public Access Computer Systems Review http://epress.lib.uh.edu/pr/pacsrev.html#history	.edu
51	Urban Library Journal http://lacuny.cuny.edu/ulj/	.edu
52	Virginia Libraries http://scholar.lib.vt.edu/ejournals/VALib/	.edu
53	Interpersonal Computing and Technology Journal http://www.helsinki.fi/science/optek/#byissue	.fi
54	Agricultural Libraries Information Notes http://webharvest.gov/peth04/20041023101316/http://www.nal.usda.gov/NewAlin/	.gov
55	Data Science Journal http://www.jstage.jst.go.jp/browse/dsj	.gov

56	DESIDOC Journal of Library & Information Science http://publications.drdo.gov.in/ojs/index.php/djlit/index	.gov
57	Journal of the American Medical Informatics Association http://www.pubmedcentral.nih.gov/tocrender.fcgi?action=archive&journal=76	.gov
58	Journal of the Medical Library association http://www.ncbi.nlm.nih.gov/pmc/journals/93/	.gov
59	Annals of Library & Information Studies http://nopr.niscair.res.in/	.in
60	Cites & Insights: Crawford at Large http://citesandinsights.info/citoc.htm	.info
61	EBIB Electronic Information Bulletin for librarians http://ebib.info/biuletyn/	.info
62	Scandinavian Public Library Quarterly http://www.splq.info/	.info
63	Webology http://www.webology.ir/	.ir
64	JLIS.it Italian Journal of Library and Information Science http://leo.cilea.it/index.php/jlis/article/view/4539/4416	.it
65	Digital Document Quarterly http://home.pacbell.net/hgladney/ddqstart.htm	.net
66	Electronic Journal of Health Informatics http://www.ejhi.net/ojs/index.php/ejhi	.net
67	Information Research: An International Electronic Journal http://informationr.net/ir/	.net
68	International Journal of Digital Curation http://www.ijdc.net/./ijdc/issue/current	.net
69	International Review of Information Ethics http://www.i-r-i-e.net/	.net
70	Journal of the European Association for Health Information and Libraries http://www.eahil.net/journal/	.net

71	Informing Science The International Journal of an Emerging Transdiscipline http://inform.nu/	.nu
72	College and Research Libraries http://crl.acrl.org/	.org
73	Journal of Artificial Intelligence Research http://www.jair.org/	.org
74	Alki: The Washington Library Association Journal http://www.wla.org/alki/	.org
75	Australian Academic and Research Libraries http://www.alia.org.au/publishing/aarl/index.html	.org
76	Australian Library Journal http://alia.org.au/publishing/alj/	.org
77	Christian Library Journal http://www.christianlibraryj.org/pdf/index.htm	.org
78	Collaborative Librarianship http://www.collaborativelibrarianship.org/index.html	.org
79	Communications in Information Literacy http://www.comminfolit.org/index.php/cil/issue/archive	.org
80	Computer and Information Science http://journal.ccsenet.org/index.php/cis/index	.org
81	Current Cites http://lists.webjunction.org/currentcites/	.org
82	Cybermetrics : International Journal of Scientometrics, Informetrics and Bibliometrics http://www.cindoc.csic.es/cybermetrics/	.org
83	E-JASL: The Electronic Journal of Academic and Special Librarianship http://southernlibrarianship.icaap.org/	.org
84	Electronic Journal on Information Systems in Developing Countries http://www.ejisdc.org/ojs2/index.php/ejisdc	.org
85	Firstmonday http://firstmonday.org/	.org

86	IFLA Journal http://www.ifla.org/V/iflaj/index.htm	.org
87	Information for Social Change **http://libr.org/isc/journal.html**	.org
88	Information Scotland: The Journal of the Chartered Institute of Library and Information Professionals in Scotland http://www.slainte.org.uk/publications/serials/infoscot/vol1(1)/vol1(1)contents.html	.org
89	Information Technologies and International Development http://itidjournal.org/itid	.org
90	Information Technology and Libraries **http://www.ala.org/ala/mgrps/divs/lita/ital/italinformation.cfm**	.org
91	Informing Faculty: An International Journal of Higher Education Discussion Cases http://informingfaculty.org/	.org
92	Inter-Actions: UCLA Journal of Education and Information Studies http://repositories.cdlib.org/gseis/interactions/	.org
93	Interdisciplinary Journal of E-Learning and Learning Objects http://ijklo.org/	.org
94	Interdisciplinary Journal of Information, Knowledge, and Management http://www.ijikm.org/	.org
95	International Journal of Communication http://ijoc.org/ojs/index.php/ijoc/about/editorialPolicies#focusAndScope	.org
96	International Journal of Computer and Information Engineering http://www.waset.org/journals/ijcie/	.org
97	International Journal of Computer Science and Information Technology **http://airccse.org/journal/ijcsit.html**	.org
98	International Journal of Doctoral Studies (IJDS) http://ijds.org/	.org

99	International Journal of Library and Information Science **http://www.academicjournals.org/ijlis/index.htm**	.org
100	International Journal of Managing Public Sector Information and Communication Technologies **http://airccse.org/journal/mpict/ijmpict.html**	.org
101	International Journal of Multimedia and Its Applications **http://airccse.org/journal/ijma_index.html**	.org
102	International Review of Research in Open and Distance Learning http://www.irrodl.org/index.php/irrodl	.org
103	Issues in Informing Science and Information Technology http://iisit.org/	.org
104	Issues in science and Technology Librarianship http://www.istl.org/	.org
105	IT&Society http://www.itandsociety.org/index.html	.org
106	JEP: The Journal of Electronic Publishing http://www.journalofelectronicpublishing.org/	.org
107	Journal of Digital Information http://jodi.ecs.soton.ac.uk/r or http://journals.tdl.org/jodi	.org
108	Journal of eLiteracy http://www.jelit.org/index.html	.org
109	Journal of Health Informatics in Developing Countries http://www.jhidc.org/index.php/jhidc	.org
110	Journal of Information Architecture http://journalofia.org/archives/	.org
111	Journal of Information Literacy http://ojs.lboro.ac.uk/ojs/index.php/JIL/index	.org
112	Journal of Information Technology Education (JITE: Research) http://www.informingscience.us/icarus/journals/jiteresearch/publications	.org
113	Journal of Information, Information Technology, and Organizations http://jiito.org/	.org

114	Journal of Library Innovation http://www.libraryinnovation.org/about/contact	.org
115	Journal of Medical Internet Research http://www.jmir.org/	.org
116	Journal of Research and Practice in Information Technology http://ws.acs.org.au/jrpit/JRPIT_Volumes.html	.org
117	Journal of Staff Development http://learningforward.org/publications/jsd#.UUQguzcynUc	.org
118	Journal of Virtual Worlds Research http://www.jvwresearch.org/index.html	.org
119	Law Library Journal http://www.aallnet.org/products/pub_journal.asp	.org
120	LIBER Quarterly Journal of European Research Libraries http://liber.library.uu.nl/index.html	.org
121	Library Journal http://www.libraryjournal.com	.org
122	Library Resources & Technical Services (LRTS) http://www.ala.org/ala/mgrps/divs/alcts/resources/lrts/index.cfm	.org
123	Library Student Journal http://www.librarystudentjournal.org/index.php/lsj/index	.org
124	LIBRI: International Journal of Libraries and Information Services http://www.librijournal.org/	.org
125	Mississippi Libraries http://www.misslib.org/index.php/publications/mississippi-libraries/	.org
126	MLA Forum http://www.mlaforum.org/	.org
127	Multimedia Information and Technology Journal (MmIT) http://www.cilip.org.uk/get-involved/special-interest-groups/multimedia/journal/pages/default.aspx	.org
128	Progressive Librarian http://libr.org/pl/	.org
129	RBM Journal of Rare Books , Manuscripts, and Cultural Heritage http://rbm.acrl.org/content/2/2	.org

130	School Library Research http://www.ala.org/aasl/slr	.org
131	Special Libraries http://www.sla.org/content/shop/speclibs.cfm#1910	.org
132	Technology Electronic Reviews, TER http://www.ala.org/ala/mgrps/divs/lita/ter/tertechnology.cfm	.org
133	Texas library journal http://www.txla.org/TLJ	.org
134	Code4Lib Journal http://journal.code4lib.org/	.org
135	The Idaho Librarian: A Publication of the Idaho Library Association http://www.idaholibraries.org/idlibrarian/index.php/idaho-librarian/index	.org
136	The International Journal of Database Management Systems http://airccse.org/journal/ijdms/ijdms.html	.org
137	The International Journal of Managing Information Technology http://airccse.org/journal/ijmit/ijmit.html	.org
138	World Libraries http://www.worlib.org/	.org
139	Library & Information Research: Research into Practice for Information & Library Services http://www.lirg.org.uk/lir/ojs/index.php/lir	.org
140	Informatica Economica Journal http://revistaie.ase.ro/index.html	.ro
141	Electronic Transactions on Artificial Intelligence http://www.ida.liu.se/ext/etai/	.se
142	Human IT: Journal for Information Technology Studies as a Human Science**http://etjanst.hb.se/bhs/ith//info-eng.htm**	.se
143	NPO Journal/NPO E-Journal http://www.bl.uk/blpac/publicationsjournals.html	.uk
144	Chinese Librarianship: An International Electronic Journal http://www.iclc.us/cliej/	.us

145	MELA Notes: The Journal of the Middle East Librarians Association http://www.mela.us/MELANotes/MELANotesIntro.html	.us

E-Magazines

1	Ariadne http://www.ariadne.ac.uk/	.ac
2	Provenance http://www.provenance.ca/about-provenance/index.html	.ca
3	The Marginal http://www.gslis.mcgill.ca/marginal/	.ca
4	Book business http://www.bookbusinessmag.com/	.com
5	Computer in Libraries http://www.infotoday.com/cilmag/default.shtml	.com
6	Ex Libris http://marylaine.com/exlibris/	.com
7	Information Today http://www.infotoday.com/IT/nov08/index.shtml	.com
8	Knowledge Management World http://www.kmworld.com/index.cfm	.com
9	Link-Up http://www.infotoday.com/linkup/default.shtml	.com
10	Online http://www.infotoday.com/online/default.shtml	.com
11	Searcher: The Magazine for Database Professionals http://www.infotoday.com/searcher/default.asp	.com
12	EDUCAUSE Review http://www.educause.edu/	.edu
13	Virginia Tech Magazine http://www.vtmagazine.vt.edu/	.edu
14	Access http://www.aardvarknet.info/access/number46/index.cfm	.info

15	Research Information http://www.researchinformation.info/	.info
16	E-Content http://www.ecmag.net/	.net
17	AALL Spectrum http://www.aallnet.org/main-menu/Publications/spectrum	.org
18	American Libraries http://americanlibrariesmagazine.org/	.org
19	Book Links http://www.ala.org/ala/aboutala/hqops/publishing/booklinks/index.cfm	.org
20	CHOICE http://www.ala.org/ala/mgrps/divs/acrl/publications/choice/previousissues/previousissues.cfm	.org
21	Cultivate Interactive http://www.cultivate-int.org/index-2.html	.org
22	D-Lib Magazine http://www.dlib.org/dlib/september08/09contents.html	.org
23	Exploit Interactive http://www.exploit-lib.org/	.org
24	inCite http://alia.org.au/publishing/incite/archive.html	.org
25	Library Juice http://libr.org/juice/	.org
26	The Bulletin of the American Society for Information Science and Technology http://www.asis.org/bulletin.html	.org

Newsletters and other E-Resources

1	ALCTS Network News http://bubl.ac.uk/archive/journals/alctsnn/	.ac
2	Cataloging and Classification Quarterly http://bubl.ac.uk/archive/journals/cacq/	.ac
3	Internet Resources Newsletter http://www.hw.ac.uk/libwww/irn/irn.html	.ac
4	Against the grain http://www.against-the-grain.com/d/TOC	.com
5	Biblia's Warrior Librarian Weekly http://warriorlibrarian.com/ARCHIVE/00archives.html	.com
6	Biblio-Tech Review http://www.ringgold.com/biblio-tech/si_pd.cfm?pid=2	.com
7	CIT Infobits http://serials.infomotions.com/infobits/	.com
8	Free Pint http://www.freepint.com/	.com
9	Internet on a Disk http://www.samizdat.com/ioad.html	.com
10	MLS: Marketing Library Services http://www.infotoday.com/MLS/default.shtml	.com
11	Serials E-News http://www.ringgold.com/UKSG/si_pd.cfm	.com
12	The Wired Librarian's Newsletter http://www.wiredlibrarian.com/wln/wlnfront.htm	.com
13	Abbey Newsletter http://cool.conservation-us.org/byorg/abbey/an/	.edu
14	SPARC Open Access Newsletter or Free Online Scholarship Newsletter http://www.earlham.edu/~peters/fos/index.htm	.edu
15	Conserline http://www.loc.gov/acq/conser/consrlin.html	.gov
16	Information today and Tomorrow http://www.dsir.gov.in/pubs/itt/index.htm	.gov

17	LC Cataloging Newsline http://www.loc.gov/catdir/lccn/	.gov
18	NLM Technical Bulletin http://www.nlm.nih.gov/pubs/techbull/current_issue.html	.gov
19	ABAA Newsletter http://hq.abaa.org/books/antiquarian/abaapages/newsletter	.org
20	ALAWON. The ALA Washington Office Electronic Newsline http://www.ala.org/ala/aboutala/offices/wo/washnews/archivea/archive.cfm	.org
21	ARL: A bimonthly newsletter for library issues and action http://www.arl.org/resources/pubs/br/index.shtml	.org
22	Business and Finance Division Bulletin http://bf.sla.org/resources/the-bulletin/	.org
23	RLG DigiNews http://www.oclc.org/programs/publications/newsletters/diginews.htm	.org
24	Sprouts: Working Papers on Information Systems http://sprouts.aisnet.org/home.html	.org

E-Resources published from different country have greater importance. E-Resources Published from USA, UK, Japan, German has more weight age then journal publish form India, Bangladesh, Shri Lanka. Domain has greater Impact Factor on publication of E-Resources. Author has found various domain Authorities of These 195 E-Resources.

Summary Table: Authoritative Ranking of E-Resources

.ac	6	3%
.ca	6	3%
.com	30	15%
.edu	36	18%

.gov	9	5%
.info	5	3%
.org	84	43%
Net	10	5%
Others	9	5%
Total	**195**	**100%**

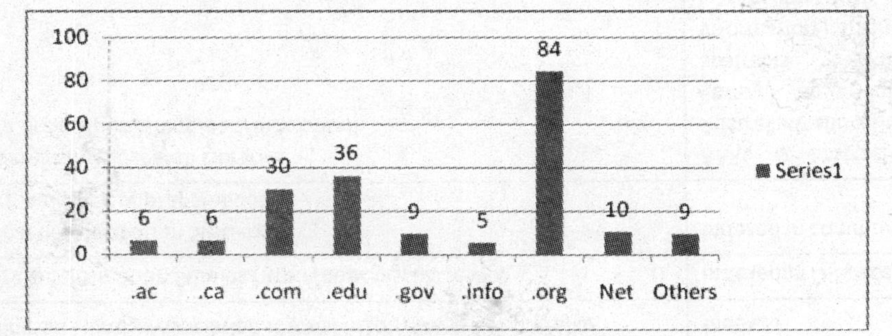

Fig: Authoritative Ranking of E-Resources

This chart shows that maximum 84 (43%) E-Resources are of .org, edu 36 (18%) and .com 30 (15%).

3.6. E-RESOURCES INDEXED IN OTHER DATABASES

E-Journals

1	African Journal of Information & Communication Technology http://epress.lib.uts.edu.au/ojs/index.php/ajict/	Indexed in Niscair online publication repository, LISA, UK, ILISA India, Doaj.
2	Alki: The Washington Library Association Journal http://www.wla.org/alki/	Indexed
3	Annals of Library & Information Studies http://nopr.niscair.res.in/	Indexed in D-Space at NISCAIR
4	Australian Journal of Information Systems http://dl.acs.org.au/index.php/ajis/about	Indexed in common attributes database
5	Australian Academic and Research Libraries http://www.alia.org.au/publishing/aarl/index.html	AARL is abstracted or indexed in Australian education index, Australian library and information science abstracts, APAIS, Library and information science abstracts, and Library literature.
6	B Sides http://ir.uiowa.edu/bsides/	Indexed in Research Now, Doaj, Database of network Institutional Repository

7	Chinese Librarianship: An International Electronic Journal http://www.iclc.us/cliej/	Indexed in: Ebsco's Library, Information Science & Technology Abstracts (LISTA), Wislon's Library and Information Science Index (LISI), CSA's Library and Information Science Abstracts (LISA), Listed in: Ulrich's and Cabell's
8	Collaborative Librarianship http://www.collaborativelibrarianship.org/index.html	Indexed
9	Communications in Information Literacy http://www.comminfolit.org/index.php/cil/issue/archive	Catalogued in world Catalogue OCLC PKP, Ulrich online Directory, Indexed in Directory of Open Access Journals, Elsevier EBSCO (Library, Information Science & Technology Abstracts), Elsevier Science (SCOPUS), Google Scholar, H.W. Wilson (Library Literature & Information Science Full Text), Proquest (Library Science)
10	Computer and Information Science http://journal.ccsenet.org/index.php/cis/index	Indexed in DOAJ, PKP, J-Gate, LOCKSS etc.
11	Coordinates: Online Journal of the Map and Geography Round Table of the American Library Association. Series A and B http://www.sunysb.edu/libmap/coordinates.htm	Articles in Coordinates are indexed in The Directory of Open Access Journals
12	Current Issues in Education http://cie.asu.edu/index.php	Indexed

13	DESIDOC Journal of Library & Information Science http://publications.drdo.gov.in/ojs/index.php/djlit/index	Indexed in LISA
14	E-JASL: The Electronic Journal of Academic and Special Librarianship http://southernlibrarianship.icaap.org/	Form 1996-2000 was known as "Journal of southern academic and special librarianship" Archived in National Library of Canada's Electronic Publications Collection. Listed in the DOAJ. Indexed in LISA.
15	Electronic Journal of Health Informatics http://www.ejhi.net/ojs/index.php/ejhi	Indexed
16	Electronic Journal on Information Systems in Developing Countries http://www.ejisdc.org/ojs2/index.php/ejisdc	Indexed
17	Evidence Based Library and Information Practice http://ejournals.library.ualberta.ca/index.php/EBLIP/index	Indexed in LISTA, LISA, DOAJ, Information Librarian Onlie, LLIS etc.
18	First monday http://firstmonday.org/	Indexed in Communication Abstracts, Computer & Communications Security Abstracts, INSPEC, ISTA, LISA, PAIS, DDIS and other services etc.
19	Health Information and Libraries Journal http://www3.interscience.wiley.com/journal/120118368/grouphome/home.html	Indexed in Thomsan ISI, LISTa CSA, Medline, Infotrac, Inspec, LISA, Scopus (Elsievier) etc.

20	Human IT: Journal for Information Technology Studies as a Human Sciencehttp://etjanst.hb.se/bhs/ith//info-eng.htm	Indexed
21	Informatica Economica Journal http://revistaie.ase.ro/index.html	Listed in the DOAJ. Cabell's Directories of Publishing Opportunities EBSCO (Business Source Complete) ICAAP Index Copernicus Index of Information Systems Journals Inspec Open J-Gate ProQuest Computing Urlich's Periodicals Directory
22	Information Research: An International Electronic Journal http://informationr.net/ir/	Indexed by Google Scholar, INSPEC: Engineering Village, Library Information Science & Technology Abstracts, LISA. It is also indexed for ISI's Web of Knowledge
23	Information Technologies and International Development http://itidjournal.org/itid	Indexed in EBSCO Host, Proquest etc.
24	Interdisciplinary Journal of E-Learning and Learning Objects http://ijklo.org/	Indexed in Cabells, Ulrichs, EBSCO, Doaj
25	Interdisciplinary Journal of Information, Knowledge, and Management http://www.ijikm.org/	Indexed in Cabells, Ulrichs, EBSCO, Doaj

26	International Journal of Communication http://ijoc.org/ojs/index.php/ijoc/about/editorialPolicies#focusAndScope	Indexed in various databases
27	International Journal of Communication Networks and Information Security http://www.ijcnis.org/index.php/ijcnis	Indexed in DOAJ, Inspec, Proquest etc. It is Peer Review and Reffered journal
28	International Journal of Computer Science and Information Technology http://airccse.org/journal/ijcsit.html	Indexed in Google, Scirus, Doaj, Pubmget, Pubjone, Inspec, Ulrich, PKP etc.
29	International Journal of Digital Curation http://www.ijdc.net/./ijdc/issue/current	Indexed and available in OJS
30	International Journal of Doctoral Studies (IJDS) http://ijds.org/	IJDS is proudly listed in the following indices: Cabell's Directory of Publishing Opportunities in Educational Curriculum and Methods, Cabell's Directory of Publishing Opportunities in Educational Psychology and Administration, EBSCO, DOAJ.
31	International Journal of Managing Public Sector Information and Communication Technologies http://airccse.org/journal/mpict/ijmpict.html	Indexed in getcited, Pubget, Pub zone, .doc star, citeceer, ulrichs web global serials directory
32	International Journal of Multimedia and Its Applications http://airccse.org/journal/ijma_index.html	Indexed in Inspec, Google Scholar, Open Jgate, Scirus etc.
33	International Journal of Special Libraries http://forge.fh-potsdam.de/~IFLA/INSPEL/intro.htm	Indexed

34	International Review of Research in Open and Distance Learning http://www.irrodl.org/index.php/irrodl	Indexed
35	Issues in Informing Science and Information Technology http://iisit.org/	Issues in Informing Science and Information Technology is indexed in the following databases: EBSCO Computers & Applied Sciences Complete, EBSCO Vocational Studies Complete, Cabell's Directories Educational Technology, Cabell's Library Science and Management, AMSER (Applied Math and Science Education Repository), The Index of Information Systems Journals, Intute, Ulrich, DOAJ, Magistri et Scholares, Smithsonian Institution Libraries, Open J-Gate.
36	Issues in Science and Technology Librarianship http://www.library.ucsb.edu/istl/ Or http://www.istl.org/	Indexed
37	JLIS.it Italian Journal of Library and Information Science http://leo.cilea.it/index.php/jlis/article/view/4539/4416	Indexed IN lisa, lista,Ulrich, World Cat, Google Scholar, Doaj, EZB, NewJour,TicTocs, Informed Librarian Online, Journaltocs etc
38	Journal of Artificial Intelligence Research http://www.jair.org/	Indexed

39	Journal of Digital Information http://jodi.ecs.soton.ac.uk/r or http://journals.tdl.org/jodi	Indexed in Compendex, Scopus, Inspec, DBLP
40	Journal of Educational Media & Library Sciences http://joemls.tku.edu.tw/index_e.htm	The JoEMLS is indexed or abstracted in Index to Chinese Periodicals, Chinese Electronic Periodicals Service (CEPS), Ulrich's Periodicals Directory, Public Affairs Information Services (PAIS), Library & Information Sciences Abstracts (LISA), Library Literature & Information Science (LLIS), H.W. Wilson Database, Directory of Open Access Journal (DOAJ), Library, Information Science & Technology Abstract (LISTA), and Scopus.
41	Journal of Health Informatics in Developing Countries http://www.jhidc.org/index.php/jhidc	Indexed
42	Journal of Information Architecture http://journalofia.org/archives/	Indexed
43	Journal of Information Law and Technology http://www2.warwick.ac.uk/fac/soc/law/elj/jilt/ or European Journal of Law and Technology http://ejlt.org//issue/archive	Indexed
44	Journal of Information Literacy http://ojs.lboro.ac.uk/ojs/index.php/JIL/index	Indexed
45	Journal of Information Technology Education (JITE: Research) http://www.informingscience.us/icarus/journals/jiteresearch/publications	JITE is listed in Applied Math and Science Education Repository (AMSER),

		Cabell's , DOAJ, EBSCO etc
46	Journal of Information, Information Technology, and Organizations http://jiito.org/	Indexed
47	Journal of Library Innovation http://www.libraryinnovation.org/about/contact	Indexed DOAJ, Google Scholar, The Informed Librarian online, Library Literature and Information Fulltext, LISTA
48	Journal of Medical Internet Research http://www.jmir.org/	JMIR is indexed in MEDLINE and numerous other databases, Permanently report archived in research central.
49	Journal of Research and Practice in Information Technology http://ws.acs.org.au/jrpit/JRPIT_Volumes.html	Indexed by Applied Mechanics Reviews, Applied Mechanics Reviews, Compumath Citation Index etc.
50	Journal of the American Medical Informatics Association http://www.pubmedcentral.nih.gov/tocrender.fcgi?action=archive&journal=76	Indexed
51	Journal of the Association for History and Computing http://quod.lib.umich.edu/j/jahc/browse.html	Index by Subject, Author, Articles, Columns, Editorials, Reviews, Books Reviewed by Title, Books Reviewed by Author, Software Reviewed.
52	Journal of the Medical Library association http://www.ncbi.nlm.nih.gov/pmc/journals/93/	Indexed

53	Journal of Virtual Worlds Research http://www.jvwresearch.org/index.html	The Journal of Virtual Worlds Research is indexed by EBSCO.
54	Library & Information Research: Research into Practice for Information & Library Services http://www.lirgjournal.org.uk/lir/ojs/index.php/lir	Indexed PKP
55	Library Philosophy and Practice http://www.webpages.uidaho.edu/~mbolin/lpp.htm	LPP is indexed in LISTA, DOAJ, Library Literature & Information Science, and SCOPUS.
56	Library Student Journal http://www.librarystudentjournal.org/index.php/lsj/index	The Law Library Journal is available on Lexis-Nexis®, WESTLAW, H.W. Wilson and HeinOnline.
57	LIBRES: Library and Information Science Research Electronic Journal http://libres.curtin.edu.au/	Libres is distributed through a listserver, and an ftp site. LISA, EBSCO, and SPI index it.
58	LIBRI: International Journal of Libraries and Information Services http://www.librijournal.org/	Abstracted or indexed in: Social Sciences Citation Index/Research Alert, Current Contents: Social & Behavioral Sciences, Library & Information Science Abstracts, Information Science Abstracts, Library Literature.
59	Mississippi Libraries http://www.misslib.org/index.php/publications/mississippi-libraries/	Indexed
60	MLA Forum http://www.mlaforum.org/	It is indexed in Library Literature, LISA

61	New Knowledge Environments http://journals.uvic.ca/index.php/INKE	Indexed
62	North Carolina Libraries http://www.ncl.ecu.edu/index.php/NCL	Indexed
63	Partnership: The Canadian Journal of Library and Information Practice and Research http://journal.lib.uoguelph.ca/index.php/perj/index	Indexed
64	Progressive Librarian http://libr.org/pl/	Indexed
65	Simile: Studies in Media and Information Literacy Education http://utpjournals.metapress.com/content/120764/	Abstracting and Indexing in Academic Search Premier CBCA Education CEPIEC, EBSCO. Vol. 2, N. 1-4, 2002-Vol. 8, N.1and3, 2008 are not open access.
66	South African Journal of Information Management http://www.sajim.co.za/index.php/sajim/issue/current	Indexed in DOAJ, Google Scholar, Jgate, Sa epublications etc
67	Technological Librarianship: An Online Journal of the American Theological Library Association http://journal.atla.com/ojs/index.php/theolib/index	Indexed
68	The Bonefolder: An outgrowth of the Book Arts Web http://www.philobiblon.com/bonefolder/	The Bonefolder is listed in the Directory of Open Access Journals (DOAJ) and is archived as part of the New York University Library's contribution to LOCKSS (Lots of Copies Keep Stuff Safe)
69	The Idaho Librarian: A Publication of the Idaho Library Association http://www.idaholibraries.org/idlibrarian/index.php/idaho-librarian/index	Indexed

70	The International Journal of Database Management Systems http://airccse.org/journal/ijdms/ijdms.html	Indexed in Open Jgate, EBSCO, Inspac, Google etc.
71	The International Journal of Managing Information Technology http://airccse.org/journal/ijmit/ijmit.html	Indexed in Google, EBSCO, Pub Zone, PKP, Scirus, Citeseer, EZB, Pubget, .docstar, getcited, Scribed, Pubzone, Worldcat etc.
72	The Journal of the Rutgers University Library http://jrul.libraries.rutgers.edu/index.php/jrul/index	Indexed
73	Webology http://www.webology.ir/	Indexed
74	International Journal of Computer and Information Engineering http://www.waset.org/journals/ijcie/	Indexed in Google Scholar, Scopus, Compendex, Thomson Reuters,WorldCat, EBSCO, GALE, Embase, Reaxys, Engineering Village/Engineering Index(EI), DOAJ, Library of Congress, Electronic Journals Library

E-Magazines

1	American Libraries http://americanlibrariesmagazine.org/	American Libraries is available full-text from ProQuest, EBSCO Publishing, Knowledge Quest, LexisNexis, and Information Access. A full-text searchable database of issues from 2003 to the present is available online free through Ebrary.
2	Computer in Libraries http://www.infotoday.com/cilmag/default.shtml	Indexed and abstracted in Computer Review Index, Internet & Personal Computing Abstracts, Guide to Computing Literature, Library Literature, Information Science & Technology Abstracts, Library and Information Science Abstracts, Information Technology Review, and Computer Database. Computers in Libraries are available full-text through CAS/STN, Dialog, EBSCO, Factiva, Gale, Intelligence Data, LexisNexis, Northern Light Technology, Profound, ProQuest, Reuters, Westlaw, and H.W. Wilson.

Newsletters and other E-Resources

1	Business and Finance Division Bulletin http://bf.sla.org/resources/the-bulletin/	Bulletin is indexed in Library and Information Science Abstracts (LISA), Library Literature, and Information Science Abstracts

Indexed, Peer Reviewed and Refereed Journals have greater use by the academicians and Researchers. Authors always wish to publish their articles in Refereed, Indexed and Peer Reviewed Journals because articles published in these journals have appraisal performance indicator scores high in compare to journals not having these features. Researcher has found out that 77 (39%) E-Resources are indexed in other Data bases out of which E-Journals are 74, E-Magazines are 2, and E-Newsletter is 1.

Summary Table: Distribution of Indexed E-Resources

S.N.	Indexed E-Resources	No.	Percentage
1	E-Journals	74	96%
2	E-Magazines	2	3%
3	E-Newsletters &Other E-Resources	1	1%
	Total	**77**	**100%**

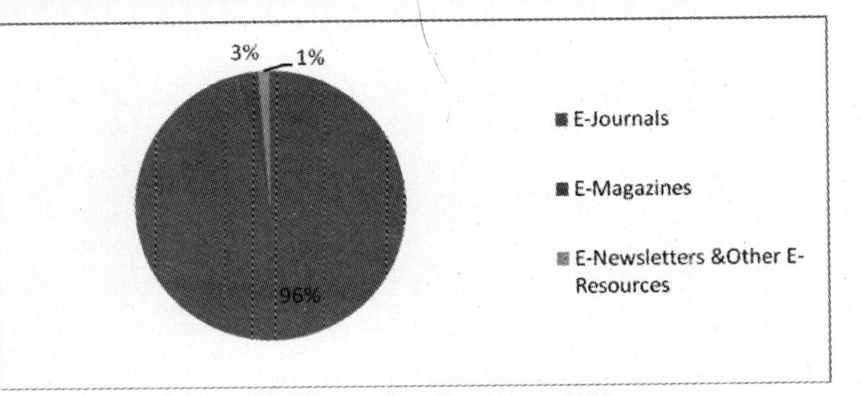

Fig.: E-Resources Indexed in Other Databases

This chart shows that, out of 195 Open Access E-Resources Indexed are 77 (39%). Out of total 145 E-Journals, Indexed E-Journals are 74 (51%), Out of total 26 E-Magazines Indexed E-Magazines are 2 (7%), & out of 24 E-Newsletters Indexed E-Newsletters is 1 (3%).

3.7. INDEXING OF OPEN ACCESS E-RESOURCES IN LIS

E-Journals

Sl. No.	URL	INDEX
1	Annals of Library & Information Studies http://nopr.niscair.res.in/	Issue

2	Coordinates: Online Journal of the Map and Geography Round Table of the American Library Association. Series A and B http://www.sunysb.edu/libmap/coordinates.htm	Issue
3	DIGITHUM: The Humanities in Digital Age http://www.uoc.edu/digithum/7/eng/numeros.html	Issue
4	Malaysian Journal of Library & Information Sciencehttp://ejum.fsktm.um.edu.my/VolumeListing.aspx?JournalID=3	Issue
5	Mississippi Libraries http://www.misslib.org/index.php/publications/mississippi-libraries/	Issue
6	Journal of Information Law and Technology http://www2.warwick.ac.uk/fac/soc/law/elj/jilt/ or European Journal of Law and Technology http://ejlt.org//issue/archive	Issue and Year.
7	Internet Writing Journal http://www.internetwritingjournal.com/	Issue and Year.
8	NPO Journal/NPO E-Journal http://www.bl.uk/blpac/publicationsjournals.html	Issue and Year.
9	Partnership: The Canadian Journal of Library and Information Practice and Research http://journal.lib.uoguelph.ca/index.php/perj/index	Issue and then Year
10	Scandinavian Public Library Quarterly http://www.splq.info/	Issue and Title
11	Health Information and Libraries Journal http://www3.interscience.wiley.com/journal/120118368/grouphome/home.html	Issue and Year
12	Code4Lib Journal http://journal.code4lib.org/	Issue and Year
13	Alki: The Washington Library Association Journal http://www.wla.org/alki/	Issue indexing
14	American Archivist http://archivists.metapress.com/home/main.mpx	Issue indexing

15	Journal of Knowledge Management Practice http://www.tlainc.com/boutjkmp.htm	Issue indexing
16	European Journal of ePractice http://www.epracticejournal.eu/	Issue indexing
17	IT&Society http://www.itandsociety.org/index.html	Issue indexing
18	School Library Journal Online http://www.schoollibraryjournal.com/	Issue indexing has been done.
19	Chinese Librarianship: An International Electronic Journal http://www.iclc.us/cliej/	Issue number wise
20	B Sides http://ir.uiowa.edu/bsides/	Issue Spring, Fall, Summer, Winter
21	Issues in Science and Technology Librarianship http://www.library.ucsb.edu/istl/ Or http://www.istl.org/	Issue Summer, Winter, Fall, Spring.
22	Current Cites http://lists.webjunction.org/currentcites/	Issue wise
23	Journal of Information Literacy http://ojs.lboro.ac.uk/ojs/index.php/JIL/index	Issue, after by Volume
24	DESIDOC Journal of Library & Information Science http://publications.drdo.gov.in/ojs/index.php/djlit/index	Issue, Author and Title arrange information.
25	Progressive Librarian http://libr.org/pl/	Issue, Author and title indexing
26	The Journal of the Rutgers University Library http://jrul.libraries.rutgers.edu/index.php/jrul/index	Issue, Author and Title indexing

27	Journal of Philippine Librarianship http://journals.upd.edu.ph/index.php/jpl/issue/current	Issue, Author and Title indexing
28	LIBRES: Library and Information Science Research Electronic Journal http://libres.curtin.edu.au/	Issue, Author and title indexing
29	Library Journal http://www.libraryjournal.com	Issue, Author and title indexing has been given.
30	Interpersonal Computing and Technology Journal http://www.helsinki.fi/science/optek/#byissue	Issue, author.
31	Information for Social Change http://libr.org/isc/journal.html	Issue, Vol and Year
32	Cites & Insights: Crawford at Large http://citesandinsights.info/citoc.htm	Volume
33	Cybermetrics : International Journal of Scientometrics, Informetrics and Bibliometrics http://www.cindoc.csic.es/cybermetrics/	Volume
34	Electronic Journal of Africana Bibliography http://ir.uiowa.edu/ejab/all_issues.html	Volume
35	International Journal of Communication http://ijoc.org/ojs/index.php/ijoc/about/editorialPolicies#focusAndScope	Volume
36	International Journal of Library and Information Science http://www.academicjournals.org/ijlis/index.htm	Volume
37	LIBER Quarterly Journal of European Research Libraries http://liber.library.uu.nl/index.html	Volume
38	ALAN Review http://scholar.lib.vt.edu/ejournals/ALAN/	Volume

39	African Journal of Information & Communication Technology http://epress.lib.uts.edu.au/ojs/index.php/ajict/	Volume
40	Journal of Information Technology Education (JITE: Research) http://www.informingscience.us/icarus/journals/jiteresearch/publications	Volume & Year
41	Journal of Technology Studies http://scholar.lib.vt.edu/ejournals/JOTS/	Volume and Year.
42	Journal of the American Medical Informatics Association http://www.pubmedcentral.nih.gov/tocrender.fcgi?action=archive&journal=76	Volume and Year.
43	North Carolina Libraries http://www.ncl.ecu.edu/index.php/NCL	Volume and Year.
44	School libraries in Canada (SLIC): A Journal of the Canadian Association for School Libraries http://www.clatoolbox.ca/casl/slic/links.html	Volume and Year.
45	Firstmonday http://firstmonday.org/	Volume and issue wise
46	World Libraries http://www.worlib.org/	Volume and No wise
47	Colby Quarterly (formerly: Colby Library Quarterly) http://digitalcommons.colby.edu/	Volume and Number
48	Collaborative Librarianship http://www.collaborativelibrarianship.org/index.html	Volume and Number
49	Agricultural Libraries Information Notes http://webharvest.gov/peth04/20041023101316/http://www.nal.usda.gov/NewAlin/	Volume and Number.

50	International Journal of Computer and Information Engineering http://www.waset.org/journals/ijcie/	Volume and then Number wise.
51	New Knowledge Environments http://journals.uvic.ca/index.php/INKE	Volume and then Number.
52	Journal of Virtual Worlds Research http://www.jvwresearch.org/index.html	Volume and then particular article title.
53	Australian Academic and Research Libraries http://www.alia.org.au/publishing/aarl/index.html	Volume and year wise
54	Australian Library Journal http://alia.org.au/publishing/alj/	Volume and year wise.
55	International Review of Research in Open and Distance Learning http://www.irrodl.org/index.php/irrodl	Volume and year wise. Author, Issue and Title indexing has been given.
56	Electronic Journal on Information Systems in Developing Countries http://www.ejisdc.org/ojs2/index.php/ejisdc	Volume and year.
57	Information Technology and Disabilities http://people.rit.edu/easi/itd.htm	Volume and Year.
58	Journal of Health Informatics in Developing Countries http://www.jhidc.org/index.php/jhidc	Volume and year-wise
59	Data Science Journal http://www.jstage.jst.go.jp/browse/dsj	Volume indexing

60	Digital Document Quarterly http://home.pacbell.net/hgladney/ddqstart.htm	Volume indexing
61	EDUCAUSE Quarterly http://www.educause.edu/eq	Volume wise
62	E-JASL: The Electronic Journal of Academic and Special Librarianship http://southernlibrarianship.icaap.org/	Volume wise
63	Electronic Journal of Knowledge Management http://www.ejkm.com/	Volume wise
64	Information Research: An International Electronic Journal http://informationr.net/ir/	Volume wise
65	International Journal of Computer Science and Information Technology http://airccse.org/journal/ijcsit.html	Volume wise
66	International Journal of Digital Curation http://www.ijdc.net/./ijdc/issue/current	Volume wise
67	International Journal of Doctoral Studies (IJDS) http://ijds.org/	Volume wise
68	International Review of Information Ethics http://www.i-r-i-e.net/	Volume wise
69	Journal of Artificial Intelligence Research http://www.jair.org/	Volume wise
70	Journal of eLiteracy http://www.jelit.org/index.html	Volume wise
71	Journal of Information, Information Technology, and Organizations http://jiito.org/	Volume wise
72	Journal of Medical Internet Research http://www.jmir.org/	Volume wise
73	Library Resources & Technical Services (LRTS) http://alcts.metapress.com/home/main.mpx	Volume wise
74	Multimedia Information and Technology Journal (MmIT) http://www.cilip.org.uk/get-involved/special-interest-groups/multimedia/journal/pages/default.aspx	Volume wise

75	Northwestern Journal of Technology and Intellectual Property http://www.law.northwestern.edu/journals/njtip/issues.htm	Volume wise
76	Simile: Studies in Media and Information Literacy Education http://utpjournals.metapress.com/content/120764/	Volume wise
77	South African Journal of Information Management http://www.sajim.co.za/index.php/sajim/issue/current	Volume wise
78	Special Libraries http://www.sla.org/content/shop/speclibs.cfm#1910	Volume wise
79	Studies in Bibliography http://etext.lib.virginia.edu/bsuva/sb	Volume wise
80	Technological Librarianship: An Online Journal of the American Theological Library Association http://journal.atla.com/ojs/index.php/theolib/index	Volume wise
81	Technology Electronic Reviews (TER) http://www.ala.org/lita/publications/archive/ter	Volume wise
82	The Bonefolder: An outgrowth of the Book Arts Web http://www.philobiblon.com/bonefolder/	Volume wise
83	The Idaho Librarian: A Publication of the Idaho Library Association http://www.idaholibraries.org/idlibrarian/index.php/idaho-librarian/index	Volume wise
84	Urban Library Journal http://lacuny.cuny.edu/ulj/	Volume wise
85	Virginia Libraries http://scholar.lib.vt.edu/ejournals/VALib/	Volume wise
86	Library Student Journal http://www.librarystudentjournal.org/index.php/lsj/index	Volume wise
87	Australian Journal of Information Systems http://dl.acs.org.au/index.php/ajis/about	Volume wise, Author and Title

88	Christian Library Journal http://www.christianlibraryj.org/pdf/index.htm	Volume wise.
89	Electronic Transactions on Artificial Intelligence http://www.ida.liu.se/ext/etai/	Volume wise.
90	Human IT: Journal for Information Technology Studies as a Human Sciencehttp://etjanst.hb.se/bhs/ith//info-eng.htm	Volume wise.
91	IFLA Journal http://www.ifla.org/V/iflaj/index.htm	Volume wise.
92	Information Scotland: The Journal of the Chartered Institute of Library and Information Professionals in Scotland http://www.slainte.org.uk/publications/serials/infoscot/vol1(1)/vol1(1)contents.html	Volume wise.
93	Information Technology and Libraries http://www.ala.org/ala/mgrps/divs/lita/ital/italinformation.cfm	Volume wise.
94	Informing Faculty: An International Journal of Higher Education Discussion Cases http://informingfaculty.org/	Volume wise.
95	Informing Science The International Journal of an Emerging Transdiscipline http://inform.nu/	Volume wise.
96	Inter-Actions: UCLA Journal of Education and Information Studies http://repositories.cdlib.org/gseis/interactions/	Volume wise.
97	Interdisciplinary Journal of E-Learning and Learning Objects http://ijklo.org/	Volume wise.
98	Interdisciplinary Journal of Information, Knowledge, and Management http://www.ijikm.org/	Volume wise.
99	International Journal of Multimedia and Its Applications http://airccse.org/journal/ijma_index.html	Volume wise.
100	International Journal of Special Libraries http://forge.fh-potsdam.de/~IFLA/INSPEL/intro.htm	Volume wise.
101	Issues in Informing Science and Information Technology http://iisit.org/	Volume wise.

102	Journal of Internet Cataloguing http://www.internetcataloging.com/home.html	Volume wise.
103	Journal of Research and Practice in Information Technology http://ws.acs.org.au/jrpit/JRPIT_Volumes.html	Volume wise.
104	Journal of Staff Development http://learningforward.org/publications/jsd#.UUQguzcynUc	Volume wise.
105	LASIE: Library Automated Systems Information Exchange http://search.informit.com.au/browseJournalTitle;res=E-LIBRARY;issn=0047-3774	Volume wise.
106	Library & Information Research: Research into Practice for Information & Library Services http://www.lirgjournal.org.uk/lir/ojs/index.php/lir	Volume wise.
107	LIBRI: International Journal of Libraries and Information Services http://www.librijournal.org/	Volume wise.
108	MC Journal: The Journal of Academic Media Librarianship http://wings.buffalo.edu/publications/mcjrnl/	Volume wise.
109	MELA Notes: The Journal of the Middle East Librarians Association http://www.mela.us/MELANotes/MELANotesIntro.html	Volume wise.
110	RBM Journal of Rare Books , Manuscripts, and Cultural Heritage http://rbm.acrl.org/content/2/2	Volume wise.
111	School Library Research http://www.ala.org/aasl/slr	Volume wise.
112	Journal of the Association for History and Computing http://quod.lib.umich.edu/j/jahc/browse.html	Volume wise.
113	Informatica Economica Journal http://revistaie.ase.ro/index.html	Volume wise.
114	Journal of Library Innovation http://www.libraryinnovation.org/about/contact	Volume, Issue and Year

115	JEP: The Journal of Electronic Publishing http://www.journalofelectronicpublishing.org/	Volume, Issue and Year
116	Journal of East Asian Libraries http://www.lib.byu.edu/dlib/spc/jeal/	Volume, Issue and year wise
117	JLIS.it Italian Journal of Library and Information Science http://leo.cilea.it/index.php/jlis/article/view/4539/4416	Volume, No and Year
118	Journal of Digital Information http://jodi.ecs.soton.ac.uk/r or http://journals.tdl.org/jodi	Volume, No, Year
119	International Journal of Legal Information http://scholarship.law.cornell.edu/ijli/vol33/iss1/	Volume, No, And Year.
120	Journal of the Medical Library association http://www.ncbi.nlm.nih.gov/pmc/journals/93/	Volume, No, and Year.
121	Computer and Information Science http://journal.ccsenet.org/index.php/cis/index	Volume, No, and year wise.
122	Current Issues in Education http://cie.asu.edu/index.php	Volume, No. and year wise.
123	Information Technologies and International Development http://itidjournal.org/itid	Volume, No. and year wise.
124	International Journal of Communication Networks and Information Security http://www.ijcnis.org/index.php/ijcnis	Volume, No. and year wise.
125	The International Journal of Database Management Systems http://airccse.org/journal/ijdms/ijdms.html	Volume, No. and year wise.

126	The International Journal of Managing Information Technology http://airccse.org/journal/ijmit/ijmit.html	Volume, No. and year wise.
127	Journal of Information Architecture http://journalofia.org/archives/	Volume, No. and year-wise
128	The Public Access Computer Systems Review http://epress.lib.uh.edu/pr/pacsrev.html#history	Volume, Number, Year
129	Communications in Information Literacy http://www.comminfolit.org/index.php/cil/issue/archive	Volume.
130	EBIB Electronic Information Bulletin for librarians http://ebib.info/biuletyn/	Year
131	Webology http://www.webology.ir/	Year and Volume wise.
132	High Energy Physics Libraries Webzine http://library.web.cern.ch/library/Webzine/index.shtml	Year and issue wise.
133	Texas library journal http://www.txla.org/TLJ	Year and issue wise.
134	Research Management Review http://www.ncura.edu/content/news/rmr/archive.php	Year and Volume
135	Law Library Journal http://www.aallnet.org/products/pub_journal.asp	Year, volume and then Number.
136	ITALICS: Innovations in Teaching and Learning in Information and Computer Sciences http://www.ics.heacademy.ac.uk/italics/	Year, Vol and Issue.
137	International Journal of Managing Public Sector Information and Communication Technologies http://airccse.org/journal/mpict/ijmpict.html	Year, Volume and then by No.

138	Learned Publishing http://www.ingentaconnect.com/content/alpsp/lp	Year, Volume and then Number
139	College and Research Libraries http://crl.acrl.org/	Year, Volume, and No arrange Articles
140	Journal of the European Association for Health Information and Libraries http://www.eahil.net/journal/	Year, Volume, Issue
141	Evidence Based Library and Information Practice http://ejournals.library.ualberta.ca/index.php/EBLIP/index	Year, Volume, No
142	Electronic Journal of Health Informatics http://www.ejhi.net/ojs/index.php/ejhi	Year, Volume, No
143	Journal of Educational Media & Library Sciences http://joemls.tku.edu.tw/index_e.htm	Year, Volume, Number
144	MLA Forum http://www.mlaforum.org/	Year.
145	Library Philosophy and Practice http://www.webpages.uidaho.edu/~mbolin/lpp.htm	Year-wise

E-Magazines

1	Access http://www.aardvarknet.info/access/number46/index.cfm	Issue
2	Exploit Interactive http://www.exploit-lib.org/	Issue and Year.
3	Information Today http://www.infotoday.com/IT/nov08/index.shtml	Issue indexing has been done.

4	The Marginal http://www.gslis.mcgill.ca/marginal/	Issue Indexing has been done.
5	Cultivate Interactive http://www.cultivate-int.org/index-2.html	Issue wise.
6	D-Lib Magazine http://www.dlib.org/dlib/september08/09contents.html	Issue wise.
7	Ex Libris http://marylaine.com/exlibris/	Issue wise.
8	Library Juice http://libr.org/juice/	Issue wise.
9	Ariadne http://www.ariadne.ac.uk/	Issues indexing
10	Link-Up http://www.infotoday.com/linkup/default.shtml	Volume
11	Provenance http://www.provenance.ca/about-provenance/index.html	Volume
12	Research Information http://www.researchinformation.info/	Volume and Year.
13	Knowledge Management World http://www.kmworld.com/index.cfm	Volume and Issue
14	AALL Spectrum http://www.aallnet.org/main-menu/Publications/spectrum	Volume and Issue.
15	Book Links http://www.ala.org/ala/aboutala/offices/publishing/booklinks/archiveonline/archive_of_online_articles.cfm	Volume and year wise
16	EDUCAUSE Review http://www.educause.edu/	Volume and year.
17	American Libraries http://americanlibrariesmagazine.org/	Volume wise.
18	Computer in Libraries http://www.infotoday.com/cilmag/default.shtml	Volume wise.
19	Online http://www.infotoday.com/online/default.shtml	Volume wise.

20	CHOICE http://www.ala.org/ala/mgrps/divs/acrl/publications/choice/previousissues/previousissues.cfm	Volume, No, Year.
21	Book business http://www.bookbusinessmag.com/	Year
22	Virginia Tech Magazine http://www.vtmagazine.vt.edu/	Year
23	E-Content http://www.ecmag.net/	Year wise.
24	Searcher: The Magazine for Database Professionals http://www.infotoday.com/searcher/default.asp	Year wise.
25	inCite http://alia.org.au/publishing/incite/archive.html	Year, Volume and then Month
26	The Bulletin of the American Society for Information Science and Technology http://www.asis.org/bulletin.html	Year, Volume, Number-wise

Newsletters and other E-Resources

1	RLG DigiNews http://www.oclc.org/programs/publications/newsletters/diginews.htm	Issue, Author, Title index has been given
2	Biblia's Warrior Librarian Weekly http://warriorlibrarian.com/ARCHIVE/00archives.html	Issue
3	Cataloging and Classification Quarterly http://bubl.ac.uk/archive/journals/cacq/	Issue indexing has been done.
4	Free Pint http://www.freepint.com/	Issue No and year.

5	Serials E-News http://www.ringgold.com/UKSG/si_pd.cfm	Issue, Date, Month, Year
6	Internet on a Disk http://www.samizdat.com/ioad.html	Issue.
7	Internet Resources Newsletter http://www.hw.ac.uk/libwww/irn/irn.html	Issue.
8	SPARC Open Access Newsletter or Free Online Scholarship Newsletter http://www.earlham.edu/~peters/fos/index.htm	Issue.
9	Against the grain http://www.against-the-grain.com/d/TOC	Volume
10	LC Cataloging Newsline http://www.loc.gov/catdir/lccn/	Volume and then Number.
11	Abbey Newsletter http://cool.conservation-us.org/byorg/abbey/an/	Volume and Year
12	Information today and Tomorrow http://www.dsir.gov.in/pubs/itt/index.htm	Volume and year.
13	Business and Finance Division Bulletin http://bf.sla.org/resources/the-bulletin/	Volume wise.
14	Conserline http://www.loc.gov/acq/conser/consrlin.html	Year
15	ABAA Newsletter http://hq.abaa.org/books/antiquarian/abaapages/newsletter	Year and Issue.
16	ARL: A bimonthly newsletter for library issues and action http://www.arl.org/resources/pubs/br/index.shtml	Year and issue wise.
17	ALCTS Network News http://bubl.ac.uk/archive/journals/alctsnn/	Year and volume-wise

18	Biblio-Tech Review http://www.ringgold.com/biblio-tech/si_pd.cfm?pid=2	Year wise indexing has been done.
19	The Wired Librarian's Newsletter http://www.wiredlibrarian.com/wln/wlnfront.htm	Year wise.
20	Sprouts: Working Papers on Information Systems http://sprouts.aisnet.org/home.html	Year, Subject, Tag and organization have done arrange
21	ALAWON. The ALA Washington Office Electronic Newsline http://www.ala.org/ala/aboutala/offices/wo/washnews/archivea/archive.cfm	Year.
22	CIT Infobits http://serials.infomotions.com/infobits/	Year.
23	MLS: Marketing Library Services http://www.infotoday.com/MLS/default.shtml	Year.
24	NLM Technical Bulletin http://www.nlm.nih.gov/pubs/techbull/current_issue.html	Year.

Table shows that all 195 E-Resources are having Indexing. Indexing by Volume is 114, by Issue 48 by year 33.

Summary Table: Distribution of E-Resources having Indexing Facility

S.N.	Indexing of E-Resources	No.
1	Volume	114
2	Issue	48
3	Year	33
	Total	**195**

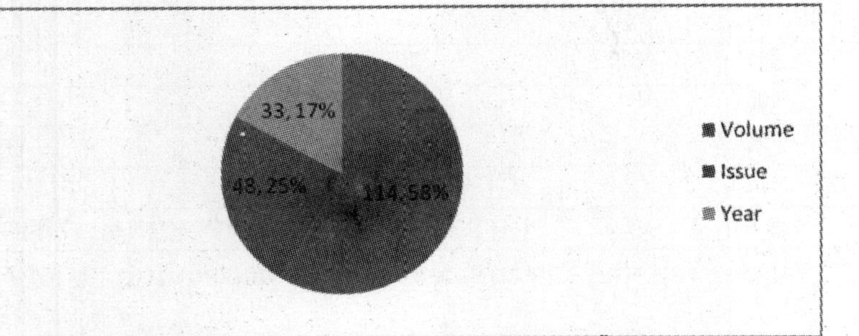

Fig.: Resources Indexing

This chart shows that Indexing by Volume is114 (58%), indexing by Issue is 48 (25%), Indexing by Year 33 (17%).

3.8. OPEN ACCESS E-RESOURCES HAVING ISSN

E-Journals

Sl. No.	TITLE	ISBN
1	College and Research Libraries http://crl.acrl.org/	2150-6701 online, 0010-0870
2	African Journal of Information & Communication Technology http://epress.lib.uts.edu.au/ojs/index.php/ajict/	1449-2679

3	ALAN Review http://scholar.lib.vt.edu/ejournals/ALAN/	1547-741X
4	Alki: The Washington Library Association Journal http://www.wla.org/alki/	0975-2404
5	American Archivist http://archivists.metapress.com/home/main.mpx	0001-253X
6	Annals of Library & Information Studies http://nopr.niscair.res.in/	0975-2404 (Online), 0972-5423 (Print)
7	Australian Journal of Information Systems http://dl.acs.org.au/index.php/ajis/about	1077-6613
8	Australian Academic and Research Libraries http://www.alia.org.au/publishing/aarl/index.html	0004-8623
9	Australian Library Journal http://alia.org.au/publishing/alj/	0004-9670
10	B Sides http://ir.uiowa.edu/bsides/	2155-6687
11	Christian Library Journal http://www.christianlibraryj.org/pdf/index.htm	1 0 9 7–1 2 6 2
12	Cites & Insights: Crawford at Large http://citesandinsights.info/citoc.htm	1534-0937
13	Collaborative Librarianship http://www.collaborativelibrarianship.org/index.html	1943-7528
14	Communications in Information Literacy http://www.comminfolit.org/index.php/cil/issue/archive	1933-5954
15	Computer and Information Science http://journal.ccsenet.org/index.php/cis/index	1913-8989 (Print) 1913-8997 (Online)
16	Coordinates: Online Journal of the Map and Geography Round Table of the American Library Association. Series A and B http://www.sunysb.edu/libmap/coordinates.htm	A-1553-3247, B-1553-3255

17	Current Cites http://lists.webjunction.org/currentcites/	1060-2356
18	Cybermetrics : International Journal of Scientometrics, Informetrics and Bibliometrics http://www.cindoc.csic.es/cybermetrics/	*1137-5019*
19	Data Science Journal http://www.jstage.jst.go.jp/browse/dsj	1683-1470
20	Digital Document Quarterly http://home.pacbell.net/hgladney/ddqstart.htm	978-3-540-37886-0
21	DIGITHUM: The Humanities in Digital Age http://www.uoc.edu/digithum/7/eng/numeros.html	1575-2275
22	EDUCAUSE Quarterly http://www.educause.edu/eq	1528-5324
23	E-JASL: The Electronic Journal of Academic and Special Librarianship http://southernlibrarianship.icaap.org/	1704-8532
24	Electronic Journal of Africana Bibliography http://ir.uiowa.edu/ejab/all_issues.html	1092-9576
25	Electronic Journal of Health Informatics http://www.ejhi.net/ojs/index.php/ejhi	1446-4381
26	Electronic Journal of Knowledge Management http://www.ejkm.com/	1479-4411
27	Electronic Journal on Information Systems in Developing Countries http://www.ejisdc.org/ojs2/index.php/ejisdc	1681-4835
28	Evidence Based Library and Information Practice http://ejournals.library.ualberta.ca/index.php/EBLIP/index	1715-720X
29	Firstmonday http://firstmonday.org/	1396-0466
30	Health Information and Libraries Journal http://www3.interscience.wiley.com/journal/120118368/grouphome/home.html	1471-1842 Online, 1471-1834 Print

31	High Energy Physics Libraries Webzine http://library.web.cern.ch/library/Webzine/index.shtml	1424-2729
32	Human IT: Journal for Information Technology Studies as a Human Sciencehttp://etjanst.hb.se/bhs/ith//info-eng.htm	1402-151X
33	IFLA Journal http://www.ifla.org/V/iflaj/index.htm	Online 1745-2651, Print 0340-0352
34	Informatica Economica Journal http://revistaie.ase.ro/index.html	Online- 1842-8088, Print-1453-1305
35	Information for Social Change http://libr.org/isc/journal.html	1756-901X (online), 1364-694X (print)
36	Information Scotland: The Journal of the Chartered Institute of Library and Information Professionals in Scotland http://www.slainte.org.uk/publications/serials/infoscot/vol1(1)/vol1(1)contents.html	1743-5471
37	Information Technologies and International Development http://itidjournal.org/itid	1544-7529
38	Information Technology and Libraries http://www.ala.org/ala/mgrps/divs/lita/ital/italinformation.cfm	0730-9295
39	Informing Faculty: An International Journal of Higher Education Discussion Cases http://informingfaculty.org/	1559-758X (Online), 1559-727X (Print), 1559-7598 (CD)
40	Informing Science The International Journal of an Emerging Transdiscipline http://inform.nu/	1521-4772
41	Inter-Actions: UCLA Journal of Education and Information Studies http://repositories.cdlib.org/gseis/interactions/	1548-3320

42	Interdisciplinary Journal of E-Learning and Learning Objects http://ijklo.org/	Online 1552-2237: print 1552-2210: CD-ROM 1552-2229
43	Interdisciplinary Journal of Information, Knowledge, and Management http://www.ijikm.org/	online 1555-1237: print 1555-1229: CD-ROM 1555-1245
44	International Journal of Communication http://ijoc.org/ojs/index.php/ijoc/about/editorialPolicies#focusAndScope	1932-8036
45	International Journal of Communication Networks and Information Security http://www.ijcnis.org/index.php/ijcnis	ISSN: 2076-0930 (Print)ISSN: 2073-607X (Online)
46	International Journal of Computer and Information Engineering http://www.waset.org/journals/ijcie/	eISSN 2010-393X, pISSN 2010-3921
47	International Journal of Computer Science and Information Technology http://airccse.org/journal/ijcsit.html	0975-3826(online); 0975-4660 (Print)
48	International Journal of Doctoral Studies (IJDS) http://ijds.org/	Online 1556-8873: print 1556-8881: CD-ROM 1556-8865
49	International Journal of Library and Information Science http://www.academicjournals.org/ijlis/index.htm	2141-2537
50	International Journal of Managing Public Sector Information and Communication Technologies http://airccse.org/journal/mpict/ijmpict.html	0976 - 9773 (Online) ; 2230 - 7958 (Print)

51	International Journal of Multimedia and Its Applications http://airccse.org/journal/ijma_index.html	0975-5578(Online); 0975-5934 (Print)
52	International Journal of Special Libraries http://forge.fh-potsdam.de/~IFLA/INSPEL/intro.htm	0019-0217
53	International Review of Information Ethics http://www.i-r-i-e.net/	1614-1687
54	International Review of Research in Open and Distance Learning http://www.irrodl.org/index.php/irrodl	1614-1687
55	Internet Writing Journal http://www.internetwritingjournal.com/	1095-3973
56	Issues in Informing Science and Information Technology http://iisit.org/	1547-5867 Online, CD edition: 1547-5859, Print edition: 1547-5840
57	Issues in Science and Technology Librarianship http://www.library.ucsb.edu/istl/ Or http://www.istl.org/	1092-1206
58	IT&Society http://www.itandsociety.org/index.html	d0000080
59	JEP; The Journal of Electronic Publishing http://www.journalofelectronicpublishing.org/	1080-2711
60	JLIS.it Italian Journal of Library and Information Science http://leo.cilea.it/index.php/jlis/article/view/4539/4416	2038-1026
61	Journal of Artificial Intelligence Research http://www.jair.org/	1076 - 9757
62	Journal of Digital Information http://jodi.ecs.soton.ac.uk/r or http://journals.tdl.org/jodi	1368-7506
63	Journal of Educational Media & Library Sciences http://joemls.tku.edu.tw/index_e.htm	1013090X

64	Journal of eLiteracy http://www.jelit.org/index.html	1745-4360
65	Journal of Health Informatics in Developing Countries http://www.jhidc.org/index.php/jhidc	1778-4407
66	Journal of Information Architecture http://journalofia.org/archives/	1903-7260
67	Journal of Information Law and Technology http://www2.warwick.ac.uk/fac/soc/law/elj/jilt/ or European Journal of Law and Technology http://ejlt.org//issue/archive	1361-4169
68	Journal of Information Literacy http://ojs.lboro.ac.uk/ojs/index.php/JIL/index	1750-5968
69	Journal of Information Technology Education (JITE: Research) http://www.informingscience.us/icarus/journals/jiteresearch/publications	1539-3585 Online, 1547-9714 Print
70	Journal of Information, Information Technology, and Organizations http://jiito.org/	online 1557-1327: print 1557-1319:
71	Journal of Knowledge Management Practice http://www.tlainc.com/boutjkmp.htm	1705-9232
72	Journal of Library Innovation http://www.libraryinnovation.org/about/contact	1947-525X
73	Journal of Medical Internet Research http://www.jmir.org/	1438-8871
74	Journal of Philippine Librarianship http://journals.upd.edu.ph/index.php/jpl/issue/current	0022-359x
75	Journal of Research and Practice in Information Technology http://ws.acs.org.au/jrpit/JRPIT_Volumes.html	1443-458X
76	Journal of Technology Studies http://scholar.lib.vt.edu/ejournals/JOTS/	ISSN 1071-6084 (Print), ISSN 1541-9258 (Online)

77	Journal of the American Medical Informatics Association http://www.pubmedcentral.nih.gov/tocrender.fcgi?action=archive&journal=76	ISSN1527-974X
78	Journal of the Association for History and Computing http://quod.lib.umich.edu/j/jahc/browse.html	1937-5905
79	Journal of the European Association for Health Information and Libraries http://www.eahil.net/journal/	1841- 0715
80	Journal of the Medical Library association http://www.ncbi.nlm.nih.gov/pmc/journals/93/	0025-7338
81	Journal of Virtual Worlds Research http://www.jvwresearch.org/index.html	1941-8477
82	LASIE: Library Automated Systems Information Exchange http://search.informit.com.au/browseJournalTitle;res=E-LIBRARY;issn=0047-3774	0047-3774
83	Learned Publishing http://www.ingentaconnect.com/content/alpsp/lp	ISSN 0953-1513, Online ISSN: 1741-4857
84	LIBER Quarterly Journal of European Research Libraries http://liber.library.uu.nl/index.html	1435-5205
85	Library & Information Research: Research into Practice for Information & Library Services http://www.lirgjournal.org.uk/lir/ojs/index.php/lir	1756-1086 (Online)
86	Library Philosophy and Practice http://www.webpages.uidaho.edu/~mbolin/lpp.htm	1522-0222
87	Library Resources & Technical Services (LRTS) http://alcts.metapress.com/home/main.mpx	0024-2527
88	Library Student Journal http://www.librarystudentjournal.org/index.php/lsj/index	1931-6100
89	LIBRES: Library and Information Science Research Electronic Journal http://libres.curtin.edu.au/	1058-6768

90	LIBRI: International Journal of Libraries and Information Services http://www.librijournal.org/	0024-2667
91	Malaysian Journal of Library & Information Sciencehttp://ejum.fsktm.um.edu.my/VolumeListing.aspx?JournalID=3	1394-6234
92	MC Journal: The Journal of Academic Media Librarianship http://wings.buffalo.edu/publications/mcjrnl/	1069-6792
93	MELA Notes: The Journal of the Middle East Librarians Association http://www.mela.us/MELANotes/MELANotesIntro.html	0364-2410
94	Missisippi Libraries http://www.misslib.org/index.php/publications/mississippi-libraries/	0194-388X
95	MLA Forum http://www.mlaforum.org/	1539-4123
96	Partnership: The Canadian Journal of Library and Information Practice and Research http://journal.lib.uoguelph.ca/index.php/perj/index	1911-9593
97	Progressive Librarian http://libr.org/pl/	1051-5722
98	RBM Journal of Rare Books , Manuscripts, and Cultural Heritage http://rbm.acrl.org/content/2/2	2150-668X Online, 1529-6407 Print
99	School libraries in Canada (SLIC): A Journal of the Canadian Association for School Libraries http://www.clatoo box.ca/casl/slic/links.html	7010-8535
100	Simile: Studies in Media and Information Literacy Education http://utpjournals.metapress.com/content/120764/	1496-6603
101	South African Journal of Information Management http://www.sajim.co.za/index.php/sajim/issue/current	1560-683X Online, 2078-1865 Print

102	Special Libraries http://www.sla.org/content/shop/speclibs.cfm#1910	0038-6723
103	Technological Librarianship :An Online Journal of the American Theological Library Association http://journal.atla.com/ojs/index.php/theolib/index	1937-8904
104	Technology Electronic Reviews (TER) http://www.ala.org/lita/publications/archive/ter	1533-9165
105	The Bonefolder: An outgrowth of the Book Arts Web http://www.philobiblon.com/bonefolder/	1555-6565
106	Code4Lib Journal http://journal.code4lib.org/	1940-5758
107	The Idaho Librarian: A Publication of the Idaho Library Association http://www.idaholibraries.org/idlibrarian/index.php/idaho-librarian/index	2151-7738
108	The International Journal of Database Management Systems http://airccse.org/journal/ijdms/ijdms.html	0975-5705 (Online); 0975-5985(Print)
109	The International Journal of Managing Information Technology http://airccse.org/journal/ijmit/ijmit.html	0975-5586 (Online) ;0975-5926 (Print)
110	The Journal of the Rutgers University Library http://jrul.libraries.rutgers.edu/index.php/jrul/index	0036-0473.
111	The Public Access Computer Systems Review http://epress.lib.uh.edu/pr/pacsrev.html#history	1048-6542
112	Urban Library Journal http://lacuny.cuny.edu/ulj/	1944-9682 Online, 1044-9674 Print
113	Virginia Libraries http://scholar.lib.vt.edu/ejournals/VALib/	1086-9751
114	Webology http://www.webology.ir/	1735-188x

115	World Libraries http://www.worlib.org/	2155-7896

E-Magazines

1	Access http://www.aardvarknet.info/access/number46/index.cfm	0217-5673
2	American Libraries http://americanlibrariesmagazine.org/	0002-9769
3	Book Links http://www.ala.org/ala/aboutala/offices/publishing/booklinks/archiveonline/ archive_of_online_articles.cfm	0009-4978
4	CHOICE http://www.ala.org/ala/mgrps/divs/acrl/publications/choice/previousissues/previousissues.cfm	0009-4978
5	Computer in Libraries http://www.infotoday.com/cilmag/default.shtml	1471-3225
6	Cultivate Interactive http://www.cultivate-int.org/index-2.html	1082-9873
7	Knowledge Management World http://www.kmworld.com/index.cfm	0-9778617-3-2
8	Link-Up http://www.infotoday.com/linkup/default.shtml	*1203 - 8954*
9	Virginia Tech Magazine http://www.vtmagazine.vt.edu/	1527-6619

Newsletters and other E-Resources

1	ABAA Newsletter http://hq.abaa.org/books/antiquarian/abaapages/newsletter	1070-7000X)
2	Against the grain http://www.against-the-grain.com/d/TOC	1043-2094
3	ALCTS Network News http://bubl.ac.uk/archive/journals/alctsnn/	1056-6694

4	Biblia's Warrior Librarian Weekly http://warriorlibrarian.com/ARCHIVE/00archives.html	1445-9124
5	Biblio-Tech Review http://www.ringgold.com/biblio-tech/si_pd.cfm?pid=2	1463-7146
6	Cataloging and Classification Quarterly http://bubl.ac.uk/archive/journals/cacq/	0163-9374
7	Conserline http://www.loc.gov/acq/conser/consrlin.html	1072-611X)
8	Free Pint http://www.freepint.com/	1546-7821
9	Internet on a Disk http://www.samizdat.com/ioad.html	0971-7102
10	MLS: Marketing Library Services http://www.infotoday.com/MLS/default.shtml	1066-8829
11	RLG DigiNews http://www.oclc.org/programs/publications/newsletters/diginews.htm	0146-3055
12	Serials E-News http://www.ringgold.com/UKSG/si_pd.cfm	1093-5371
13	SPARC Open Access Newsletter or Free Online Scholarship Newsletter http://www.earlham.edu/~peters/fos/index.htm	1476-0576
14	Sprouts: Working Papers on Information Systems http://sprouts.aisnet.org/home.html	1535-6078

Researcher has found out that 138 (70%) E-Resources are having ISSN, E-Journals are 115 E-Magazines are 9, and E-Newsletter is 14.

Summary Table: Distribution of E-Resources by ISSN

S.N.	E-Resources by ISSN	No.	Percentage
1	E-Journals	115	79%
2	E-Magazines	9	34%
3	E-Newsletters & other E-Resources	14	58%
	Total	**141**	

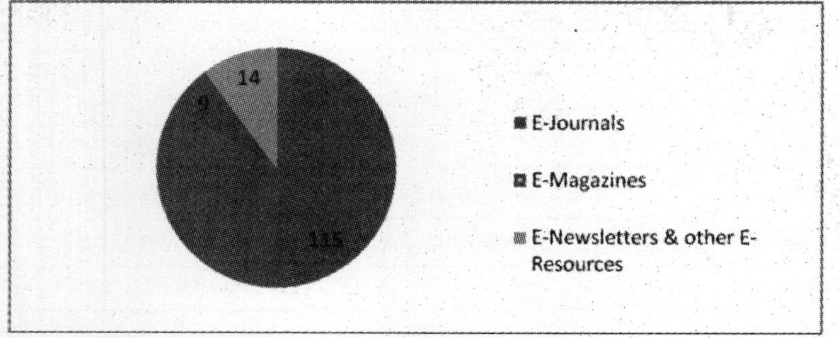

Fig: E-Resources having ISSN Number

This chart shows that out of 145 E-Journals 118 (79%) E-Journals have ISSN, Out of 26 E-Magazine 9 (34%) has ISSN, Out of 24 E-Newsletters & Other E-Resources 14 (58%) have ISSN Numbers.

OPEN ACCESS E-RESOURCES HAVING PERIODICITY

S.No.	Title	Periodicity
1	Special Libraries http://www.sla.org/content/shop/speclibs.cfm#1910	10/Y
2	Alki: The Washington Library Association Journal http://www.wla.org/alki/	3/y
3	Australian Journal of Information Systems http://dl.acs.org.au/index.php/ajis/about	3/y
4	E-JASL: The Electronic Journal of Academic and Special Librarianship http://southernlibrarianship.icaap.org/	3/Y
5	Human IT: Journal for Information Technology Studies as a Human Sciencehttp://etjanst.hb.se/bhs/ith//info-eng.htm	3/Y
6	International Journal of Communication Networks and Information Security http://www.ijcnis.org/index.php/ijcnis	3/y
7	International Journal of Legal Information http://scholarship.law.cornell.edu/ijli/vol33/iss1/	3/Y
8	ITALICS: Innovations in Teaching and Learning in Information and Computer Sciences http://www.ics.heacademy.ac.uk/italics/	3/Y
9	JEP: The Journal of Electronic Publishing http://www.journalofelectronicpublishing.org/	3/Y
10	Journal of Artificial Intelligence Research http://www.jair.org/	3/Y
11	Journal of Information Law and Technology http://www2.warwick.ac.uk/fac/soc/law/elj/jilt/ or European Journal of Law and Technology http://ejlt.org//issue/archive	3/Y
12	Journal of the Association for History and Computing http://quod.lib.umich.edu/j/jahc/browse.html	3/Y

13	Library & Information Research: Research into Practice for Information & Library Services http://www.lirgjournal.org.uk/lir/ojs/index.php/lir	3/Y
14	Malaysian Journal of Library & Information Sciencehttp://ejum.fsktm.um.edu.my/VolumeListing.aspx?JournalID=3	3/Y
15	School libraries in Canada (SLIC): A Journal of the Canadian Association for School Libraries http://www.clatoolbox.ca/casl/slic/links.html	3/Y
16	The International Journal of Managing Information Technology http://airccse.org/journal/ijmit/ijmit.html	3/y
17	ALAN Review http://scholar.lib.vt.edu/ejournals/ALAN/	3/Y
18	International Review of Research in Open and Distance Learning http://www.irrodl.org/index.php/irrodl	3/Y
19	Electronic Journal on Information Systems in Developing Countries http://www.ejisdc.org/ojs2/index.php/ejisdc	5/Y
20	International Journal of Computer Science and Information Technology http://airccse.org/journal/ijcsit.html	5/Y
21	Cybermetrics : International Journal of Scientometrics, Informetrics and Bibliometrics http://www.cindoc.csic.es/cybermetrics/	A
22	DIGITHUM: The Humanities in Digital Age http://www.uoc.edu/digithum/7/eng/numeros.html	A
23	Electronic Journal of Africana Bibliography http://ir.uiowa.edu/ejab/all_issues.html	A
24	Informing Science The International Journal of an Emerging Transdiscipline http://inform.nu/	A

25	Interdisciplinary Journal of E-Learning and Learning Objects http://ijklo.org/	A
26	Interdisciplinary Journal of Information, Knowledge, and Management http://www.ijikm.org/	A
27	International Journal of Communication http://ijoc.org/ojs/index.php/ijoc/about/editorialPolicies#focusAndScope	A
28	International Journal of Doctoral Studies (IJDS) http://ijds.org/	A
29	Issues in Informing Science and Information Technology http://iisit.org/	A
30	Journal of Information Technology Education (JITE: Research) http://www.informingscience.us/icarus/journals/jiteresearch/publications	A
31	Library Philosophy and Practice http://www.webpages.uidaho.edu/~mbolin/lpp.htm	A
32	Library Student Journal http://www.librarystudentjournal.org/index.php/lsj/index	A
33	MELA Notes: The Journal of the Middle East Librarians Association http://www.mela.us/MELANotes/MELANotesIntro.html	A
34	Progressive Librarian http://libr.org/pl/	A
35	School Library Research http://www.ala.org/aasl/slr	A
36	South African Journal of Information Management http://www.sajim.co.za/index.php/sajim/issue/current	A
37	Studies in Bibliography http://etext.lib.virginia.edu/bsuva/sb	A
38	The Journal of the Rutgers University Library http://jrul.libraries.rutgers.edu/index.php/jrul/index	A
39	Journal of Philippine Librarianship http://journals.upd.edu.ph/index.php/jpl/issue/current	A

40	IFLA Journal http://www.ifla.org/V/iflaj/index.htm	BM
41	Information Scotland: The Journal of the Chartered Institute of Library and Information Professionals in Scotland http://www.slainte.org.uk/publications/serials/infoscot/vol1(1)/vol1(1)contents.html	BM
42	College and Research Libraries http://crl.acrl.org/	BM
43	Christian Library Journal http://www.christianlibraryj.org/pdf/index.htm	BM
44	DESIDOC Journal of Library & Information Science http://publications.drdo.gov.in/ojs/index.php/djlit/index	BM
45	Internet Writing Journal http://www.internetwritingjournal.com/	BM
46	Journal of Staff Development http://learningforward.org/publications/jsd#.UUQguzcynUc	BM
47	Journal of Technology Studies http://scholar.lib.vt.edu/ejournals/JOTS/	BM
48	Journal of the American Medical Informatics Association http://www.pubmedcentral.nih.gov/tocrender.fcgi?action=archive&journal=76	BM
49	Research Management Review http://www.ncura.edu/content/news/rmr/archive.php	HY
50	International Journal of Digital Curation http://www.ijdc.net/./ijdc/issue/current	HY
51	International Review of Information Ethics http://www.i-r-i-e.net/	HY
52	JLIS.it Italian Journal of Library and Information Science http://leo.cilea.it/index.php/jlis/article/view/4539/4416	HY
53	Journal of eLiteracy http://www.jelit.org/index.html	HY
54	Journal of Health Informatics in Developing Countries http://www.jhidc.org/index.php/jhidc	HY

55	Journal of Information Architecture http://journalofia.org/archives/	HY
56	LIBRES: Library and Information Science Research Electronic Journal http://libres.curtin.edu.au/	HY
57	MC Journal: The Journal of Academic Media Librarianship http://wings.buffalo.edu/publications/mcjrnl/	HY
58	New Knowledge Environments http://journals.uvic.ca/index.php/INKE	HY
59	North Carolina Libraries http://www.ncl.ecu.edu/index.php/NCL	HY
60	NPO Journal/NPO E-Journal http://www.bl.uk/blpac/publicationsjournals.html	HY
61	RBM Journal of Rare Books , Manuscripts, and Cultural Heritage http://rbm.acrl.org/content/2/2	HY
62	Technological Librarianship: An Online Journal of the American Theological Library Association http://journal.atla.com/ojs/index.php/theolib/index	HY
63	The Bonefolder: An outgrowth of the Book Arts Web http://www.philobiblon.com/bonefolder/	HY
64	The Idaho Librarian: A Publication of the Idaho Library Association http://www.idaholibraries.org/idlibrarian/index.php/idaho-librarian/index	HY
65	Urban Library Journal http://lacuny.cuny.edu/ulj/	HY
66	World Libraries http://www.worlib.org/	HY
67	Partnership: The Canadian Journal of Library and Information Practice and Research http://journal.lib.uoguelph.ca/index.php/perj/index	HY
68	American Archivist http://archivists.metapress.com/home/main.mpx	HY
69	Chinese Librarianship: An International Electronic Journal http://www.iclc.us/cliej/	HY
70	Communications in Information Literacy http://www.comminfolit.org/index.php/cil/issue/archive	HY

71	Electronic Journal of Health Informatics http://www.ejhi.net/ojs/index.php/ejhi	HY
72	Information for Social Change http://libr.org/isc/journal.html	HY
73	Inter-Actions: UCLA Journal of Education and Information Studies http://repositories.cdlib.org/gseis/interactions/	HY
74	Journal of Library Innovation http://www.libraryinnovation.org/about/contact	HY
75	B Sides http://ir.uiowa.edu/bsides/	HY
76	Agricultural Libraries Information Notes http://webharvest.gov/peth04/20041023101316/http://www.nal.usda.gov/NewAlin/	M
77	Cites & Insights: Crawford at Large http://citesandinsights.info/citoc.htm	M
78	Current Cites http://lists.webjunction.org/currentcites/	M
79	EBIB Electronic Information Bulletin for librarians http://ebib.info/biuletyn/	M
80	Firstmonday http://firstmonday.org/	M
81	International Journal of Library and Information Science http://www.academicjournals.org/ijlis/index.htm	M
82	Library Journal http://www.libraryjournal.com	M
83	Northwestern Journal of Technology and Intellectual Property http://www.law.northwestern.edu/journals/njtip/issues.htm	M
84	School Library Journal Online http://www.schoollibraryjournal.com/	M
85	Annals of Library & Information Studies http://nopr.niscair.res.in/	Q

86	Australian Academic and Research Libraries http://www.alia.org.au/publishing/aarl/index.html	Q
87	Australian Library Journal http://alia.org.au/publishing/alj/	Q
88	Colby Quarterly (formerly: Colby Library Quarterly) http://digitalcommons.colby.edu/	Q
89	Collaborative Librarianship http://www.collaborativelibrarianship.org/index.html	Q
90	Computer and Information Science http://journal.ccsenet.org/index.php/cis/index	Q
91	Digital Document Quarterly http://home.pacbell.net/hgladney/ddqstart.htm	Q
92	EDUCAUSE Quarterly http://www.educause.edu/eq	Q
93	Evidence Based Library and Information Practice http://ejournals.library.ualberta.ca/index.php/EBLIP/index	Q
94	Health Information and Libraries Journal http://www3.interscience.wiley.com/journal/120118368/grouphome/home.html	Q
95	Informatica Economica Journal http://revistaie.ase.ro/index.html	Q
96	Information Research: An International Electronic Journal http://informationr.net/ir/	Q
97	Information Technologies and International Development http://itidjournal.org/itid	Q
98	Information Technology and Libraries http://www.ala.org/ala/mgrps/divs/lita/ital/italinformation.cfm	Q
99	International Journal of Computer and Information Engineering http://www.waset.org/journals/ijcie/	Q
100	International Journal of Multimedia and Its Applications http://airccse.org/journal/ijma_index.html	Q
101	International Journal of Special Libraries http://forge.fh-potsdam.de/~IFLA/INSPEL/intro.htm	Q

102	Interpersonal Computing and Technology Journal http://www.helsinki.fi/science/optek/#byissue	Q
103	Issues in Science and Technology Librarianship http://www.library.ucsb.edu/istl/ Or http://www.istl.org/	Q
104	Journal of Digital Information http://jodi.ecs.soton.ac.uk/r or http://journals.tdl.org/jodi	Q
105	Journal of East Asian Libraries http://www.lib.byu.edu/dlib/spc/jeal/	Q
106	Journal of Educational Media & Library Sciences http://joemls.tku.edu.tw/index_e.htm	Q
107	Journal of Information Literacy http://ojs.lboro.ac.uk/ojs/index.php/JIL/index	Q
108	Journal of Information, Information Technology, and Organizations http://jiito.org/	Q
109	Journal of Internet Cataloguing http://www.internetcataloging.com/home.html	Q
110	Journal of Knowledge Management Practice http://www.tlainc.com/boutjkmp.htm	Q
111	Journal of Medical Internet Research http://www.jmir.org/	Q
112	Journal of Research and Practice in Information Technology http://ws.acs.org.au/jrpit/JRPIT_Volumes.html	Q
113	Journal of the European Association for Health Information and Libraries http://www.eahil.net/journal/	Q
114	Journal of the Medical Library association http://www.ncbi.nlm.nih.gov/pmc/journals/93/	Q
115	Journal of Virtual Worlds Research http://www.jvwresearch.org/index.html	Q
116	LASIE: Library Automated Systems Information Exchange http://search.informit.com.au/browseJournalTitle;res=E-LIBRARY;issn=0047-3774	Q
117	Law Library Journal http://www.aallnet.org/products/pub_journal.asp	Q

118	Learned Publishing http://www.ingentaconnect.com/content/alpsp/lp	Q
119	LIBER Quarterly Journal of European Research Libraries http://liber.library.uu.nl/index.html	Q
120	Library Resources & Technical Services (LRTS) http://alcts.metapress.com/home/main.mpx	Q
121	LIBRI: International Journal of Libraries and Information Services http://www.librijournal.org/	Q
122	Mississippi Libraries http://www.misslib.org/index.php/publications/mississippi-libraries/	Q
123	MLA Forum http://www.mlaforum.org/	Q
124	Multimedia Information and Technology Journal (MmIT) http://www.cilip.org.uk/get-involved/special-interest-groups/multimedia/journal/pages/default.aspx	Q
125	Scandinavian Public Library Quarterly http://www.splq.info/	Q
126	Simile: Studies in Media and Information Literacy Education http://utpjournals.metapress.com/content/120764/	Q
127	Texas library journal http://www.txla.org/TLJ	Q
128	The International Journal of Database Management Systems http://airccse.org/journal/ijdms/ijdms.html	Q
129	Virginia Libraries http://scholar.lib.vt.edu/ejournals/VALib/	Q
130	Webology http://www.webology.ir/	Q
131	African Journal of Information & Communication Technology http://epress.lib.uts.edu.au/ojs/index.php/ajict/	Q
132	International Journal of Managing Public Sector Information and Communication Technologies http://airccse.org/journal/mpict/ijmpict.html	Q

E-Magazines

1	E-Content http://www.ecmag.net/	10/Y
2	Provenance http://www.provenance.ca/about-provenance/index.html	3/Y
3	American Libraries http://americanlibrariesmagazine.org/	BM
4	Book Links http://www.ala.org/ala/aboutala/offices/publishing/booklinks/archiveonline/ archive_of_online_articles.cfm	BM
5	EDUCAUSE Review http://www.educause.edu/	BM
6	Research Information http://www.researchinformation.info/	BM
7	The Bulletin of the American Society for Information Science and Technology http://www.asis.org/bulletin.html	BM
8	Link-Up http://www.infotoday.com/linkup/default.shtml	FN
9	AALL Spectrum http://www.aallnet.org/main-menu/Publications/spectrum	M
10	CHOICE http://www.ala.org/ala/mgrps/divs/acrl/publications/choice/previousissues/previousissues.cfm	M
11	Computer in Libraries http://www.infotoday.com/cilmag/default.shtml	M
12	D-Lib Magazine http://www.dlib.org/dlib/september08/09contents.html	M
13	inCite http://alia.org.au/publishing/incite/archive.html	M
14	Information Today http://www.infotoday.com/IT/nov08/index.shtml	M
15	Knowledge Management World http://www.kmworld.com/index.cfm	M

16	Online http://www.infotoday.com/online/default.shtml	M
17	Searcher: The Magazine for Database Professionals http://www.infotoday.com/searcher/default.asp	M
18	Access http://www.aardvarknet.info/access/number46/index.cfm	Q
19	Ariadne http://www.ariadne.ac.uk/	Q
20	The Marginal http://www.gslis.mcgill.ca/marginal/	Q
21	Virginia Tech Magazine http://www.vtmagazine.vt.edu/	Q

Newsletters and other E-Resources

1	Business and Finance Division Bulletin http://bf.sla.org/resources/the-bulletin/	3/Y
2	ARL: A bimonthly newsletter for library issues and action **http://www.arl.org/resources/pubs/br/** index.shtml	BM
3	MLS: Marketing Library Services http://www.infotoday.com/MLS/default.shtml	BM
4	NLM Technical Bulletin http://www.nlm.nih.gov/pubs/techbull/current_issue.html	BM
5	Abbey Newsletter http://cool.conservation-us.org/byorg/abbey/an/	BM
6	Against the grain http://www.against-the-grain.com/d/TOC	BM
7	RLG DigiNews http://www.oclc.org/programs/publications/newsletters/diginews.htm	BM
8	Serials E-News http://www.ringgold.com/UKSG/si_pd.cfm	FN
9	ALCTS Network News http://bubl.ac.uk/archive/journals/alctsnn/	FN
10	CIT Infobits http://serials.infomotions.com/infobits/	M

11	Internet Resources Newsletter http://www.hw.ac.uk/libwww/irn/irn.html	M
12	ABAA Newsletter http://hq.abaa.org/books/antiquarian/abaapages/newsletter	Q
13	Information today and Tomorrow http://www.dsir.gov.in/pubs/itt/index.htm	Q

Table shows that out that out of 195 E-Resources 166 (85%) having Periodicity and 29 (15%) not having Periodicity. Out of 145 E-Journals 132 (91%), Out of 26 E-Magazine 21 (80%) and Out of 24 E-Newsletter and others 13 (54%) are having Periodicity.

Summary Table: E-Resources having Periodicity

S.N.	E-Resources	Percentage %	No.
1	E-Journals	85%	132
2	E-Magazines	84%	22
3	Other E-Resources	54%	13
	Total		**166**

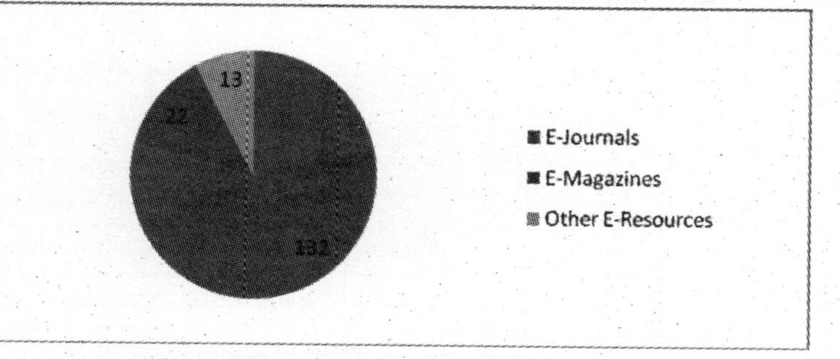

Fig.: E-Resources having Periodicity

The chart shows those E-Journals are 85%, E-Magazines are 80%, E-Newsletters are 54% having Periodicity.

3.10. OPEN ACCESS INTERNATIONAL E-RESOURCES

E-Journals

SL. No.	Title/URL	Peer Reviewed	Indexed	Title/ Name
1	Annals of Library & Information Studies http://nopr.niscair.res.in/	Y	Y	N
2	Australian Journal of Information Systems http://dl.acs.org.au/index.php/ajis/about	Y	Y	N

3	Australian Academic and Research Libraries http://www.alia.org.au/publishing/aarl/index.html	Y	Y	N
4	B Sides http://ir.uiowa.edu/bsides/	Y	Y	N
5	Collaborative Librarianship http://www.collaborativelibrarianship.org/index.html	Y	Y	N
6	Communications in Information Literacy http://www.comminfolit.org/index.php/cil/issue/archive	Y	Y	N
7	Computer and Information Science http://journal.ccsenet.org/index.php/cis/index	Y	Y	N
8	Coordinates: Online Journal of the Map and Geography Round Table of the American Library Association. Series A and B http://www.sunysb.edu/libmap/coordinates.htm	Y	Y	N
9	Current Issues in Education http://cie.asu.edu/index.php	Y	Y	N
10	DESIDOC Journal of Library & Information Science http://publications.drdo.gov.in/ojs/index.php/djlit/index	Y	Y	N
11	Electronic Journal of Health Informatics http://www.ejhi.net/ojs/index.php/ejhi	Y (D)	Y	N
12	European Journal of ePractice http://www.epracticejournal.eu/	Y	Y	N
13	Evidence Based Library and Information Practice http://ejournals.library.ualberta.ca/index.php/EBLIP/index	Y	Y	N
14	Firstmonday http://firstmonday.org/	Y	Y	N
15	International Review of Research in Open and Distance Learning http://www.irrodl.org/index.php/irrodl	Y	Y	N

16	Issues in Informing Science and Information Technology http://iisit.org/	Y	Y	N
17	Issues in Science and Technology Librarianship http://www.library.ucsb.edu/istl/ Or http://www.istl.org/	Y	Y	N
18	Journal of Digital Information http://jodi.ecs.soton.ac.uk/r or http://journals.tdl.org/jodi	Y	Y	N
19	Journal of Health Informatics in Developing Countries http://www.jhidc.org/index.php/jhidc	Y	Y	N
20	Journal of Information Law and Technology http://www2.warwick.ac.uk/fac/soc/law/elj/jilt/ or European Journal of Law and Technology http://ejlt.org//issue/archive	Y	Y	N
21	Journal of Information Literacy (JIL) http://www.informationliteracy.org.uk/JIL.aspx	Y	Y	N
22	Journal of Information Technology Education (JITE: Research) http://www.informingscience.us/icarus/journals/jiteresearch/publications	Y	Y	N
23	Journal of Information, Information Technology, and Organizations http://jiito.org/	Y	Y	N
24	Journal of Library Innovation http://www.libraryinnovation.org/about/contact	Y	Y	N
25	Journal of Medical Internet Research http://www.jmir.org/	Y	Y	N
26	Journal of the American Medical Informatics Association http://www.pubmedcentral.nih.gov/tocrender.fcgi?action=archive&journal=76	Y	Y	N
27	Library & Information Research: Research into Practice for Information & Library Services http://www.lirg.org.uk/lir/ojs/index.php/lir	Y	Y	N
28	Library Philosophy and Practice http://www.webpages.uidaho.edu/~mbolin/lpp.htm	Y	Y	N

29	Library Student Journal http://www.librarystudentjournal.org/index.php/lsj/index	Y	Y	N
30	New Knowledge Environments http://journals.uvic.ca/index.php/INKE	Y	Y	N
31	North Carolina Libraries http://www.ncl.ecu.edu/index.php/NCL	Y	Y	N
32	Partnership: The Canadian Journal of Library and Information Practice and Research http://journal.lib.uoguelph.ca/index.php/perj/index	Y	Y	N
33	Simile: Studies in Media and Information Literacy Education http://www.utpjournals.com/simile/simile.html	Y	Y	N
34	South African Journal of Information Management http://general.rau.ac.za/infosci/raujournal/	Y	Y	N
35	Technological Librarianship: An Online Journal of the American Theological Library Association http://journal.atla.com/ojs/index.php/theolib/index	Y	Y	N
36	The Idaho Librarian: A Publication of the Idaho Library Association http://www.idaholibraries.org/idlibrarian/index.php/idaho-librarian/index	Y	Y	N
37	Journal of Educational Media & Library Sciences http://joemls.tku.edu.tw/index_e.htm	Y	Y	Y
38	African Journal of Information & Communication Technology http://epress.lib.uts.edu.au/ojs/index.php/ajict/	Y	Y	Y
39	Information Research: An International Electronic Journal http://informationr.net/ir/	Y	Y	Y
40	Information Technologies and International Development http://itidjournal.org/itid	Y	Y	Y
41	International Journal of Communication http://ijoc.org/ojs/index.php/ijoc/about/editorialPolicies#focusAndScope	Y	Y	Y

42	International Journal of Communication Networks and Information Security http://www.ijcnis.org/index.php/ijcnis	Y	Y	Y
43	International Journal of Computer and Information Engineering http://www.waset.org/journals/ijcie/	Y	Y	Y
44	International Journal of Digital Curation http://www.ijdc.net/./ijdc/issue/current	Y	Y	Y
45	International Journal of Managing Public Sector Information and Communication Technologies http://airccse.org/journal/mpict/ijmpict.html	Y	Y	Y
46	JLIS.it Italian Journal of Library and Information Science http://leo.cilea.it/index.php/jlis/article/view/4539/4416	Y	Y	Y
47	The International Journal of Managing Information Technology http://airccse.org/journal/ijmit/ijmit.html	Y	Y	Y
48	The Journal of the Rutgers University Library http://jrul.libraries.rutgers.edu/index.php/jrul/index	Y	Y	Y
49	Australian Library Journal http://alia.org.au/publishing/alj/	N	N	Y
50	Chinese Librarianship: An International Electronic Journal http://www.iclc.us/cliej/	N	N	Y
51	Cybermetrics : International Journal of Scientometrics, Informetrics and Bibliometrics http://www.cindoc.csic.es/cybermetrics/	N	N	Y
52	Electronic Journal on Information Systems in Developing Countries http://www.ejisdc.org/ojs2/index.php/ejisdc	N	N	Y

53	Health Information and Libraries Journal http://www3.interscience.wiley.com/journal/120118368/grouphome/home.html	N	N	Y
54	Informing Science The International Journal of an Emerging Transdiscipline http://inform.nu/	N	N	Y
55	International Journal of Computer Science and Information Technology http://airccse.org/journal/ijcsit.html	N	N	Y
56	International Journal of Doctoral Studies (IJDS) http://ijds.org/	N	N	Y
57	International Journal of Legal Information http://scholarship.law.cornell.edu/ijli/vol33/iss1/	N	N	Y
58	International Journal of Library and Information Science http://www.academicjournals.org/ijlis/index.htm	N	N	Y
59	International Journal of Multimedia and Its Applications http://airccse.org/journal/ijma_index.html	N	N	Y
60	International Journal of Special Libraries http://forge.fh-potsdam.de/~IFLA/INSPEL/intro.htm	N	N	Y
61	International Review of Information Ethics http://www.i-r-i-e.net/	N	N	Y
62	Journal of Internet Cataloguing http://www.internetcataloging.com/home.html	N	N	Y
63	Journal of Research and Practice in Information Technology http://acs.org.au/jrpit/index.html	N	N	Y
64	LIBRES: Library and Information Science Research Electronic Journal http://libres.curtin.edu.au/	N	N	Y

65	LIBRI: International Journal of Libraries and Information Services http://www.librijournal.org/	N	N	Y
66	The International Journal of Database Management Systems http://airccse.org/journal/ijdms/ijdms.html	N	N	Y
Newsletters and other E-Resources				
1	Business and Finance Division Bulletin http://units.sla.org/division/dbf/resources/bulletin.html	Y	Y	N

E-Resources have International standards have greater accumulation compare to national Published journals. International Journals are mostly preferred by academicians and researchers. These have their own characteristics than the national Journals. Table shows 67 International E-Resources on the bases of Peer Reviewed, Indexed, Name/ Title.

Summary Table: Distribution of National and International E-Resources

S.N.	E-Resources	No.
1	National E-Resources	128
2	International E-Resources	67

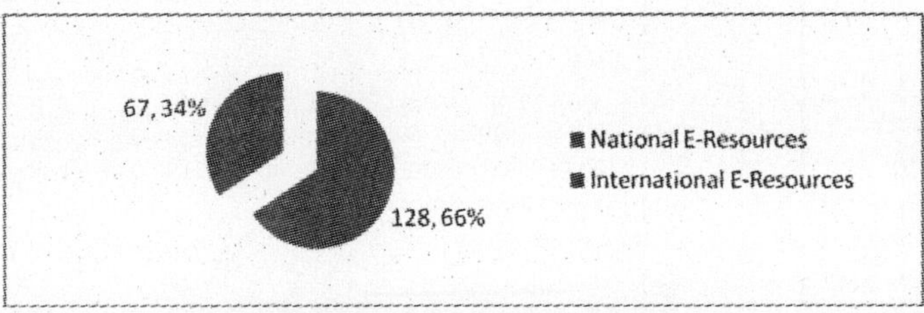

Fig: National and International E-Resources

The above chart shows that 34% E-Resources are International and 66% E-Resources are National.

Summary Table: Distribution of International E-Resources

S.N.	International E-Resources	No.
1	Peer Reviewed & Indexed	49
2	Peer Reviewed, Index, Title/Name	12
3	E-Resources on Title/Name but not Peer Reviewed and Indexed	17
4	National E-Resources	128
5	International E-Resources	67

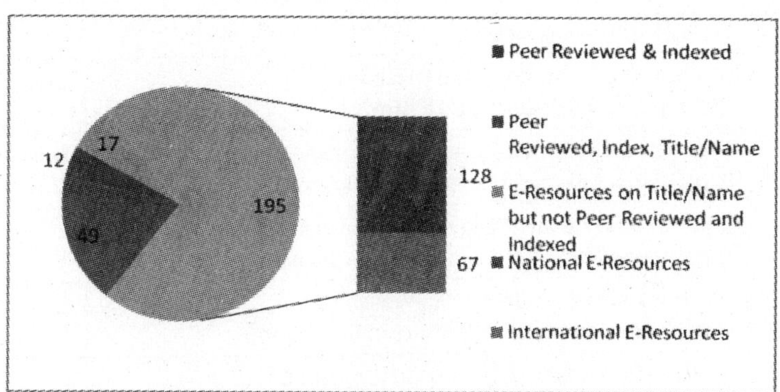

Fig.: International E-Resources

This chart shows 128 (66%) National and 67 (34%) International E-Resources, Peer Reviewed & indexed 49, Peer Reviewed, Index, Title/Name 12, and E-Resources on Title/Name but not peer Reviewed & indexed are 17.

3.11. FORMAT OF OPEN ACCESS E-RESOURCES

There are basically four main format s in which Electronic Journals are available.

ASCII

PDF

E-Text

HTML

E-Journals

SL. No.	Title/URL	Format
1	Chinese Librarianship: An International Electronic Journal http://www.iclc.us/cliej/	E-Text
2	Cites & Insights: Crawford at Large http://citesandinsights.info/citoc.htm	E-Text
3	Current Cites http://lists.webjunction.org/currentcites/	E-Text
4	Digital Document Quarterly http://home.pacbell.net/hgladney/ddqstart.htm	E-Text
5	Information Research: An International Electronic Journal	E-Text

	http://informationr.net/ir/	
6	Information Technology and Disabilities http://people.rit.edu/easi/itd.htm	E-Text
7	Interpersonal Computing and Technology Journal http://www.helsinki.fi/science/optek/#byissue	E-Text
8	Issues in Science and Technology Librarianship http://www.library.ucsb.edu/istl/ Or http://www.istl.org/	E-Text
9	JEP: The Journal of Electronic Publishing http://www.journalofelectronicpublishing.org/	E-Text
10	Journal of the Association for History and Computing http://quod.lib.umich.edu/j/jahc/browse.html	E-Text
11	Library Journal http://www.libraryjournal.com	E-Text
12	MLA Forum http://www.mlaforum.org/	E-Text
13	NPO Journal/NPO E-Journal http://www.bl.uk/blpac/publicationsjournals.html	E-Text
14	Progressive Librarian http://libr.org/pl/	E-Text
15	Scandinavian Public Library Quarterly http://www.splq.info/	E-Text
16	School Library Journal Online http://www.schoollibraryjournal.com/	E-Text
17	Studies in Bibliography http://etext.lib.virginia.edu/bsuva/sb	E-Text
18	Code4Lib Journal http://journal.code4lib.org/	E-Text
19	Webology http://www.webology.ir/	E-text
20	World Libraries http://www.worlib.org/	E-text
21	EBIB Electronic Information Bulletin for librarians http://ebib.info/biuletyn/	E-Text
22	Agricultural Libraries Information Notes http://webharvest.gov/peth04/20041023101316/http://www.nal.usda.gov/NewAlin/	html
23	Australian Library Journal http://alia.org.au/publishing/alj/	html
24	Current Issues in Education http://cie.asu.edu/index.php	Html
25	High Energy Physics Libraries Webzine http://library.web.cern.ch/library/Webzine/index.shtml	Html
26	Information Scotland: The Journal of the Chartered Institute of Library and Information Professionals in Scotland http://www.slainte.org.uk/publications/serials/infoscot/vol1	HTML

	1)/vol1(1)contents.html	
27	Internet Writing Journal http://www.internetwritingjournal.com/	Html
28	IT&Society http://www.itandsociety.org/index.html	Html
29	Journal of Digital Information http://jodi.ecs.soton.ac.uk/r or http://journals.tdl.org/jodi	Html
30	Journal of Internet Cataloguing http://www.internetcataloging.com/home.html	Html
31	Journal of Knowledge Management Practice http://www.tlainc.com/boutjkmp.htm	Html
32	Journal of Medical Internet Research http://www.jmir.org/	Html
33	School Library Research http://www.ala.org/aasl/slr	Html
34	South African Journal of Information Management http://www.sajim.co.za/index.php/sajim/issue/current	Html
35	Technological Librarianship: An Online Journal of the American Theological Library Association http://journal.atla.com/ojs/index.php/theolib/index	Html
36	The Public Access Computer Systems Review http://epress.lib.uh.edu/pr/pacsrev.html#history	Html
37	E-JASL: The Electronic Journal of Academic and Special Librarianship http://southernlibrarianship.icaap.org/	Html
38	Coordinates: Online Journal of the Map and Geography Round Table of the American Library Association. Series A and B http://www.sunysb.edu/libmap/coordinates.htm	Html & Pdf
39	Cybermetrics : International Journal of Scientometrics, Informetrics and Bibliometrics http://www.cindoc.csic.es/cybermetrics/	Html & Pdf
40	Informing Science The International Journal of an Emerging Transdiscipline http://inform.nu/	Html & Pdf
41	Alki: The Washington Library Association Journal http://www.wla.org/alki/	Pdf
42	American Archivist http://archivists.metapress.com/home/main.mpx	Pdf
43	Annals of Library & Information Studies http://nopr.niscair.res.in/	Pdf
44	Australian Journal of Information Systems	Pdf

	http://dl.acs.org.au/index.php/ajis/about	
45	Australian Academic and Research Libraries http://www.alia.org.au/publishing/aarl/index.html	Pdf
46	Christian Library Journal http://www.christianlibraryj.org/Pdf/index.htm	Pdf
47	Colby Quarterly (formerly: Colby Library Quarterly) http://digitalcommons.colby.edu/	Pdf
48	Collaborative Librarianship http://www.collaborativelibrarianship.org/index.html	Pdf
49	Communications in Information Literacy http://www.comminfolit.org/index.php/cil/issue/archive	Pdf
50	Computer and Information Science http://journal.ccsenet.org/index.php/cis/index	Pdf
51	DESIDOC Journal of Library & Information Science http://publications.drdo.gov.in/ojs/index.php/djlit/index	Pdf
52	DIGITHUM: The Humanities in Digital Age http://www.uoc.edu/digithum/7/eng/numeros.html	Pdf
53	Electronic Journal of Africana Bibliography http://ir.uiowa.edu/ejab/all_issues.html	Pdf
54	Electronic Journal of Health Informatics http://www.ejhi.net/ojs/index.php/ejhi	Pdf
55	Electronic Journal of Knowledge Management http://www.ejkm.com/	Pdf
56	Electronic Journal on Information Systems in Developing Countries http://www.ejisdc.org/ojs2/index.php/ejisdc	Pdf
57	Electronic Transactions on Artificial Intelligence http://www.ida.liu.se/ext/etai/	Pdf
58	European Journal of ePractice http://www.epracticejournal.eu/	Pdf
59	Evidence Based Library and Information Practice http://ejournals.library.ualberta.ca/index.php/EBLIP/index	Pdf
60	Human IT: Journal for Information Technology Studies as a Human Science http://etjanst.hb.se/bhs/ith//info-eng.htm	Pdf
61	IFLA Journal http://www.ifla.org/V/iflaj/index.htm	Pdf
62	Informatica Economica Journal http://revistaie.ase.ro/index.html	Pdf

63	Information for Social Change http://libr.org/isc/journal.html	Pdf
64	Information Technologies and International Development http://itidjournal.org/itid	Pdf
65	Information Technology and Libraries http://www.ala.org/ala/mgrps/divs/lita/ital/italinformation.cfm	Pdf
66	Informing Faculty: An International Journal of Higher Education Discussion Cases http://informingfaculty.org/	Pdf
67	Inter-Actions: UCLA Journal of Education and Information Studies http://repositories.cdlib.org/gseis/interactions/	Pdf
68	Interdisciplinary Journal of E-Learning and Learning Objects http://ijklo.org/	Pdf
69	Interdisciplinary Journal of Information, Knowledge, and Management http://www.ijikm.org/	Pdf
70	International Journal of Communication http://ijoc.org/ojs/index.php/ijoc/about/editorialPolicies#focusAndScope	Pdf
71	International Journal of Communication Networks and Information Security http://www.ijcnis.org/index.php/ijcnis	Pdf
72	International Journal of Computer and Information Engineering http://www.waset.org/journals/ijcie/	Pdf
73	International Journal of Computer Science and Information Technology http://airccse.org/journal/ijcsit.html	Pdf
74	International Journal of Digital Curation http://www.ijdc.net/./ijdc/issue/current	Pdf
75	International Journal of Doctoral Studies (IJDS) http://ijds.org/	Pdf
76	International Journal of Legal Information http://scholarship.law.cornell.edu/ijli/vol33/iss1/	Pdf
77	International Journal of Library and Information Science http://www.academicjournals.org/ijlis/index.htm	Pdf
78	International Journal of Managing Public Sector Information and Communication Technologies http://airccse.org/journal/mpict/ijmpict.html	Pdf
79	International Journal of Multimedia and Its Applications http://airccse.org/journal/ijma_index.html	Pdf

80	International Journal of Special Libraries http://forge.fh-potsdam.de/~IFLA/INSPEL/intro.htm	Pdf
81	International Review of Information Ethics http://www.i-r-i-e.net/	Pdf
82	Issues in Informing Science and Information Technology http://iisit.org/	Pdf
83	ITALICS: Innovations in Teaching and Learning in Information and Computer Sciences http://www.ics.heacademy.ac.uk/italics/	Pdf
84	JLIS.it Italian Journal of Library and Information Science http://leo.cilea.it/index.php/jlis/article/view/4539/4416	Pdf
85	Journal of East Asian Libraries http://www.lib.byu.edu/dlib/spc/jeal/	Pdf
86	Journal of Educational Media & Library Sciences http://joemls.tku.edu.tw/index_e.htm	Pdf
87	Journal of eLiteracy http://www.jelit.org/index.html	Pdf
88	Journal of Health Informatics in Developing Countries http://www.jhidc.org/index.php/jhidc	Pdf
89	Journal of Information Architecture http://journalofia.org/archives/	Pdf
90	Journal of Information Literacy http://ojs.lboro.ac.uk/ojs/index.php/JIL/index	Pdf
91	Journal of Information Technology Education (JITE: Research) http://www.informingscience.us/icarus/journals/jiteresearch/publications	Pdf
92	Journal of Information, Information Technology, and Organizations http://jiito.org/	Pdf
93	Journal of Library Innovation http://www.libraryinnovation.org/about/contact	Pdf
94	Journal of Philippine Librarianship http://journals.upd.edu.ph/index.php/jpl/issue/current	Pdf
95	Journal of Research and Practice in Information Technology http://ws.acs.org.au/jrpit/JRPIT_Volumes.html	Pdf
96	Journal of Staff Development http://learningforward.org/publications/jsd#.UUQguzcynUc	Pdf
97	Journal of Technology Studies	Pdf

	http://scholar.lib.vt.edu/ejournals/JOTS/	
98	Journal of the European Association for Health Information and Libraries http://www.eahil.net/journal/	Pdf
99	Journal of the Medical Library association http://www.ncbi.nlm.nih.gov/pmc/journals/93/	Pdf
100	Journal of Virtual Worlds Research http://www.jvwresearch.org/index.html	Pdf
101	LASIE: Library Automated Systems Information Exchange http://search.informit.com.au/browseJournalTitle;res=E-LIBRARY;issn=0047-3774	Pdf
102	Law Library Journal http://www.aallnet.org/products/pub_journal.asp	Pdf
103	Learned Publishing http://www.ingentaconnect.com/content/alpsp/lp	Pdf
104	LIBER Quarterly Journal of European Research Libraries http://liber.library.uu.nl/index.html	Pdf
105	Library & Information Research: Research into Practice for Information & Library Services http://www.lirg.org.uk/lir/ojs/index.php/lir	Pdf
106	Library Philosophy and Practice http://www.webpages.uidaho.edu/~mbolin/lpp.htm	Pdf
107	Library Resources & Technical Services (LRTS) http://alcts.metapress.com/home/main.mpx	Pdf
108	LIBRES: Library and Information Science Research Electronic Journal http://libres.curtin.edu.au/	Pdf
109	LIBRI: International Journal of Libraries and Information Services http://www.librijournal.org/	Pdf
110	Malaysian Journal of Library & Information Sciencehttp://ejum.fsktm.um.edu.my/VolumeListing.aspx?JournalID=3	Pdf
111	MC Journal: The Journal of Academic Media Librarianship http://wings.buffalo.edu/publications/mcjrnl/	Pdf
112	MELA Notes: The Journal of the Middle East Librarians Association http://www.mela.us/MELANotes/MELANotesIntro.html	Pdf
113	Mississippi Libraries http://www.misslib.org/index.php/publications/mississippi-libraries/	Pdf

114	Multimedia Information and Technology Journal (MmIT) http://www.cilip.org.uk/get-involved/special-interest-groups/multimedia/journal/pages/default.aspx	Pdf
115	New Knowledge Environments http://journals.uvic.ca/index.php/INKE	Pdf
116	North Carolina Libraries http://www.ncl.ecu.edu/index.php/NCL	Pdf
117	Northwestern Journal of Technology and Intellectual Property http://www.law.northwestern.edu/journals/njtip/issues.htm	Pdf
118	RBM Journal of Rare Books , Manuscripts, and Cultural Heritage http://rbm.acrl.org/content/2/2	Pdf
119	Research Management Review http://www.ncura.edu/content/news/rmr/archive.php	Pdf
120	School libraries in Canada (SLIC): A Journal of the Canadian Association for School Libraries http://www.clatoolbox.ca/casl/slic/links.html	Pdf
121	Simile: Studies in Media and Information Literacy Education http://utpjournals.metapress.com/content/120764/	Pdf
122	Special Libraries http://www.sla.org/content/shop/speclibs.cfm#1910	Pdf
123	Technology Electronic Reviews (TER) http://www.ala.org/lita/publications/archive/ter	Pdf
124	Texas library journal http://www.txla.org/TLJ	Pdf
125	The Bonefolder: An outgrowth of the Book Arts Web http://www.philobiblon.com/bonefolder/	Pdf
126	The International Journal of Database Management Systems http://airccse.org/journal/ijdms/ijdms.html	Pdf
127	The International Journal of Managing Information Technology http://airccse.org/journal/ijmit/ijmit.html	Pdf
128	The Journal of the Rutgers University Library http://jrul.libraries.rutgers.edu/index.php/jrul/index	Pdf
129	College and Research Libraries http://crl.acrl.org/	Pdf
130	African Journal of Information & Communication Technology http://epress.lib.uts.edu.au/ojs/index.php/ajict/	Pdf
131	B Sides http://ir.uiowa.edu/bsides/	Pdf
132	Data Science Journal http://www.jstage.jst.go.jp/browse/dsj	Pdf

133	Journal of Artificial Intelligence Research http://www.jair.org/	Pdf
134	Journal of Information Law and Technology http://www2.warwick.ac.uk/fac/soc/law/elj/jilt/ or European Journal of Law and Technology http://ejlt.org//issue/archive	Pdf
135	ALAN Review http://scholar.lib.vt.edu/ejournals/ALAN/	Pdf & Html
136	EDUCAUSE Quarterly http://www.educause.edu/eq	Pdf & Html
137	Firstmonday http://firstmonday.org/	Pdf & Html
138	Health Information and Libraries Journal http://www3.interscience.wiley.com/journal/120118368/grouphome/home.html	Pdf & Html
139	International Review of Research in Open and Distance Learning http://www.irrodl.org/index.php/irrodl	Pdf and Html
140	Journal of the American Medical Informatics Association http://www.pubmedcentral.nih.gov/tocrender.fcgi?action=archive&journal=76	Pdf and Html
141	Library Student Journal http://www.librarystudentjournal.org/index.php/lsj/index	Pdf and Html
142	Partnership: The Canadian Journal of Library and Information Practice and Research http://journal.lib.uoguelph.ca/index.php/perj/index	Pdf and Html
143	The Idaho Librarian: A Publication of the Idaho Library Association http://www.idaholibraries.org/idlibrarian/index.php/idaho-librarian/index	Pdf and Html
144	Urban Library Journal http://lacuny.cuny.edu/ulj/	Pdf and Html
145	Virginia Libraries http://scholar.lib.vt.edu/ejournals/VALib/	Pdf and Html

E-Magazines

1	American Libraries http://americanlibrariesmagazine.org/	E-text
2	Ariadne http://www.ariadne.ac.uk/	E-text
3	Cultivate Interactive http://www.cultivate-int.org/index-	E-Text

	2.html	
4	D-Lib Magazine http://www.dlib.org/dlib/september08/09contents.html	E-text
5	E-Content http://www.ecmag.net/	E-text
6	EDUCAUSE Review http://www.educause.edu/	E-Text
7	Ex Libris http://marylaine.com/exlibris/	E-text
8	Knowledge Management World http://www.kmworld.com/index.cfm	E-text
9	Library Juice http://libr.org/juice/	E-Text
10	Online http://www.infotoday.com/online/default.shtml	E-text
11	Provenance http://www.provenance.ca/about-provenance/index.html	E-text
12	Research Information http://www.researchinformation.info/	E-Text
13	Searcher: The Magazine for Database Professionals http://www.infotoday.com/searcher/default.asp	E-text
14	The Marginal http://www.gslis.mcgill.ca/marginal/	E-Text
15	Book business http://www.bookbusinessmag.com/	Html
16	CHOICE http://www.ala.org/ala/mgrps/divs/acrl/publications/choice/previousissues/previousissues.cfm	Html
17	Exploit Interactive http://www.exploit-lib.org/	Html
18	inCite http://alia.org.au/publishing/incite/archive.html	Html
19	Virginia Tech Magazine http://www.vtmagazine.vt.edu/	Html
19	AALL Spectrum http://www.aallnet.org/main-menu/Publications/spectrum	Pdf
20	Access http://www.aardvarknet.info/access/number46/index.cfm	Pdf
21	Computer in Libraries http://www.infotoday.com/cllmag/default.shtml	Pdf
22	Link-Up http://www.infotoday.com/linkup/default.shtml	Pdf
23	Book Links http://www.ala.org/ala/aboutala/offices/publishing/booklinks/archiveonline/archive_of_online_articles.cfm	Pdf and Html
24	The Bulletin of the American Society for Information Science and Technology http://www.asis.org/bulletin.html	Pdf and Html

25	Information Today http://www.infotoday.com/IT/nov08/index.shtml	Pdf and html

E-Newsletters and others

1	Abbey Newsletter http://cool.conservation-us.org/byorg/abbey/an/	E-text
2	ALCTS Network News http://bubl.ac.uk/archive/journals/alctsnn/	E-Text
3	Biblia's Warrior Librarian Weekly http://warriorlibrarian.com/ARCHIVE/00archives.html	E-text
4	Biblio-Tech Review http://www.ringgold.com/biblio-tech/si_pd.cfm?pid=2	E-Text
5	Cataloging and Classification Quarterly http://bubl.ac.uk/archive/journals/cacq/	E-Text
6	CIT Infobits http://serials.infomotions.com/infobits/	E-text
7	Internet on a Disk http://www.samizdat.com/ioad.html	E-Text
8	Internet Resources Newsletter http://www.hw.ac.uk/libwww/irn/irn.html	E-text
9	MLS: Marketing Library Services http://www.infotoday.com/MLS/default.shtml	E-Text
10	Serials E-News http://www.ringgold.com/UKSG/si_pd.cfm	E-text
11	The Wired Librarian's Newsletter http://www.wiredlibrarian.com/wln/wlnfront.htm	E-text
12	Conserline http://www.loc.gov/acq/conser/consrlin.html	Html
13	Free Pint http://www.freepint.com/	Html
14	Information today and Tomorrow http://www.dsir.gov.in/pubs/itt/index.htm	Html
15	SPARC Open Access Newsletter or Free Online Scholarship Newsletter http://www.earlham.edu/~peters/fos/index.htm	Html
16	ABAA Newsletter http://hq.abaa.org/books/antiquarian/abaapages/newsletter	Pdf
17	ALAWON. The ALA Washington Office Electronic Newsline http://www.ala.org/ala/aboutala/offices/wo/washnews/archivea/archive.cfm	Pdf
18	Business and Finance Division Bulletin http://bf.sla.org/resources/the-bulletin/	Pdf

19	LC Cataloging Newsline http://www.loc.gov/catdir/lccn/	Pdf
20	RLG DigiNews http://www.oclc.org/programs/publications/newsletters/diginews.htm	Pdf
21	Sprouts: Working Papers on Information Systems http://sprouts.aisnet.org/home.html	Pdf
22	Against the grain http://www.against-the-grain.com/d/TOC	Pdf and Html
23	ARL: A bimonthly newsletter for library issues and action http://www.arl.org/resources/pubs/br/index.shtml	Pdf and Html
24	NLM Technical Bulletin http://www.nlm.nih.gov/pubs/techbull/current_issue.html	Pdf and Html

E-Resources are different types of format such as Pdf, Html, E-Text etc. These formats are mostly preferred by the publishers, they intent to choose them at their convenient. Mostly E-resources are published in PDF because format author and publisher want to protect their Intellectual property. Table shows that out of 200 E-Resources 106 are in Pdf, 48 in E-Text, 25 in Html and 21 in Html and Pdf.

Summary Table: Distribution of E-Resources by Format

Sl.No	Format	NO.
1	Pdf	104
2	Html	25
3	E-Text	46
4	Html and Pdf	20
	Total	**195**

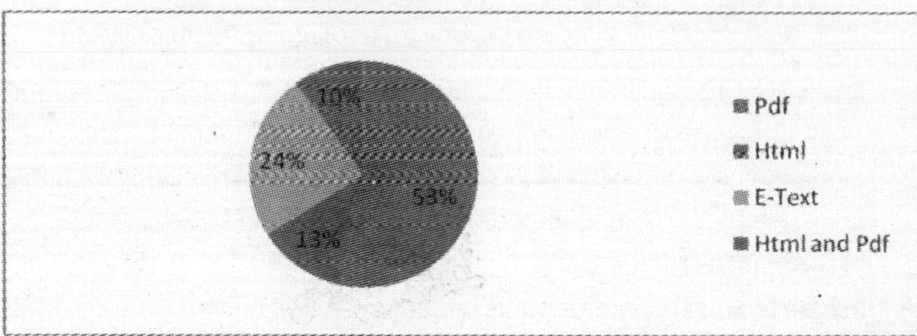

Fig: Distribution of E-Resources by Format

This chart shows that 53% E-Resources are providing PDF, 13 % Html, 24% E-Text, and 10% Html and PDF.

3.12. OPEN ACCESS E-RESOURCES BY GEOGRAPHICAL REGION

E-Journals

Sl.No.	URL	Geographical
1	College and Research Libraries http://crl.acrl.org/	America
2	Agricultural Libraries Information Notes http://webharvest.gov/peth04/20041023101316/http://www.nal.usda.gov/NewAlin/	America
3	Alki: The Washington Library Association Journal http://www.wla.org/alki/	America
4	American Archivist http://archivists.metapress.com/home/main.mpx	America
5	B Sides http://ir.uiowa.edu/bsides/	America
6	Chinese Librarianship: An International Electronic Journal http://www.iclc.us/cliej/	America
7	Colby Quarterly (formerly: Colby Library Quarterly) http://digitalcommons.colby.edu/	America
8	Collaborative Librarianship http://www.collaborativelibrarianship.org/index.html	America
9	Communications in Information Literacy http://www.comminfolit.org/index.php/cil/issue/archive	America
10	Coordinates: Online Journal of the Map and Geography Round Table of the American Library Association. Series A and B http://www.sunysb.edu/libmap/coordinates.htm	America
11	Current Cites http://lists.webjunction.org/currentcites/	America
12	Current Issues in Education http://cie.asu.edu/index.php	America
13	Digital Document Quarterly http://home.pacbell.net/hgladney/ddqstart.htm	America
14	EDUCAUSE Quarterly http://www.educause.edu/eq	America
15	Electronic Journal of Africana Bibliography http://ir.uiowa.edu/ejab/all_issues.html	America
16	Electronic Journal of Knowledge Management http://www.ejkm.com/	America

17	Firstmonday http://firstmonday.org/	America
18	Information Technologies and International Development http://itidjournal.org/itid	America
19	Information Technology and Disabilities http://people.rit.edu/easi/itd.htm	America
20	Information Technology and Libraries http://www.ala.org/ala/mgrps/divs/lita/ital/italinformation.cfm	America
21	Informing Faculty: An International Journal of Higher Education Discussion Cases http://informingfaculty.org/	America
22	Informing Science The International Journal of an Emerging Transdiscipline http://inform.nu/	America
23	Inter-Actions: UCLA Journal of Education and Information Studies http://repositories.cdlib.org/gseis/interactions/	America
24	Interdisciplinary Journal of E-Learning and Learning Objects http://ijklo.org/	America
25	Interdisciplinary Journal of Information, Knowledge, and Management http://www.ijikm.org/	America
26	International Journal of Communication http://ijoc.org/ojs/index.php/ijoc/about/editorialPolicies#focusAndScope	America
27	International Journal of Computer Science and Information Technology http://airccse.org/journal/ijcsit.html	America
28	International Journal of Doctoral Studies (IJDS) http://ijds.org/	America
29	International Journal of Legal Information http://scholarship.law.cornell.edu/ijli/vol33/iss1/	America
30	International Journal of Multimedia and Its Applications http://airccse.org/journal/ijma_index.html	America
31	Internet Writing Journal http://www.internetwritingjournal.com/	America
32	Issues in Informing Science and Information Technology http://iisit.org/	America
33	Issues in Science and Technology Librarianship http://www.library.ucsb.edu/istl/ Or http://www.istl.org/	America
34	JEP: The Journal of Electronic Publishing http://www.journalofelectronicpublishing.org/	America

35	JLIS.it Italian Journal of Library and Information Science http://leo.cilea.it/index.php/jlis/article/view/4539/4416	America
36	Journal of East Asian Libraries http://www.lib.byu.edu/dlib/spc/jeal/	America
37	Journal of Educational Media & Library Sciences http://joemls.tku.edu.tw/index_e.htm	America
38	Journal of eLiteracy http://www.jelit.org/index.html	America
39	Journal of Information Law and Technology http://www2.warwick.ac.uk/fac/soc/law/elj/jilt/ or European Journal of Law and Technology http://ejlt.org//issue/archive	America
40	Journal of Information, Information Technology, and Organizations http://jiito.org/	America
41	Journal of Internet Cataloguing http://www.internetcataloging.com/home.html	America
42	Journal of Library Innovation http://www.libraryinnovation.org/about/contact	America
43	Journal of Staff Development http://learningforward.org/publications/jsd#.UUQguzcynUc	America
44	Journal of Technology Studies http://scholar.lib.vt.edu/ejournals/JOTS/	America
45	Journal of the American Medical Informatics Association http://www.pubmedcentral.nih.gov/tocrender.fcgi?action=archive&journal=76	America
46	Journal of the Association for History and Computing http://quod.lib.umich.edu/j/jahc/browse.html	America
47	Journal of the European Association for Health Information and Libraries http://www.eahil.net/journal/	America
48	Journal of the Medical Library association http://www.ncbi.nlm.nih.gov/pmc/journals/93/	America
49	Journal of Virtual Worlds Research http://www.jvwresearch.org/index.html	America
50	Law Library Journal http://www.aallnet.org/products/pub_journal.asp	America
51	Library Journal http://www.libraryjournal.com	America
52	Library Philosophy and Practice	America

	http://www.webpages.uidaho.edu/~mbolin/lpp.htm	
53	Library Resources & Technical Services (LRTS) http://alcts.metapress.com/home/main.mpx	America
54	Library Student Journal http://www.librarystudentjournal.org/index.php/lsj/index	America
55	Malaysian Journal of Library & Information Sciencehttp://ejum.fsktm.um.edu.my/VolumeListing.aspx?JournalID=3	America
56	MC Journal: The Journal of Academic Media Librarianship http://wings.buffalo.edu/publications/mcjrnl/	America
57	Mississippi Libraries http://www.misslib.org/index.php/publications/mississipp-libraries/	America
58	MLA Forum http://www.mlaforum.org/	America
59	North Carolina Libraries http://www.ncl.ecu.edu/index.php/NCL	America
60	Northwestern Journal of Technology and Intellectual Property http://www.law.northwestern.edu/journals/njtip/issues.htm	America
61	RBM Journal of Rare Books , Manuscripts, and Cultural Heritage http://rbm.acrl.org/content/2/2	America
62	Research Management Review http://www.ncura.edu/content/news/rmr/archive.php	America
63	School Library Journal Online http://www.schoollibraryjournal.com/	America
64	School Library Research http://www.ala.org/aasl/slr	America
65	Special Libraries http://www.sla.org/content/shop/speclibs.cfm#1910	America
66	Studies in Bibliography http://etext.lib.virginia.edu/bsuva/sb	America
67	Technological Librarianship: An Online Journal of the American Theological Library Association http://journal.atla.com/ojs/index.php/theolib/index	America
68	Technology Electronic Reviews (TER) http://www.ala.org/lita/publications/archive/ter	America

69	Texas library journal http://www.txla.org/TLJ	America
70	The Bonefolder: An outgrowth of the Book Arts Web http://www.philobiblon.com/bonefolder/	America
71	Code4Lib Journal http://journal.code4lib.org/	America
72	The Idaho Librarian: A Publication of the Idaho Library Association http://www.idaholibraries.org/idlibrarian/index.php/idaho-librarian/index	America
73	The Journal of the Rutgers University Library http://jrul.libraries.rutgers.edu/index.php/jrul/index	America
74	The Public Access Computer Systems Review http://epress.lib.uh.edu/pr/pacsrev.html#history	America
75	Urban Library Journal http://lacuny.cuny.edu/ulj/	America
76	Virginia Libraries http://scholar.lib.vt.edu/ejournals/VALib/	America
77	Webology http://www.webology.ir/	America
78	World Libraries http://www.worlib.org/	America
79	ALAN Review http://scholar.lib.vt.edu/ejournals/ALAN/	America
80	Journal of Philippine Librarianship http://journals.upd.edu.ph/index.php/jpl/issue/current	Asia (Philippine)
81	Annals of Library & Information Studies http://nopr.niscair.res.in/	Asia (India)
82	DESIDOC Journal of Library & Information Science http://publications.drdo.gov.in/ojs/index.php/djlit/index	Asia (India)
83	International Journal of Communication Networks and Information Security http://www.ijcnis.org/index.php/ijcnis	Asia (Pakistan)
84	Journal of Digital Information http://jodi.ecs.soton.ac.uk/r or http://journals.tdl.org/jodi	Europe (UK)
85	Australian Academic and Research Libraries http://www.alia.org.au/publishing/aarl/index.html	Europe
86	Christian Library Journal http://www.christianlibraryj.org/pdf/index.htm	Europe
87	Cites & Insights: Crawford at Large http://citesandinsights.info/citoc.htm	Europe
88	Computer and Information Science http://journal.ccsenet.org/index.php/cis/index	Europe

89	Cybermetrics : International Journal of Scientometrics, Informetrics and Bibliometrics http://www.cindoc.csic.es/cybermetrics/	Europe
90	Data Science Journal http://www.jstage.jst.go.jp/browse/dsj	Europe
91	DIGITHUM: The Humanities in Digital Age http://www.uoc.edu/digithum/7/eng/numeros.html	Europe
92	EBIB Electronic Information Bulletin for librarians http://ebib.info/biuletyn/	Europe
93	E-JASL: The Electronic Journal of Academic and Special Librarianship http://southernlibrarianship.icaap.org/	Europe
94	Electronic Journal on Information Systems in Developing Countries http://www.ejisdc.org/ojs2/index.php/ejisdc	Europe
95	Electronic Transactions on Artificial Intelligence http://www.ida.liu.se/ext/etai/	Europe
96	European Journal of ePractice http://www.epracticejournal.eu/	Europe
97	Evidence Based Library and Information Practice http://ejournals.library.ualberta.ca/index.php/EBLIP/index	Europe
98	Health Information and Libraries Journal http://www3.interscience.wiley.com/journal/120118368/grouphome/home.html	Europe
99	High Energy Physics Libraries Webzine http://library.web.cern.ch/library/Webzine/index.shtml	Europe
100	Human IT: Journal for Information Technology Studies as a Human Science http://etjanst.hb.se/bhs/ith//info-eng.htm	Europe
101	IFLA Journal http://www.ifla.org/V/iflaj/index.htm	Europe
102	Informatica Economica Journal http://revistaie.ase.ro/index.html	Europe
103	Information for Social Change http://libr.org/isc/journal.html	Europe
104	Information Research: An International Electronic Journal http://informationr.net/ir/	Europe
105	Information Scotland: The Journal of the Chartered Institute of Library and Information Professionals in Scotland http://www.slainte.org.uk/publications/serials/infoscot/vol1(1)/vol1(1)contents.html	Europe

106	International Journal of Computer and Information Engineering http://www.waset.org/journals/ijcie/	Europe
107	International Journal of Digital Curation http://www.ijdc.net/./ijdc/issue/current	Europe
108	International Journal of Library and Information Science http://www.academicjournals.org/ijlis/index.htm	Europe
109	International Journal of Special Libraries http://forge.fh-potsdam.de/~IFLA/INSPEL/intro.htm	Europe
110	International Review of Information Ethics http://www.i-r-i-e.net/	Europe
111	International Review of Research in Open and Distance Learning http://www.irrodl.org/index.php/irrodl	Europe
112	Interpersonal Computing and Technology Journal http://www.helsinki.fi/science/optek/#byissue	Europe
113	IT&Society http://www.itandsociety.org/index.html	Europe
114	ITALICS: Innovations in Teaching and Learning in Information and Computer Sciences http://www.ics.heacademy.ac.uk/italics/	Europe
115	Journal of Artificial Intelligence Research http://www.jair.org/	Europe
116	Journal of Health Informatics in Developing Countries http://www.jhidc.org/index.php/jhidc	Europe
117	Journal of Information Literacy http://ojs.lboro.ac.uk/ojs/index.php/JIL/index	Europe
118	Journal of Information Technology Education (JITE: Research) http://www.informingscience.us/icarus/journals/jiteresearch/publications	Europe
119	Journal of Knowledge Management Practice http://www.tlainc.com/boutjkmp.htm	Europe
120	Journal of Medical Internet Research http://www.jmir.org/	Europe
121	Learned Publishing http://www.ingentaconnect.com/content/alpsp/lp	Europe
122	Library & Information Research: Research into Practice for Information & Library Services http://www.lirgjournal.org.uk/lir/ojs/index.php/lir	Europe
123	LIBRI: International Journal of Libraries and Information	Europe

	Services http://www.librijournal.org/	
124	MELA Notes: The Journal of the Middle East Librarians Association http://www.mela.us/MELANotes/MELANotesIntro.html	Europe
125	Multimedia Information and Technology Journal (MmIT) http://www.cilip.org.uk/get-involved/special-interest-groups/multimedia/journal/pages/default.aspx	Europe
126	New Knowledge Environments http://journals.uvic.ca/index.php/INKE	Europe
127	NPO Journal/NPO E-Journal http://www.bl.uk/blpac/publicationsjournals.html	Europe
128	Partnership: The Canadian Journal of Library and Information Practice and Research http://journal.lib.uoguelph.ca/index.php/perj/index	Europe
129	Progressive Librarian http://libr.org/pl/	Europe
130	Scandinavian Public Library Quarterly http://www.splq.info/	Europe
131	School libraries in Canada (SLIC): A Journal of the Canadian Association for School Libraries http://www.clatoolbox.ca/casl/slic/links.html	Europe
132	Simile: Studies in Media and Information Literacy Education http://utpjournals.metapress.com/content/120764/	Europe
133	South African Journal of Information Management http://www.sajim.co.za/index.php/sajim/issue/current	Europe
134	African Journal of Information & Communication Technology http://epress.lib.uts.edu.au/ojs/index.php/ajict/	Oceania (Australia)
135	Australian Journal of Information Systems http://dl.acs.org.au/index.php/ajis/about	Oceania (Australia)
136	Australian Library Journal http://alia.org.au/publishing/alj/	Oceania (Australia)
137	Electronic Journal of Health Informatics http://www.ejhi.net/ojs/index.php/ejhi	Oceania (Australia)
138	Journal of Research and Practice in Information Technology http://ws.acs.org.au/jrpit/JRPIT_Volumes.html	Oceania (Australia)
139	LASIE: Library Automated Systems Information Exchange http://search.informit.com.au/browseJournalTitle;res=E-	Oceania (Australia)

	LIBRARY;issn=0047-3774	
140	LIBRES: Library and Information Science Research Electronic Journal http://libres.curtin.edu.au/	Oceania (Australia)
141	The International Journal of Database Management Systems http://airccse.org/journal/ijdms/ijdms.html	Oceania (Australia)
142	The International Journal of Managing Information Technology http://airccse.org/journal/ijmit/ijmit.html	Oceania (Australia)
143	International Journal of Managing Public Sector Information and Communication Technologies http://airccse.org/journal/mpict/ijmpict.html	Oceania (Australia)
144	Journal of Information Architecture http://journalofia.org/archives/	Oceania (New Zealand)
145	LIBER Quarterly Journal of European Research Libraries http://liber.library.uu.nl/index.html	Oceania (New Zealand)

E-Magazines

1	AALL Spectrum http://www.aallnet.org/main-menu/Publications/spectrum	America
2	American Libraries http://americanlibrariesmagazine.org/	America
3	Book business http://www.bookbusinessmag.com/	America
4	Book Links http://www.ala.org/ala/aboutala/offices/publishing/booklinks/archiveonline/archive_of_online_articles.cfm	America
5	CHOICE http://www.ala.org/ala/mgrps/divs/acrl/publications/choice/previousissues/previousissues.cfm	America
6	Computer in Libraries http://www.infotoday.com/cilmag/default.shtml	America
7	E-Content http://www.ecmag.net/	America
8	EDUCAUSE Review http://www.educause.edu/	America
9	Ex Libris http://marylaine.com/exlibris/	America
10	Information Today http://www.infotoday.com/IT/nov08/index.shtml	America
11	Knowledge Management World http://www.kmworld.com/index.cfm	America

12	Library Juice http://libr.org/juice/	America
13	Link-Up http://www.infotoday.com/linkup/default.shtml	America
14	Online http://www.infotoday.com/online/default.shtml	America
15	Searcher: The Magazine for Database Professionals http://www.infotoday.com/searcher/default.asp	America
16	The Bulletin of the American Society for Information Science and Technology http://www.asis.org/bulletin.html	America
17	The Marginal http://www.gslis.mcgill.ca/marginal/	America
18	Virginia Tech Magazine http://www.vtmagazine.vt.edu/	America
19	Access http://www.aardvarknet.info/access/number46/index.cfm	Asia
20	Ariadne http://www.ariadne.ac.uk/	Europe
21	Cultivate Interactive http://www.cultivate-int.org/index-2.html	Europe
22	D-Lib Magazine http://www.dlib.org/dlib/september08/09contents.html	Europe
23	Exploit Interactive http://www.exploit-lib.org/	Europe
24	Provenance http://www.provenance.ca/about-provenance/index.html	Europe
25	Research Information http://www.researchinformation.info/	Europe
26	inCite http://alia.org.au/publishing/incite/archive.html	Oceania (Australia)

Newsletters and other E-Resources

1	ABAA Newsletter http://hq.abaa.org/books/antiquarian/abaapages/newsletter	America
2	Abbey Newsletter http://cool.conservation-us.org/byorg/abbey/an/	America
3	Against the grain http://www.against-the-grain.com/d/TOC	America
4	ALAWON. The ALA Washington Office Electronic Newsline http://www.ala.org/ala/aboutala/offices/wo/washnews/archivea/archive.cfm	America
5	ARL: A bimonthly newsletter for library issues and action http://www.arl.org/resources/pubs/br/index.shtml	America

6	Business and Finance Division Bulletin http://units.sla.org/division/dbf/resources/bulletin.html	America
7	CIT Infobits http://serials.infomotions.com/infobits/	America
8	Conserline http://www.loc.gov/acq/conser/consrlin.html	America
9	Internet on a Disk http://www.samizdat.com/ioad.html	America
10	LC Cataloging Newsline http://www.loc.gov/catdir/lccn/	America
11	MLS: Marketing Library Services http://www.infotoday.com/MLS/default.shtml	America
12	NLM Technical Bulletin http://www.nlm.nih.gov/pubs/techbull/current_issue.html	America
13	RLG DigiNews http://www.oclc.org/programs/publications/newsletters/diginews.htm	America
14	SPARC Open Access Newsletter or Free Online Scholarship Newsletter http://www.earlham.edu/~peters/fos/index.htm	America
15	The Wired Librarian's Newsletter http://www.wiredlibrarian.com/wln/wlnfront.htm	America
16	Information today and Tomorrow http://www.dsir.gov.in/pubs/itt/index.htm	Asia (India)
17	ALCTS Network News http://bubl.ac.uk/archive/journals/alctsnn/	Europe
18	Biblio-Tech Review http://www.ringgold.com/biblio-tech/si_pd.cfm?pid=2	Europe
19	Cataloging and Classification Quarterly http://bubl.ac.uk/archive/journals/cacq/	Europe
20	Free Pint http://www.freepint.com/	Europe
21	Internet Resources Newsletter http://www.hw.ac.uk/libwww/irn/irn.html	Europe
22	Serials E-News http://www.ringgold.com/UKSG/si_pd.cfm	Europe
23	Sprouts: Working Papers on Information Systems http://sprouts.aisnet.org/home.html	Europe
24	Biblia's Warrior Librarian Weekly http://warriorlibrarian.com/ARCHIVE/00archives.html	Oceania (Australia)

E-Resources published from different Geographical Region have their own weightage &potency. Mostly E-resources are published from American region compare to others. The region is Categorize in to four regions, American E-Resource 115, European E-Resources 65, Oceania E-Resources 14, and Asian E-Resources 6.

Summary Table: Distribution of E-Resources by Geographical Areas

Sl. No.	Geographical E-resources	No
1	America	112
2	Europe	63
3	Oceania	14
4	Asia	6
	Total	**195**

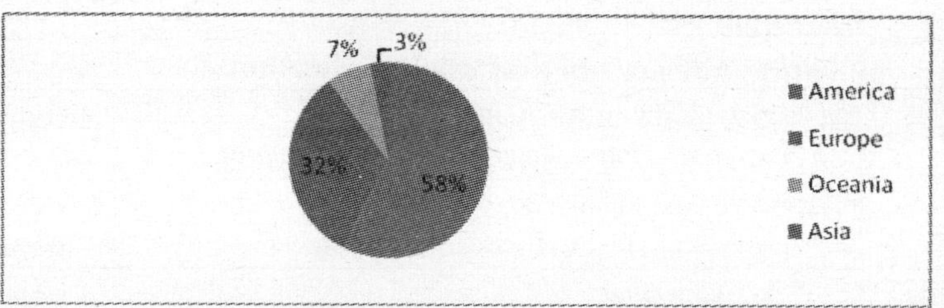

Fig: E-Resources in Four Geographical Regions

These Chart Shows Areas, American E-Resource are 58%, European E-Resources are 32%, Oceania E-Resources 7%, and Asian E-Resources are 3%.

Summary Table: Distribution of American E-Resources

Researcher has categorize 112 E-Resources American Geographical Areas, American

E-Journals are 81, American E-Magazines are 19, and American E-Newsletters are 15.

S.N	American E-Resources	No	
1	American Journals	79	(145)
2	American Magazines	18	(26)
3	American Newsletter	15	(24)
	Total	**112**	**(195)**

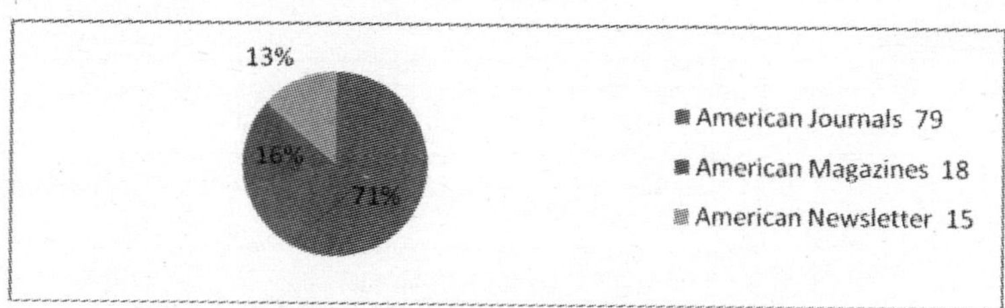

Fig.: E-Resources in American Geographical Regions

This chart shows that out of Total 145 E-Journals only America Region contributes 79 (54%), Out of total 26 E-Magazines 19(73%), & Out of total E-Newsletters 15 (62%).

3.13. CONTRIBUTION OF COUNTRIES IN OPEN ACCESS E-RESOURCES

E-Journals

SL. No	URL	COUNTRY
1	Special Libraries http://www.sla.org/content/shop/speclibs.cfm#1910	Alexandria, America
2	Agricultural Libraries Information Notes http://webharvest.gov/peth04/20041023101316/http://www.nal.usda.gov/NewAlin/	America
3	American Archivist http://archivists.metapress.com/home/main.mpx	America
4	Current Cites http://lists.webjunction.org/currentcites/	America
5	Electronic Journal of Africana Bibliography http://ir.uiowa.edu/ejab/all_issues.html	America
6	Electronic Journal of Knowledge Management http://www.ejkm.com/	America
7	Information Technology and Libraries http://www.ala.org/ala/mgrps/divs/lita/ital/italinformation.cfm	America
8	International Journal of Computer Science and Information Technology http://airccse.org/journal/ijcsit.html	America
9	International Journal of Doctoral Studies (IJDS) http://ijds.org/	America

10	International Journal of Multimedia and Its Applications http://airccse.org/journal/ijma_index.html	America
11	Issues in Informing Science and Information Technology http://iisit.org/	America
12	Issues in Science and Technology Librarianship http://www.library.ucsb.edu/istl/ Or http://www.istl.org/	America
13	Journal of East Asian Libraries http://www.lib.byu.edu/dlib/spc/jeal/	America
14	Journal of Information Law and Technology http://www2.warwick.ac.uk/fac/soc/law/elj/jilt/ or European Journal of Law and Technology http://ejlt.org//issue/archive	America
15	Journal of the American Medical Informatics Association http://www.pubmedcentral.nih.gov/tocrender.fcgi?action =archive&journal=76	America
16	Journal of the Medical Library association http://www.ncbi.nlm.nih.gov/pmc/journals/93/	America
17	Journal of Virtual Worlds Research http://www.jvwresearch.org/index.html	America
18	MLA Forum http://www.mlaforum.org/	America
19	The Bonefolder: An outgrowth of the Book Arts Web http://www.philobiblon.com/bonefolder/	America
20	Code4Lib Journal http://journal.code4lib.org/	America
21	Urban Library Journal http://lacuny.cuny.edu/ulj/	America
22	Webology http://www.webology.ir/	America
23	DESIDOC Journal of Library & Information Science http://publications.drdo.gov.in/ojs/index.php/djlit/index	Asia (India)
24	International Journal of Communication Networks and Information Security http://www.ijcnis.org/index.php/ijcnis	Asia (Pakistan)
25	Journal of Digital Information http://jodi.ecs.soton.ac.uk/r or http://journals.tdl.org/jodi	UK
26	E-JASL: The Electronic Journal of Academic and Special Librarianship http://southernlibrarianship.icaap.org/	Athabasca, Canada, Europe

27	International Review of Research in Open and Distance Learning http://www.irrodl.org/index.php/irrodl	Athabasca, Europe
28	Texas library journal http://www.txla.org/TLJ	Austin, Texas, America
29	Australian Library Journal http://alia.org.au/publishing/alj/	Australia (Oceania)
30	Australian Academic and Research Libraries http://www.alia.org.au/publishing/aarl/index.html	Barton, Europe
31	JLIS.it Italian Journal of Library and Information Science http://leo.cilea.it/index.php/jlis/article/view/4539/4416	Binghamton, NY
32	International Journal of Computer and Information Engineering http://www.waset.org/journals/ijcie/	Blackpool Victoria Hospital, United Kingdom, Europe
33	Journal of Technology Studies http://scholar.lib.vt.edu/ejournals/JOTS/	Blacksburg, VA, America
34	The Idaho Librarian: A Publication of the Idaho Library Association http://www.idaholibraries.org/idlibrarian/index.php/idaho-librarian/index	Boise, Idaho, America
35	The Journal of the Rutgers University Library http://jrul.libraries.rutgers.edu/index.php/jrul/index	Brunswick, America
36	Informatica Economica Journal http://revistaie.ase.ro/index.html	Bucharest, Romaina, Europe
37	Journal of Library Innovation http://www.libraryinnovation.org/about/contact	Buffalo, New York, America
38	MC Journal: The Journal of Academic Media Librarianship http://wings.buffalo.edu/publications/mcjrnl/	Buffalo, New York, America
39	Journal of Information, Information Technology, and Organizations http://jiito.org/	California, America

40	Information Technologies and International Development http://itidjournal.org/itid	California, America
41	Informing Faculty: An International Journal of Higher Education Discussion Cases http://informingfaculty.org/	California, America
42	Inter-Actions: UCLA Journal of Education and Information Studies http://repositories.cdlib.org/gseis/interactions/	California, America
43	Interdisciplinary Journal of E-Learning and Learning Objects http://ijklo.org/	California, America
44	Interdisciplinary Journal of Information, Knowledge, and Management http://www.ijikm.org/	California, America
45	Journal of Internet Cataloguing http://www.internetcataloging.com/home.html	California, America
46	Journal of the European Association for Health Information and Libraries http://www.eahil.net/journal/	Cambridge, America
47	Computer and Information Science http://journal.ccsenet.org/index.php/cis/index	Canada, Europe
48	Journal of Medical Internet Research http://www.jmir.org/	Canada, Europe
49	Partnership: The Canadian Journal of Library and Information Practice and Research http://journal.lib.uoguelph.ca/index.php/perj/index	Canada, Europe
50	School libraries in Canada (SLIC): A Journal of the Canadian Association for School Libraries http://www.clatoolbox.ca/casl/slic/links.html	Canada, Europe
51	Simile: Studies in Media and Information Literacy Education http://www.utpjournals.com/simile/simile.html	Canada, Europe
52	Journal of Knowledge Management Practice http://www.tlainc.com/boutjkmp.htm	Canada, UK, Europe
53	College and Research Libraries http://crl.acrl.org/	Chicago, America
54	Firstmonday http://firstmonday.org/	Chicago, America
55	Informing Science The International Journal of an Emerging Transdiscipline http://inform.nu/	Chicago, America
56	Law Library Journal http://www.aallnet.org/products/pub_journal.asp	Chicago, America

57	Library Resources & Technical Services (LRTS) http://alcts.metapress.com/home/main.mpx	Chicago, America
58	RBM Journal of Rare Books , Manuscripts, and Cultural Heritage http://rbm.acrl.org/content/2/2	Chicago, America
59	School Library Research http://www.ala.org/aasl/slr	Chicago, America
60	Technological Librarianship: An Online Journal of the American Theological Library Association http://journal.atla.com/ojs/index.php/theolib/index	Chicago, Illinois, America
61	Cites & Insights: Crawford at Large http://citesandinsights.info/citoc.htm	Crawford, Europe
62	World Libraries http://www.worlib.org/	Dominican, America
63	Electronic Transactions on Artificial Intelligence http://www.ida.liu.se/ext/etai/	Europe
64	High Energy Physics Libraries Webzine http://library.web.cern.ch/library/Webzine/index.shtml	Europe
65	ITALICS: Innovations in Teaching and Learning in Information and Computer Sciences http://www.ics.heacademy.ac.uk/italics/	Europe
66	Interpersonal Computing and Technology Journal http://www.helsinki.fi/science/optek/#byissue	Finland, Europe
67	Scandinavian Public Library Quarterly http://www.splq.info/	Finland, Europe
68	Journal of Artificial Intelligence Research http://www.jair.org/	Florence
69	Christian Library Journal http://www.christianlibraryj.org/pdf/index.htm	Florence, Europe
70	International Journal of Special Libraries http://forge.fh-potsdam.de/~IFL4/INSPEL/intro.htm	Germany, Europe
71	International Review of Information Ethics http://www.i-r-i-e.net/	Germany, Europe
72	North Carolina Libraries http://www.ncl.ecu.edu/index.php/NCL	Greenville, NC, America

73	Journal of Educational Media & Library Sciences http://joemls.tku.edu.tw/index_e.htm	Harold B. Lee Library, Provo, UT, America
74	Electronic Journal on Information Systems in Developing Countries http://www.ejisdc.org/ojs2/index.php/ejisdc	Hong Kong, Europe
75	The Public Access Computer Systems Review http://epress.lib.uh.edu/pr/pacsrev.html#history	Houston, America
76	Annals of Library & Information Studies http://nopr.niscair.res.in/	India (Asia)
77	International Journal of Legal Information http://scholarship.law.cornell.edu/ijli/vol33/iss1/	Ithaca, NY America
78	Australian Journal of Information Systems http://dl.acs.org.au/index.php/ajis/about	KANSAS, America
79	Information Technology and Disabilities http://people.rit.edu/easi/itd.htm	Lake Forest CA , America
80	NPO Journal/NPO E-Journal http://www.bl.uk/blpac/publicationsjournals.html	London, Europe
81	Library & Information Research: Research into Practice for Information & Library Services http://www.lirg.org.uk/lir/ojs/index.php/lir	London, UK, Europe
82	International Journal of Communication http://ijoc.org/ojs/index.php/ijoc/about/editorialPolicies#focusAndScope	Los Angeles, CA, America
83	Malaysian Journal of Library & Information Sciencehttp://ejum.fsktm.um.edu.my/VolumeListing.aspx?JournalID=3	Malaya, America
84	Colby Quarterly (formerly: Colby Library Quarterly) http://digitalcommons.colby.edu/	Mayflower Hill, Waterville, ME, America
85	JEP: The Journal of Electronic Publishing http://www.journalofelectronicpublishing.org/	Michigan, America
86	Mississippi Libraries http://www.misslib.org/index.php/publications/mississippi-libraries/	Mississippi, America

87	MELA Notes: The Journal of the Middle East Librarians Association http://www.mela.us/MELANotes/MELANotesIntro.html	MLISSA, Europe
88	LIBRI: International Journal of Libraries and Information Services http://www.librijournal.org/	Muchen, Germany, Europe
89	IFLA Journal http://www.ifla.org/V/iflaj/index.htm	Netherland , Europe
90	School Library Journal Online http://www.schoollibraryjournal.com/	New York, America
91	Library Journal http://www.libraryjournal.com	New York, NY, America
92	Learned Publishing http://www.ingentaconnect.com/content/alpsp/lp	North America and Germany
93	Northwestern Journal of Technology and Intellectual Property http://www.law.northwestern.edu/journals/njtip/issues.htm	Northwestern, America
94	Electronic Journal of Health Informatics http://www.ejhi.net/ojs/index.php/ejhi	Oceania (Australia)
95	Journal of Research and Practice in Information Technology http://acs.org.au/jrpit/index.html	Oceania (Australia)
96	LASIE: Library Automated Systems Information Exchange http://search.informit.com.au/browseJournalTitle;res=E-LIBRARY;issn=0047-3774	Oceania (Australia)
97	LIBRES: Library and Information Science Research Electronic Journal http://libres.curtin.edu.au/	Oceania (Australia)
98	Journal of Information Architecture http://journalofia.org/archives/	Oceania (New Zealand)
99	LIBER Quarterly Journal of European Research Libraries http://liber.library.uu.nl/index.html	Oceania (New Zealand)
100	Journal of Staff Development http://learningforward.org/publications/jsd#.UUQguzcynUc	Oxford, OH, America
101	EBIB Electronic Information Bulletin for librarians	Poland

	http://ebib.info/biuletyn/	
102	Collaborative Librarianship http://www.collaborativelibrarianship.org/index.html	Regis University Regis Blvd. Denver, America
103	Progressive Librarian http://libr.org/pl/	Ruskin, FL, Europe
104	Digital Document Quarterly http://home.pacbell.net/hgladney/ddqstart.htm	Saratoga, CA , America
105	Journal of Health Informatics in Developing Countries http://www.jhidc.org/index.php/jhidc	Scotland , United Kingdom, Europe
106	Information Scotland: The Journal of the Chartered Institute of Library and Information Professionals in Scotland http://www.slainte.org.uk/publications/serials/infoscot/vol1(1)/vol1(1)contents.html	Scotland, Europe
107	South African Journal of Information Management http://www.sajim.co.za/index.php/sajim/issue/current	South Africa
108	Cybermetrics : International Journal of Scientometrics, Informetrics and Bibliometrics http://www.cindoc.csic.es/cybermetrics/	Spain, Europe
109	European Journal of ePractice http://www.epracticejournal.eu/	Spain, Europe
110	IT&Society http://www.itandsociety.org/index.html	Stanford
111	Human IT: Journal for Information Technology Studies as a Human Science http://etjanst.hb.se/bhs/ith//info-eng.htm	Sweden, Europe
112	Information Research: An International Electronic Journal http://informationr.net/ir/	Sweden, United Kingdom, Europe
113	African Journal of Information & Communication Technology http://epress.lib.uts.edu.au/ojs/index.php/ajict/	Sydney, Australia (Oceania)
114	Journal of eLiteracy http://www.jelit.org/index.html	Taiwan
115	Current Issues in Education http://cie.asu.edu/index.php	Tempe AZ,

		America
116	Internet Writing Journal http://www.internetwritingjournal.com/	Texas, America
117	DIGITHUM: The Humanities in Digital Age http://www.uoc.edu/digithum/7/eng/numeros.html	Tibidabo, Europe 08035 Barcelona
118	Communications in Information Literacy http://www.comminfolit.org/index.php/cil/issue/archive	Tulsa, OK, America
119	Health Information and Libraries Journal http://www3.interscience.wiley.com/journal/120118368/grouphome/home.html	UK, Europe
120	Information for Social Change http://libr.org/isc/journal.html	UK, Europe
121	Multimedia Information and Technology Journal (MmIT) http://www.cilip.org.uk/get-involved/special-interest-groups/multimedia/journal/pages/default.aspx	UK, Europe
122	Data Science Journal http://www.jstage.jst.go.jp/browse/dsj	Unesco, Europe
123	International Journal of Digital Curation http://www.ijdc.net/./ijdc/issue/current	United Kingdom, Europe
124	Journal of Information Technology Education (JITE: Research) http://www.informingscience.us/icarus/journals/jiteresearch/publications	United Kingdom, Europe
125	Library Philosophy and Practice http://www.webpages.uidaho.edu/~mbolin/lpp.htm	United States
126	B Sides http://ir.uiowa.edu/bsides/	United States, America
127	Chinese Librarianship: An International Electronic Journal http://www.iclc.us/cliej/	United States, America
128	Coordinates: Online Journal of the Map and Geography Round Table of the American Library Association. Series A and B http://www.sunysb.edu/libmap/coordinates.htm	United States, America
129	Technology Electronic Reviews (TER) http://www.ala.org/lita/publications/archive/ter	United States,

		America
130	Journal of Information Literacy http://ojs.lboro.ac.uk/ojs/index.php/JIL/index	Universities of Warwic, United Kingdom, Europe
131	Evidence Based Library and Information Practice http://ejournals.library.ualberta.ca/index.php/EBLIP/index	University of Alberta Edmonton, Europe
132	Library Student Journal http://www.librarystudentjournal.org/index.php/lsj/index	University of Illinois, Urbana-Champaign, America
133	Journal of the Association for History and Computing http://quod.lib.umich.edu/j/jahc/browse.html	University of Michigan, America
134	International Journal of Library and Information Science http://www.academicjournals.org/ijlis/index.htm	Victoria Island, Lagos, Europe
135	The International Journal of Database Management Systems http://airccse.org/journal/ijdms/ijdms.html	Victoria, Australia, Oceania (Australia)
136	The International Journal of Managing Information Technology http://airccse.org/journal/ijmit/ijmit.html	Victoria, Australia, Oceania (Australia)
137	New Knowledge Environments http://journals.uvic.ca/index.php/INKE	Victoria, Europe
138	Studies in Bibliography http://etext.lib.virginia.edu/bsuva/sb	Virginia, America
139	Virginia Libraries http://scholar.lib.vt.edu/ejournals/VALib/	Virginia, America
140	Alki: The Washington Library Association Journal http://www.wla.org/alki/	Washington, America

141	EDUCAUSE Quarterly http://www.educause.edu/eq	Washington, D.C. America
142	Research Management Review http://www.ncura.edu/content/news/rmr/archive.php	Washington, D.C. America
143	ALAN Review http://scholar.lib.vt.edu/ejournals/ALAN/	Blacksburg, VA, America
144	Journal of Philippine Librarianship http://journals.upd.edu.ph/index.php/jpl/issue/current	Philippine, Manila (Asia)
145	International Journal of Managing Public Sector Information and Communication Technologies http://airccse.org/journal/mpict/ijmpict.html	Victoria, Australia, Oceania (Australia)

E-Magazines

1	AALL Spectrum http://www.aallnet.org/main-menu/Publications/spectrum	America
2	Computer in Libraries http://www.infotoday.com/cilmag/default.shtml	America
3	D-Lib Magazine http://www.dlib.org/dlib/september08/09contents.html	America
4	E-Content http://www.ecmag.net/	America
5	Ex Libris http://marylaine.com/exlibris/	America
6	Information Today http://www.infotoday.com/IT/nov08/index.shtml	America
7	Knowledge Management World http://www.kmworld.com/index.cfm	America
8	Library Juice http://libr.org/juice/	America
9	Link-Up http://www.infotoday.com/linkup/default.shtml	America
10	Online http://www.infotoday.com/online/default.shtml	America
11	Searcher: The Magazine for Database Professionals http://www.infotoday.com/searcher/default.asp	America
12	Access http://www.aardvarknet.info/access/number46/index.cfm	England, UK

13	Ariadne http://www.ariadne.ac.uk/	Bath, UK, Europe
14	Provenance http://www.provenance.ca/about-provenance/index.html	Canada, Europe
15	American Libraries http://americanlibrariesmagazine.org/	Chicago, America
16	Book Links http://www.ala.org/ala/aboutala/offices/publishing/booklinks/archiveonline/archive_of_online_articles.cfm	Chicago, America
17	CHOICE http://www.ala.org/ala/mgrps/divs/acrl/publications/choice/ previousissues/previousissues.cfm	Chicago, America
18	The Bulletin of the American Society for Information Science and Technology http://www.asis.org/bulletin.html	Maryland, America
19	The Marginal http://www.gslis.mcgill.ca/marginal/	Montreal, Quebec, America
20	inCite http://alia.org.au/publishing/incite/archive.html	Oceania (Australia)
21	Book business http://www.bookbusinessmag.com/	Philadelphia, PA, America
22	Cultivate Interactive http://www.cultivate-int.org/index-2.html	UK, Europe
23	Exploit Interactive http://www.exploit-lib.org/	UK, Europe
24	Research Information http://www.researchinformation.info/	UK, Europe
25	Virginia Tech Magazine http://www.vtmagazine.vt.edu/	Virginia
26	EDUCAUSE Review http://www.educause.edu/	Washington, D.C. America

Newsletters and other E-Resources

1	Against the grain http://www.against-the-grain.com/d/TOC	America
2	Business and Finance Division Bulletin http://units.sla.org/division/dbf/resources/bulletin.html	America

3	NLM Technical Bulletin http://www.nlm.nih.gov/pubs/techbull/current_issue.html	America
4	SPARC Open Access Newsletter or Free Online Scholarship Newsletter http://www.earlham.edu/~peters/fos/index.htm	America
5	Sprouts: Working Papers on Information Systems http://sprouts.aisnet.org/home.html	Amsterdam Netherlands, Europe
6	Free Pint http://www.freepint.com/	Ashford Middlesex TW15 2QN United Kingdom,
7	Information today and Tomorrow http://www.dsir.gov.in/pubs/itt/index.htm	Asia (India)
8	Biblio-Tech Review http://www.ringgold.com/biblio-tech/si_pd.cfm?pid=2	Bristol, UK, Europe
9	CIT Infobits http://serials.infomotions.com/infobits/	Chapel Hill, America
10	ALAWON. The ALA Washington Office Electronic Newsline http://www.ala.org/ala/aboutala/offices/wo/washnews/archivea/archive.cfm	Washington, America
11	The Wired Librarian's Newsletter http://www.wiredlibrarian.com/wln/wlnfront.htm	Chicago, America
12	RLG DigiNews http://www.oclc.org/programs/publications/newsletters/diginews.htm	Dublin, Ohio, America
13	MLS: Marketing Library Services http://www.infotoday.com/MLS/default.shtml	Medford, NJ, America
14	ABAA Newsletter http://hq.abaa.org/books/antiquarian/abaapages/newsletter	New York, America
15	Abbey Newsletter http://cool.conservation-us.org/byorg/abbey/an/	Standford, New York, America
16	Serials E-News http://www.ringgold.com/UKSG/si_pd.cfm	UK, Europe
17	ALCTS Network News http://bubl.ac.uk/archive/journals/alctsnn/	UK, Europe
18	Cataloging and Classification Quarterly http://bubl.ac.uk/archive/journals/cacq/	UK, Europe

19	Internet Resources Newsletter http://www.hw.ac.uk/libwww/irn/irn.html	UK, Europe
20	ARL: A bimonthly newsletter for library issues and action http://www.arl.org/resources/pubs/br/index.shtml	Washington D.C. America
21	Conserline http://www.loc.gov/acq/conser/consrlin.html	Washington D.C. America
22	LC Cataloging Newsline http://www.loc.gov/catdir/lccn/	Washington, DC America
23	Biblia's Warrior Librarian Weekly http://warriorlibrarian.com/ARCHIVE/00archives.html	Wentworthville NSW , Oceania (Australia)
24	Internet on a Disk http://www.samizdat.com/ioad.html	West Roxbury, MA (Boston), America

Table shows that Maximum 112 Free E-Resources are covered by American Countries. Out of 112 Chicago contributes 13, followed by Washington 8, California 7, New York 6, Virginia 3, besides that countries from America (Names are not specified) 37 and Single country both contributes 38 respectively.

Summary Table: Contribution in Open Access E-Resources by American Countries

Sl. No.	American Countries	No
1	Chicago	13
2	Washington	8
3	California	7
4	New York	6
5	Virginia	3
6	America but not specify Country Name	37
7	Single Country	38
	Total	**112**

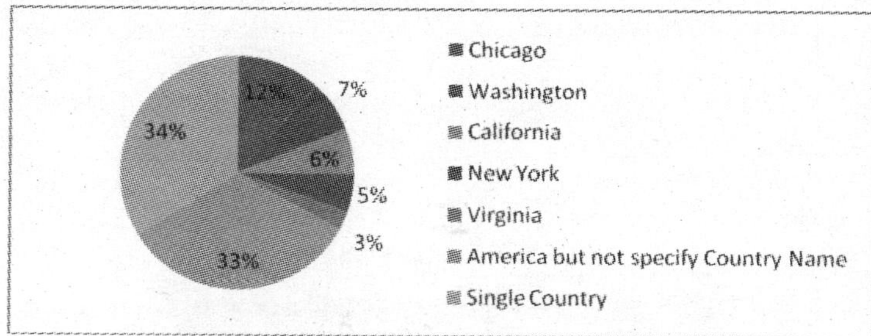

Fig: Geographical Distribution of Free Resources

American Countries Contribution in Open Access E-Resources chart shows that Maximum 112 (58%) Open Access E-Resources are covered by American Countries. Out of them Chicago contributes (12%), followed by Washington (7%) California (6%), New York (5%), Virginia (3%), besides that countries from America but not specified country name and Single country contributes (34%) respectively.

3.14. RANKING OF OPEN ACCESS E-JOURNALS

Sl. No.	Title	Ranking
1	Journal of Knowledge Management Practice http://www.tlainc.com/boutjkmp.htm	A 2009 survey to rank the top 21 Knowledge Management and Intellectual Capital academic journals rated JKMP seventh; JKMP was the top rated online open access journal [Bontis, N., & Serenko, A. (2009), A follow-up ranking of academic journals, Journal of Knowledge Management, 13(1), pp.16-26.] And in 2008 another survey, ranked the top 20 Knowledge Management and Intellectual Capital academic journals rated JKMP eighth.
2	Northwestern Journal of Technology and Intellectual Property http://www.law.northwestern.edu/journals/ njtip/ issues.htm	It is among the top ranked intellectual property and technology journals in the country.

3	School Library Research http://www.ala.org/aasl/slr	SLMR is ranked by Deans of Library and Information Science as a respected research journal. See College and Research Libraries July 2005
4	Journal of Medical Internet Research http://www.jmir.org/	The new JMIR Impact Factor released in 2009 is 3.9 by Thomson Reuters Journal Citation
5	Library Resources & Technical Services (LRTS) http://alcts.metapress.com/home/main.mpx	2008: 0.698 (Journal Citation Reports® 2009, published by Thomson Scientific.

Table shows ranking of E-Journals according to Website Information, out of 195 E-Resources Five E-Journals ranked in the highest order.

3.15. E-RESOURCES HAVING SEARCH WITH PERSONALIZATION FEATURE

SL. No.	Title	Search Engine	Personalize
1	College and Research Libraries http://crl.acrl.org/	Y	Y
2	African Journal of Information & Communication Technology http://epress.lib.uts.edu.au/ojs/index.php/ajict/	Y	Y
3	American Archivist http://archivists.metapress.com/home/main.mpx	Y	Y
4	Annals of Library & Information Studies http://nopr.niscair.res.in/	Y	Y
5	Australian Journal of Information Systems http://dl.acs.org.au/index.php/ajis/about	Y	Y
6	Australian Library Journal http://alia.org.au/publishing/alj/	Y	Y
7	B Sides http://ir.uiowa.edu/bsides/	Y	Y
8	Colby Quarterly (formerly: Colby Library Quarterly) http://digitalcommons.colby.edu/	Y	Y
9	Collaborative Librarianship http://www.collaborativelibrarianship.org/index.html	Y	Y

10	Current Cites http://lists.webjunction.org/currentcites/	Y	Y
11	Electronic Journal of Knowledge Management http://www.ejkm.com/	Y	Y
12	European Journal of ePractice http://www.epracticejournal.eu/	Y	Y
13	Evidence Based Library and Information Practice http://ejournals.library.ualberta.ca/index.php/EBLIP/index	Y	Y
14	Firstmonday http://firstmonday.org/	Y	Y
15	Health Information and Libraries Journal http://www3.interscience.wiley.com/journal/120118368/grouphome/home.html	Y	Y
16	Information Technologies and International Development http://itidjournal.org/itid	Y	Y
17	Internet Writing Journal http://www.internetwritingjournal.com/	Y	Y
18	JEP: The Journal of Electronic Publishing http://www.journalofelectronicpublishing.org/	Y	Y
19	JLIS.it Italian Journal of Library and Information Science http://leo.cilea.it/index.php/jlis/article/view/4539/4416	Y	Y
20	Journal of Digital Information http://jodi.ecs.soton.ac.uk/r or http://journals.tdl.org/jodi	Y	Y
21	Journal of East Asian Libraries http://www.lib.byu.edu/dlib/spc/jeal/	Y	Y
22	Journal of the American Medical Informatics Association http://www.pubmedcentral.nih.gov/tocrender.fcgi?action=archive&journal=76	Y	Y
23	Journal of the Association for History and Computing http://quod.lib.umich.edu/j/jahc/browse.html	Y	Y
24	Journal of Virtual Worlds Research http://www.jvwresearch.org/index.html	Y	Y
25	LASIE: Library Automated Systems Information Exchange http://search.informit.com.au/browseJournalTitle;res=E-LIBRARY;issn=0047-3774	Y	Y

26	Learned Publishing http://www.ingentaconnect.com/content/alpsp/lp	Y	Y
27	Library & Information Research: Research into Practice for Information & Library Services http://www.lirgjournal.org.uk/lir/ojs/index.php/lir	Y	Y
28	Library Journal http://www.libraryjournal.com	Y	Y
29	Library Philosophy and Practice http://www.webpages.uidaho.edu/~mbolin/lpp.htm	Y	Y
30	Multimedia Information and Technology Journal (MmIT) http://www.cilip.org.uk/get-involved/special-interest-groups/multimedia/journal/pages/default.aspx	Y	Y
31	New Knowledge Environments http://journals.uvic.ca/index.php/INKE	Y	Y
32	Northwestern Journal of Technology and Intellectual Property http://www.law.northwestern.edu/journals/njtip/issues.htm	Y	Y
33	RBM Journal of Rare Books , Manuscripts, and Cultural Heritage http://rbm.acrl.org/content/2/2	Y	Y
34	School Library Journal Online http://www.schoollibraryjournal.com/	Y	Y
35	South African Journal of Information Management http://www.sajim.co.za/index.php/sajim/issue/current	Y	Y
36	Special Libraries http://www.sla.org/content/shop/speclibs.cfm#1910	Y	Y
37	Technological Librarianship: An Online Journal of the American Theological Library Association http://journal.atla.com/ojs/index.php/theolib/index	Y	Y

E-Magazines

1	AALL Spectrum http://www.aallnet.org/main-menu/Publications/spectrum	Y	Y
2	American Libraries http://americanlibrariesmagazine.org/	Y	Y
3	Ariadne http://www.ariadne.ac.uk/	Y	Y
4	Book business http://www.bookbusinessmag.com/	Y	Y

5	E-Content http://www.ecmag.net/	Y	Y
6	EDUCAUSE Review http://www.educause.edu/	Y	Y
7	Knowledge Management World http://www.kmworld.com/index.cfm	Y	Y
8	Library Juice http://libr.org/juice/	Y	Y
9	Research Information http://www.researchinformation.info/	Y	Y

Newsletters and other E-Resources

1	Against the grain http://www.against-the-grain.com/d/TOC	Y	Y
2	ARL: A bimonthly newsletter for library issues and action http://www.arl.org/resources/pubs/br/index.shtml	Y	Y
3	Free Pint http://www.freepint.com/	Y	Y
4	NLM Technical Bulletin http://www.nlm.nih.gov/pubs/techbull/current_issue.html	Y	Y
5	Sprouts: Working Papers on Information Systems http://sprouts.aisnet.org/home.html	Y	Y

E-Resources having Personalize features mostly prepared by the academicians and researchers because Personalization provides RSS, Marked Item, order History, Alerts etc. Besides that E-resources having Easy searching with keywords are mostly referred by the users for quick access. Sometimes some search has internal search engine to find out accurate information about that particular E-resource. Users mostly choose those E-Resources which are having Searching, Personalization, and both Searching with Personalization. Author has found out that 52 (26%) E-Resources are having Search with Personalize features, E-Journals are 38, E-Magazines are 9, and Other E-Resources are 5.

Summary Table: Distribution of E-Resources having Search with Personalization

S.N.	E-Resources	No	Total E-Res.
1	E-Journals	37	-145
2	E-Magazines	5	-26
3	E-Newsletters	9	-24
	Total	**51**	**195**

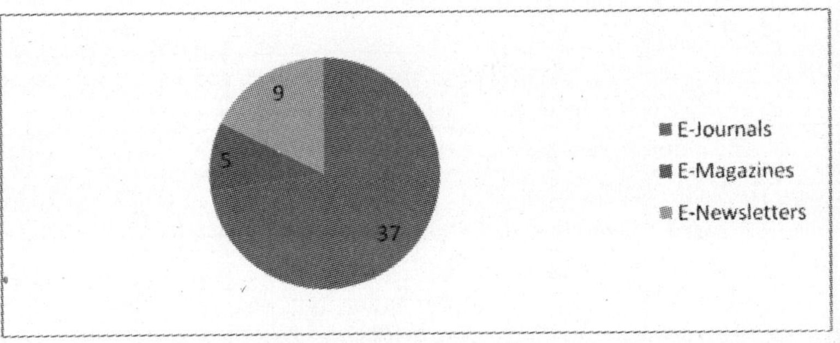

Fig: E-Resources having Search with Personalization Features

This chart shows that out of total 145 E-Journals 37 (25%), Out of total 26 E-Magazines 5 (18%), and Out of total 24 E-Newsletters 9 (37%) have Search with Personalize features.

3.16. OPEN ACCESS E-RESOURCES HAVING PERSONALIZE FACILITY

Author has found out that 62 (31%) E-Resources are having Personalize Features, E-Journals are 47, E-Magazines are 9, and E-Newsletter is 6.

College and Research Libraries http://crl.acrl.org/

African Journal of Information & Communication Technology http://epress.lib.uts.edu.au/ojs/index.php/ajict/

American Archivist http://archivists.metapress.com/ home/main.mpx

Annals of Library & Information Studies http://nopr.niscair.res.in/

Associates: The Electronic Library Support Staff Journal http://associates.ucr.edu/journal/

Australian Library Journal http://alia.org.au/publishing/ alj/

B Sides http://ir.uiowa.edu/bsides/

Colby Quarterly (formerly: Colby Library Quarterly) http:// digitalcommons.colby.edu/

Collaborative Librarianship http://www.collaborative librarianship.org/index.html

Current Cites http://lists.webjunction.org/currentcites/

Current Issues in Education http://cie.asu.edu/index.php

EBIB Electronic Information Bulletin for librarians http:// ebib.info/biuletyn/

EDUCAUSE Quarterly http://www.educause.edu/eq

Electronic Journal of Africana Bibliography http:// ir.uiowa.edu/ejab/all_issues.html

Electronic Journal of Knowledge Management http:// www.ejkm.com/

European Journal of ePractice http://www. epracticejournal.eu/

Evidence Based Library and Information Practice http:// ejournals.library.ualberta.ca/index.php/ EBLIP/index

Firstmonday http://firstmonday.org/

Health Information and Libraries Journal http://www3. interscience.wiley.com/journal/120118368/ grouphome/ home.html

Information Technologies and International Development http://itidjournal.org/itid

Inter-Actions: UCLA Journal of Education and Information Studies http://repositories.cdlib.org/gseis/interactions/

International Journal of Legal Information http:// scholarship.law.cornell.edu/ijli/vol33/iss1/

Internet Writing Journal http://www. internetwriting journal.com/

JEP: The Journal of Electronic Publishing http://www. journalofelectronicpublishing.org/

JLIS.it Italian Journal of Library and Information Science http://leo.cilea.it/index.php/ jlis/article/view/4539/4416

Journal of Digital Information http://jodi.ecs.soton.ac.uk/ r or http://journals.tdl.org/jodi

Journal of East Asian Libraries http://www.lib.byu. edu/dlib/ spc/jeal/

Journal of Information Literacy http://ojs.lboro.ac.uk/ojs/ index.php/JIL/index

Journal of Library Innovation http://www. libraryinnovation.org/about/contact

Journal of Medical Internet Research http://www. jmir.org/

Journal of the American Medical Informatics Association http://www.pubmedcentral.nih.gov/ tocrender.fcgi?action= archive&journal=76

Journal of the Association for History and Computing http:/ /quod.lib.umich.edu/j/jahc/browse.html

Journal of Virtual Worlds Research http:// www.jvwresearch.org/index.html

LASIE: Library Automated Systems Information Exchange http://search.informit.com.au/ browseJournalTitle;res=E-LIBRARY;issn=0047-3774

Learned Publishing http://www.ingentaconnect.com/ content/alpsp/lp

Library & Information Research: Research into Practice for Information & Library Services http://www.lirgjournal. org.uk/lir/ ojs/index.php/lir

Library Journal http://www.libraryjournal.com

Library Philosophy and Practice http://www.webpages.

uidaho.edu/~mbolin/lpp.htm

Multimedia Information and Technology Journal (MmIT) http://www.cilip.org.uk/get-involved/special-interest-groups/multimedia/journal/pages/default.aspx

New Knowledge Environments http://journals.uvic.ca/index.php/INKE

Northwestern Journal of Technology and Intellectual Property http://www.law.northwestern.edu/journals/njtip/issues.htm

RBM Journal of Rare Books , Manuscripts, and Cultural Heritage http://rbm.acrl.org/content/2/2

School Library Journal Online http://www.schoollibrary journal.com/

Simile: Studies in Media and Information Literacy Education http://utpjournals.metapress.com/ content/120764/

South African Journal of Information Management http://www.sajim.co.za/index.php/ sajim/issue/current

Special Libraries http://www.sla.org/content/shop/speclibs.cfm#1910

Technological Librarianship: An Online Journal of the American Theological Library Association http://journal. atla.com/ojs/index.php/theolib/index

E-Magazines

AALL Spectrum http://www.aallnet.org/main-menu/Publications/spectrum

American Libraries http://americanlibrariesmagazine.org/

Ariadne http://www.ariadne.ac.uk/

Book business http://www.bookbusinessmag.com/

E-Content http://www.ecmag.net/

EDUCAUSE Review http://www.educause.edu/

Knowledge Management World http://www.kmworld.com/index.cfm

Library Juice http://libr.org/juice/

Research Information http://www.researchinformation.info/

Newsletters and other E-Resources

Against the grain http://www.against-the-grain.com/ d/TOC

ARL: A Bimonthly Newsletter for Library Issues and Action http://www.arl.org/resources/pubs/br/index.shtml

Free Pint http://www.freepint.com/

NLM Technical Bulletin http://www.nlm.nih.gov/pubs/techbull/current_issue.html

RLG DigiNews http://www.oclc.org/programs/ publications/newsletters/diginews.htm

Sprouts: Working Papers on Information Systems http://sprouts.aisnet.org/home.html

Summary: Distribution of E-Resources having Personalize Features

S.N.	E-Resources	No	Total E-Res.
1	E-Journals	47	-145
2	E-Magazines	9	-26
3	Other E-Resources	6	-24
	Total	62	195

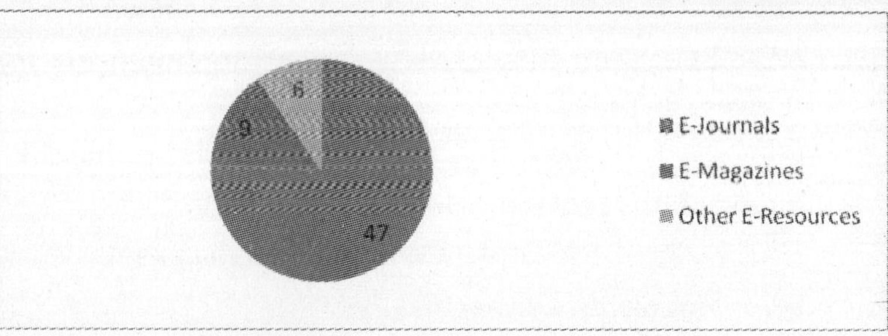

Fig.: E-Resources having Personalize Features

The chart show that out of 145 total E-Resources 47 (32%), Out of total 26 E-Magazines 10 (34%), and Out of total 24 E-

Newsletters 6 (25%) are having Personalize features.

3.17. PEER REVIEWED OPEN ACCESS E-RESOURCES

It is found that Peer Reviewed Open access E-Resources out of 195 E-Resources are 71 (36%) Peer Reviewed E-Resources. Out of 145 E-Journals 71 (48), E-Newsletter 1 (4%).

African Journal of Information & Communication Technology http://epress.lib.uts.edu.au/ojs/ index.php/ajict/

American Archivist http://archivists.metapress.com/ home/ main.mpx

Australian Journal of Information Systems http://dl.acs. org.au/index.php/ajis/about

Australian Academic and Research Libraries http:// www.alia.org.au/publishing/aarl/index.html

B Sides http://ir.uiowa.edu/bsides/

Christian Library Journal http://www.christianlibraryj.org/ pdf/index.htm

Collaborative Librarianship http://www.collaborative librarianship.org/index.html

Communications in Information Literacy http://www. comminfolit.org/index.php/cil/issue/archive

Computer and Information Science http://journal. ccsenet.org/index.php/cis/index

Coordinates : Online Journal of the Map and Geography Round Table of the American Library Association. Series A and B http://www.sunysb.edu/libmap/coordinates.htm

Current Issues in Education http://cie.asu.edu/index.php

Cybermetrics : International Journal of Scientometrics, Informetrics and Bibliometrics http://www.cindoc.csic.es/ cybermetrics/

Data Science Journal http://www.jstage.jst.go.jp/ browse/ dsj

DESIDOC Journal of Library & Information Science http://publications.drdo.gov.in/ ojs/index.php/djlit/index

EDUCAUSE Quarterly http://www.educause.edu/eq

Electronic Journal of Africana Bibliography http://ir.uiowa.edu/ejab/all_issues.html

Electronic Journal of Health Informatics http://www.ejhi.net/ojs/index.php/ejhi

Electronic Journal of Knowledge Management http://www.ejkm.com/

European Journal of ePractice http://www. epractice journal.eu/

Evidence Based Library and Information Practice http://ejournals.library.ualberta.ca/ index.php/EBLIP/index

Firstmonday http://firstmonday.org/

Health Information and Libraries Journal http://www3.interscience.wiley.com/journal/120118368/grouphome/home.html

Information Research: An International Electronic Journal http://informationr.net/ir/

Information Technologies and International Development http://itidjournal.org/itid

Information Technology and Disabilities http://people.rit.edu/easi/itd.htm

Informing Science The International Journal of an Emerging Transdiscipline http://inform.nu/

Inter-Actions: UCLA Journal of Education and Information Studies http://repositories.cdlib.org/gseis/ interactions/

Interdisciplinary Journal of E-Learning and Learning Objects http://ijklo.org/

Interdisciplinary Journal of Information, Knowledge, and Management http://www.ijikm.org/

International Journal of Communication http://ijoc.org/ ojs/ index.php/ijoc/about/ editorialPolicies#focusAndScope

International Journal of Communication Networks and Information Security http://www.ijcnis.org/index.php/ijcnis

International Journal of Computer and Information Engineering http://www.waset.org/journals/ijcie/

International Journal of Computer Science and Information Technology http://airccse.org/journal/ ijcsit.html

International Journal of Digital Curation http://www.ijdc. net/./ijdc/issue/current

International Journal of Doctoral Studies (IJDS) http:// ijds.org/

International Journal of Library and Information Science http://www.academicjournals.org/ ijlis/index.htm

International Journal of Managing Public Sector Information and Communication Technologies http://airccse.org/journal/ mpict/ijmpict.html

International Review of Research in Open and Distance Learning http://www.irrodl.org/index.php/ irrodl

Interpersonal Computing and Technology Journal http:// www.helsinki.fi/science/optek/#byissue

Issues in Informing Science and Information Technology http://iisit.org/

Issues in Science and Technology Librarianship http:// www.library.ucsb.edu/istl/ Or http://www.istl. org/

ITALICS: Innovations in Teaching and Learning in Information and Computer Sciences http://www.ics. heacademy.ac.uk/italics/

JLIS.it Italian Journal of Library and Information Science http://leo.cilea.it/index.php/jlis/article/ view/4539/4416

Journal of Digital Information http://jodi.ecs.soton.ac. uk/r or http://journals.tdl.org/jodi

Journal of Educational Media & Library Sciences http://

joemls.tku.edu.tw/index_e.htm

Journal of Health Informatics in Developing Countries http:/ /www.jhidc.org/index.php/jhidc

Journal of Information Architecture http://journalofia. org/ archives/

Journal of Information Law and Technology http:// www2.warwick.ac.uk/fac/soc/law/elj/jilt/ or European Journal of Law and Technology http://ejlt.org//issue/archive

Journal of Information Literacy http://ojs.lboro.ac.uk/ ojs/ index.php/JIL/index

Journal of Information Technology Education (JITE: Research) http://www.informingscience.us/icarus/journals/ jiteresearch/publications

Journal of Information, Information Technology, and Organizations http://jiito.org/

Journal of Library Innovation http://www. libraryinnovation. org/about/contact

Journal of Medical Internet Research http://www.jmir. org/

Journal of Research and Practice in Information Technology http://ws.acs.org.au/jrpit/JRPIT_ Volumes.html

Journal of Technology Studies http://scholar.lib.vt. edu/ ejournals/JOTS/

Journal of the American Medical Informatics Association http://www.pubmedcentral.nih.gov/tocrender.fcgi?action= archive&journal=76

Library & Information Research: Research into Practice for Information & Library Services http://www.lirgjournal. org.uk/lir/ ojs/index.php/lir

Library Philosophy and Practice http://www.webpages. uidaho.edu/~mbolin/lpp.htm

Library Student Journal http://www. librarystudent journal.org/index.php/lsj/index

MC Journal: The Journal of Academic Media Librarianship http://wings.buffalo.edu/ publications/mcjrnl/

North Carolina Libraries http://www.ncl.ecu.edu/index.php/NCL

Partnership: The Canadian Journal of Library and Information Practice and Research http://journal.lib. uoguelph.ca/ index.php/perj/index

Simile: Studies in Media and Information Literacy Education http://utpjournals.metapress.com/ content/120764/

South African Journal of Information Management http://www.sajim.co.za/index.php/ sajim/issue/current

Technological Librarianship: An Online Journal of the American Theological Library Association http://journal. atla.com/ ojs/index.php/theolib/index

The Idaho Librarian: A Publication of the Idaho Library Association http://www.idaholibraries.org/ idlibrarian/ index.php/ idaho-librarian/index

The International Journal of Managing Information Technology http://airccse.org/journal/ijmit/ ijmit.html

The Journal of the Rutgers University Library http://jrul.libraries.rutgers.edu/index.php/jrul/index

Webology http://www.webology.ir/

World Libraries http://www.worlib.org/

Newsletters and other E-Resources

Business and Finance Division Bulletin http://bf.sla.org/ resources/the-bulletin/Out of 195E-Resources 36% are Peer Reviewed.

Summary Table: Peer Reviewed Open Access E-Resources

S.N	Peer Reviewed E-Resource	No
1	E-Journals	70
2	E-Newsletter	1
	Total	71

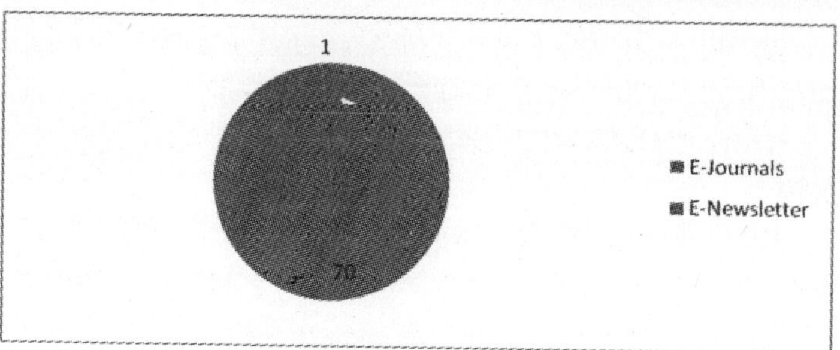

Fig.: Peer Reviewed E-Resources

The chart shows out of total 145 E-Journals 48% and Out of total 24 E-Newsletters 1(4%) are Peer Reviewed.

3.18. REFEREED OPEN ACCESS E-RESOURCES

Author has found that out of 145 E-Journals 22 (13%) are Refereed E-Journal, No Magazines and Newsletters found to be the features of Refereed.

Australian Academic and Research Libraries http://www.alia.org.au/publishing/aarl/index.html

Communications in Information Literacy http://www.comminfolit.org/index.php/cil/issue/archive

E-JASL: The Electronic Journal of Academic and Special Librarianship http://southernlibrarianship.icaap.org/

Electronic Journal of Africana Bibliography http://ir.uiowa.edu/ejab/all_issues.html

Information Technoogy and Libraries http://www.ala.org/ala/mgrps/divs/lita/ital/italinformation.cfm

Informing Science The International Journal of an Emerging Transdiscipline http://inform.nu/

Interdisciplinary Journal of E-Learning and Learning Objects http://ijklo.org/

Interdisciplinary Journal of Information, Knowledge, and Management http://www.ijikm.org/

International Journal of Communication Networks and Information Security http://www.ijcnis.org/index.php/ijcnis

International Journal of Computer and Information Engineering http://www.waset.org/journals/ijcie/

International Journal of Doctoral Studies (IJDS) http://ijds.org/

International Journal of Managing Public Sector Information and Communication Technologies http://airccse. org/journal/mpict/ijmpict.html

Issues in Informing Science and Information Technology http://iisit.org/

Journal of Artificial Intelligence Research http://www.jair.org/

Journal of Information Technology Education (JITE: Research) http://www.informingscience.us/icarus/ journals/jiteresearch/publications

Journal of Information, Information Technology, and Organizations http://jiito.org/

Library & Information Research: Research into Practice for Information & Library Services http://www.lirgjournal. org.uk/lir/ojs/index.php/lir

LIBRES: Library and Information Science Research Electronic Journal http://libres.curtin.edu.au/

Simile: Studies in Media and Information Literacy Education http://utpjournals.metapress.com/ content/120764/

The International Journal of Managing Information Technology http://airccse.org/journal/ ijmit/ijmit.html

The Public Access Computer Systems Review http://epress.lib.uh.edu/pr/pacsrev.html#history

Urban Library Journal http://lacuny.cuny.edu/ulj/

Summary: Distribution of Refereed E-Resources

S.N.	Refereed E-Resources	No.
1	E-Journals	145
2	Refereed	22

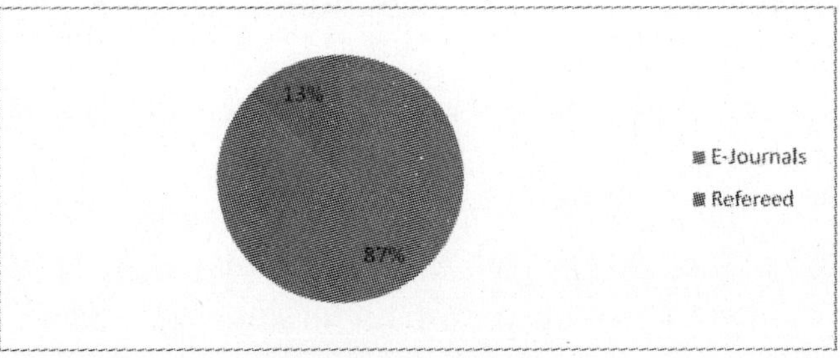

Fig.: Refereed E-Resources

The above chart shows that Refereed E-Journals are 22 (13%). 173 (87%) E-Resources are not refereed.

3.19. OPEN ACCESS E-RESOURCES HAVING LINKS

E-Resources having Links features sometimes have greater advantage. Sometime some of the E-resources have Internal links or external links form their websites to other websites. This is like a feature of facilitating the user to extract more useful Information from one website and the same website linking to other websites. Author has found out 105 (53%) E-Resources having links for other E-Resources, E-Journals are 81, and E-Magazines 16 and Other E-Resources are 8.

African Journal of Information & Communication Technology http://epress.lib.uts.edu.au/ojs/ index.php/ajict/

ALAN Review http://scholar.lib.vt.edu/ejournals/ALAN/

Annals of Library & Information Studies http://nopr.niscair.res.in/

Australian Journal of Information Systems http://dl.acs.org.au/index.php/ajis/about

Australian Academic and Research Libraries http://www.alia.org.au/publishing/aarl/index.html

Australian Library Journal http://alia.org.au/publishing/ alj/

B Sides http://ir.uiowa.edu/bsides/

Chinese Librarianship: An International Electronic Journal http://www.iclc.us/cliej/

Colby Quarterly (formerly: Colby Library Quarterly) http://digitalcommons.colby.edu/

Collaborative Librarianship http://www. collaborative librarianship.org/index.html

Communications in Information Literacy http://www. comminfolit.org/index.php/cil/issue/archive

Computer and Information Science http://journal. ccsenet.org/index.php/cis/index

Current Issues in Education http://cie.asu.edu/index.php

DESIDOC Journal of Library & Information Science http://publications.drdo.gov.in/ojs/ index.php/djlit/index

EDUCAUSE Quarterly http://www.educause.edu/eq

E-JASL: The Electronic Journal of Academic and Special Librarianship http://southernlibrarianship. icaap.org/

Electronic Journal of Health Informatics http://www.ejhi. net/ojs/index.php/ejhi

Electronic Journal on Information Systems in Developing Countries http://www.ejisdc.org/ ojs2/index.php/ejisdc

Evidence Based Library and Information Practice http://ejournals.library.ualberta.ca/index.php/ EBLIP/index

Firstmonday http://firstmonday.org/

Health Information and Libraries Journal http://www3. interscience.wiley.com/journal/120118368/ grouphome/ home. html

High Energy Physics Libraries Webzine http://library. web.cern.ch/library/Webzine/index.shtml

IFLA Journal http://www.ifla.org/V/iflaj/index.htm

Information for Social Change http://libr.org/isc/journal.html

Information Technologies and International Development http://itidjournal.org/itid

Informing Science The International Journal of an Emerging Transdiscipline http://inform.nu/

Inter-Actions: UCLA Journal of Education and Information Studies http://repositories.cdlib.org/ gseis/interactions/

Interdisciplinary Journal of E-Learning and Learning Objects http://ijklo.org/

Interdisciplinary Journal of Information, Knowledge, and Management http://www.ijikm.org/

International Journal of Communication http://ijoc.org/ ojs/index.php/ijoc/about/editorialPolicies# focusAndScope

International Journal of Computer and Information Engineering http://www.waset.org/journals/ijcie/

International Journal of Digital Curation http://www.ijdc.net/./ijdc/issue/current

International Journal of Doctoral Studies (IJDS) http://ijds.org/

International Journal of Library and Information Science http://www.academicjournals.org/ ijlis/index.htm

International Journal of Managing Public Sector Information and Communication Technologies http://airccse. org/journal/mpict/ijmpict.html

International Review of Research in Open and Distance Learning http://www.irrodl.org/index.php/irrodl

Issues in Informing Science and Information Technology http://iisit.org/

IT&Society http://www.itandsociety.org/index.html

JEP: The Journal of Electronic Publishing http://www.

journalofelectronicpublishing.org/

JLIS.it Italian Journal of Library and Information Science http://leo.cilea.it/index.php/jlis/article/ view/4539/4416

Journal of Digital Information http://jodi.ecs.soton.ac.uk/ r or http://journals.tdl.org/jodi

Journal of Health Informatics in Developing Countries http:/ /www.jhidc.org/index.php/jhidc

Journal of Information Law and Technology http://www2. warwick.ac.uk/fac/soc/law/elj/jilt/ or European Journal of Law and Technology http://ejlt.org//issue/archive

Journal of Information Literacy http://ojs.lboro.ac.uk/ ojs/ index.php/JIL/index

Journal of Information Technology Education (JITE: Research) http://www.informingscience.us/icarus/journals/ jiteresearch/publications

Journal of Information, Information Technology, and Organizations http://jiito.org/

Journal of Library Innovation http://www. library innovation.org/about/contact

Journal of Medical Internet Research http://www. jmir.org/

Journal of Philippine Librarianship http://journals.upd. edu.ph/index.php/jpl/issue/current

Journal of Technology Studies http://scholar.lib.vt. edu/ ejournals/JOTS/

Journal of the American Medical Informatics Association http://www.pubmedcentral.nih.gov/tocrender.fcgi?action= archive&journal=76

Journal of the Association for History and Computing http:/ /quod.lib.umich.edu/j/jahc/browse.html

Journal of the European Association for Health Information and Libraries http://www.eahil.net/ journal/

Journal of the Medical Library association http://www.

ncbi.nlm.nih.gov/pmc/journals/93/

LASIE: Library Automated Systems Information Exchange http://search.informit.com.au/browseJournalTitle;res=E LIBRARY; issn=0047-3774

Law Library Journal http://www.aallnet.org/products/ pub_journal.asp

LIBER Quarterly Journal of European Research Libraries http://liber.library.uu.nl/index.html

Library & Information Research: Research into Practice for Information & Library Services http://www.lirgjournal. org.uk/lir/ ojs/index.php/lir

Library Journal http://www.libraryjournal.com

Library Student Journal http://www. librarystudentjournal.org/index.php/lsj/index

MLA Forum http://www.mlaforum.org/

Malaysian Journal of Library & Information Sciencehttp:// ejum.fsktm.um.edu.my/ VolumeListing.aspx?JournalID=3

Multimedia Information and Technology Journal (MmIT) http://www.cilip.org.uk/get-involved/special-interest-groups/ multimedia/journal/pages/default.aspx

New Knowledge Environments http://journals.uvic. ca/ index.php/INKE

North Carolina Libraries http://www.ncl.ecu.edu/ index.php/NCL

NPO Journal/NPO E-Journal http://www.bl.uk/blpac/ publicationsjournals.html

Partnership: The Canadian Journal of Library and Information Practice and Research http://journal.lib. uoguelph.ca/ index.php/perj/index

Research Management Review http://www.ncura.edu/ content/news/rmr/archive.php

School libraries in Canada (SLIC): A Journal of the Canadian

Association for School Libraries http://www. clatoolbox.ca/casl/ slic/links.html

School Library Journal Online http://www.schoollibrary journal.com/

Simile: Studies in Media and Information Literacy Education http://utpjournals.metapress.com/ content/120764/

South African Journal of Information Management http:// www.sajim.co.za/index.php/ sajim/issue/current

Technological Librarianship: An Online Journal of the American Theological Library Association http://journal.atla. com/ ojs/index.php/theolib/index

Technology Electronic Reviews (TER) http://www.ala.org/ lita/publications/archive/ter

The Idaho Librarian: A Publication of the Idaho Library Association http://www.idaholibraries.org/idlibrarian/index. php/ idaho-librarian/index

The International Journal of Database Management Systems http://airccse.org/journal/ijdms/ ijdms.html

The International Journal of Managing Information Technology http://airccse.org/journal/ ijmit/ijmit.html

International Journal of Communication Networks and Information Security http://www.ijcnis.org/index.php/ijcnis

The Journal of the Rutgers University Library http:// jrul.libraries.rutgers.edu/index.php/jrul/index

Virginia Libraries http://scholar.lib.vt.edu/ejournals/ VALib/

Webology http://www.webology.ir/

E-Magazines

AALL Spectrum http://www.aallnet.org/main-menu/ Publications/spectrum

Access http://www.aardvarknet.info/access/number46/ index.cfm

American Libraries http://americanlibrariesmagazine.org/

Book business http://www.bookbusinessmag.com/

Book Links http://www.ala.org/ala/aboutala/offices/publishing/booklinks/archiveonline/ archive_of_online_articles.cfm

CHOICE http://www.ala.org/ala/mgrps/divs/acrl/publications/choice/previousissues/previousissues. cfm

Computer in Libraries http://www.infotoday.com/cilmag/default.shtml

E-Content http://www.ecmag.net/

EDUCAUSE Review http://www.educause.edu/

Information Today http://www.infotoday.com/IT/nov08/index.shtml

Knowledge Management World http://www.kmworld.com/index.cfm

Link-Up http://www.infotoday.com/linkup/default.shtml

Online http://www.infotoday.com/online/default.shtml

Research Information http://www.researchinformation.info/

Searcher: The Magazine for Database Professionals http://www.infotoday.com/searcher/default.asp

Virginia Tech Magazine http://www.vtmagazine.vt.edu/

Newsletters and other E-Resources

Abbey Newsletter http://cool.conservation-us.org/byorg/abbey/an/

Against the grain http://www.against-the-grain.com/ d/TOC

ALAWON. The ALA Washington Office Electronic Newsline http://www.ala.org/ala/aboutala/offices/wo/washnews/archivea/archive.cfm

ALCTS Network News http://bubl.ac.uk/archive/ journals/alctsnn/

ARL: A Bimonthly Newsletter for Library Issues and Action http://www.arl.org/ resources/pubs/br/index.shtml

Cataloging and Classification Quarterly http://bubl.ac.uk/archive/journals/cacq/

MLS: Marketing Library Services http://www.infotoday.com/MLS/default.shtml

RLG DigiNews http://www.oclc.org/programs/ publications/newsletters/diginews.htm

Summary Table: Distribution of E-Resources having Links of other E-Resources

S.N.	E-resources	No
1	E-Journals	81
2	E-Magazines	16
3	Other E-resources	8
	Total	105

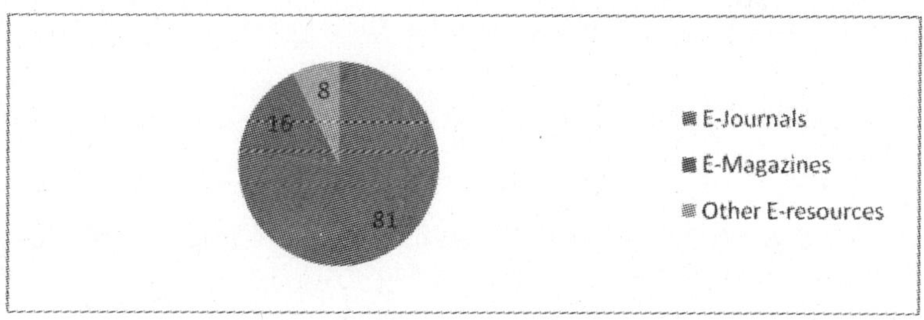

Fig.: E-Resources having links for other E-Resources

This chart shows that out of total 145 E-journal 81(55%), Out of total 26 E-Magazine 16 (61%) and out of total 24 E-newsletters 8 (33%) are having links for other E-Resources.

3.20. OPEN ACCESS E-RESOURCES HAVING SPECIAL FEATURES

Researcher has find out that 146 (73%) E-Resources having Special Features, E-Journals are 112, and E-Magazines 23 and Other E-Resources are 11.

College and Research Libraries http://crl.acrl.org/

African Journal of Information & Communication Technology http://epress.lib.uts.edu.au/ojs/ index.php/ajict/

ALAN Review http://scholar.lib.vt.edu/ejournals/ALAN/

Annals of Library & Information Studies http://nopr.niscair.res.in/

Australian Journal of Information Systems http://dl.acs.org.au/index.php/ajis/about

B Sides http://ir.uiowa.edu/bsides/

Chinese Librarianship: An International Electronic Journal http://www.iclc.us/cliej/

Colby Quarterly (formerly: Colby Library Quarterly) http://digitalcommons.colby.edu/

Collaborative Librarianship http://www.collaborative librarianship.org/index.html

Communications in Information Literacy http://www.comminfolit.org/index.php/cil/issue/archive

Computer and Information Science http://journal.ccsenet.org/index.php/cis/index

Current Cites http://lists.webjunction.org/currentcites/

Current Issues in Education http://cie.asu.edu/index.php

Cybermetrics : International Journal of Scientometrics, Informetrics and Bibliometrics http://www.cindoc.csic.es/cybermetrics/

Data Science Journal http://www.jstage.jst.go.jp/browse/dsj

DESIDOC Journal of Library & Information Science http://publications.drdo.gov.in/ojs/ index.php/djlit/index

EDUCAUSE Quarterly http://www.educause.edu/eq

E-JASL: The Electronic Journal of Academic and Special Librarianship http://southernlibrarianship.icaap.org/

Electronic Journal of Africana Bibliography http://ir.uiowa.edu/ejab/all_issues.html

Electronic Journal of Health Informatics http://www.ejhi.net/ojs/index.php/ejhi

Electronic Journal of Knowledge Management http://www.ejkm.com/

Electronic Journal on Information Systems in Developing Countries http://www.ejisdc.org/ojs2/ index.php/ejisdc

European Journal of ePractice http://www.epracticejournal.eu/

Evidence Based Library and Information Practice http://ejournals.library.ualberta.ca/ index.php/EBLIP/index

Firstmonday http://firstmonday.org/

Health Information and Libraries Journal http://www3.interscience.wiley.com/journal/ 120118368/grouphome/home.html

High Energy Physics Libraries Webzine http://library.web.cern.ch/library/Webzine/index.shtml

IFLA Journal http://www.ifla.org/V/iflaj/index.htm

Information for Social Change http://libr.org/isc/journal.html

Information Research: An International Electronic Journal http://informationr.net/ir/

Information Technologies and International Development http://itidjournal.org/itid

Informing Science The International Journal of an Emerging Transdiscipline http://inform.nu/

Inter-Actions: UCLA Journal of Education and Information Studies http://repositories.cdlib.org/ gseis/interactions/

Interdisciplinary Journal of E-Learning and Learning Objects http://ijklo.org/

Interdisciplinary Journal of Information, Knowledge, and Management http://www.ijikm.org/

International Journal of Communication http://ijoc.org/ ojs/ index.php/ijoc/about/ editorialPolicies# focusAndScope

International Journal of Communication Networks and Information Security http://www.ijcnis.org/ index.php/ijcnis

International Journal of Computer and Information Engineering http://www.waset.org/journals/ijcie/

International Journal of Computer Science and Information Technology http://airccse.org/journal/ ijcsit.html

International Journal of Digital Curation http://www. ijdc.net/./ijdc/issue/current

International Journal of Doctoral Studies (IJDS) http://ijds. org/

International Journal of Legal Information http:// scholarship.law.cornell.edu/ijli/vol33/iss1/

International Journal of Library and Information Science http://www.academicjournals.org/ ijlis/index.htm

International Journal of Multimedia and Its Applications http://airccse.org/journal/ijma_index.html

International Review of Information Ethics http://www.i-r-i-e.net/

International Review of Research in Open and Distance Learning http://www.irrodl.org/ index.php/irrodl

Interpersonal Computing and Technology Journal http:// www.helsinki.fi/science/optek/#byissue

Issues in Informing Science and Information Technology http://iisit.org/

Issues in Science and Technology Librarianship http:// www.library.ucsb.edu/istl/ Or http://www.istl.org/

IT&Society http://www.itandsociety.org/index.html

JEP: The Journal of Electronic Publishing http://www. journalofelectronicpublishing.org/

JLIS.it Italian Journal of Library and Information Science http://leo.cilea.it/index.php/ jlis/article/view/4539/4416

Journal of Artificial Intelligence Research http://www. jair.org/

Journal of Digital Information http://jodi.ecs.soton. ac.uk/r or http://journals.tdl.org/jodi

Journal of East Asian Libraries http://www.lib.byu.edu/ dlib/ spc/jeal/

Journal of Educational Media & Library Sciences http:// joemls.tku.edu.tw/index_e.htm

Journal of eLiteracy http://www.jelit.org/index.html

Journal of Health Informatics in Developing Countries http:/ /www.jhidc.org/index.php/jhidc

Journal of Information Architecture http://journalofia. org/ archives/

Journal of Information Law and Technology http:// www2.warwick.ac.uk/fac/soc/law/elj/jilt/ or European Journal of Law and Technology http://ejlt.org//issue/archive

Journal of Information Literacy http://ojs.lboro.ac. uk/ojs/ index.php/JIL/index

Journal of Information Technology Education (JITE: Research) http://www.informingscience.us/ icarus/journals/ jiteresearch/publications

Journal of Information, Information Technology, and Organizations http://jiito.org/

Journal of Internet Calaloguing http://www. internetcataloging.com/home.html

Journal of Library Innovation http://www. libraryinnovation.org/about/contact

Journal of Medical Internet Research http://www. jmir.org/

Journal of Philippine Librarianship http://journals.upd. edu.ph/index.php/jpl/issue/current

Journal of Research and Practice in Information Technology http://ws.acs.org.au/jrpit/ JRPIT_Volumes.html

Journal of Technology Studies http://scholar.lib. vt.edu/ ejournals/JOTS/

Journal of the American Medical Informatics Association http://www.pubmedcentral.nih.gov/tocrender.fcgi?action= archive&journal=76

Journal of the Association for History and Computing http:/ /quod.lib.umich.edu/j/jahc/browse.html

Journal of the European Association for Health Information and Libraries http://www.eahil.net/ journal/

Journal of the Medical Library association http://www. ncbi.nlm.nih.gov/pmc/journals/93/

Journal of Virtual Worlds Research http://www. jvwresearch.org/index.html

LASIE: Library Automated Systems Information Exchange http://search.informit.com.au/browseJournalTitle;res=E-LIBRARY; issn=0047-3774

Law Library Journal http://www.aallnet.org/products/ pub_journal.asp

Learned Publishing http://www.ingentaconnect.com/ content/alpsp/lp

LIBER Quarterly Journal of European Research Libraries http://liber.library.uu.nl/index.html

Library & Information Research: Research into Practice for Information & Library Services http://www.lirgjournal. org.uk/lir/ ojs/index.php/lir

Library Journal http://www.libraryjournal.com

Library Philosophy and Practice http://www.webpages. uidaho.edu/~mbolin/lpp.htm

Library Student Journal http://www.librarystudent journal.org/index.php/lsj/index

LIBRES: Library and Information Science Research Electronic Journal http://libres.curtin.edu.au/

LIBRI: International Journal of Libraries and Information Services http://www.librijournal.org/

Malaysian Journal of Library & Information Sciencehttp:// ejum.fsktm.um.edu.my/ VolumeListing.aspx?JournalID=3

MC Journal: The Journal of Academic Media Librarianship http://wings.buffalo.edu/ publications/mcjrnl/

Mississippi Libraries http://www.misslib.org/index.php/ publications/mississippi-libraries/

MLA Forum http://www.mlaforum.org/

Multimedia Information and Technology Journal (MmIT) http://www.cilip.org.uk/get-involved/special-interest-groups/ multimedia/journal/pages/default.aspx

New Knowledge Environments http://journals.uvic.ca/ index.php/INKE

North Carolina Libraries http://www.ncl.ecu.edu/ index.php/NCL

Northwestern Journal of Technology and Intellectual Property http://www.law.northwestern.edu/ journals/njtip/ issues.htm

NPO Journal/NPO E-Journal http://www.bl.uk/blpac/ publicationsjournals.html

Partnership: The Canadian Journal of Library and Information Practice and Research http://journal.lib.uoguelph. ca/ index.php/perj/index

Progressive Librarian http://libr.org/pl/

RBM Journal of Rare Books , Manuscripts, and Cultural Heritage http://rbm.acrl.org/content/2/2

Scandinavian Public Library Quarterly http://www. splq.info/

School libraries in Canada (SLIC): A Journal of the Canadian Association for School Libraries http://www. clatoolbox.ca/casl/

slic/links.html

School Library Journal Online http://www.schoollibrary journal.com/

School Library Research http://www.ala.org/aasl/slr

Simile: Studies in Media and Information Literacy Education http://utpjournals.metapress.com/ content/120764/

South African Journal of Information Management http:// www.sajim.co.za/index.php/sajim/ issue/current

Special Libraries http://www.sla.org/content/shop/ speclibs.cfm#1910

Technological Librarianship: An Online Journal of the American Theological Library Association http://journal.atla. com/ ojs/index.php/theolib/index

The Idaho Librarian: A Publication of the Idaho Library Association http://www.idaholibraries.org/ idlibrarian/index. php/ idaho-librarian/index

The International Journal of Database Management Systems http://airccse.org/journal/ijdms/ijdms.html

The International Journal of Managing Information Technology http://airccse.org/journal/ ijmit/ijmit.html

The Journal of the Rutgers University Library http://jrul. libraries.rutgers.edu/index.php/jrul/index

Urban Library Journal http://lacuny.cuny.edu/ulj/

Webology http://www.webology.ir/

World Libraries http://www.worlib.org/

E-Magazines

AALL Spectrum http://www.aallnet.org/main-menu/ Publications/spectrum

Access http://www.aardvarknet.info/access/number46/ index.cfm

American Libraries http://americanlibrariesmagazine.org/

Ariadne http://www.ariadne.ac.uk/

Book business http://www.bookbusinessmag.com/

Book Links http://www.ala.org/ala/aboutala/offices/publishing/booklinks/archiveonline/ archive_of_ online_articles.cfm

CHOICE http://www.ala.org/ala/mgrps/divs/acrl/publications/choice/previousissues/ previousissues.cfm

Computer in Libraries http://www.infotoday.com/ cilmag/default.shtml

D-Lib Magazine http://www.dlib.org/dlib/september08/09contents.html

E-Content http://www.ecmag.net/

EDUCAUSE Review http://www.educause.edu/

Information Today http://www.infotoday.com/IT/nov08/index.shtml

Knowledge Management World http://www.kmworld.com/index.cfm

Library Juice http://libr.org/juice/

Link-Up http://www.infotoday.com/linkup/default.shtml

Online http://www.infotoday.com/online/default.shtml

Provenance http://www.provenance.ca/about-provenance/index.html

Research Information http://www.researchinformation.info/

Searcher: The Magazine for Database Professionals http://www.infotoday.com/searcher/default.asp

The Bulletin of the American Society for Information Science and Technology http://www.asis.org/ bulletin.html

Virginia Tech Magazine http://www.vtmagazine.vt.edu/

International Journal of Managing Public Sector Information and Communication Technologies http://airccse. org/journal/mpict/ijmpict.html

Newsletters and other E-Resources

ABAA Newsletter http://hq.abaa.org/books/antiquarian/abaapages/newsletter

Against the grain http://www.against-the-grain.com/ d/TOC

ALAWON. The ALA Washington Office Electronic Newsline http://www.ala.org/ala/aboutala/offices/wo/washnews/archivea/archive.cfm

ALCTS Network News http://bubl.ac.uk/archive/ journals/alctsnn/

ARL: A Bimonthly Newsletter for Library Issues and Action http://www.arl.org/resources/ pubs/br/index.shtml

Business and Finance Division Bulletin http://bf.sla.org/resources/the-bulletin/

Free Pint http://www.freepint.com/

MLS: Marketing Library Services http://www.infotoday.com/MLS/default.shtml

NLM Technical Bulletin http://www.nlm.nih.gov/pubs/techbull/current_issue.html

RLG DigiNews http://www.oclc.org/programs/ publications/newsletters/diginews.htm

Sprouts: Working Papers on Information Systems http://sprouts.aisnet.org/home.html

Summary Table: E-Resources having Special features

S.N	E-Resources	No.
1	E-Journals	111
2	E-Magazines	22
3	Other E-resources	11
4	Total	144

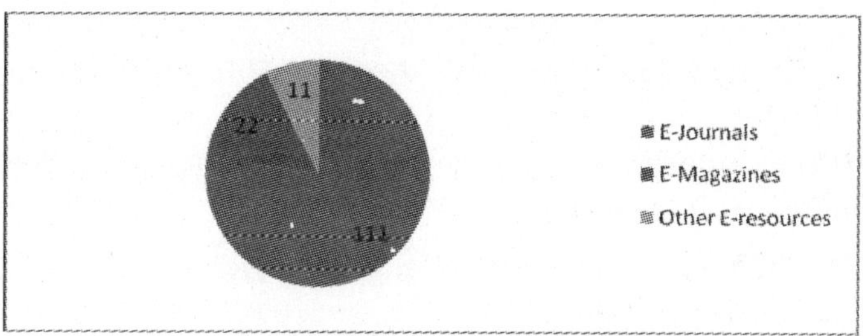

Fig.: E-Resources having Special Features

The chart shows that out of total 145 E-Journals 111(76%), Out of total 26 E-Magazines 22 (84%) and Out of 24 E-Newsletters 11 (45%) have Special Features.

3.21. OPEN ACCESS E-RESOURCES HAVING INTERNAL SEARCH ENGINE

College and Research Libraries http://crl.acrl.org/

African Journal of Information & Communication Technology http://epress.lib.uts.edu.au/ojs/ index.php/ajict/

Agricultural Libraries Information Notes http:// webharvest.gov/peth04/20041023101316/ http://www. nal.usda.gov/NewAlin/

ALAN Review http://scholar.lib.vt.edu/ejournals/ALAN/

Alki: The Washington Library Association Journal http:// www.wla.org/alki/

American Archivist http://archivists.metapress.com/ home/ main.mpx

Annals of Library & Information Studies http://nopr. niscair.res.in/

Associates: The Electronic Library Support Staff Journal http://associates.ucr.edu/journal/

Australian Journal of Information Systems http://dl.acs. org.au/index.php/ajis/about

Australian Library Journal http://alia.org.au/ publishing/alj/

B Sides http://ir.uiowa.edu/bsides/

Christian Library Journal http://www.christianlibraryj. org/pdf/index.htm

Colby Quarterly (formerly: Colby Library Quarterly) http://digitalcommons.colby.edu/

Collaborative Librarianship http://www. collaborative librarianship.org/index.html

Communications in Information Literacy http://www. comminfolit.org/index.php/cil/issue/archive

Computer and Information Science http://journal. ccsenet.org/index.php/cis/index

Current Cites http://lists.webjunction.org/currentcites/

Current Issues in Education http://cie.asu.edu/index.php

Data Science Journal http://www.jstage.jst.go. jp/browse/dsj

DESIDOC Journal of Library & Information Science http://publications.drdo.gov.in/ ojs/index.php/djlit/index

EBIB Electronic Information Bulletin for librarians http://ebib.info/biuletyn/

EDUCAUSE Quarterly http://www.educause.edu/eq

Electronic Journal of Africana Bibliography http://ir. uiowa.edu/ejab/all_issues.html

Electronic Journal of Health Informatics http://www. ejhi.net/ojs/index.php/ejhi

Electronic Journal of Knowledge Management http://www.ejkm.com/

Electronic Journal on Information Systems in Developing Countries http://www.ejisdc.org/ojs2/ index.php/ejisdc

European Journal of ePractice http://www.epractice journal.eu/

Evidence Based Library and Information Practice http://ejournals.library.ualberta.ca/ index.php/EBLIP/index

Firstmonday http://firstmonday.org/

Health Information and Libraries Journal http://www3.interscience.wiley.com/journal/ 120118368/grouphome/home.html

IFLA Journal http://www.ifla.org/V/iflaj/index.htm

Information for Social Change http://libr.org/ isc/journal.html

Information Research: An International Electronic Journal http://informationr.net/ir/

Information Scotland: The Journal of the Chartered Institute of Library and Information Professionals in Scotland http://www.slainte.org.uk/publications/serials/infoscot/vol1(1)/vol1(1)contents.html

Information Technologies and International Development http://itidjournal.org/itid

Informing Science The International Journal of an Emerging Tran discipline http://inform.nu/

Inter-Actions: UCLA Journal of Education and Information Studies http://repositories.cdlib.org/ gseis/interactions/

Interdisciplinary Journal of E-Learning and Learning Objects http://ijklo.org/

Interdisciplinary Journal of Information, Knowledge, and Management http://www.ijikm.org/

International Journal of Communication http://ijoc.org/ ojs/index.php/ijoc/about/ editorialPolicies#focusAndScope

International Journal of Communication Networks and Information Security http://www.ijcnis.org/index.php/ ijcnis

International Journal of Computer Science and Information Technology http://airccse.org/journal/ ijcsit.html

International Journal of Digital Curation http://www.ijdc.net/./ijdc/issue/current

International Journal of Doctoral Studies (IJDS) http://

ijds.org/

International Journal of Legal Information http://scholarship.law.cornell.edu/ijli/vol33/iss1/

International Journal of Library and Information Science http://www.academicjournals.org/ ijlis/index.htm

International Journal of Multimedia and Its Applications http://airccse.org/journal/ijma_index.html

International Review of Information Ethics http://www.i-r-i-e.net/

International Review of Research in Open and Distance Learning http://www.irrodl.org/ index.php/irrodl

Internet Writing Journal http://www. internetwriting journal.com/

Issues in Informing Science and Information Technology http://iisit.org/

Issues in Science and Technology Librarianship http://www.library.ucsb.edu/istl/ Or http://www.istl.org/

ITALICS: Innovations in Teaching and Learning in Information and Computer Sciences http://www.ics. heacademy.ac.uk/italics/

JEP: The Journal of Electronic Publishing http://www.journalofelectronicpublishing.org/

JLIS.it Italian Journal of Library and Information Science http://leo.cilea.it/index.php/jlis/article/view/4539/4416

Journal of Artificial Intelligence Research http://www.jair.org/

Journal of Digital Information http://jodi.ecs.soton.ac.uk/ r or http://journals.tdl.org/jodi

Journal of East Asian Libraries http://www.lib.byu.edu/ dlib/spc/jeal/

Journal of Educational Media & Library Sciences http://joemls.tku.edu.tw/index_e.htm

Journal of eLiteracy http://www.jelit.org/index.html

Journal of Health Informatics in Developing Countries http://www.jhidc.org/index.php/jhidc

Journal of Information Law and Technology http://www2.warwick.ac.uk/fac/soc/law/elj/jilt/ or European Journal of Law and Technology http://ejlt.org//issue/archive

Journal of Information Literacy http://ojs.lboro.ac.uk/ ojs/index.php/JIL/index

Journal of Information Technology Education (JITE: Research) http://www.informingscience.us/icarus/ journals/jiteresearch/publications

Journal of Information, Information Technology, and Organizations http://jiito.org/

Journal of Library Innovation http://www.library innovation.org/about/contact

Journal of Medical Internet Research http://www. jmir.org/

Journal of Philippine Librarianship http://journals.upd.edu.ph/index.php/jpl/issue/current

Journal of Research and Practice in Information Technology http://ws.acs.org.au/jrpit/ JRPIT_Volumes.html

Journal of Technology Studies http://scholar.lib.vt. edu/ejournals/JOTS/

Journal of the American Medical Informatics Association http://www.pubmedcentral.nih.gov/tocrender.fcgi?action=archive&journal=76

Journal of the Association for History and Computing http://quod.lib.umich.edu/j/jahc/browse.html

Journal of the European Association for Health Information and Libraries http://www.eahil.net/ journal/

Journal of the Medical Library association http://www.ncbi.nlm.nih.gov/pmc/journals/93/

Journal of Virtual Worlds Research http://www.jvwresearch.org/index.html

LASIE: Library Automated Systems Information Exchange http://search.informit.com.au/ browseJournalTitle;res=E-LIBRARY; issn=0047-3774

Law Library Journal http://www.aallnet.org/ products/ pub_journal.asp

Learned Publishing http://www.ingentaconnect.com/ content/alpsp/lp

LIBER Quarterly Journal of European Research Libraries http://liber.library.uu.nl/index.html

Library & Information Research: Research into Practice for Information & Library Services http://www. lirgjournal.org.uk/lir/ ojs/index.php/lir

Library Journal http://www.libraryjournal.com

Library Philosophy and Practice http://www. webpages.uidaho.edu/~mbolin/lpp.htm

Library Resources & Technical Services (LRTS) http://alcts. metapress.com/home/main.mpx

Library Student Journal http://www.librarystudent journal.org/index.php/lsj/index

LIBRES: Library and Information Science Research Electronic Journal http://libres.curtin.edu.au/

LIBRI: International Journal of Libraries and Information Services http://www.librijournal.org/

Malaysian Journal of Library & Information Sciencehttp:// ejum.fsktm.um.edu.my/VolumeListing.aspx? JournalID=3

MC Journal: The Journal of Academic Media Librarianship http://wings.buffalo.edu/publications/ mcjrnl/

Mississippi Libraries http://www.misslib.org/index.php/ publications/mississippi-libraries/

Multimedia Information and Technology Journal (MmIT) http://www.cilip.org.uk/get-involved/special-interest-groups/ multimedia/journal/pages/default.aspx

New Knowledge Environments http://journals.uvic.ca/index.php/INKE

North Carolina Libraries http://www.ncl.ecu.edu/index.php/NCL

Northwestern Journal of Technology and Intellectual Property http://www.law.northwestern.edu/ journals/njtip/issues.htm

NPO Journal/NPO E-Journal http://www.bl.uk/blpac/publicationsjournals.html

Partnership: The Canadian Journal of Library and Information Practice and Research http://journal.lib. uoguelph.ca/index.php/perj/index

Progressive Librarian http://libr.org/pl/

RBM Journal of Rare Books , Manuscripts, and Cultural Heritage http://rbm.acrl.org/content/2/2

Scandinavian Public Library Quarterly http://www. splq.info/

School libraries in Canada (SLIC): A Journal of the Canadian Association for School Libraries http://www. clatoolbox.ca/casl/slic/links.html

School Library Journal Online http://www. schoollibrary journal.com/

School Library Research http://www.ala.org/aasl/slr

South African Journal of Information Management http://www.sajim.co.za/index.php/sajim/ issue/current

Special Libraries http://www.sla.org/content/shop/speclibs.cfm#1910

Studies in Bibliography http://etext.lib.virginia.edu/ bsuva/sb

Technological Librarianship: An Online Journal of the American Theological Library Association http://journal. atla.com/ojs/index.php/theolib/index

Technology Electronic Reviews (TER) http://www.ala. org/

lita/publications/archive/ter

Texas library journal http://www.txla.org/TLJ

The Bonefolder: An outgrowth of the Book Arts Web http://www.philobiblon.com/bonefolder/

Code4Lib Journal http://journal.code4lib.org/

The Idaho Librarian: A Publication of the Idaho Library Association http://www.idaholibraries.org/ idlibrarian/index. php/ idaho-librarian/index

The International Journal of Database Management Systems http://airccse.org/journal/ ijdms/ijdms.html

The International Journal of Managing Information Technology http://airccse.org/journal/ ijmit/ijmit.html

The Journal of the Rutgers University Library http://jrul.libraries.rutgers.edu/index.php/jrul/index

The Public Access Computer Systems Review http://epress.lib.uh.edu/pr/pacsrev.html#history

Urban Library Journal http://lacuny.cuny.edu/ulj/

Virginia Libraries http://scholar.lib.vt.edu/ejournals/ VALib/

Webology http://www.webology.ir/

E-Magazines

AALL Spectrum http://www.aallnet.org/main-menu/Publications/spectrum

Access http://www.aardvarknet.info/access/number46/index.cfm

American Libraries http://americanlibrariesmagazine.org/

Ariadne http://www.ariadne.ac.uk/

Book business http://www.bookbusinessmag.com/

Book Links http://www.ala.org/ala/aboutala/offices/publishing/booklinks/archiveonline/ archive_of_online_articles.cfm

Computer in Libraries http://www.infotoday.com/ cilmag/default.shtml

Cultivate Interactive http://www.cultivate-int.org/index-2.html

D-Lib Magazine http://www.dlib.org/dlib/september08/09contents.html

E-Content http://www.ecmag.net/

EDUCAUSE Review http://www.educause.edu/

inCite http://alia.org.au/publishing/incite/archive.html

Information Today http://www.infotoday.com/IT/ nov08/index.shtml

Knowledge Management World http://www.kmworld.com/index.cfm

Library Juice http://libr.org/juice/

Link-Up http://www.infotoday.com/linkup/default.shtml

Online http://www.infotoday.com/online/default.shtml

Provenance http://www.provenance.ca/about-provenance/index.html

Research Information http://www.researchinformation.info/

Searcher: The Magazine for Database Professionals http://www.infotoday.com/searcher/default.asp

The Bulletin of the American Society for Information Science and Technology http://www.asis.org/bulletin.html

Virginia Tech Magazine http://www.vtmagazine.vt.edu/

Newsletters and other E-Resources

ABAA Newsletter http://hq.abaa.org/books/antiquarian/abaapages/newsletter

Abbey Newsletter http://cool.conservation-us.org/byorg/abbey/an/

Against the grain http://www.against-the-grain.com/d/ TOC

ALAWON. The ALA Washington Office Electronic Newsline http://www.ala.org/ala/aboutala/offices/wo/washnews/

archivea/archive.cfm

ARL: A Bimonthly Newsletter for Library Issues and Action http://www.arl.org/resources/ pubs/br/index.shtml

Biblia's Warrior Librarian Weekly http://warriorlibrarian.com/ARCHIVE/00archives.html

Biblio-Tech Review http://www.ringgold.com/biblio-tech/si_pd.cfm?pid=2

Conserline http://www.loc.gov/acq/conser/consrlin.html

Free Pint http://www.freepint.com/

Internet Resources Newsletter http://www.hw.ac.uk/libwww/irn/irn.html

LC Cataloging Newsline http://www.loc.gov/catdir/lccn/

MLS: Marketing Library Services http://www.infotoday.com/MLS/default.shtml

NLM Technical Bulletin http://www.nlm.nih.gov/pubs/techbull/current_issue.html

Serials E-News http://www.ringgold.com/UKSG/si_pd.cfm

SPARC Open Access Newsletter or Free Online Scholarship Newsletter http://www.earlham.edu/ ~peters/fos/ index.htm

Sprouts: Working Papers on Information Systems http://sprouts.aisnet.org/home.html

The Wired Librarian's Newsletter http://www.wiredlibrarian.com/wln/wlnfront.htm

Summary Table: E-Resources having Internal Search Engine

S.N.	E-Resources	No
1	E-Journals	117
2	E-Magazines	21
3	Other E-resources	17
	Total	155

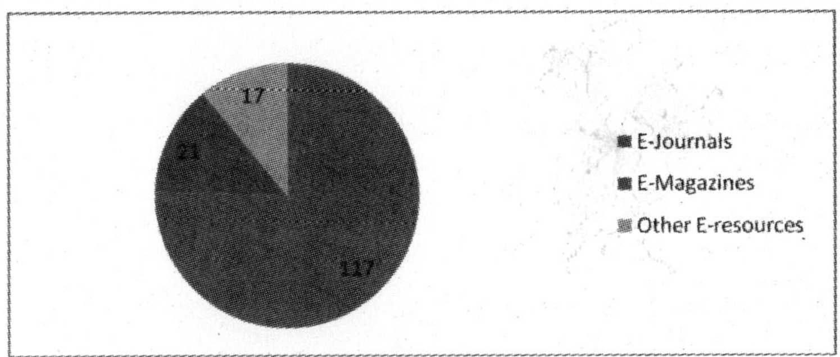

Fig.: E-Resources having Internal Search Engine

The chart shows that out of total 145 E-Journals 117 (60%), Out of total 26 E-Magazines 21 (80%) and out of total 24 E-Newsletters 17 (70%) are having Internal Search Engine.

4

Parameters Covering By Open Access E-resources

4.1. DIFFERENT PARAMETERS COVERING OPEN ACCESS E-RESOURCES

E-journals

	1	2	3	4	5	6	7	8	9	10	11	12	13	14	15	16	17	18	19	20	21	22	23	24	25	26	27	28	29	30	31	32	33	34	35	36	37	38	39	40	
S. No.	Title	URL	Authority	Publisher(organization, editor, host)	Geographical Area/Country	Scope/Coverage	Accessibility & Reliability	Browsebility	Networkability	Format	Design & Layout	Treatment	Accuracy	Objectivity	Arrangement(sequence, alphabetization, index)	Response Time	Structure	Link	Periodicity/Frequency	Special Features	Help	download	Currency	Internal Search Engine	Specific guidelines(content, output)	Review (maintenance, easy to use, equipment)	Standards	Information: Primary or Secondary	Information: Factual or Opinion	Latest and Currents Trends	Archiving	Indexed	Searching	Personalization (Marked Items, Alerts, Rss)	International	Refereed E-Resources	Peer Reviewed	ISSN	Search with Personalization	Peer Review + Indexed = International	Maximum Parameters Covered
1	College and Research Libraries http://crl.acrl.org/	Y	Y	Y	Y	Y	Y	Y	Y	Y	Y	Y	Y	Y	Y	Y	Y	N	Y	Y	Y	Y	Y	Y	Y	Y	Y	Y	Y	Y	Y	N	Y	Y	N	N	N	Y	Y		34

2	African Journal of Information & Communication Technology http://epress.lib.uts.edu.au/ojs/index.php/ajict/	Y	Y	Y	Y	Y	Y	Y	Y	Y	Y	Y	Y	Y	Y	Y	Y	Y	Y	Y	Y	Y	Y	Y	Y	Y	Y	Y	Y	Y	Y	Y	Y	Y	Y	N	Y	Y	Y		39
3	Agricultural Libraries Information Notes http://webharvest.gov/peth04/20041023101316/http://www.nal.usda.gov/NewAlin/	Y	Y	Y	Y	Y	Y	Y	Y	Y	Y	Y	Y	Y	Y	Y	Y	N	Y	N	Y	Y	N	Y	Y	Y	Y	Y	Y	N	Y	N	Y	N	N	N	N	N	N		28
4	ALAN Review http://scholar.lib.vt.edu/ejournals/ALAN/	Y	Y	Y	Y	Y	Y	Y	Y	Y	Y	Y	Y	Y	Y	Y	Y	Y	Y	Y	Y	Y	Y	Y	Y	Y	Y	Y	Y	Y	Y	N	Y	N	N	N	N	Y	N		33
5	Alki: The Washington Library Association Journal http://www.wla.org/alki/	Y	Y	Y	Y	Y	Y	Y	Y	Y	Y	Y	Y	Y	Y	Y	Y	N	Y	N	Y	Y	N	Y	Y	Y	Y	Y	Y	N	Y	Y	Y	N	N	N	N	Y	N		30
6	American Archivist http://archivists.metapress.com/home/main.mpx	Y	Y	Y	Y	Y	Y	Y	Y	Y	Y	Y	Y	Y	Y	Y	Y	N	Y	N	Y	Y	N	Y	Y	Y	Y	Y	Y	N	Y	N	Y	Y	N	N	Y	Y	Y		32
7	Annals of Library & Information Studies http://nopr.niscair.res.in/	Y	Y	Y	Y	Y	Y	Y	Y	Y	Y	Y	Y	Y	Y	Y	Y	Y	Y	Y	Y	Y	Y	Y	Y	Y	Y	Y	Y	Y	Y	Y	Y	Y	N	N	N	Y	Y	Y	37

8	Australian Journal of Information Systems http://dl.acs.org.au/index.php/ajis/about	Y	Y	Y	Y	Y	Y	Y	Y	Y	Y	Y	Y	Y	Y	Y	Y	N	Y	N	Y	Y	Y	Y	Y	Y	Y	Y	Y	Y	Y	N	Y	Y	N	N	N	Y	Y		33
9	Australian Academic and Research Libraries http://www.alia.org.au/publishing/aarl/index.html	Y	Y	Y	Y	Y	Y	Y	Y	Y	Y	Y	Y	Y	Y	Y	Y	Y	Y	N	N	Y	Y	N	Y	Y	Y	Y	Y	Y	Y	Y	N	N	N	Y	Y	Y	N	Y	33
10	Australian Library Journal http://alia.org.au/publishing/alj/	Y	Y	Y	Y	Y	Y	Y	Y	Y	Y	Y	Y	Y	Y	Y	Y	Y	Y	N	Y	Y	N	Y	Y	Y	Y	Y	Y	N	Y	N	Y	Y	Y	N	N	Y	Y		32
11	B Sides http://ir.uiowa.edu/bsides/	Y	Y	Y	Y	Y	Y	Y	Y	Y	Y	Y	Y	Y	Y	Y	Y	Y	Y	Y	Y	Y	Y	Y	Y	Y	Y	Y	Y	Y	Y	Y	Y	Y	N	N	Y	Y	Y	Y	38
12	Chinese Librarianship: an International Electronic Journal http://www.iclc.us/cliej/	Y	Y	Y	Y	Y	Y	Y	Y	Y	Y	Y	Y	Y	Y	Y	Y	Y	Y	Y	N	Y	Y	N	Y	Y	Y	Y	Y	Y	Y	Y	N	N	Y	N	N	N	N		31
13	Christian Library Journal http://www.christianlibraryj.org/pdf/index.htm	Y	Y	Y	Y	Y	Y	Y	Y	Y	Y	Y	Y	Y	Y	Y	Y	N	Y	N	Y	Y	Y	Y	Y	Y	Y	Y	Y	Y	Y	N	Y	N	N	N	Y	Y	N		32
14	Cites & Insights: Crawford at Large http://citesandinsights.info/citoc.htm	Y	Y	Y	Y	Y	Y	Y	Y	Y	Y	Y	Y	Y	Y	Y	Y	N	Y	N	N	Y	N	N	Y	Y	Y	Y	Y	N	Y	N	N	N	N	N	N	Y	N		26

15	Colby Quarterly (formerly: Colby Library Quarterly) http://digitalcommons.colby.edu/	Y	Y	Y	Y	Y	Y	Y	Y	Y	Y	Y	Y	Y	Y	Y	Y	Y	Y	Y	Y	Y	N	Y	Y	Y	Y	Y	Y	N	Y	N	Y	Y	N	N	N	N	Y		32
16	Collaborative Librarianshiphttp://www.collaborativelibrarianship.org/index.html	Y	Y	Y	Y	Y	Y	Y	Y	Y	Y	Y	Y	Y	Y	Y	Y	Y	Y	Y	Y	Y	Y	Y	Y	Y	Y	Y	Y	Y	Y	Y	Y	Y	N	N	Y	Y	Y	Y	38
17	Communications in information literacy http://www.comminfolit.org/index.php/cil/index	Y	Y	Y	Y	Y	Y	Y	Y	Y	Y	Y	Y	Y	Y	Y	Y	Y	Y	Y	Y	Y	Y	Y	Y	Y	Y	Y	Y	Y	Y	Y	Y	N	N	Y	Y	Y	N	Y	37
18	Computer and Information Science http://journal.ccsenet.org/index.php/cis/index	Y	Y	Y	Y	Y	Y	Y	Y	Y	Y	Y	Y	Y	Y	Y	Y	Y	Y	Y	Y	Y	Y	Y	Y	Y	Y	Y	Y	Y	Y	Y	Y	N	N	N	Y	Y	N	Y	36
19	Coordinates: Online Journal of the Map and Geography Round Table of the American Library Association. Series A and B http://www.sunysb.edu/libmap/coordinates.htm	Y	Y	Y	Y	Y	Y	Y	Y	Y	Y	Y	Y	Y	Y	Y	Y	N	N	N	N	Y	Y	N	Y	Y	Y	Y	Y	Y	Y	Y	N	N	N	N	Y	Y	N	Y	30
20	Current Cites http://lists.webjunction.org	Y	Y	Y	Y	Y	Y	Y	Y	Y	Y	Y	Y	Y	Y	Y	Y	N	Y	Y	Y	Y	Y	Y	Y	Y	Y	Y	Y	Y	Y	N	Y	Y	N	N	N	Y	Y		34

21	Current Issues in Education http://cie.asu.edu/index.php	Y	Y	Y	Y	Y	Y	Y	Y	Y	Y	Y	Y	Y	Y	Y	Y	Y	N	Y	Y	Y	Y	Y	Y	Y	Y	Y	Y	Y	Y	Y	Y	Y	N	N	Y	N	N	Y	35
22	Cybermetrics : International Journal of Scientometrics, Informetrics and Bibliometrics http://www.cindoc.csic.es/cybermetrics/	Y	Y	Y	Y	Y	Y	Y	Y	Y	Y	Y	Y	Y	Y	N	Y	N	Y	Y	N	Y	Y	N	Y	Y	Y	Y	Y	Y	Y	N	N	N	Y	N	Y	Y	N		30
23	Data Science Journal http://www.datasciencejournal.org/	Y	Y	Y	Y	Y	Y	Y	Y	Y	Y	Y	Y	Y	Y	Y	Y	N	N	Y	Y	Y	Y	Y	Y	Y	Y	Y	Y	Y	Y	N	Y	N	N	N	Y	Y	N		32
24	DESIDOC Journal of Library & Information Science http://publications.drdo.gov.in/ojs/index.php/djlit/index	Y	Y	Y	Y	Y	Y	Y	Y	Y	Y	Y	Y	Y	Y	Y	Y	Y	Y	Y	Y	Y	Y	Y	Y	Y	Y	Y	Y	Y	Y	Y	Y	N	N	N	Y	N	N	Y	35
25	Digital Document Quarterly http://home.pacbell.net/hgladney/ddqstart.htm	Y	Y	Y	Y	Y	Y	Y	Y	Y	Y	Y	Y	Y	Y	Y	Y	N	Y	N	N	Y	N	N	Y	Y	Y	Y	Y	N	Y	N	N	N	N	N	N	Y	N		26
26	DIGITHUM: The Humanities in Digital Age http://www.uoc.edu/digithum/7/eng/index.html	Y	Y	Y	Y	Y	Y	Y	Y	Y	Y	Y	Y	Y	Y	Y	Y	N	Y	N	N	Y	N	N	Y	Y	Y	Y	Y	N	Y	N	N	N	N	N	N	Y	N		26

27	EBIB Electronic Information Bulletin for librarians http://ebib.info/biuletyn/	Y	Y	Y	Y	Y	Y	Y	Y	Y	Y	Y	Y	Y	Y	Y	Y	N	Y	N	Y	Y	N	Y	Y	Y	Y	Y	Y	N	Y	N	Y	Y	N	N	N	N	N		29
28	EDUCAUSE Quarterly http://connect.educause.edu/apps/eq/index.asp	Y	Y	Y	Y	Y	Y	Y	Y	Y	Y	Y	Y	Y	Y	Y	Y	Y	Y	Y	Y	Y	Y	Y	Y	Y	Y	Y	Y	Y	Y	N	Y	Y	N	N	Y	Y	N		35
29	E-JASL: The Electronic Journal of Academic and Special Librarianship http://southernlibrarianship.icaap.org/	Y	Y	Y	Y	Y	Y	Y	Y	Y	Y	Y	Y	Y	Y	Y	Y	Y	Y	Y	N	Y	Y	N	Y	Y	Y	Y	Y	Y	Y	Y	N	N	N	Y	N	Y	N		32
30	Electronic Journal of Africana Bibliography http://ir.uiowa.edu/ejab/all_issues.html	Y	Y	Y	Y	Y	Y	Y	Y	Y	Y	Y	Y	Y	Y	Y	Y	N	Y	Y	Y	Y	Y	Y	Y	Y	Y	Y	Y	Y	Y	N	Y	Y	N	Y	Y	Y	N		35
31	Electronic Journal of Health Informatics http://www.ejhi.net/ojs/index.php/ejhi	Y	Y	Y	Y	Y	Y	Y	Y	Y	Y	Y	Y	Y	Y	Y	Y	Y	Y	Y	Y	Y	Y	Y	Y	Y	Y	Y	Y	Y	Y	Y	Y	N	N	N	Y	Y	N	Y	36
32	Electronic Journal of Knowledge Management http://www.ejkm.com/	Y	Y	Y	Y	Y	Y	Y	Y	Y	Y	Y	Y	Y	Y	Y	Y	N	N	Y	Y	Y	N	Y	Y	Y	Y	Y	Y	N	Y	N	Y	Y	N	N	Y	Y	Y		32
33	Electronic Journal on Information Systems in Developing Countries http://www.ejisdc.org/ojs2/index.php/ejisdc	Y	Y	Y	Y	Y	Y	Y	Y	Y	Y	Y	Y	Y	Y	Y	Y	Y	Y	Y	Y	Y	Y	Y	Y	Y	Y	Y	Y	Y	Y	Y	Y	N	Y	N	N	Y	N		35

34	Electronic Transactions on Artificial Intlelligence http://www.ida.liu.se/ext/etai/	Y	Y	Y	Y	Y	Y	Y	Y	Y	Y	Y	Y	Y	Y	Y	Y	N	N	N	N	Y	N	N	Y	Y	Y	Y	Y	N	Y	N	N	N	N	N	N	N	N		24
35	European Journal of ePractice http://www.epracticejournal.eu/	Y	Y	Y	Y	Y	Y	Y	Y	Y	Y	Y	Y	Y	Y	Y	Y	N	N	Y	Y	Y	Y	Y	Y	Y	Y	Y	Y	Y	Y	N	Y	Y	N	N	Y	N	Y	Y	34
36	Evidence Based Library and Information Practice http://ejournals.library.ualberta.ca/index.php/EBLIP/index	Y	Y	Y	Y	Y	Y	Y	Y	Y	Y	Y	Y	Y	Y	Y	Y	Y	Y	Y	Y	Y	Y	Y	Y	Y	Y	Y	Y	Y	Y	Y	Y	Y	N	N	Y	Y	Y	Y	38
37	Firstmonday http://firstmonday.org/ (journal)	Y	Y	Y	Y	Y	Y	Y	Y	Y	Y	Y	Y	Y	Y	Y	Y	Y	Y	Y	Y	Y	Y	Y	Y	Y	Y	Y	Y	Y	Y	Y	Y	Y	N	N	Y	Y	Y	Y	38
38	Health Information and Libraries Journal http://www3.Intlerscience.wiley.com/journal/120118368/grouphome/home.html	Y	Y	Y	Y	Y	Y	Y	Y	Y	Y	Y	Y	Y	Y	Y	Y	Y	Y	Y	Y	Y	Y	Y	Y	Y	Y	Y	Y	Y	Y	Y	Y	Y	Y	N	Y	Y	Y		39
39	High Energy Physics Libraries Webzine http://library.web.cern.ch/library/Webzine/index.shtml	Y	Y	Y	Y	Y	Y	Y	Y	Y	Y	Y	Y	Y	Y	Y	Y	Y	N	Y	N	Y	N	N	Y	Y	Y	Y	Y	N	Y	N	N	N	N	N	N	Y	N		27

40	Human IT: Journal for Information Technology Studies as a Human Sciencehttp://etjanst.hb.se/bhs/ith//info-eng.htm	Y	Y	Y	Y	Y	Y	Y	Y	Y	Y	Y	Y	Y	Y	Y	Y	N	Y	N	N	Y	Y	N	Y	Y	Y	Y	Y	Y	Y	Y	N	N	N	N	N	Y	N		29
41	IFLA Journal http://www.ifla.org/V/iflaj/index.htm	Y	Y	Y	Y	Y	Y	Y	Y	Y	Y	Y	Y	Y	Y	N	Y	Y	Y	Y	Y	Y	N	Y	Y	Y	Y	Y	Y	N	Y	N	Y	N	N	N	N	Y	N		30
42	Informatica Economica Journal http://revistaie.ase.ro/index.html	Y	Y	Y	Y	Y	Y	Y	Y	Y	Y	Y	Y	Y	Y	Y	Y	N	Y	N	N	Y	Y	N	Y	Y	Y	Y	Y	Y	Y	Y	N	N	N	N	N	Y	N		29
43	Information for Social Change http://libr.org/isc/journal.html	Y	Y	Y	Y	Y	Y	Y	Y	Y	Y	Y	Y	Y	Y	Y	Y	Y	Y	Y	Y	Y	Y	Y	Y	Y	Y	Y	Y	Y	Y	N	Y	N	N	N	N	Y	N		33
44	Information Research: an International Electronic Journal http://informationr.net/ir/	Y	Y	Y	Y	Y	Y	Y	Y	Y	Y	Y	Y	Y	Y	Y	Y	N	Y	Y	Y	Y	Y	Y	Y	Y	Y	Y	Y	Y	Y	Y	Y	N	Y	N	Y	N	N		34
45	Information Scotland: The Journal of the Chartered Institute of Library and Information Professionals in Scotland http://www.slaintle.org.uk/publications/serials/infoscot/vol1(1)/vol1(1)contents.h	Y	Y	Y	Y	Y	Y	Y	Y	Y	Y	Y	Y	Y	Y	Y	Y	N	Y	N	Y	Y	Y	Y	Y	Y	Y	Y	Y	Y	Y	N	Y	N	N	N	N	Y	N		31

	tml																																								
46	Information Technologies and International Development http://itidjournal.org/itid	Y	Y	Y	Y	Y	Y	Y	Y	Y	Y	Y	Y	Y	Y	Y	Y	Y	Y	Y	Y	Y	Y	Y	Y	Y	Y	Y	Y	Y	Y	Y	Y	Y	Y	N	Y	Y	Y		39
47	Information Technology and Disabilities http://people.rit.edu/easi/itd.htm	Y	Y	Y	Y	Y	Y	Y	Y	Y	Y	Y	Y	Y	Y	Y	Y	N	N	N	N	Y	N	N	Y	Y	Y	Y	Y	N	Y	N	N	N	N	N	Y	N	N		25
48	Information Technology and Libraries http://www.ala.org/ala/mgrps/divs/lita/italinformation.cfm	Y	Y	Y	Y	Y	Y	Y	Y	Y	Y	Y	Y	Y	Y	Y	Y	N	Y	N	N	Y	N	N	Y	Y	Y	Y	Y	N	Y	N	N	N	N	Y	N	Y	N		27
49	Informing Faculty: An International Journal of Higher Education Discussion Cases http://informingfaculty.org/	Y	Y	Y	Y	Y	Y	Y	Y	Y	Y	Y	Y	Y	Y	Y	Y	N	N	N	N	Y	N	N	Y	Y	Y	Y	Y	N	Y	N	N	N	N	N	N	Y	N		25
50	Informing Science The International Journal of an Emerging Transdiscipline http://inform.nu/	Y	Y	Y	Y	Y	Y	Y	Y	Y	Y	Y	Y	Y	Y	Y	Y	Y	Y	Y	Y	Y	Y	Y	Y	Y	Y	Y	Y	Y	Y	N	Y	N	Y	Y	Y	Y	N		36

51	Inter-Actions: UCLA Journal of Education and Information Studies http://repositories.cdlib.org/gseis/Intleractions/	Y	Y	Y	Y	Y	Y	Y	Y	Y	Y	Y	Y	Y	Y	Y	Y	Y	Y	Y	Y	Y	Y	Y	Y	Y	Y	Y	Y	Y	Y	N	Y	Y	N	N	Y	Y	N		35
52	Interdisciplinary Journal of E-Learning and Learning Objects http://ijklo.org/	Y	Y	Y	Y	Y	Y	Y	Y	Y	Y	Y	Y	Y	Y	Y	Y	Y	Y	Y	Y	Y	Y	Y	Y	Y	Y	Y	Y	Y	Y	Y	Y	N	N	Y	Y	Y	N		36
53	Interdisciplinary Journal of Information, Knowledge, and Management http://www.ijikm.org/	Y		Y		Y	Y	Y	Y	Y	Y	Y	Y	Y	Y		Y	Y	Y	Y	Y	Y	Y	Y	Y	Y	Y	Y	Y	Y	Y	Y	Y	N	N	Y	Y	Y	N		36
54	International Journal of Communication http://ijoc.org/ojs/index.php/ijoc/about/editorialPolicies#focusAndScope	Y	Y	Y	Y	Y	Y	Y	Y	Y	Y	Y	Y	Y	Y	Y	Y	Y	Y	Y	Y	Y	Y	Y	Y	Y	Y	Y	Y	Y	Y	Y	Y	N	Y	N	Y	Y	N		36
55	International Journal of Communication Networks and Information Security http://www.ijcnis.org/index.php/ijcnis	Y	Y	Y	Y	Y	Y	Y	Y	Y	Y	Y	Y	Y	Y	Y	Y	Y	Y	Y	Y	Y	Y	Y	Y	Y	Y	Y	Y	Y	Y	Y	Y	N	Y	Y	Y	Y	N		37
56	International Journal of Computer and Information Engineering http://www.waset.org/journals/ijcie/	Y	Y	Y	Y	Y	Y	Y	Y	Y	Y	Y	Y	Y	Y	Y	Y	Y	Y	Y	Y	Y	Y	N	Y	Y	Y	Y	Y	Y	Y	Y	N	N	Y	Y	Y	Y	Y		36

57	International Journal of Computer Science and Information Technology http://airccse.org/journal/ijcsit.html	Y	Y	Y	Y	Y	Y	Y	Y	Y	Y	Y	Y	Y	Y	Y	Y	N	Y	Y	Y	Y	Y	Y	Y	Y	Y	Y	Y	Y	Y	Y	Y	N	Y	N	Y	Y	N		35
58	International Journal of Digital Curation http://www.ijdc.net/./ijdc/issue/current	Y	Y	Y	Y	Y	Y	Y	Y	Y	Y	Y	Y	Y	Y	Y	Y	Y	Y	Y	Y	Y	Y	Y	Y	Y	Y	Y	Y	Y	Y	Y	Y	N	Y	N	Y	N	N		35
59	International Journal of Doctoral Studies (IJDS) http://ijds.org/	Y	Y	Y	Y	Y	Y	Y	Y	Y	Y	Y	Y	Y	Y	Y	Y	Y	Y	Y	Y	Y	Y	Y	Y	Y	Y	Y	Y	Y	Y	Y	Y	N	Y	Y	Y	Y	N		37
60	Intlernational Journal of Legal Information http://scholarship.law.cornell.edu/ijli/vol33/iss1/	Y	Y	Y	Y	Y	Y	Y	Y	Y	Y	Y	Y	Y	Y	Y	Y	N	Y	Y	Y	Y	Y	Y	Y	Y	Y	Y	Y	Y	N	Y	Y	Y	N	N	N	N		33
61	International Journal of Library and Information Science http://www.academicjournals.org/ijlis/index.htm	Y	Y	Y	Y	Y	Y	Y	Y	Y	Y	Y	Y	Y	Y	Y	Y	Y	Y	Y	Y	Y	Y	Y	Y	Y	Y	Y	Y	Y	N	Y	N	Y	N	Y	Y	N		35
62	International Journal of Managing Public Sector Information and Communication Technologies http://airccse.org/journal/	Y	Y	Y	Y	Y	Y	Y	Y	Y	Y	Y	Y	Y	Y	Y	Y	Y	Y	Y	N	Y	Y	N	Y	Y	Y	Y	Y	Y	Y	Y	Y	N	Y	Y	Y	Y	N		35

	mpict/ijmpict.html																																							
63	International Journal of Multimedia and Its Applications http://airccse.org/journal/ijma_index.html	Y	Y	Y	Y	Y	Y	Y	Y	Y	Y	Y	Y	Y	Y	Y	Y	N	Y	Y	Y	Y	Y	Y	Y	Y	Y	Y	Y	Y	Y	Y	N	Y	N	N	Y	N		34
64	Intlernational Journal of Special Libraries http://forge.fh-potsdam.de/~IFLA/INSPEL/Intlro.htm	Y	Y	Y	Y	Y	Y	Y	Y	Y	Y	Y	Y	Y	Y	Y	Y	N	Y	N	N	Y	N	N	Y	Y	Y	Y	Y	N	Y	Y	N	N	Y	N	N	Y	N		28
65	International Review of Information Ethics http://www.i-r-i-e.net/	Y	Y	Y	Y	Y	Y	Y	Y	Y	Y	Y	Y	Y	Y	Y	Y	N	Y	Y	Y	Y	Y	Y	Y	Y	Y	Y	Y	Y	Y	N	Y	N	Y	N	N	Y	N		33
66	Intlernational Review of Research in Open and Distance Learning http://www.irrodl.org/index.php/irrodl	Y	Y	Y	Y	Y	Y	Y	Y	Y	Y	Y	Y	Y	Y	Y	Y	Y	Y	Y	Y	Y	Y	Y	Y	Y	Y	Y	Y	Y	Y	Y	Y	N	Y	N	Y	Y	N	Y	37
67	Intlernet Writing Journal http://www.Intlernetwritingjournal.com/	Y	Y	Y	Y	Y	Y	Y	Y	Y	Y	Y	Y	Y	Y	Y	Y	N	Y	N	Y	Y	N	Y	Y	Y	Y	Y	Y	N	Y	N	Y	Y	N	N	N	Y	Y		31
68	Intlerpersonal Computing and Technology Journal http://www.helsinki.fi/science/optek/#byissue	Y	Y	Y	Y	Y	Y	Y	Y	Y	Y	Y	Y	Y	Y	Y	Y	N	Y	Y	N	Y	N	N	Y	Y	Y	Y	Y	N	Y	N	N	N	N	N	Y	N	N		27

69	Issues in Informing Science and Information Technology http://iisit.org/	Y	Y	Y	Y	Y	Y	Y	Y	Y	Y	Y	Y	Y	Y	Y	Y	Y	Y	Y	Y	Y	Y	Y	Y	Y	Y	Y	Y	Y	Y	Y	Y	N	N	Y	Y	Y	N	Y	37
70	Issues in Science and Technology Librarianship http://www.library.ucsb.edu/istl/ Or http://www.istl.org/	Y	Y	Y	Y	Y	Y	Y	Y	Y	Y	Y	Y	Y	Y	Y	Y	N	Y	Y	Y	Y	Y	Y	Y	Y	Y	Y	Y	Y	Y	Y	Y	N	N	N	Y	Y	N	Y	35
71	IT&Society http://www.stanford.edu/group/siqss/itandsociety/	Y	Y	Y	Y	Y	Y	Y	Y	Y	Y	Y	Y	Y	Y	Y	Y	Y	N	Y	N	Y	Y	N	Y	Y	Y	Y	Y	Y	Y	N	N	N	N	N	N	Y	N		29
72	ITALICS: Innovations in Teaching and Learning in Information and Computer Sciences http://www.ics.ltsn.ac.uk/pub/italics/index.html Now http://www.ics.heacademy.ac.uk/.	Y	Y	Y	Y	Y	Y	Y	Y	Y	Y	Y	Y	Y	Y	Y	Y	N	Y	N	Y	Y	N	Y	Y	Y	Y	Y	Y	N	Y	N	Y	N	N	N	Y	N	N		29
73	JEP: The Journal of Electronic Publishing http://www.journalofelectronicpublishing.org/	Y	Y	Y	Y	Y	Y	Y	Y	Y	Y	Y	Y	Y	Y	Y	Y	Y	Y	Y	Y	Y	Y	Y	Y	Y	Y	Y	Y	Y	Y	N	Y	Y	N	N	N	Y	Y		35

74	JLIS.it Italian Journal of Library and Information Science http://leo.cilea.it/index.php/jlis/article/view/4539/4416	Y	Y	Y	Y	Y	Y	Y	Y	Y	Y	Y	Y	Y	Y	Y	Y	Y	Y	Y	Y	Y	Y	Y	Y	Y	Y	Y	Y	Y	Y	Y	Y	Y	Y	Y	Y	Y	N	Y	Y	Y		39
75	Journal of Artificial Intlelligence Research http://www.jair.org/	Y	Y	Y	Y	Y	Y	Y	Y	Y	Y	Y	Y	Y	Y	Y	Y	N	Y	Y	Y	Y	Y	Y	Y	Y	Y	Y	Y	Y	Y	Y	Y	Y	Y	Y	N	N	Y	N	Y	Y		35
76	Journal of Digital Information http://journals.tdl.org/jodi	Y	Y	Y	Y	Y	Y	Y	Y	Y	Y	Y	Y	Y	Y	Y	Y	Y	Y	Y	Y	Y	Y	Y	Y	Y	Y	Y	Y	Y	Y	Y	Y	Y	Y	Y	Y	N	N	Y	Y	Y	Y	38
77	Journal of East Asian Libraries http://www.lib.byu.edu/dlib/spc/jeal/	Y	Y	Y	Y	Y	Y	Y	Y	Y	Y	Y	Y	Y	Y	Y	Y	N	Y	Y	Y	Y	Y	Y	Y	Y	Y	Y	Y	Y	Y	Y	Y	Y	N	Y	Y	N	N	N	N	Y		33
78	Journal of Educational Media & Library Sciences http://joemls.tku.edu.tw/index_e.htm	Y	Y	Y	Y	Y	Y	Y	Y	Y	Y	Y	Y	Y	Y	Y	Y	N	Y	Y	Y	Y	Y	Y	Y	Y	Y	Y	Y	Y	Y	Y	Y	Y	Y	Y	N	Y	N	Y	Y	N		35
79	Journal of eLiteracy http://www.jelit.org/index.html	Y	Y	Y	Y	Y	Y	Y	Y	Y	Y	Y	Y	Y	Y	Y	Y	N	Y	Y	Y	Y	N	Y	Y	N	Y	Y	Y	Y	Y	Y	N	Y	N	Y	N	N	N	N	Y	N		30
80	Journal of Health Informatics in Developing Countries http://www.jhidc.org/index	Y	Y	Y	Y	Y	Y	Y	Y	Y	Y	Y	Y	Y	Y	Y	Y	Y	Y	Y	Y	Y	Y	Y	Y	Y	Y	Y	Y	Y	Y	Y	Y	Y	Y	Y	N	N	N	Y	Y	N	Y	35

	.php/jhidc																																								
81	Journal of Information Architecture http://journalofia.org/archives/	Y	Y	Y	Y	Y	Y	Y	Y	Y	Y	Y	Y	Y	Y	Y	Y	N	Y	Y	N	Y	Y	N	Y	Y	Y	Y	Y	Y	Y	Y	N	N	N	N	Y	Y	N		31
82	Journal of Information Law and Technology http://www2.warwick.ac.uk/fac/soc/law/elj/jilt/ or European Journal of Law and Technology http://ejlt.org//issue/archive	Y	Y	Y	Y	Y	Y	Y	Y	Y	Y	Y	Y	Y	Y	Y	Y	Y	Y	Y	Y	Y	Y	Y	Y	Y	Y	Y	Y	Y	Y	Y	Y	N	N	N	Y	Y	N	Y	35
83	Journal of Information Literacy (JIL) http://ojs.lboro.ac.uk/ojs/index.php/JIL/index	Y	Y	Y	Y	Y	Y	Y	Y	Y	Y	Y	Y	Y	Y	Y	Y	Y	Y	Y	Y	Y	Y	Y	Y	Y	Y	Y	Y	Y	Y	Y	Y	Y	N	N	Y	Y	N	Y	36
84	Journal of Information Technology Education (JITE: Research) http://www.informingscience.us/icarus/journals/jiteresearch/publications	Y	Y	Y	Y	Y	Y	Y	Y	Y	Y	Y	Y	Y	Y	Y	Y	Y	Y	Y	Y	Y	Y	Y	Y	Y	Y	Y	Y	Y	Y	Y	Y	N	N	Y	Y	Y	N	Y	36
85	Journal of Information, Information Technology, and Organizations http://jiito.org/	Y	Y	Y	Y	Y	Y	Y	Y	Y	Y	Y	Y	Y	Y	Y	Y	Y	Y	Y	Y	Y	Y	Y	Y	Y	Y	Y	Y	Y	Y	N	Y	N	N	Y	Y	Y	N	Y	35

86	Journal of Internetcataloguing http://www.Intlernetcataloging.com/jicissu.html	Y	Y	Y	Y	Y	Y	Y	Y	Y	Y	Y	Y	Y	Y	Y	Y	N	Y	Y	N	Y	N	N	Y	Y	Y	Y	Y	N	Y	N	N	N	Y	N	N	N	N		27
87	Journal of Knowledge Management Practice http://www.tlainc.com/boutjkmp.htm	Y	Y	Y	Y	Y	Y	Y	Y	Y	Y	Y	Y	Y	Y	Y	Y	N	Y	N	N	Y	Y	N	Y	Y	Y	Y	Y	Y	Y	N	N	N	N	N	N	Y	N		28
88	Journal of Library Innovation http://www.libraryinnovation.org/about/contact	Y	Y	Y	Y	Y	Y	Y	Y	Y	Y	Y	Y	Y	Y	Y	Y	Y	Y	Y	Y	Y	Y	Y	Y	Y	Y	Y	Y	Y	Y	Y	Y	Y	N	N	Y	Y	N	Y	36
89	Journal of Medical Internet Research http://www.jmir.org/	Y	Y	Y	Y	Y	Y	Y	Y	Y	Y	Y	Y	Y	Y	Y	Y	Y	Y	Y	Y	Y	Y	Y	Y	Y	Y	Y	Y	Y	Y	Y	Y	Y	N	N	Y	Y	N	Y	36
90	Journal of Philippine Librarianship http://journals.upd.edu.ph/index.php/jpl/issue/current	Y	Y	Y	Y	Y	Y	Y	Y	Y	Y	Y	Y	Y	Y	Y	Y	Y	Y	Y	Y	Y	Y	Y	Y	Y	Y	Y	Y	Y	Y	N	Y	N	N	N	N	Y	N		33
91	Journal of Research and Practice in Information Technology http://ws.acs.org.au/jrpit/JRPIT_Volumes.html	Y	Y	Y	Y	Y	Y	Y	Y	Y	Y	Y	Y	Y	Y	Y	Y	N	Y	Y	Y	Y	Y	Y	Y	Y	Y	Y	Y	Y	Y	Y	Y	N	Y	N	Y	Y	N		35
92	Journal of Staff Development http://learningforward.org/	Y	Y	Y	Y	Y	Y	Y	Y	Y	Y	Y	Y	Y	Y	Y	Y	N	Y	N	N	Y	Y	N	Y	Y	Y	Y	Y	Y	Y	N	N	N	N	N	N	N	N		27

	publications/jsd#.UUQguzcynUc																																								
93	Journal of Technology Studies http://scholar.lib.vt.edu/ejournals/JOTS/	Y	Y	Y	Y	Y	Y	Y	Y	Y	Y	Y	Y	Y	Y	Y	Y	Y	Y	Y	Y	Y	Y	Y	Y	Y	Y	Y	Y	Y	Y	N	Y	N	N	N	Y	Y	N		34
94	Journal of the American Medical Informatics Association http://www.pubmedcentral.nih.gov/tocrender.fcgi?action=archive&journal=76	Y	Y	Y	Y	Y	Y	Y	Y	Y	Y	Y	Y	Y	Y	Y	Y	Y	Y	Y	Y	Y	Y	Y	Y	Y	Y	Y	Y	Y	Y	Y	Y	Y	N	N	Y	Y	Y	Y	38
95	Journal of the Association for History and Computing http://mcel.pacificu.edu/jahc/	Y	Y	Y	Y	Y	Y	Y	Y	Y	Y	Y	Y	Y	Y	Y	Y	Y	Y	Y	Y	Y	Y	Y	Y	Y	Y	Y	Y	Y	Y	Y	Y	Y	N	N	N	Y	Y		36
96	Journal of the European Association for Health Information and Libraries http://www.eahil.net/journal/	Y	Y	Y	Y	Y	Y	Y	Y	Y	Y	Y	Y	Y	Y	Y	Y	Y	Y	Y	Y	Y	Y	Y	Y	Y	Y	Y	Y	Y	Y	N	Y	N	N	N	N	Y	N		33
97	Journal of the Medical Library association http://www.pubmedcentral.nih.gov/tocrender.fcgi?journal=93	Y	Y	Y	Y	Y	Y	Y	Y	Y	Y	Y	Y	Y	Y	Y	Y	Y	Y	Y	Y	Y	N	Y	Y	Y	Y	Y	Y	N	Y	Y	Y	N	N	N	N	Y	N		32

98	Journal of Virtual Worlds Research http://www.jvwresearch.org/index.html	Y	Y	Y	Y	Y	Y	Y	Y	Y	Y	Y	Y	Y	Y	Y	Y	N	Y	Y	Y	Y	Y	Y	Y	Y	Y	Y	Y	Y	Y	Y	Y	Y	N	N	N	Y	Y		35
99	LASIE: Library Automated Systems Information Exchange http://search.informit.com.au/browseJournalTitle;res=E-LIBRARY;issn=0047-3774	Y	Y	Y	Y	Y	Y	Y	Y	Y	Y	Y	Y	Y	Y	Y	Y	Y	Y	Y	Y	Y	N	Y	Y	Y	Y	Y	Y	N	Y	N	Y	Y	N	N	N	Y	Y		33
100	Law Library Journal http://www.aallnet.org/products/pub_journal.asp	Y	Y	Y	Y	Y	Y	Y	Y	Y	Y	Y	Y	Y	Y	Y	Y	Y	Y	Y	Y	Y	Y	Y	Y	Y	Y	Y	Y	Y	Y	N	Y	N	N	N	N	N	N		32
101	Learned Publishing http://www.ingentaconnect.com/content/alpsp/lp	Y	Y	Y	Y	Y	Y	Y	Y	Y	Y	Y	Y	Y	Y	Y	Y	N	Y	Y	Y	Y	Y	Y	Y	Y	Y	Y	Y	Y	Y	N	Y	Y	N	N	N	Y	Y		34
102	LIBER Quarterly Journal of European Research Libraries http://liber.library.uu.nl/index.html	Y	Y	Y	Y	Y	Y	Y	Y	Y	Y	Y	Y	Y	Y	Y	Y	Y	Y	Y	Y	Y	Y	Y	Y	Y	Y	Y	Y	Y	Y	N	Y	N	N	N	N	Y	N		33
103	Library & Information Research: Research Intlo Practice for Information & Library Services http://www.lirg.org.uk/lir/	Y	Y	Y	Y	Y	Y	Y	Y	Y	Y	Y	Y	Y	Y	Y	Y	Y	Y	Y	Y	Y	Y	Y	Y	Y	Y	Y	Y	Y	Y	Y	Y	Y	N	Y	Y	Y	Y	Y	39

	ojs/index.php/lir																																								
104	Library Journal http://www.libraryjournal.com/csp/cms/sites/LJ/LJInPrIntl/Archive/archive2002.csp	Y	Y	Y	Y	Y	Y	Y	Y	Y	Y	Y	Y	Y	Y	Y	Y	Y	Y	Y	Y	Y	Y	Y	Y	Y	Y	Y	Y	Y	Y	N	Y	Y	N	N	N	N	Y		34
105	Library Philosophy and Practice http://www.webpages.uidaho.edu/~mbolin/lpp.htm	Y	Y	Y	Y	Y	Y	Y	Y	Y	Y	Y	Y	Y	Y	Y	Y	N	Y	Y	Y	Y	Y	Y	Y	Y	Y	Y	Y	Y	Y	Y	Y	Y	N	N	Y	Y	Y	Y	37
106	Library Resources & Technical Services (LRTS) http://alcts.metapress.com/home/main.mpx	Y	Y	Y	Y	Y	Y	Y	Y	Y	Y	Y	Y	Y	Y	Y	Y	N	Y	N	Y	Y	N	Y	Y	Y	Y	Y	Y	N	Y	N	Y	N	N	N	N	Y	N		29
107	Library Student Journal http://www.librarystudentjournal.org/index.php/lsj/index	Y	Y	Y	Y	Y	Y	Y	Y	Y	Y	Y	Y	Y	Y	Y	Y	Y	Y	Y	Y	Y	Y	Y	Y	Y	Y	Y	Y	Y	Y	Y	Y	N	N	N	Y	Y	N	Y	36
108	LIBRES: Library and Information Science Research Electronic Journal http://libres.curtin.edu.au/	Y	Y	Y	Y	Y	Y	Y	Y	Y	Y	Y	Y	Y	Y	Y	Y	N	Y	Y	Y	Y	Y	Y	Y	Y	Y	Y	Y	Y	Y	Y	Y	N	Y	Y	N	Y	N		35
109	LIBRI: International Journal of Libraries and Information Services http://www.librijournal.org/	Y	Y	Y	Y	Y	Y	Y	Y	Y	Y	Y	Y	Y	Y	Y	Y	N	Y	Y	Y	Y	Y	Y	Y	Y	Y	Y	Y	Y	Y	Y	Y	N	Y	N	N	Y	N		34

110	Malaysian Journal of Library & Information Science Malaysian Journal of Library & Information Science http://ejum.fsktm.um.edu.my/Default.aspx	Y	Y	Y	Y	Y	Y	Y	Y	Y	Y	Y	Y	Y	Y	Y	Y	Y	Y	Y	Y	Y	Y	Y	Y	Y	Y	Y	Y	Y	Y	N	Y	N	N	N	N	Y	N		33
111	MC Journal: The Journal of Academic Media Librarianship http://wings.buffalo.edu/publications/mcjrnl/	Y	Y	Y	Y	Y	Y	Y	Y	Y	Y	Y	Y	Y	Y	Y	Y	N	Y	Y	Y	Y	N	Y	Y	Y	Y	Y	Y	N	Y	N	Y	N	N	N	Y	Y	N		31
112	MELA Notes: The Journal of the Middle East Librarians Association http://www.mela.us/MELANotes/MELANotesIntro.html	Y	Y	Y	Y	Y	Y	Y	Y	Y	Y	Y	Y	Y	Y	Y	Y	N	Y	N	N	Y	Y	N	Y	Y	Y	Y	Y	Y	Y	N	N	N	N	N	N	Y	N		28
113	Mississippi Libraries http://www.misslib.org/index.php/publications/mississippi-libraries/mississippi-libraries/ml-archives/	Y	Y	Y	Y	Y	Y	Y	Y	Y	Y	Y	Y	Y	Y	N	Y	N	Y	Y	Y	Y	Y	Y	Y	Y	Y	Y	Y	Y	Y	Y	Y	N	N	N	N	Y	N		32
114	MLA Forum http://www.mlaforum.org/	Y	Y	Y	Y	Y	Y	Y	Y	Y	Y	Y	Y	Y	Y	N	Y	Y	Y	Y	Y	Y	Y	Y	Y	Y	Y	Y	Y	Y	Y	Y	N	N	N	N	N	Y	N		32

115	Multimedia Information and Technology (MmIT)http://mmitblog.wordpress.com/	Y	Y	Y	Y	Y	Y	Y	Y	Y	Y	Y	Y	Y	Y	Y	Y	Y	Y	Y	Y	Y	Y	Y	Y	Y	Y	Y	Y	Y	Y	N	Y	Y	N	N	N	N	Y		34
116	New Knowledge Environments http://journals.uvic.ca/index.php/INKE	Y	Y	Y	Y	Y	Y	Y	Y	Y	Y	Y	Y	Y	Y	Y	Y	Y	Y	Y	Y	Y	Y	Y	Y	Y	Y	Y	Y	Y	Y	Y	Y	Y	N	N	N	N	Y	Y	36
117	North Carolina Libraries http://www.nclaonline.org/NCL/	Y	Y	Y	Y	Y	Y	Y	Y	Y	Y	Y	Y	Y	Y	Y	Y	Y	Y		Y	Y	Y	Y	Y	Y	Y	Y	Y	Y	Y	Y	Y	N	N	N	Y	N	N	Y	35
118	Northwestern Journal of Technology and Intlellectual Property http://www.law.northwestern.edu/journals/njtip/issues.htm	Y	Y	Y	Y	Y	Y	Y	Y	Y	Y	Y	Y	Y	Y	Y	Y	N	Y	Y	Y	Y	Y	Y	Y	Y	Y	Y	Y	Y	Y	N	Y	Y	N	N	N	N	Y		33
119	NPO E-journals / National Preservation Office http://www.bl.uk/npo/journaltemp.html	Y	Y	Y	Y	Y	Y	Y	Y	Y	Y	Y	Y	Y	Y	Y	Y	Y	Y	Y	Y	Y	N	Y	Y	Y	Y	Y	Y	N	Y	N	Y	N	N	N	N	N	N		30
120	Partnership: The Canadian Journal of Library and Information Practice and Research http://journal.lib.uoguelph.ca/index.php/perj/index	Y	Y	Y	Y	Y	Y	Y	Y	Y	Y	Y	Y	Y	Y	Y	Y	Y	Y	Y	Y	Y	Y	Y	Y	Y	Y	Y	Y	Y	Y	Y	Y	N	N	N	Y	Y	N	Y	35

121	Progressive Librarian http://libr.org/pl/	Y	Y	Y	Y	Y	Y	Y	Y	Y	Y	Y	Y	Y	Y	Y	Y	N	Y	Y	Y	Y	N	Y	Y	Y	Y	Y	Y	N	Y	Y	Y	N	N	N	N	Y	N		31
122	RBM Journal of Rare Books & Manuscripts http://rbm.acrl.org/content /2/2Librarianship http://rbm.acrl.org/content /2/2	Y	Y	Y	Y	Y	Y	Y	Y	Y	Y	Y	Y	Y	Y	Y	Y	N	Y	Y	Y	Y	Y	Y	Y	Y	Y	Y	Y	Y	N	Y	Y	N	N	N	Y	Y		34
123	Research Management Review http://www.ncura.edu/con tent/news/rmr/archive php	Y	Y	Y	Y	Y	Y	Y	Y	Y	Y	Y	Y	Y	Y	Y	Y	Y	Y	N	N	Y	N	N	Y	Y	Y	Y	Y	N	Y	N	N	N	N	N	N	N	N		26
124	Scandinavian Public Library Quarterly http://www.splq.info/	Y	Y	Y	Y	Y	Y	Y	Y	Y	Y	Y	Y	Y	Y	Y	Y	N	Y	Y	Y	Y	Y	Y	Y	Y	Y	Y	Y	Y	N	Y	N	N	N	N	N	N		31
125	School libraries in Canada (SLIC): A Journal of the Canadian Association for School Libraries http://www.clatoolbox.ca/c asl/slic/links.html	Y	Y	Y	Y	Y	Y	Y	Y	Y	Y	Y	Y	Y	Y	Y	Y	Y	Y	Y	Y	Y	Y	Y	Y	Y	Y	Y	Y	Y	N	Y	N	N	N	N	Y	N		33
126	School Library Journal Online http://www.schoollibraryjo urnal.com/	Y	Y	Y	Y	Y	Y	Y	Y	Y	Y	Y	Y	Y	Y	Y	Y	Y	Y	Y	Y	Y	Y	Y	Y	Y	Y	Y	Y	Y	N	Y	Y	N	N	N	N	Y		34
127	School Library Research http://www.ala.org/aasl/slr	Y	Y	Y	Y	Y	Y	Y	Y	Y	Y	Y	Y	Y	Y	Y	Y	N	Y	Y	Y	Y	Y	Y	Y	Y	Y	Y	Y	Y	N	Y	N	N	N	N	N	N		31

128	Simile: Studies in Media and Information Literacy Education http://utpjournals.metapress.com/content/120764/	Y	Y	Y	Y	Y	Y	Y	Y	Y	Y	Y	Y	Y	Y	Y	Y	Y	Y	Y	N	Y	Y	N	Y	Y	Y	Y	Y	Y	Y	Y	N	Y	N	Y	Y	Y	N	Y	35
129	South African Journal of Information Management http://general.rau.ac.za/infosci/raujournal/	Y	Y	Y	Y	Y	Y	Y	Y	Y	Y	Y	Y	Y	Y	Y	Y	Y	Y	Y	Y	Y	Y	Y	Y	Y	Y	Y	Y	Y	Y	Y	Y	Y	N	N	Y	Y	Y	Y	38
130	Special Libraries http://www.sla.org/content/shop/speclibs.cfm#1910	Y	Y	Y	Y	Y	Y	Y	Y	Y	Y	Y	Y	Y	Y	Y	Y	N	Y	Y	Y	Y	N	Y	Y	Y	Y	Y	Y	N	Y	N	Y	Y	N	N	N	Y	Y		32
131	Studies in Bibliography http://etext.lib.virginia.edu/bsuva/sb	Y	Y	Y	Y	Y	Y	Y	Y	Y	Y	Y	Y	Y	Y	Y	Y	N	Y	N	Y	Y	N	Y	Y	Y	Y	Y	Y	N	Y	N	Y	N	N	N	N	N	N		28
132	Technological Librarianship :An Online Journal of the American Theological Library Association http://journal.atla.com/ojs/index.php/theolib/index	Y	Y	Y	Y	Y	Y	Y	Y	Y	Y	Y	Y	Y	Y	Y	Y	Y	Y	Y	Y	Y	Y	Y	Y	Y	Y	Y	Y	Y	Y	Y	Y	Y	N	N	Y	Y	Y	Y	38
133	Technology Electronic Reviews (TER) http://www.ala.org/lita/publications/archive/ter	Y	Y	Y	Y	Y	Y	Y	Y	Y	Y	Y	Y	Y	Y	Y	Y	Y	N	N	Y	Y	N	Y	Y	Y	Y	Y	Y	N	Y	N	Y	N	N	N	N	Y	N		29

134	Texas library journal http://www.txla.org/TLJ	Y	Y	Y	Y	Y	Y	Y	Y	Y	Y	Y	Y	Y	Y	Y	Y	N	Y	N	Y	Y	Y	Y	Y	Y	Y	Y	Y	Y	Y	N	Y	N	N	N	N	N	N		30
135	The Bonefolder: An outgrowth of the Book Arts Web http://www.philobiblon.com/bonefolder/index.html	Y	Y	Y	Y	Y	Y	Y	Y	Y	Y	Y	Y	Y	Y	Y	Y	N	Y	N	Y	Y	Y	Y	Y	Y	Y	Y	Y	Y	Y	Y	Y	N	N	N	N	Y	N		32
136	Code4Lib Journal http://journal.code4lib.org/	Y	Y	Y	Y	Y	Y	Y	Y	Y	Y	Y	Y	Y	Y	N	Y	N	N	N	Y	Y	Y	Y	Y	Y	Y	Y	Y	Y	Y	N	Y	N	N	N	N	Y	N		29
137	The Idaho Librarian: A Publication of the Idaho Library Association http://www.idaholibraries.org/idlibrarian/index.php/idaho-librarian/index	Y	Y	Y	Y	Y	Y	Y	Y	Y	Y	Y	Y	Y	Y	Y	Y	Y	Y	Y	Y	Y	Y	Y	Y	Y	Y	Y	Y	Y	Y	Y	Y	N	N	N	Y	Y	N	Y	36
138	The International Journal of Database Management Systems http://airccse.org/journal/ijdms/ijdms.html	Y	Y	Y	Y	Y	Y	Y	Y	Y	Y	Y	Y	Y	Y	Y	Y	Y	Y	Y	Y	Y	Y	Y	Y	Y	Y	Y	Y	Y	Y	Y	Y	N	Y	N	N	Y	N		35
139	The International Journal of Managing Information Technology http://airccse.org/journal/ijmit/ijmit.html	Y	Y	Y	Y	Y	Y	Y	Y	Y	Y	Y	Y	Y	Y	Y	Y	Y	Y	Y	Y	Y	Y	Y	Y	Y	Y	Y	Y	Y	Y	Y	Y	N	Y	Y	Y	Y	N		37

140	The journal of the Rutgers University Library. http://jrul.libraries.rutgers.edu/index.php/jrul/index	Y	Y	Y	Y	Y	Y	Y	Y	Y	Y	Y	Y	Y	Y	Y	Y	Y	Y	Y	Y	Y	N	Y	Y	Y	Y	Y	Y	N	Y	Y	Y	N	N	N	Y	Y	N		33
141	The Public Access Computer Systems Review http://epress.lib.uh.edu/pr/pacsrev.html	Y	Y	Y	Y	Y	Y	Y	Y	Y	Y	Y	Y	Y	Y	Y	Y	N	N	N	Y	Y	N	Y	Y	Y	Y	Y	Y	N	Y	N	Y	N	N	Y	N	Y	N		29
142	Urban Library Journal http://lacuny.cuny.edu/ulj/	Y	Y	Y	Y	Y	Y	Y	Y	Y	Y	Y	Y	Y	Y	Y	Y	N	Y	Y	Y	Y	Y	Y	Y	Y	Y	Y	Y	Y	Y	N	Y	N	N	Y	N	Y	N		33
143	Virginia Libraries http://scholar.lib.vt.edu/ejournals/VALib/	Y	Y	Y	Y	Y	Y	Y	Y	Y	Y	Y	Y	Y	Y	Y	Y	Y	Y	N	Y	Y	Y	Y	Y	Y	Y	Y	Y	Y	Y	N	Y	N	N	N	N	Y	N		32
144	Webology http://www.webology.ir/	Y	Y	Y	Y	Y	Y	Y	Y	Y	Y	Y	Y	Y	Y	Y	Y	Y	Y	Y	Y	Y	Y	Y	Y	Y	Y	Y	Y	Y	Y	Y	Y	N	N	N	Y	Y	N		35
145	World Libraries http://www.worlib.org/	Y	Y	Y	Y	Y	Y	Y	Y	Y	Y	Y	Y	Y	Y	Y	Y	N	Y	Y	N	Y	Y	N	Y	Y	Y	Y	Y	Y	Y	N	N	N	N	N	Y	Y	N		30

E-Magazines

1	AALL Spectrum http://www.aallnet.org/main-menu/Publications/spectrum	Y	Y	Y	Y	Y	Y	Y	Y	Y	Y	Y	Y	Y	Y	Y	Y	Y	Y	Y	Y	Y	Y	Y	Y	Y	Y	Y	Y	Y	Y	N	Y	Y	N	N	N	N	Y		34

2	Access http://www.aardvarknet.info/access/number46/index.cfm	Y	Y	Y	Y	Y	Y	Y	Y	Y	Y	Y	Y	Y	Y	Y	Y	Y	Y	Y	Y	Y	Y	Y	Y	Y	Y	Y	Y	Y	Y	N	Y	N	N	N	N	Y	N		33
3	American Libraries http://americanlibrariesmagazine.org/	Y	Y	Y	Y	Y	Y	Y	Y	Y	Y	Y	Y	Y	Y	Y	Y	Y	Y	Y	Y	Y	Y	Y	Y	Y	Y	Y	Y	Y	Y	Y	Y	Y	N	N	N	Y	Y		37
4	Ariadne http://www.ariadne.ac.uk/	Y	Y	Y	Y	Y	Y	Y	Y	Y	Y	Y	Y	Y	Y	Y	Y	N	Y	Y	Y	Y	Y	Y	Y	Y	Y	Y	Y	Y	Y	N	Y	Y	N	N	N	N	Y		34
5	Book business http://www.bookbusinessmag.com/	Y	Y	Y	Y	Y	Y	Y	Y	Y	Y	Y	Y	Y	Y	Y	Y	Y	N	Y	Y	Y	Y	Y	Y	Y	Y	Y	Y	Y	Y	N	Y	Y	N	N	N	N	Y		34
6	Book Links http://www.ala.org/ala/aboutala/offices/publishing/booklinks/archiveonline/archive_of_online_articles.cfm	Y	Y	Y	Y	Y	Y	Y	Y	Y	Y	Y	Y	Y	Y	Y	Y	Y	Y	Y	Y	Y	Y	Y	Y	Y	Y	Y	Y	Y	Y	N	Y	N	N	N	N	Y	N		33
7	CHOICE http://www.ala.org/ala/mgrps/divs/acrl/publications/choice/previousissues/previousissues.cfm	Y	Y	Y	Y	Y	Y	Y	Y	Y	Y	Y	Y	Y	Y	Y	Y	Y	Y	Y	N	Y	Y	N	Y	Y	Y	Y	Y	Y	Y	N	N	N	N	N	N	Y	N		30
8	Computer in Libraries http://www.infotoday.com/cilmag/default.shtml	Y	Y	Y	Y	Y	Y	Y	Y	Y	Y	Y	Y	Y	Y	Y	Y	Y	Y	Y	Y	Y	Y	Y	Y	Y	Y	Y	Y	Y	Y	Y	Y	N	N	N	N	Y	N		34

9	Cultivate Interactive http://www.cultivate-Intl.org/index-2.html	Y	Y	Y	Y	Y	Y	Y	Y	Y	Y	Y	Y	Y	Y	Y	Y	N	N	N	Y	Y	N	Y	Y	Y	Y	Y	Y	N	Y	N	Y	N	N	N	N	Y	N		28
10	D-Lib Magazine http://www.dlib.org/dlib/september08/09contents.html	Y	Y	Y	Y	Y	Y	Y	Y	Y	Y	Y	Y	Y	Y	Y	Y	N	Y	Y	Y	Y	Y	Y	Y	Y	Y	Y	Y	Y	Y	N	Y	N	N	N	N	N	N		31
11	E-Content http://www.ecmag.net/	Y	Y	Y	Y	Y	Y	Y	Y	Y	Y	Y	Y	Y	Y	Y	Y	Y	Y	Y	Y	Y	Y	Y	Y	Y	Y	Y	Y	Y	Y	N	Y	Y	N	N	N	N	Y		34
12	EDUCAUSE Review http://www.educause.edu/	Y	Y	Y	Y	Y	Y	Y	Y	Y	Y	Y	Y	Y	Y	Y	Y	Y	Y	Y	Y	Y	Y	Y	Y	Y	Y	Y	Y	Y	Y	N	Y	Y	N	N	N	N	Y		34
13	Ex Libris http://marylaine.com/exlibris/	Y	Y	Y	Y	Y	Y	Y	Y	Y	Y	Y	Y	Y	Y	Y	Y	N	N	N	N	Y	N	N	Y	Y	Y	Y	Y	N	Y	N	N	N	N	N	N	N	N		24
14	Exploit Intleractive http://www.exploit-lib.org/	Y	Y	Y	Y	Y	Y	Y	Y	Y	Y	Y	Y	Y	Y	Y	Y	N	N	N	N	Y	N	N	Y	Y	Y	Y	Y	N	Y	N	N	N	N	N	N	N	N		24
15	inCite http://alia.org.au/publishing/incite/archive.html	Y	Y	Y	Y	Y	Y	Y	Y	Y	Y	Y	Y	Y	Y	Y	Y	N	Y	N	Y	Y	Y	Y	Y	Y	Y	Y	Y	Y	Y	N	Y	N	N	N	N	N	N		30
16	Information Today http://www.infotoday.com/IT/nov08/index.shtml	Y	Y	Y	Y	Y	Y	Y	Y	Y	Y	Y	Y	Y	Y	Y	Y	Y	Y	Y	Y	Y	Y	Y	Y	Y	Y	Y	Y	Y	Y	N	Y	N	N	N	N	N	N		32
17	Knowledge Management World http://www.kmworld.com/	Y	Y	Y	Y	Y	Y	Y	Y	Y	Y	Y	Y	Y	Y	Y	Y	Y	Y	Y	Y	Y	Y	Y	Y	Y	Y	Y	Y	Y	Y	N	Y	Y	N	N	N	Y	Y		36

	index.cfm																																								
18	Library Juice http://libr.org/juice/	Y	Y	Y	Y	Y	Y	Y	Y	Y	Y	Y	Y	Y	Y	Y	Y	N	N	Y	Y	Y	N	Y	Y	Y	Y	Y	Y	N	Y	N	Y	Y	N	N	N	N	Y		30
19	Link-Up http://www.infotoday.com /linkup/default.shtml	Y	Y	Y	Y	Y	Y	Y	Y	Y	Y	Y	Y	Y	Y	Y	Y	Y	Y	Y	Y	Y	Y	Y	Y	Y	Y	Y	Y	Y	Y	N	Y	N	N	N	N	Y	N		33
20	Online http://www.infotoday.com /online/default.shtml	Y	Y	Y	Y	Y	Y	Y	Y	Y	Y	Y	Y	Y	Y	N	Y	Y	Y	Y	Y	Y	Y	Y	Y	Y	Y	Y	Y	Y	Y	N	Y	N	N	N	N	N	N		31
21	Provenance http://www.provenance.ca /about- provenance/index.html	Y	Y	Y	Y	Y	Y	Y	Y	Y	Y	Y	Y	Y	Y	Y	Y	N	Y	Y	Y	Y	Y	Y	Y	Y	Y	Y	Y	Y	Y	N	Y	N	N	N	N	N	N		31
22	Research Information http://www.researchinfor mation.info/	Y	Y	Y	Y	Y	Y	Y	Y	Y	Y	Y	Y	Y	Y	Y	Y	Y	Y	Y	Y	Y	Y	Y	Y	Y	Y	Y	Y	Y	Y	N	Y	Y	N	N	N	N	Y		34
23	Searcher: The Magazine for Database Professionals http://www.infotoday.com /searcher/default.asp	Y	Y	Y	Y	Y	Y	Y	Y	Y	Y	Y	Y	Y	Y	Y	Y	Y	Y	Y	Y	Y	Y	Y	Y	Y	Y	Y	Y	Y	Y	N	Y	N	N	N	N	N	N		32
24	The Bulletin of the American Society for Information Science and Technology http://www.asis.org/bulleti n.html	Y	Y	Y	Y	Y	Y	Y	Y	Y	Y	Y	Y	Y	Y	Y	Y	N	Y	Y	Y	Y	Y	Y	Y	Y	Y	Y	Y	Y	Y	N	Y	N	N	N	N	N	N		31

25	The Marginal http://www.gslis.mcgill.ca/marginal/	Y	Y	Y	Y	Y	Y	Y	Y	Y	Y	Y	Y	Y	Y	Y	Y	N	Y	N	N	Y	Y	N	Y	Y	Y	Y	Y	Y	Y	N	N	N	N	N	N	N	N		27
26	Virginia Tech Magazine (current issue) http://www.vtmagazine.vt.edu/wlntler09/index.html	Y	Y	Y	Y	Y	Y	Y	Y	Y	Y	Y	Y	Y	Y	Y	Y	Y	Y	Y	Y	Y	Y	Y	Y	Y	Y	Y	Y	Y	Y	N	Y	N	N	N	N	Y	N		33

Newsletters and other E-Resources

1	ABAA Newsletter http://hq.abaa.org/books/antiquarian/abaapages/newsletter	Y	Y	Y	Y	Y	Y	Y	Y	Y	Y	Y	Y	Y	Y	Y	Y	N	Y	Y	Y	Y	Y	Y	Y	Y	Y	Y	Y	Y	Y	N	Y	N	N	N	N	Y	N		32
2	Abbey Newsletter http://cool.conservation-us.org/byorg/abbey/an/	Y	Y	Y	Y	Y	Y	Y	Y	Y	Y	Y	Y	Y	Y	Y	Y	Y	Y	N	Y	Y	N	Y	Y	Y	Y	Y	Y	N	Y	N	Y	N	N	N	N	N	N		29
3	Against the grain http://www.against-the-grain.com/d/TOC	Y	Y	Y	Y	Y	Y	Y	Y	Y	Y	Y	Y	Y	Y	Y	Y	Y	Y	Y	Y	Y	Y	Y	Y	Y	Y	Y	Y	Y	Y	N	Y	Y	N	N	N	Y	Y		36
4	ALAWON. The ALA Washington Office Electronic Newsline http://www.ala.org/ala/aboutala/offices/wo/washnews/archivea/archive.cfm	Y	Y	Y	Y	Y	Y	Y	Y	Y	Y	Y	Y	Y	Y	Y	Y	Y	N	Y	Y	Y	Y	Y	Y	Y	Y	Y	Y	Y	Y	N	Y	N	N	N	N	N	N		31

5	ALCTS Network News http://bubl.ac.uk/archive/journals/alctsnn/	Y	Y	Y	Y	Y	Y	Y	Y	Y	Y	Y	Y	Y	Y	Y	Y	Y	Y	Y	N	Y	N	N	Y	Y	Y	Y	Y	N	Y	N	N	N	N	N	N	Y	N		28
6	ARL: A bimonthly newsletter for library issues and action http://www.arl.org/resources/pubs/br/index.shtml	Y	Y	Y	Y	Y	Y	Y	Y	Y	Y	Y	Y	Y	Y	Y	Y	Y	Y	Y	Y	Y	N	Y	Y	Y	Y	Y	Y	N	Y	N	Y	Y	N	N	N	N	Y		32
7	Biblia's Warrior Librarian Weekly http://warriorlibrarian.com/ARCHIVE/00archives.html	Y	Y	Y	Y	Y	Y	Y	Y	Y	Y	Y	Y	Y	Y	Y	Y	N	N	N	Y	Y	N	Y	Y	Y	Y	Y	Y	N	Y	N	Y	N	N	N	N	Y	N		28
8	Biblio-Tech Review http://www.ringgold.com/biblio-tech/si_pd.cfm?pid=2	Y	Y	Y	Y	Y	Y	Y	Y	Y	Y	Y	Y	Y	Y	Y	Y	N	N	N	Y	Y	Y	Y	Y	Y	Y	Y	Y	Y	Y	N	Y	N	N	N	N	Y	N		30
9	Business and Finance Division Bulletin http://bf.sla.org/resources/the-bulletin/	Y	Y	Y	Y	Y	Y	Y	Y	Y	Y	Y	Y	Y	Y	Y	Y	N	Y	Y	N	Y	Y	N	Y	Y	Y	Y	Y	Y	Y	Y	N	N	N	N	Y	N	N	Y	31
10	Cataloging and Classification Quarterly http://bubl.ac.uk/archive/journals/cacq/	Y	Y	Y	Y	Y	Y	Y	Y	Y	Y	Y	Y	Y	Y	Y	Y	Y	N	N	N	Y	N	N	Y	Y	Y	Y	Y	N	Y	N	N	N	N	N	N	Y	N		26
11	CIT Infobits http://serials.infomotions.com/infobits/	Y	Y	Y	Y	Y	Y	Y	Y	Y	Y	Y	Y	Y	Y	Y	Y	N	Y	N	N	Y	N	N	Y	Y	Y	Y	Y	N	Y	N	N	N	N	N	N	N	N		25

12	Conserline http://www.loc.gov/acq/conser/consrlin.html	Y	Y	Y	Y	Y	Y	Y	Y	Y	Y	Y	Y	Y	Y	Y	Y	N	N	N	Y	Y	N	Y	Y	Y	Y	Y	Y	N	Y	N	Y	N	N	N	N	Y	N		28
13	Free PIntl http://www.freepIntl.com/	Y	Y	Y	Y	Y	Y	Y	Y	Y	Y	Y	Y	Y	Y	Y	Y	N	N	Y	Y	Y	Y	Y	Y	Y	Y	Y	Y	Y	N	Y	Y	N	N	N	Y	Y			33
14	Information today and Tomorrow http://www.dsir.gov.in/pubs/itt/index.htm	Y	Y	Y	Y	Y	Y	Y	Y	Y	Y	Y	Y	Y	Y	Y	Y	N	Y	N	N	Y	N	N	Y	Y	Y	Y	Y	N	Y	N	N	N	N	N	N	N	N		25
15	Intlernet on a Disk http://www.samizdat.com/ioad.html	Y	Y	Y	Y	Y	Y	Y	Y	Y	Y	Y	Y	Y	Y	Y	Y	N	N	N	N	Y	Y	N	Y	Y	Y	Y	Y	Y	Y	N	N	N	N	N	N	Y	N		27
16	Internet Resources Newsletter http://www.hw.ac.uk/libwww/irn/irn.html	Y	Y	Y	Y	Y	Y	Y	Y	Y	Y	Y	Y	Y	Y	Y	Y	N	Y	N	Y	Y	N	Y	Y	Y	Y	Y	Y	N	Y	N	Y	N	N	N	N	N	N		28
17	LC Cataloging Newsline http://www.loc.gov/catdir/lccn/	Y	Y	Y	Y	Y	Y	Y	Y	Y	Y	Y	Y	Y	Y	Y	Y	N	N	N	Y	Y	N	Y	Y	Y	Y	Y	Y	N	Y	N	Y	N	N	N	N	N	N		27
18	MLS: Marketing Library Services http://www.infotoday.com/MLS/default.shtml	Y	Y	Y	Y	Y	Y	Y	Y	Y	Y	Y	Y	Y	Y	Y	Y	Y	Y	Y	Y	Y	Y	Y	Y	Y	Y	Y	Y	Y	Y	N	Y	N	N	N	N	Y	N		34
19	NLM Technical Bulletin http://www.nlm.nih.gov/pubs/techbull/current_issue.	Y	Y	Y	Y	Y	Y	Y	Y	Y	Y	Y	Y	Y	Y	Y	Y	N	Y	Y	Y	Y	Y	Y	Y	Y	Y	Y	Y	Y	Y	N	Y	Y	N	N	N	N	Y		33

	html																																								
20	RLG DigiNews http://www.oclc.org/programs/publications/newsletters/diginews.htm	Y	Y	Y	Y	Y	Y	Y	Y	Y	Y	Y	Y	Y	Y	N	Y	Y	Y	Y	N	Y	Y	N	Y	Y	Y	Y	Y	Y	Y	N	N	Y	N	N	N	Y	N		30
21	Serials E-News http://www.ringgold.com/UKSG/si_pd.cfm	Y	Y	Y	Y	Y	Y	Y	Y	Y	Y	Y	Y	Y	Y	Y	Y	N	Y	N	Y	Y	Y	Y	Y	Y	Y	Y	Y	Y	Y	N	Y	N	N	N	N	Y	N		31
22	SPARC Open Access Newsletter or Free Online Scholarship Newsletter http://www.earlham.edu/~peters/fos/index.htm	Y	Y	Y	Y	Y	Y	Y	Y	Y	Y	Y	Y	Y	Y	Y	Y	N	N	N	Y	Y	N	Y	Y	Y	Y	Y	Y	N	Y	N	Y	N	N	N	N	Y	N		28
23	Sprouts: Working Papers on Information Systems http://sprouts.aisnet.org/home.html	Y	Y	Y	Y	Y	Y	Y	Y	Y	Y	Y	Y	Y	Y	Y	Y	N	N	Y	Y	Y	Y	Y	Y	Y	Y	Y	Y	Y	Y	N	Y	Y	N	N	N	Y	Y		33
24	The Wired Librarian's Newsletter http://www.wiredlibrarian.com/wln/wlnfront.htm	Y	Y	Y	Y	Y	Y	Y	Y	Y	Y	Y	Y	Y	Y	N	Y	N	N	N	Y	Y	N	Y	Y	Y	Y	Y	Y	N	Y	N	Y	N	N	N	N	N	N		26
	Y-Yes and N-No																																								

While evaluation of E-resources parameters are chosen in order to ascertaining the weightage, gravity and potency of E-resources. E-resources having maximum parameters assumed more potency weight age and gravity. This helps the users, producers, Publishers of Knowledge and the Library and Information professionals to select appropriate E-Resources. Author has adopted 40 parameters evaluate overall structure of E-resources.

Summary Table: Distribution Open Access E-Resources having maximum parameters 60% above to 90% above

S.N	E-Resources	No.
1	90 % E-Resources Covering 36-39 Parameters	39
2	80 % E-Resources Covering 32-35 Parameters	86
3	70% E-Resources Covering 28-31 Parameters	49
4	60% E-Resources Covering 24-27 Parameters	21
	Total	**195**

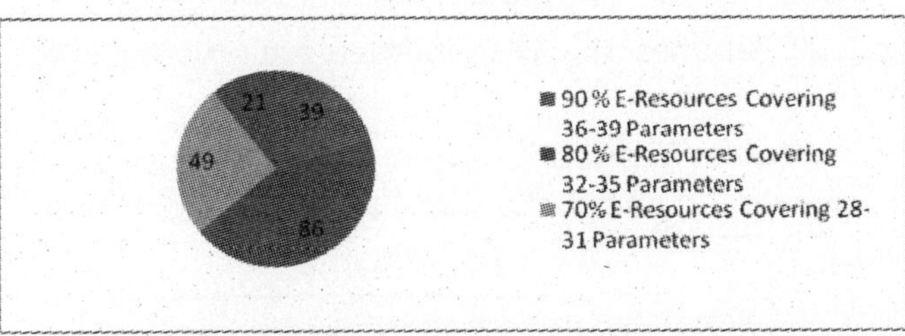

Fig.: E-Resource covering Parameters Percentage-wise

The above chart shows that 39 E-Resources are covering 90% parameters (36-39Parameters); 86 E-Resources are covering 80% parameters (32-35) E-Resources, 49 E-Resources covering 70% (28-21 Parameters); 21 E-Resources are covering 60% (24-27) parameters.

Summary Table: Distribution Open Access E-Journals having maximum parameters 60% above to 90% above

S.N.	E-Journals	No
1	90% E-Journals Covering 36-39 Parameters	36
2	80% E-Journals Covering 32-35 Parameters	67
3	70% E-Journals Covering 28-31 Parameters	30
4	60% E-Journals Covering 24-27 Parameters	12
	Total	**145**

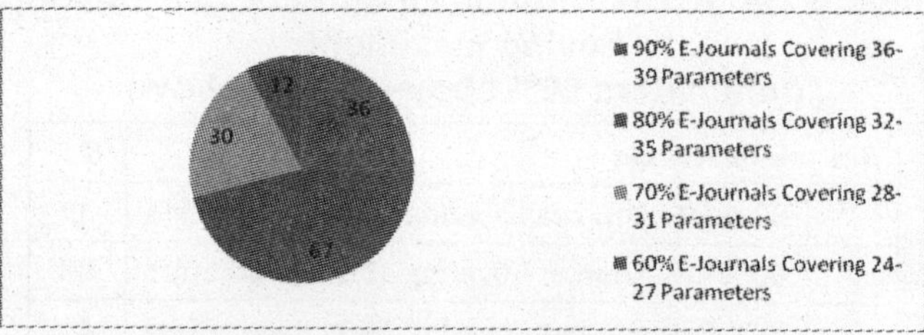

Fig: E-Journals covering Parameters Percentage-wise

This chart shows that 36 E- Journals are covering 90% parameters (36-39Parameters); 67 E- Journals are covering 80% parameters (32-35 Parameters), 30 E-Resources are Covering 70% (28-21 Parameters); 12 E- Journals are covering 60% (24-27 Parameters).

Summary Table: Distribution Open Access E-Magazines having maximum parameters 60% above to 90% above

S.N	E-Magazines	No.
1	90% E-Magazines Covering 36-39 Parameters	2
2	80% E-Magazines Covering 32-35 Parameters	13
3	70% E-Magazines Covering 28-31 Parameters	8
4	60% E-Magazines Covering 24-27 Parameters	3
	Total	26

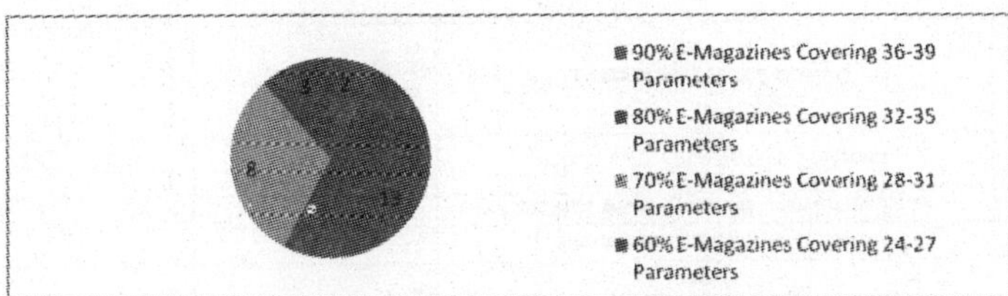

Fig.: E-Magazines covering Parameters Percentage-wise

This chart shows that 2 E- Magazines are covering 90% Parameters (36-39 Parameters), 13 E-Magazines are covering 80% parameters (32-35)Parameters), 8 E- Magazines are Covering 70% (28-21 Parameters); 3 E- Magazines are covering 60% (24-27 parameters)

Summary Table: Distribution Open Access E-Newsletters and others having maximum parameters 60% above to 90% above

S.N	E-Newsletters& others E-Resources	No
1	90% E-Newsletter & Others Covering 36-39 Parameters	1
2	80% E-Newsletter & Others Covering 32-35 Parameters	6
3	70% E-Newsletter & Others Covering 28-31 Parameters	11
4	60% E-Newsletter & Others Covering 24-27 Parameters	6
	Total	**24**

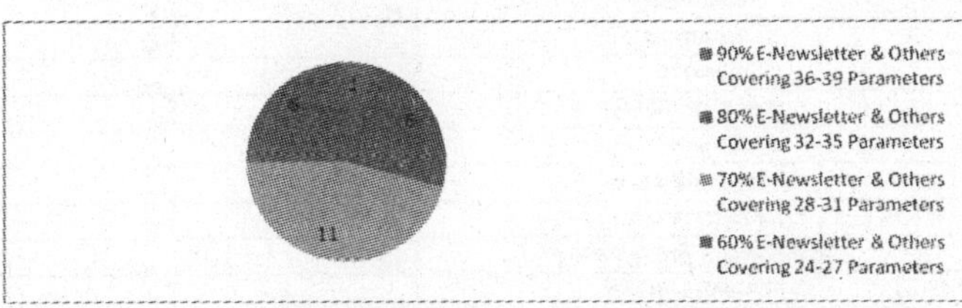

Fig: E-Newsletters & Others covering Parameters Percentage-wise

This chart shows that 1 E-Newsletters & Others are covering 90% parameters (36-39 Parameters), 6 E-Newsletters & Others are covering 80% parameters (32-35 Parameters), 11 E-Newsletters & Others are Covering 70% (28-21 Parameters), 6 E- Newsletters & Others are covering 60% (24-27 Parameters).

Most Ranked E-Resources based on Parameters Coverage

S. No.	Title	URL	Authority	Publisher(organization, editor, host)	Country	Scope/Coverage	Accessibility & Reliability	Browsebility	Networkability	Format	Design & Layout	Treatment	Accuracy	Objectivity	Arrangement(sequence, alphabetization, index)	Response Time	Structure	Link	Periodicity/Frequency	Special Features	Help	download	Currency	Internal Search Engine	Specific guidelines(content, output)	Review (maintenance, easy to use, equipment)	Standards	Information: Primary or Secondary	Information: Factual or Opinion	Latest and Currents Trends	Archiving	Indexed	Searching	Personalization (Marked Items, Alerts, Rss)	International	Refereed E-Resources	Peer Reviewed	ISSN	Search with Personalization	Peer Review + Indexed = International	Maximum Parameters Covered	Parameters Not Covered
1	Library & Information Research: Research in to Practice for Information & Library Services http://www.lirg.org.uk/lir/ojs/index.php/lir	Y	Y	Y	Y	Y	Y	Y	Y	Y	Y	Y	Y	Y	Y	Y	Y	Y	Y	Y	Y	Y	Y	Y	Y	Y	Y	Y	Y	Y	Y	Y	Y	Y	N	Y	Y	Y	Y	Y	39	Title/Name Intl
2	Information Technologies and International Development http://itidjournal.org/itid	Y	Y	Y	Y	Y	Y	Y	Y	Y	Y	Y	Y	Y	Y	Y	Y	Y	Y	Y	Y	Y	Y	Y	Y	Y	Y	Y	Y	Y	Y	Y	Y	Y	Y	N	Y	Y	Y	Y	39	Refereed

3	African Journal of Information & Communication Technology http://epress.lib.uts.edu.au/ojs/index.php/ajict/	Y	Y	Y	Y	Y	Y	Y	Y	Y	Y	Y	Y	Y	Y	Y	Y	Y	Y	Y	Y	Y	Y	Y	Y	Y	Y	Y	Y	Y	Y	Y	Y	Y	Y	**N**	Y	Y	Y	**Y**	39	Refereed
4	Health Information and Libraries Journal http://www3.interscience.wiley.com/journal/120118368/grouphome/home.html	Y	Y	Y	Y	Y	Y	Y	Y	Y	Y	Y	Y	Y	Y	Y	Y	Y	Y	Y	Y	Y	Y	Y	Y	Y	Y	Y	Y	Y	Y	Y	Y	Y	Y	**N**	Y	Y	Y	**Y**	39	Refereed
5	JLIS.it Italian Journal of Library and Information Science http://leo.cilea.it/index.php/jlis/article/view/4539/4416	Y	Y	Y	Y	Y	Y	Y	Y	Y	Y	Y	Y	Y	Y	Y	Y	Y	Y	Y	Y	Y	Y	Y	Y	Y	Y	Y	Y	Y	Y	Y	Y	Y	Y	**N**	Y	Y	Y	**Y**	39	Refereed
E-Magazines																																										
1	American Libraries http://americanlibrariesmagazine.org/	Y	Y	Y	Y	Y	Y	Y	Y	Y	Y	Y	Y	Y	Y	Y	Y	Y	Y	Y	Y	Y	Y	Y	Y	Y	Y	Y	Y	Y	Y	Y	Y	Y	N	N	N	Y	Y		37	Intl, Peer, Refereed
Newsletters and other E-Resources																																										
1	Against the grain http://www.against-the-grain.com/d/TOC	Y	Y	Y	Y	Y	Y	Y	Y	Y	Y	Y	Y	Y	Y	Y	Y	Y	Y	Y	Y	Y	Y	Y	Y	Y	Y	Y	Y	Y	Y	N	Y	Y	N	N	N	Y	Y		36	Index Intl, Peer, Refereed

Author has adopted 40 Parameters out of which, 39 parameters are Maximum Coverage. Out of 145 Free E-Journals 5 E-Journals are having Maximum coverage of 39 parameters. Out 26 E-Magazines 1 E-magazine claims to have maximum coverage of parameters. Out of 24 E-Newsletters 1 E-Newsletter claims to have maximum coverage of parameter 36.

5

Description of Open Access E-resources in LIS

5.1. DESCRIPTION OF E-JOURNALS

College and Research Libraries

College and Research Libraries http://crl.acrl.org/ is published by American Library Association, Chicago. It focuses on Latest trends and practices affecting academic and research libraries and official news magazine. Articles can be found by simple click on Issue Title. Back of file is Vol. 1, (1), 1939-v. 74, 1, Nov 2013. Vol.69, 6 not open access. Articles are arranged Issue-wise with pdf formats.

African Journal of Information & Communication Technology

African Journal of Information & Communication Technology http://epress.lib.uts.edu.au/journals/index.php/ ajict/ index is published by Faculty of Science, Technology and

Engineering La Trobe University Kingsbury Drive, Bundoora Victoria Australia. It includes material on all aspects of the design, implementation, use and management of computer and communication. Back of file is Vol. 1, 1 (2005)-

V. 6 (1) 2011 and V. 7, 1, 2013 is not open access. It is indexed, Peer Reviewed and Provides Personalize features. Articles are arranged Volume wise with pdf format and can be found on Simple click on Issue title.

Agricultural Libraries Information Notes

Agricultural Libraries Information Notes http://webharvest.gov/peth04/20041023101316/http://www.nal.usda.gov/NewAlin/ is A Publication of the National Agricultural Library. It covers almost all the aspects of Library and Information science. Back of file is V-20, No1-12, 1994- V-23, No 1-12, 1997. Information is arranged by Volume and Number. Information can be browse by simple click.

ALAN Review

ALAN Review http://scholar.lib.vt.edu/ejournals/ALAN/ is published by DLA, Virginia Tech, Virginia, US. The journal contains articles on YA literature and its teaching, interviews with authors, reports on publishing trends, current research on YA literature, a section of reviews of new books, and ALAN membership news. ALAN is made up of teachers, authors, librarians, publishers, teacher-educators and their students, and others who are particularly interested in the area of young adult literature focus on Manuscript, Library connections etc. Back of file is Vol. 21, 2, winter 1994-v. 38, 1, fall 2010. Prior to Volume 31, Number 1, fall 2003, issues of THE ALAN REVIEW were only available in HTML format. Articles can be browse by simple click. Information is arranged by year.

Alki: The Washington Library Association Journal

Alki: The Washington Library Association Journal http://www.wla.org/alki/ became the official print journal of the Washington Library Association (WLA) in 1983. It is published three times per year in March, July and December in Washington and Its Executive Director is Kristin Crowe. Alki's editors have each brought something different to the job and the intervening years have brought new production techniques, new ways of relaying content and new expectations. Alki's originators wanted a journal that was broader in scope than other library association publications, a journal that published material other state library journals and periodicals would not and that encompassed diverse people and ideas within the library community. So, from the beginning, Alki's offerings have included everything from scholarly historical pieces and conference session reports, to humor and philosophical pieces. Traditionally, each issue centers on a theme selected by the Alki Editorial Committee with one issue per year dedicated to coverage of WLA's annual conference since 1997. Alki's purpose is to communicate philosophical and substantive analyses of current and enduring issues for and about Washington libraries, personnel and advocates and to facilitate the exchange of research, opinion and information. Its Back of file is Vol.13, 2-3, July 1997-v. 28, 3. July 2012. Issue indexing has been done. Articles are available in pdf format.

American Archivist

American Archivist http://archivists.metapress.com/ home/ main.mpx is published by Society of American Archivists. It covers the American Archivist provides a forum for discussion of trends and issues in archival theory and practice. It presents current research. It includes also Peer-reviewed research articles, case studies, in-depth perspectives, and international scene papers address a wide variety of topics, such as digitization and digital preservation, electronic records, selection and appraisal, description and cataloging, reference and public services, preservation. Peer-reviewed research articles, case studies, in-depth perspectives, and international scene papers address a wide variety of topics, such as digitization and digital preservation, electronic records, selection and appraisal, description and cataloging, reference and public services, preservation. Back of file is Vol. 1, 1-4, 1938-V.75, 1-2, 2012. Fulltext is available in pdf format. Information can be browse by simple click. Information is arranged by Volume and Number.

Annals of Library & Information Studies

Annals of Library & Information Studies http://nopr.niscair.res.in/ is published by NISCAIR, New Delhi India. It includes Knowledge management, Research Aptitudes, bibliography, citation indexes etc. Back of file is Vol. 49, 2002-V. 57 2010. It is available Quarterly in NISCAIR repository. It includes Knowledge management, Research Aptitudes, bibliography, citation indexes etc. Articles can be found by simple click on Issue Title and internal search is given. Information is arranged Volume-wise with pdf format.

Australian Journal of Information Systems

Australian Journal of Information Systems http://dl.acs.org.au/index.php/ajis/about is published by Creative Commons Attribution. AJIS publishes high quality contributions to the global Information Systems (IS) discipline with an emphasis on theory and practice on the Australasian context. Information can be browse by simple click. The text issues are in Adobe Acrobat PDF format. Topics cover core IS theory development and application (the nature of data, information and knowledge; formal representations of the world, the interaction of people, organizations and information technologies; the analysis, design and deployment of information systems; the impacts of information systems on individuals, organizations and society. Information is arranged by Year and Volume. AJIS is an international quality, peer reviewed journal. Back of file is v.1, No1, 1993-V17. No2. 2012.

Australian Academic and Research Libraries

Australian Academic and Research Libraries http://www.alia.org.au/publishing/aarl/index.html is published is University of Canberra, Faculty of Communication. Australian Academic & Research Libraries is a quarterly journal devoted to all aspects of librarianship in university and college libraries. It includes the Technical and Further Education sector, and in research libraries of all types. It publishes original, refereed contributions on all aspects of librarianship past and present, pure and applied bibliography, publishing, information science and related subjects. AARL is abstracted or indexed in Australian education index, Australian library and information science abstracts, APAIS, Library and information science abstracts, and Library literature. Back of file is Vol. 32, 1-4, 2001-v. 41, 1-4, 2010. (42, 2012 & 43 2013 is not open access) available in print to subscribers only. fulltext is available in pdf format. Articles are arranged Volume and year wise. All articles appearing in AARL are fully peer-refereed and can be browse by simple click.

Australian Library Journal

Australian Library Journal http://alia.org.au/ publishing/alj/ is Australian Library and Information Association. It contains a wide coverage of Australian library issues ranging from ongoing research to day-to-day news from the workplace. It is the acknowledged flagship publication of the Australian Library and Information Association, and an appropriate vehicle for publishers, suppliers and services wishing to reach the decision-makers. The Australian Library Journal has been reaching discerning and influential Australian libraries since 1951. It is published quarterly. Vol. 48, Nov, Aug May, Feb. 1999-v. 59, (1-4) Feb., May, Aug, Nov. 2010. 2011 and 2012 are available in print to subscribers only and Full text is available in Html format. Articles are arranged Volume and year wise. Articles can be browse by simple click.

B Sides

B Sides http://ir.uiowa.edu/bsides/is published by University of Iowa, School of Library and Information Science, United States. It includes writing, images, posters, presentation slides, audio recordings, and videos. Provides a space for current students and alumni to converse about their work and contribute to the scholarly literature of Library and Information Science. ISSN is

2155-6687 and it is Peer Reviewed Journal. Its back of file is 2010-2013.

Chinese Librarianship: an International Electronic Journal

Chinese Librarianship: an International Electronic Journal http://www.iclc.us/cliej/ publishes CLIEJ, United States in various electronic channels. CLIEJ is launched with a view to facilitating information exchange among librarians and information professionals worldwide. This peer-reviewed e-journal focuses on both practical and theoretical aspects of the Chinese librarianship. It publishes research findings, theoretical explorations, and case studies by librarians, information scientists, library school faculty and students of Chinese heritage, as well as by librarians and information professionals of other nationalities on issues related to serving patrons with Chinese materials and major development of the Chinese librarianship. Author, title and web Indexing have been done. Articles are arranged Issue number wise. The fulltext is available in E-text and htm format and Back of file is N.1 June-N.2 Dec, 1996-N.25 June- N.26 Dec 2008. Author, title and web Indexing have been done. Articles are arranged by Issue number. It is Indexed in Ebsco's Library, Information Science & Technology Abstracts (LISTA), Wislon's Library and Information Science Index (LISI), CSA's Library and Information Science Abstracts (LISA), Listed in: Ulrich's and Cabell's.

Christian Library Journal

Christian Library Journal http://www.christianlibraryj.org/pdf/index.htm is published by Nancy L. Hesch Christian Library Services. It covers all subjects from picture books for little ones through in depth nonfiction for adults, fiction and other literature for all ages. It covers all nonfiction subjects, as well as fiction, picture books, fairy and folk tales, and poetry and drama. Build library collection in the Christian school, international school, home school, or church using the core collection. Back of file: Oct 1995- Oct/Dec 2010. v. XVI, No 1-2, 2012, Full text is available in pdf format and articles are arranged volume wise.

Cites & Insights: Crawford at Large

Cites & Insights: Crawford at Large http://citesandinsights.info/citoc.htm is a Web-based journal of libraries, policy, technology, and media. Its author, editor, and publisher are Walt Crawford and sponsored by YBP Library Services. Walt Crawford's commentary and annotated citations of selected articles on library and computer related issues. It's back of file is Vol.6, Jan -Dec 2006-v.13, April 2013. Current plan: At least 12 issues each year. Articles are arranged Volume wise and fulltext is available in pdf format. Articles can be browse by simple click. Articles can be browse by simple click.

Colby Quarterly (formerly: Colby Library Quarterly)

Colby Quarterly (formerly: Colby Library Quarterly) http://digitalcommons.colby.edu/ is powered by bepress. The Colby Quarterly was published from 1943 to 2003, providing a forum both for publicizing Colby's rare books and manuscripts and for literary discussion. the Quarterly, then named the Colby Library Quarterly, published lists and descriptions of books and manuscripts recently acquired by the Special Collections department of the Colby College Library. Articles included examinations of and excerpts from collections of manuscript correspondence. Information is arranged by Volume and Number. Articles were also solicited on Maine authors and Maine history, including books and authors that had influenced Maine life and letters, or were well represented in Colby's Special Collections. All aspects of literature in English, with a concentration in Maine and regional history and literature. Vol.32, 3-4, 1996 v. 39, 1-4, 2003. Fulltext is available in pdf format. Information can be browse by simple click.

Collaborative Librarianship

Collaborative Librarianship http://www.collaborativelibrarianship.org/index.html is published by Regis University. It deals with library-to-library cooperation, sharing resources and expertise, library-to-business partnerships local, regional, national and international collaboration, professional, consortium and association partnerships, history of library collaboration. Improving access to and delivery of information resources. Developing a system of sustainable ongoing resources. Enhancing human resource development. Considering what is good for Colorado. Volume and Number arrange information. The journal contains **six sections**: Editorials, Scholarly Articles, From the Field, the Collaboration Matters column, Reviews and News. Back of file is V.1 No. 1-4, 2009. Fulltext is available in pdf format. Information can be browse by simple click.

Communications in Information Literacy

Communications in Information Literacy (CIL) http://www.comminfolit.org/index.php/cil/issue/archive This Journal is published by Communications in Information Literacy, United States. It is an independent, professional, refereed electronic journal dedicated to advancing knowledge, theory, and research in information literacy. CIL is committed to the principles of information literacy as set forth by the Association of College and Research Libraries. CIL is also committed to the principles of open access for academic research. It has internal search engine Author, Title, Full text and supplementary files search is available. Search tips are also given. Abstract and full text can be browse by clicking particular volume. Information is arranged in Volume wise. Information is given for librarian, authors and readers. Its back of file is Vol.1, 1-2, 2007-v.6, 2, 2012 along with Author; Title and Issue indexes have been given.

Computer and Information Science

Computer and Information Science http://journal.ccsenet.org/index.php/cis/index is published by Canadian Center of Science. It Focus on computer, information science, e-business, internet, electronic. It publishes research papers in the fields of computer, information science, e-business, and internet, electronic and relevant subjects. It is Peer Reviewed and Indexed in DOAJ, PKP, J-Gate, LOCKSS etc. Back of file is Vol.1, 1-4, 2008-v. 6, 2, 2013. Information is arranged Volume wise with Pdf format.

Coordinates: Online Journal of the Map and Geography Round Table of the American Library Association.

Series A and B

Coordinates: is an Online Journal of the Map and Geography Round Table of the American Library Association. Series A and B http://www.sunysb.edu/libmap/coordinates.htm is an online serial publication. Contributions are published irregularly in the order received. We seek articles on a wide range of subjects relating to maps and GIS. Our target audience is primarily users and curators of maps. Appropriate subjects for articles include map and GIS librarianship, history of cartography, map cataloging and bibliography, map reading and interpretation, new developments in online mapping, and other subjects of interest to a broad spectrum of cartographically literate readers. Its aim is to take full advantage of the capabilities on the Internet. This is an "open access" publication, which is freely available to anyone who has access to the World Wide Web. Articles that include color images and links to other resources on the Web are particularly encouraged. Its Articles are divided into two groups. "Series A" consists of original, peer-reviewed articles. "Series B" includes essays and other shorter pieces, technical notes, previously published articles, and other materials of interest to our audience. This publication is produced by the Map and Geography Round Table (MAGERT) of the American Library Association. However, we encourage submissions from all interested people. Members of other map-related organizations are welcome to contribute papers, or to be considered as reviewers or members of our editorial board. Its back of file is Series A, N. 1-6-Series B, N.1-10 and Abstract and fulltext is available in html and pdf format. Articles in Coordinates are indexed inThe Directory of Open Access Journals.

Current Science

Current Science http://www.ias.ac.in/currsci/index.html, founded in 1932 is published by the Current Science Association in collaboration with the Indian Academy of Sciences. The journal is also intended as a medium for communication and discussion of important issues that concern science and scientific activity. The journal covers the bibliography of selected articles, books and digital documents in both print and digital forms on Information Technology issue. Back of file is Vol1, 1990-v. 24, 1-2, March 2013. Provision for Special Issues has been given. Information is arranged Volume wise. Fulltext is available in pdf format. Articles can be found by simple click on issue title. Internal search engine has been given.

Current Issues in Education

Current Issues in Education http://cie.asu.edu/index.php is published by Arizona State University. It is devoted to advancing scholarly thoughts in the field of education. Articles promote educational dialogue, research, practice, and policy. Strive to develop and deepen a sense of scholarship within our academic community and end the privilege to add additional articles as special topics and current events warrant extra attention to timely educational issues. Publish approximately three Issues per year. Peer reviewed and Information is arranged Volume and year wise with HTML format. Back of file is Vol. 1, 10, 1998-v. 16, 1, 2013.

Cybermetrics: International Journal of Scientometrics, Informetrics and Bibliometrics

Cybermetrics http://www.cindoc.csic.es/cybermetrics/ both an Electronic-only Journal and a Virtual Forum (The Journal) devoted to the study of the quantitative analysis of scholarly and scientific communications in the Internet. It is open to world-wide researchers to publish and discuss their findings. Internet offers them new and increased capabilities to distribute their results to a greater audience. Cybermetrics also maintains a series of directories of electronic resources (The Source), including secondary archives of interesting web papers in pdf format. The aim is to provide a reference tool to those researchers involved in the quantitative description and analysis of the Internet as a scholarly communication tool. It is also intended to add original data as a source or reference for larger studies, especially including figures about the distribution and evolution of R&D contents in the World Wide Web. Cybermetrics is a free journal published only in electronic format in the World Wide Web. No other version (printed or e-mail) is distributed. Cybermetrics is a public service for the world community of researchers in the metrics of scientific communication. Its back of file: V. 1, Issue -1, 1997-V. 12, Issue1, 2008.

Data Science Journal

Data Science Journal http://www.datasciencejournal.org/ is monthly published by International Council for Science and Its Editor-in-Chief is Dr. John Rumble, Jr.Editorial Specialist: Diane Smith. The journal includes the descriptions of data systems, their publication on the Internet application and legal issues. All of the Sciences are covered, including the Physical Sciences, Engineering, the Geosciences and the Biosciences, along with Agriculture and the Medical Science. The Journal Publishes papers about data and the data systems: it does not publish data compilation. However it may publish papers about methods data compilation or analysis. The Journal is a peer reviewed electronic publication with papers appearing throughout the year. Back of File: Vol.1, 2002-v. 12, 2013. The Journal is a peer reviewed electronic publication with papers appearing throughout the year. Data Science Journal provides information in text, RTF, Word electronic format (PDF).

DESIDOC Journal of Library & Information Science

DESIDOC Journal of Library & information science http://publications.drdo.gov.in/ojs/index.php/djlit/index is published by DESIDOC and DRDO. It endeveavours to bring recent developments in Information technology as applicable to Library and information science, to the notice of Librarians, Documentation, Information professional, students and others interested in the field. Its Back of file is Vol. 26,1-6, 2006-v. 33,1, 2013. It is biomonthly and indexed in LISA. Fulltext is available in Pdf format. Information is arranged by Issue, Author and Title. Articles can be browse by simple click on the title.

Digital Document Quarterly

Digital Document Quarterly http://home.pacbell.net/hgladney/ddqstart.htm H.M. Gladney, HMG Consulting published it quarterly. The Digital Document Quarterly topic touches the welfare of every citizen. It treats with books, newspapers, scholarly papers, scientific tables, legal briefs, medical charts, engineering designs, and government and business records, the carriers for many kinds of information. DDQ will focus, at least during 2002, on the problems that "trust", "trustworthy", and "trusted" imply and on trustworthy digital mechanisms and their limitations. Its target reader is the university graduate who reads and writes extensively, and who wants to understand and perhaps influence the "digital revolution". Digital information is a symbolic representation of something other than itself. It provides information in E-Print format. DDQ is for intelligent readers who can think about technical policy, but who have neither time nor inclination to study digital engineering. DDQ provides filtering to identify important articles, synopses comprehensible by non-technical readers, and opinions on the content. The first DDQ number starts to deal with long-range preservation of digital information and emphasizes background without which later topics might be difficult to understand or appear ill founded. The next number will continue with long-term preservation, not because it is more important than other topics, but rather because digital preservation seems timely in 2002. In the industrial nations, nearly every business, government, and academic document starts in a digital form, even if it is eventually published and saved on paper. The Digital Document Quarterly (DDQ) treats quality for digital documents. Quality is meaningful only with respect to what clients and customers want. Back of File: from 2002 to 2007.

DIGITHUM: The humanities in digital age

The electronic journal DIGITHUM http://www.uoc.edu/digithum/10/eng/index.html is designed for academics, professionals and students from the various fields relating to the humanities and social sciences and is published with the following aims in mind the following subject areas: The knowledge society, ICT, teaching and the dissemination of the humanities and social sciences. academic community and amongst its readers. It is published by Fundació per la Universitat Oberta de Catalunya (FUOC)Country: Spain. DIGITHUM is a peer-reviewed journal. Information is arranged in Issue N. wise. Each issue of DIGITHUM includes a dossier focusing on one subject, a section of miscellaneous articles and, on occasions, reviews. DIGITHUM is an annual publication that comes out in May. It is indexed by MIAR, ERCE, Latíndex (Catalogue), Redalyc, E-Revistas and others and its back of file is Issue N. 1, 1999-Issue N. 9, 2006.

EBIB Electronic Information Bulletin for librarians

EBIB Electronic Information Bulletin for librarians http://ebib.info/biuletyn/ is monthly on-line journal is published by Stowarzyszenie Bibliotekarzy Polskich Komisja Wydawnictw and Bulletin Editor-in-Chief Bo¿ena Bednarek-Michalska Country: Poland. EBIB focus on Librarianship, information, and library technologies. It includes essays, reports, announcements, letters, discussions/polemics, and agenda.. Each issue has its separate theme. Materials are published in the following departments Research, theory, views; Interviews, Law, Conference reports and others. Back of file is Abstract 1999-2008 Selected fulltext 2000-2005. Fulltext 2002 Special issue for the Frankfurt book fair 2000. Articles can browse by simple click on the title. Abstract, Selected Fulltext, fulltext 2002, and Special 2000 is available for browsing. Links are available Polish libraries, OPAC catalogues via Internet, international library services, foreign OPAC catalogues, national and virtual libraries, journals, books, publishers, and various library organizations.

EDUCAUSE Quarterly

EDUCAUSE Quarterly http://connect.educause.edu/ apps/eq/index.asp Journal is published quarterly by EDUCAUSE (a nonprofit association whose mission is to advance higher education by promoting the intelligent use of information technology). EDUCAUSE Quarterly is an online, peer-reviewed, practitioner's journal for college and university managers and users of information resources—information, technology, and services—published quarterly by EDUCAUSE. Materials related to planning for, developing, managing, evaluating, and using information resources on college and university campuses are welcomed. The EQ Editor and EQ Editorial Committee evaluate submissions for suitability. EQ publishes materials that relate to planning, developing, managing, using, and evaluating information resources in higher education. Information resources encompass technology, services, and information. Vol.23, 1-4, 2000-Vol.31, 1-4, 2008 and Full text is available in pdf and html format.

E-JASL: The Electronic Journal of Academic and Special Librarianship

E-JASL: The Electronic Journal of Academic and Special Librarianship" http://southernlibrarianship.icaap.org/ Published and Distributed by the International Consortium for the Advancement of Academic Publication (ICAAP) Country: Canada. E-JASL covers all aspects of academic and special librarianship without regard to region or country. E-JASL is an independent, professional, refereed electronic journal dedicated first and foremost to advancing knowledge and research in the areas of academic and special librarianship. Information is arranged Volume wise. Current and archive issue option has been given separately. Back of file is Vol. 1, 1996-Vol. 9 N.1-2, 2008. Form 1996-2000 was known as "Journal of southern academic and special librarianship" Archived in National Library of Canada's Electronic Publications Collection. Listed in the DOAJ. Indexed in LISA. Fulltext is available in E-print, Html and Ixml format. Articles can be browse by simple click on wanted articles.

Electronic Journal of Africana Bibliography

Electronic Journal of Africana Bibliography http://ir.uiowa.edu/ejab/all_issues.html is published by International Consortium for the Advancement of Academic Publication (ICAAP) Country: Canada. It covers all aspects of academic and special librarianship without regard to region or country. It is Independent, professional, refereed electronic journal dedicated first and foremost to advancing knowledge and research in the areas of academic and special librarianship. 1996-2000 was known as "Journal of southern academic and special librarianship". Spring, summer, winter and Listed in the DOAJ and Indexed in LISA. Back of file is Vol. 1, 1996-v.10, 1-3, winter 2009. Three issues in year spring, summer, Winter. Information is arranged volume wise with HTML format and can be found by simple click on Issue Title.

Electronic Journal of Health Informatics

The electronic Journal of Health Informatics http://www.ejhi.net/ojs/index.php/ejhi is an international journal committed to scholarly excellence and dedicated to the advancement of Health Informatics and information technology in healthcare. It is a journal for all health professions and informaticians of all levels. It is published by Central Queensland University, Australia. It provide health care workers with a readily accessible, electronic vehicle for sharing information about research, knowledge, experiences, perceptions and wisdom with colleagues involved in all facets of health informatics and health information technology. Back of file is Vol.1, 1, 2006-v.7,2, 2012 and fulltext is available in pdf format. Articles can be browse by author, Title and Issue. Internal search engine has been given And Author, Title and Issue Indexing has been given. The journal uses a single-blind peer-review process.

Electronic Journal of Knowledge Management

Electronic Journal of Knowledge Management http://www.ejkm.com/ is published by Academic Conferences International Limited publishes EJKM, United Kingdom (England). It includes topics relevant to the study, implementation and management of knowledge management. The journal contributes to the development of both theory and practice in the field of knowledge management. The journal accepts academically robust papers, topical articles and case studies that contribute to the area of research in, and practice of knowledge management. It is currently published bi-annually with a general issue and a special issue. Every paper submitted to the journal is blind-refereed by members of the editorial board or other suitably qualified readers. Its back of file is Vol. 1, 1, Sep 2003-v. 10, 3, March 2012 and Abstract and fulltext is available in pdf format. Articles are arranged Volume wise and can browse by simple click on the title. Internal search engine is available for searching.

Electronic Journal on Information Systems in Developing Countries

Electronic Journal on Information Systems in Developing Countries http://www.ejisdc.org/ojs2/index.php/ejisdc is published by Department of Information Systems, City University of Hong Kong, EJISDC) strives to become the foremost international forum for practitioners, teachers, researchers and policy makers to share their knowledge and experience and strives to become the foremost international forum for practitioners, teachers, researchers and policy makers to share their knowledge and experience in the design, development, implementation, management and evaluation of information systems and technologies in developing countries. Information is arranging by volume and year and Articles can get by simple click on particular article. Back of file is V.1, 2000- V. 55, 2012 and fulltext is available in pdf format. Information for reader, librarians, and authors has been given.

Electronic Transactions on Artificial Intelligence

Electronic Transactions on Artificial Intelligence http://www.ida.liu.se/ext/etai/ is published by Linköping University Electronic Press._The Electronic Transactions on Artificial Intelligence (ETAI) is a novel kind of scientific journal, with a radically new approach to reviewing procedures, communication between peers, information services within a research community, and even to the very concept of scientific publication. The ETAI can be reached at http://www.etaij.org/ and at http://www.etai.info/. The Info URL may eventually replace the one under. Its back of file is V. 1, N. 1-3, 4, 1997-V.5, 2001. Full text is available in pdf format. Articles can be browse by simple click on wanted articles. And Options find specific articles have been given. Information is arranged Volume wise.

European Journal of ePractice

European Journal of ePractice http://www. epracticejournal. eu/ is a peer-reviewed online publication on eTransformation, launched in November 2007. The Journal belongs to the ePractice.eu community, is sponsored by the European Commission as part of its good practice exchange activity and is run by an independent Editorial Board. The aim of European Journal of ePractice (EJeP) is to reinforce the visibility of articles as well as that of professionals in Transformation building an author's community which will strengthen the overall ePractice.eu activity. The publication will promote the diffusion and exchange of good practice in eGovernment, eHealth and eInclusion and will be open access, free of charge to all readers. We have a target audience of 50,000 professionals in Europe and beyond, and build on a community of some 14,000 members. The scope of the European Journal of ePractice reflects the three domains of the ePractice.eu: eGovernment, eHealth and eInclusion. Back of file No. 1 Nov. 2007- No. 18 Oct 2012. fulltext is available in pdf format.

Evidence Based Library and Information Practice

Evidence Based Library and Information Practice http:// ejournals.library.ualberta.ca/index.php/EBLIP/index is published by University of Alberta. Editor-in-Chief is Lindsay Glynn. Country: Canada. EBLIP focus on Evidence-based librarianship, evidence-based practice. It provides a forum for librarians and other information professionals to discover research that may contribute to decision-making in professional practice. EBLIP publishes original research and commentary on the topic of evidence based library and information practice. EBLIP is a peer reviewed open access quarterly journal. Information for Reader, librarians, Author has been given. Its back of file is Vol. 1, 1-4, 2006-v.7, 4, 2012, and is available in pdf format. Internal search engine is available. AND, OR, NOT, * Search tips have been given. Articles can be browse by author, title and Issue and it use OJS software. Author Title and Issue index have been given.

Firstmonday

Chief Editor of the Journal Firstmonday http://firstmonday.org/ is Edward Valauskas and published by University of Illinois at Chicago University Library. First Monday is one of the first openly accessible, peer–reviewed journals on the Internet, solely devoted to the Internet. First Monday publishes original research papers about the Internet and related technologies. It has published 932 papers in 147 issues; written by 1,161 different authors. It is indexed in Communication Abstracts, Computer & Communications Security Abstracts, INSPEC, ISTA, LISA, PAIS, and other services etc. Back of file is Vol. 10, 5-12 Dec 2005-v. 18, 3-4, March 2013. Full text is available in HTML format and Article can be browse by Issue, Author, and Title. Abstract and full text of articles can be searched by single click on particular article title. Information is arranged volume and issue wise. Users can get text links to Current and Archive issue. Information is categories for Authors, Librarians and Readers. Author and Title Index have been given.

Health Information and Libraries Journal

Health Information and Libraries Journal http://www3.interscience.wiley.com/journal/120118368/grouphome/home.html is published by Wiley Inter Science. Health Information and Libraries Journal (HILJ) provides practitioners, researchers, and students in library and health professions an international and interdisciplinary forum. Its objectives are to encourage discussion and to disseminate developments at the frontiers of information management and libraries. A major focus is communicating practices that are evidence based both in managing information and in supporting health care. Abstract has been given separately. Back of file is Issue Vol. 1-4, 1984-v.30, 1, March 2013. Fulltext is available in pdf and Html format. Information can be browse by simple click.

High Energy Physics Libraries Webzine

High Energy Physics Libraries Webzine http://library.web.cern.ch/library/Webzine/index.shtml is published by HEPLW Team. It includes Purchasing, cataloguing, preservation, ILL, quality control, user surveys & education, copyright, E-Journals & management, reference services, grey literature management. It is devoted to high-energy physics libraries; aim to help you in your daily activities by discussing experience in the delivery of services to users. Some of the problems we confront are unique to our field; others are of a more general nature. We are interested in knowing about effective and useful solutions to problems (and the problems), based on your experience in the following areas. Back of file is Issue 1 Mach 2000-Issue 13 Oct 2006. Information is found by simple click on Issue Title and Arranged Issue wise with HTML format.

Human IT: Journal for Information Technology Studies as a Human Science

Human IT: Journal for Information Technology Studies as a Human Science http://etjanst.hb.se/bhs/ith//info-eng.htm is published by Högskolan i Borås, Sweden. Human IT is a multi-disciplinary and scholarly journal with the goal of bringing forth-new research and discussion about digital media as communicative, aesthetic, and ludic instruments. The journal is closely aligned with the new field of research, which is alternatively referred to as humanities computing, social informatics, or informatica umanistica. Back of file is Vol. 1, 1-4, 1997- v.12, 2, 2013. It decided in 2003 to henceforth use volumes not limited to a calender year. fulltext is available in pdf format. Information is arranging volume wise and Articles can get by simple click on particular article.

IFLA Journal

IFLA Journal http://www.ifla.org/V/iflaj/index.htm is

published The Royal Library (the national library of the Netherlands) provides the facilities for IFLA headquarters. Editor is J. Stephen Parker, Netherlands. The IFLA Quarterly journal provides information about authoritative coverage and analysis of (a) the activities of IFLA and its various constituent bodies and members. (b) Completed, ongoing and proposed policies, plâns related to the development of library. Back of file Vol. 19, N.1-4, 1993-Vol.34, N.1-3, 2008. Vol. 27 (2002) and Vol. 28 (2003) are indexed. IFLA published four times in a year. Fulltext is available in pdf format. Information is arranged Volume wise and articles can be browse by simple click on wanted articles.

Informatica Economica Journal

Informatica Economica Journal http://revistaie.ase.ro/index.html is published by Inforec Association, Romania. This peer review quarterly journal published with the support of Ministry of Education, Research and Youth focusing on Economic informatics, information society, information systems, and information technology. It is founded by members of the Economic Informatics Department, Faculty of Cybernetics, Statistics and Economic Informatics Academy of Economic Studies, Bucharest. It is listed in the DOAJ. Back of file is Vol. 2, 1-4, 1998-v. 16, 4, 2012. fulltext is available in pdf format and Information is arranging volume wise. Articles can get by simple click on particular article.

Information for Social Change

Information for Social Change http://libr.org/ isc/journal.html is the publication of the organization, "Information for Social Change It focus on freedom of information and censorship; promote alternatives to mainstream. Provide a forum for the exchange of radical views, debate ethics and freedom of library and information work. Information for Social Change published twice a year summer and winter. Back of file N. 1, winter 1994-N. 31, summer 2012. Full text is available in PDF format. Articles are arranged Number wise and can be browse by simple click.

Information Research: an international electronic journal

Information Research an international electronic journal http://informationr.net/ir/ is privately published and edited by Professor T.D. Wilson. It is hosted, and given technical support, by Lund University Libraries, Sweden (United Kingdom). Information Research is an open access, international, peer-reviewed, scholarly journal, dedicated to making accessible the results of research across a wide range of information-related disciplines. It is indexed by Google Scholar, INSPEC: Engineering Village, Library Information Science & Technology Abstracts, LISA. It is also indexed for ISI's Web of Knowledge. Back of file is Vol.1, 1-3, 1995-1996-v.17, 1-4, 2012. Full text is available in E-text format and articles are arranged volume wise. Author index and subject index has been given. Internal search engine has been given. Articles can get by simple click on particular article.

Information Scotland: The Journal of the Chartered Institute of Library and Information Professionals in Scotland

Information Scotland: The Journal of the Chartered Institute of Library and Information Professionals in Scotland http://www.slainte.org.uk/publications/serials/infoscot/vol1(1)/vol1(1)contents.html is published by Chartered Institute of Library and Information Professionals in Scotland. The online edition fits in with other electronic services being developed by CILIPS. It provides tips to get to grips, Cables and connections, National Research base etc. Information can be browse by simple click. The articles are in XHTML format with presentation applied by Cascading Style Sheets (CSS). This electronic edition of the journal is designed to complement the printed issue. It offers open access to the journal's articles in electronic form and acts as an archive of this content. The content delivered in the online edition of Information Scotland has been designed following the World Wide Web Consortium's guidance on accessibility. Back f file is Vol. 1 (1-6) February 2003-Vol.7 (1-3) June 2009. A current news and events calendar is available from SLAINTE.

Information Technologies and International Development

Information Technologies and International Development http://itidjournal.org/itid is published by University of Southern California, USA. It focuses on the intersection of information and communication technologies (ICTs). It is a peer-reviewed, international, multidisciplinary quarterly designed for researchers and practitioners from the engineering and social sciences, technologists, policy makers, and development specialists. This peer-reviewed, international, multidisciplinary quarterly journal is indexed in EBSCO Host, Proquest etc. and it is Ranked 1 ICTuD Journal in the New York Study. Back of file is V.1, 1-2, 2003-V 9, 1, 2013. Articles are arranged Volume wise. Back of file is V.1, 1-2, 2003-V 9, 1, 2013 Articles are arranged Volume wise with pdf format.

Information Technology and Disabilities

Information Technology and Disabilities http://people.rit.edu/easi/itd.htm is published by E A S I: Equal Access to Software and Information, United States. ITD is a peer-reviewed e-journal covering Information technology, disabilities, education. It is accessible IT Through Podcasts, Webinars and Online Courses. Back of file is Vol. 1, 1994-Vol. 12, 2008 and fulltext is available in E-text format. Articles are arranged volume wise and can get by simple click on particular article.

Information Technology and Libraries

Information Technology and Libraries http://www.ala.org/ala/mgrps/divs/lita/ital/italinformation.cfm is published by It includes Web programming online, Africans studies, Information and technology. It focus on distance learning course in web programming discovers, Africans studies, teaching courses relating to the history of Africa and the history of genocide, discusses some of the particular challenges that his field presents. Back of file is available V.20, No 1-4, 2011 – v.29, No 1-3, 2010 But freely available from V. 23, No. 1-4 -V. 29, No1, 2010. Articles are arranged Volume wise with Pdf format.

Informing Faculty: An International Journal of Higher Education Discussion Cases

Informing Faculty: An International Journal of Higher Education Discussion Cases http://informingfaculty.org/ is Published by Informing Science Institute, Country: United States. It focus on distance learning course in web programming discovers, Africans studies, teaching courses relating to the history of Africa and the history of genocide, discusses some of the particular challenges that his field presents. Back of file is Vol.1, 2006 and Full text is available in pdf format. Articles are arranged Volume wise and can be browse by simple click.

Informing Science The International Journal of an Emerging Transdiscipline

Informing Science the International Journal of an Emerging Transdiscipline http://inform.nu/ is published by Informing Science Institute, United States. The academically peer refereed journal Informing Science endeavors to provide an understanding of the complexities in informing clientele. Fields from information systems, library science, and journalism in all its forms to education all contribute to this science. All the volumes are Indexed in Cabell, Computer Science Index, Communication Abstracts, EBSCO and others. Back of file is Vol.1 1998-v.1. 16, 2013 and full text is available in PDF format. Articles are arranged volume wise and can get by simple click on particular article.

Inter-Actions: UCLA Journal of Education and Information Studies

Inter-Actions: UCLA Journal of Education and Information Studies http://repositories.cdlib.org/gseis/interactions/ is hosted by the eScholarship initiative of the California Digital Library. It is a peer-reviewed on-line journal committed to the promotion of interdisciplinary and critical scholarship. It provides an outlet for emerging scholars in the fields of education and information studies. It focus on legal theory, literary criticism, design, and technology studies exercises a profound impact on educational, information studies research, sociology, curriculum, policy, psychological studies, systems design, information literacy, and digital preservation. InterActions is published twice yearly with funding provided by the UCLA Graduate Students Association and the UCLA Graduate School of Education & Information Studies. Back of file is Vol. 1, 1-2, 2004-v. 9, 1, 2013 and Full text is available in pdf format. Articles are arranged Volume wise and can be browse by simple click.

Interdisciplinary Journal of E-Learning and Learning Objects

Interdisciplinary Journal of E-Learning and Learning Objects http://ijklo.org/ is IJELLO is published by Informing Science Institute, United States. Interdisciplinary Journal of E-Learning and Learning Objects (formerly the Interdisciplinary Journal of Knowledge and Learning Objects) is an academically peer refereed Journal focus on Knowledge, learning objects, e-learning. The mission of the Interdisciplinary Journal of E-Learning and Learning Objects (IJELLO) is to provide readers around the world with the widest possible coverage of developments in E-Learning and Learning Objects. IJELLO is an interdisciplinary forum that publishes high quality articles on theory, practice, innovation, and research that cover all aspects of E-learning and Learning Objects. Back of file is Vol. 1, 2005-Vol. 4, 2008 and full text is available in PDF format. All submissions are blind refereed by three or more peers. Articles are arranged volume wise and can get by simple click on particular article.

Interdisciplinary Journal of Information, Knowledge, and Management

Interdisciplinary Journal of Information, Knowledge, and Management http://www.ijikm.org/ is published by Informing Science Institute, United States. Interdisciplinary Journal of Information, Knowledge, and Management is an academically peer reviewed journal. Back of file is Vol. 1, 2006-v. 7, 2012 and full text is available in PDF format. Articles are arranged volume wise and can get by simple click on Volume and then particular article.

International Journal of Communication

International Journal of Communication http://ijoc.org/ojs/index.php/ijoc/about/editorialPolicies#focusAndScope is published by International Journal of Communication (IJoC), Los Angeles, CA. It is Open and welcoming to contributions from the many disciplines and approaches that meet at the crossroads that is communication study. It is a forum for scholars when they address the wider audiences of our many sub-fields and specialties, rather than the location for the narrower conversations more appropriately conducted within more specialized journals and major focus on Communication. It is online, multi-media, academic journal that adheres to the highest standards of peer review and engages established and emerging scholars from anywhere in the world. Back of file is V.1, 2007- V.7 2013. Articles can be found by simple click on Issue Title with Pdf format.

International Journal of Communication Networks and Information Security

International Journal of Communication Networks and Information Security http://www.ijcnis.org/index.php/ijcnis is published by Institute of Information Technology, Kohat University of Science and Technology, Pakistan. It is Focusing on theories, methods, and applications in networks and information security. Provides a challenging forum for researchers, industrial professionals, engineers, managers, and policy makers working in the field to contribute and disseminate innovative new work on networks and information security. Peer reviewed, International and Indexed in DOAJ, Inspec, Proquest etc. It is Peer Review and Referred journal. Back of file is V.1 No 1-3, 2009- v. 4, No. 3, 2012. Articles are arranged Volume wise with Pdf format.

International Journal of Computer and Information Engineering

International Journal of Computer and Information Engineering http://www.waset.org/journals/ijcie/ is published by World Academy of Science, Engineering and Technology. IJCISE covers all areas of Computer and Information Science and

Engineering, publishing refereed original research articles and technical notes. IJCISE is a scholarly open access, peer-reviewed, interdisciplinary, quarterly and fully refereed journal. Back of file is International Journal of Computer and Information Engineering http://www.waset.org/journals/ijcie/ Full text is available in pdf format. Articles are arranged Volume and then Number wise and can be browse by simple click.

International Journal of Computer Science and Information Technology

International Journal of Computer Science and Information Technology http://airccse.org/journal/ijcsit.html is published by Academy & Industry Research Collaboration Center. The mission of this journal is to publish original contributions in its field in order to propagate knowledge amongst its readers and to be a reference publication. It is devoted to fields of Computer Science and Information Systems. Peer-reviewed scientific journal published in electronic form as well as print form. Back of file is V. 1, 1-2 2009- v. 5, 1- 6 2013. Information is found of simple click on Issue Title and arranged volume wise with pdf format.

International Journal of Digital Curation

International Journal of Digital Curation http://www.ijdc.net/./ijdc/issue/current is published by The Digital Curation Centre, United Kingdom. The IJDC is entirely devoted to papers, articles and news items on curation of digital objects and related issues. The journal is published in electronic form, two times a year. Back of file is V,1 ,1, 2006-v.7, 2, 2012 and full text is available in PDF format. Issues and Author Index has been given. Information for Author, Reader and Librarians has been given. Articles are arranged Volume wise. Articles can get by simple click on Volume and then particular article. Internal search engine has been given.

International Journal of Doctoral Studies (IJDS)

International Journal of Doctoral Studies (IJDS) http://ijds.org/ Published by Informing Science Institute Country: United

States. IJDS is a quality peer-reviewed scholarly journal focus on informing science, information systems, information technology, information science, information security, IT education. The editorial objective of IJDS is the facilitation of knowledge enhancement related to doctoral studies in areas such as (but not limited to): informing science, information systems, information technology, information science, decision science, information security, and IT education. IJDS is proudly listed in the following indices: Cabell's Directory of Publishing Opportunities in Educational Curriculum and Methods, Cabell's Directory of Publishing Opportunities in Educational Psychology and Administration, EBSCO, DOAJ. Back of file is Vol. 1, 2006-v. 8, 2013 and full text is available in pdf format. Articles are arranged Volume wise. All submissions are double blind refereed by four or more scholars and can get by simple click on Volume and then particular article. Internal search engine has been given.

International Journal of Legal Information

International Journal of Legal Information http://scholarship.law.cornell.edu/ijli/vol33/iss1/ is published by Published by Cornell Law Library. It focuses on Legal Issues, Behavior Economic Issues, Islamic Governance, Commercial Issues etc. It has columns for Book reviews and International calendars. Back of file is Vol. 33, No.1, spring 2005-v. 38, No. 2, spring 2010. Information is arranged volume wise with Pdf format.

International Journal of Library and Information Science

International Journal of Library and Information Science http://www.academicjournals.org/ijlis/index.htm is published by academic Journals, Victoria Island, Lagos. Its papers cover manuscripts that meet the general criteria of significance and scientific excellence. Information can be browse by simple click and internal search engine has been given. Information is Arranged volume wise with pdf format. It is Peer reviewed Journal. Back of file is V.1, No. 1-6, 2009-V. 5, No 2, 2013.

International Journal of Managing Public Sector Information and Communication Technologies

International Journal of Managing Public Sector Information and Communication Technologies http://airccse.org/journal/mpict/ijmpict.html is published by Academy & Industry Research Collaboration Center. It Contribute new results in regards to the use of information and communication technologies (ICT) in the public sector around the world. Topics of interest include, Electronic records, Information preservation, Management, Security, RFID, Privacy, Open source, Knowledge Management, Internet, Infrastructure. Provides a platform to disseminate new ideas and new research, advance theories, and propagate best practices in the management of ICT in public sector organizations. Back of file is V.1, 1- 2, Dec 2010-V.3, No2 Dec 2012. Information is arranged Year, Volume and then by No. with pdf format and can be found by simple click on Issue Title.

International Journal of Multimedia and Its Applications

International Journal of Multimedia and Its Applications http://airccse.org/journal/ijma_index.html is published by Academy & Industry Research Collaboration Center. It focuses on Technical and practical aspects of Multimedia & its applications. Bring together researchers and practitioners from academia and industry to focus on understanding recent developments this arena, and establishing new collaborations in these areas. Back of file is V.1, 1, 2009- v.5, 1, 2013. Indexed in Inspec, Google Scholar, Open Jgate, Scirus etc. and Arranged volume wise with pdf format and Information for Author, Librarian and Readers has been given. Internal search engine has been given. We can get Information by Simple click on Issue Title.

International Journal of Special Libraries

International Journal of Special Libraries http://forge.fh-potsdam.de/~IFLA/INSPEL/intro.htm is published and edited by Fachhochschule Potsdam, Country: Germany. INSPEL is for dissemination of papers written or proposed for publication by members of the IFLA Division of Special Libraries. It focuses on Library Science, Science, and Technology._It promotes and coordinates the work of particular relevance to the specific types of libraries or library activities in its Standing Committees for Art Libraries, Map Libraries, Government Libraries, Science and Technology Libraries and Social Science Libraries. Fulltext is available in pdf format and Back of file Vol.27, N. 1-4, 1993-Vol. 36, N.1-4, 2002. Print version publisher Technische Universität Berlin, Universitätsbibliothek, Abt. Publikationen Straße des 17. Juni 135, 10623 Berlin, Germany 2003 is discontinued. Information is arranged Volume wise and can be browse by simple click on wanted articles.

International Review of Information Ethics

International Review of Information Ethics http://www.i-r-i-e.net/ is published by International Center for Information Ethics, Country: Germany. It envisions an international as well as intercultural discussion focusing on the ethical impacts of information technology on human practices and thinking, social interaction, other areas of science and research and the society itself. The IRIE is the official journal of the International Center for Information Ethics (ICIE). Author index has been given. Back of file is Vol. 1, 1-2 June & Oct 2004-v.18, Dec 2012 and full text is available in PDF format. Option for Current, Archive and Next Issue has been given. Articles are arranged Volume wise and Articles can get by simple click on Volume and then particular article.

International Review of Research in Open and Distance Learning

International Review of Research in Open and Distance Learning http://www.irrodl.org/index.php/irrodl is published by Athabasca University. The International Review of Research in Open and Distance Learning is a refereed, open access e-journal that aims to disseminate research, theory, and best practice in open and distance learning worldwide. Author, Issue and Title indexing has been given. All articles are peer reviewed. Vol. 5, 1-3, 2004-v. 14, 1, 2013 and Abstract is available. Full text is available in Html and PDF format. Articles are arranged Volume and year wise. Information for author, librarian and Readers has been given. Articles can be browse by simple click. Internal search engine has been given.

Internet Writing Journal

Internet Writing Journal http://www.internetwritingjournal.com/ is published by Writers Write, Inc. the Online Magazine for Writers and Book Lovers. Information is arranged by issue and Year. Back of file is August 1997-dec-jan 2007. Information is arranged by issue and Year. Articles can be browse by simple click. Full text is available in html format.

Interpersonal Computing and Technology Journal

Interpersonal Computing and Technology Journal http://www.helsinki.fi/science/optek/#byissue is published by the Association for Educational Communications and Technology. The journal's focus is on computer-mediated communication, and the pedagogical issues surrounding the use of computers and technology in educational settings. IPCT-J is a scholarly, peer-reviewed journal and Published quarterly. Back of file is V.1, N.1, 1993-V. 5, N.2, 1997. fulltext is available in e-text format. fulltext is available in e-text format. Information is arranging by issue, author.

Issues In Informing Science and Information Technology

Issues in Informing Science and Information Technology http://iisit.org/ is published by Informing Science Institute Country: United States. The purpose of Issues in Informing Science and Information Technology is to encourage the sharing of knowledge and collaboration among the wide variety of fields that use information technology to inform clients. These areas include: Communications, Communicating Meaning, Community and Society, Computer Science, Data Communications, Distance Education, E-Commerce, Education, Government, Health Care, Medicine, History, Information Science & Library, Journalism, Justice and Law, Mathematics, Philosophical Issues, Psychology,

Public Policy, Sociology, Technology, Working Together. The articles in this publication provide insight into how best to inform clients using information technology and cover research in IT Education, such as Curriculum and Techniques for teaching IT. Back of file is Vol. 1, 2004 - v. 9, 2012 **and** full text is available in PDF format. Articles are arranged Volume wise and Articles can get by simple click on Volume and then particular article.

Issues in science and Technology Librarianship

Issues in science and Technology Librarianship http://www.library.ucsb.edu/istl/ or http://www.istl.org/ is published by Association of College and Research Libraries, United States. ISTL publishes substantive material of interest to science and technology librarians. It serves as a vehicle for science-tech librarians to share details of successful programs, materials for the delivery of information services, background information and opinions on topics of current interest, and to publish research and bibliographies on issues in science and technology libraries. Author index has been given. It published quarterly summer, winter, fall, spring. Back of file is Dec 1991- 71 Fall 2012 and Abstract and full text has been given in e-text format. Articles are arranged volume wise. Option of current and previous issue has been given. Information for author has been given and can be browse by clicking on Volume and then on particular title.

IT & Society

IT&Society http://www.stanford.edu/group/siqss/itandsociety/ is published by SIQSS, Stanford University. IT & Society is a web-based scholarly journal devoted to the scientific analysis of the social impact of information technology on society, with special emphasis on quantitative survey analysis. The intended audience for this research quarterly includes the community of scholars interested in the social impact of new technologies, as well as policy makers, media analysts, computer professionals and interested members of the general public. Issue indexing has been given. The publication of IT & Society is currently suspended. Back of file Vol. 1, Issue 2002-Vol.1, Issue7, 2004 and Full text is available in Html. Articles are arranged issue and year wise and can be browse by simple click.

ITALICS: Innovations in Teaching and Learning in Information and Computer Sciences

ITALICS: Innovations in Teaching and Learning in Information and Computer Sciences http://www.ics.ltsn. ac.uk/pub/italics/ index.html is now publishing by the Higher education academy http://www.ics.heacademy.ac.uk/. Innovation in Teaching And Learning in Information and Computer Sciences, the electronic journal of the Higher Education Academy Subject Centre for Information and Computer Sciences (ICS). ITALICS provide a vehicle for members of the ICS communities to disseminate best practice and research on learning and teaching within the subject disciplines. ITALICS aims to highlight current issues in learning and teaching Information and Computer Sciences at the Higher Education (HE) level including. It is a professional online journal for academics within the Information and Computer Sciences communities. There will be three issues of ITALICS each year, published in February, June and November. The journal will include An editorial, Peer reviewed papers, Book reviews. Back of file is Vol. 4, 1-3, 2005-v. 10, 3, 2011 and full text is available in PDF format.

JEP: The Journal of Electronic Publishing

JEP: The Journal of Electronic Publishing http:// www.journalofelectronicpublishing.org/ is published by the Scholarly Publishing Office (SPO), a unit of the University of Michigan University Library and its editor is Judith Axler Turner. It is a forum for research and discussion about contemporary publishing practices, and the impact of those practices upon users. Its major coverage is Electronic publishing. The journal provides archive of works covering current trends and issues in electronic publishing. The articles present innovative ideas, best practices, and leading-edge thinking about all aspects of publishing, authorship, and readership. Author and Title Index have been given along with quick browse option. JEP readers are publishers, scholars, librarians, journalists, students, technologists, attorneys, retailers, and others. Back of file Vol.1, 1-2, 1995-v. 15, 1-3, 2012 and Abstract and full text has given in E-text format. List of all the issues have been given in one page. Browse and search option has been given separately and have its own internal search engine. Full text, Title, author search can be made by Basic, Proximity, Boolean, Bibliography, History. Abstract and Full text can be browse by clicking on particular issue's article.

JLIS.it Italian Journal of Library and Information Science

JLIS.it Italian Journal of Library and Information Science http://leo.cilea.it/index.php/jlis/article/view/4539/4416 is published by University of Florence. It contributes in Library and Information Science, aims to valorize Italian research. It is Peer-reviewed electronic open access format, academic journal of international scope. Back of file is Vol.1, No. 1-2, 2010- V.4 No.1, 2013. Information is arranged volume wise with pdf format and can be get by Simple click on Issue Title.

Journal of Artificial Intelligence Research

Journal of Artificial Intelligence Research http://www.jair.org/ is published by AI Access Foundation, Inc._JAIR provides all areas of artificial intelligence (AI), publishing refereed research articles, survey articles, and technical notes. Author, papers, title, abstract search has been given. Back of file is Vol.1, (August 1993- June 1994) - Vol. 46, Jan 2013 and Abstract has been given. Fullext has been given in PDF and postscript format. Articles are arranged volume wise and Articles are arranged volume wise.

Journal of Digital Information

Journal of Digital Information http://jodi.ecs. soton.ac.uk/r or http://journals.tdl.org/jodi is published by Texas Digital Library, United States. The journal covers the topic of information management, information science and information technology, digital libraries, hypermedia systems, hypertext criticism, and information discovery. Issue, author, title, theme index has been given. Issue, author, title, theme index has been given. Back of file is Vol. 1, 1-2, 1997-v. 13, 1, 2012 and Abstract has been given. Fullext has been given in html format. Issue, author, Title, and theme arrange information and Articles can be browse by clicking on particular issue's article. Inter search engine for searching has been given.

Journal of East Asian Libraries

Journal of East Asian Libraries http://www.lib.byu. edu/dlib/spc/jeal/ is published by Council on East Asian Libraries and the Association for Asian Studies, Inc. Information can be browse by simple click. The text issues are in Adobe Acrobat PDF format. It basically focuses on Asian Libraries perspectives. Information is arranged by V.1, No1, 1963- No. 156, No.1 Feb 2013.

Journal of Educational Media & Library Sciences

Journal of Educational Media & Library Sciences http://joemls.tku.edu.tw/index_e.htm is published by Tamkang University Press and co-published with the Department of Information & Library Science (DILS) and Chueh Sheng Memorial Library was formerly the Bulletin of Educational Media Science, Country: Taiwan. This peer reviewed journal cover all the aspects of Library science, information science, and information technology. Scopus, LISTA, DOAJ, H.W. Wilson Database, LLIS, LISA, PAIS, Ulrich's, Chinese ERIC, THCI, and CEPS index it. Back of file is Vol. 28, 1-4, 1991-1990-v. 50, 2, 2012. Articles are arranged Volume wise and Articles can get by simple click on Volume and then particular article.

Journal of eLiteracy

Journal of eLiteracy http://www.jelit.org/index.html Published by University of Glasgow, United Kingdom. This peer review Journal discuss on topics relevant to JeLit themes involving a theoretical, comparative, overview or critical element. Case Studies, Research Reports, Reviews. JeLit is the acronym for Journal of eLiteracy. Back of file is Vol. 1, Issue 1, 2004-Vol.2, Issue1-2, 2005. Articles are arranged Volume wise and Articles can get by simple click on Volume and then particular article. Internal search engine has been given for searching.

Journal of Health Informatics in Developing Countries

Journal of Health Informatics in Developing Countries http://www.jhidc.org/index.php/jhidc Published by University of Otago, Country: New Zealand. The objective of this journal is to share and promote academic knowledge in the field. One of its aims is also to encourage writers from developing countries to contribute their writings Author, Title and Issue index has been given. Back of file is Vol.1,1, 2007-v.7,1, 2013. Information is given for author, Reader, Librarians. Articles are arranged Volume wise. Current and Archive option has been given and Articles can be browse by Author, Title and Issue. Internal search engine with search tips has been given for searching.

Journal of Information Architecture

Journal of Information Architecture http://journalofia.org/archives/ is published by REG-iA, the Research & Education Group in IA and Sponsored by the Information Architecture Institute & by Copenhagen Business School. It Facilitate the systematic development of the scientific body of knowledge in the field of information architecture. Its main focus is on Research and sharing of good ideas and case studies that are useful to the field's researchers, practitioners, students, and all other interested parties and focus information architecture research and development in all types of shared information environments, such as for example social networks, web sites, intranets, mobile and Rich Internet Applications. It is Indexed and Peer-reviewed scholarly Journal, Published twice in Year. Back of file is V.1, 1 spring 2009- V.3, 1 spring 2011. Information is arranged volume wise with pdf format and can get simple click on Issue Title. Internal search engine has been given.

Journal of Information Law and Technology/ European Journal of Law and Technology

Journal of Information Law and Technology / European Journal of Law and Technology http://www2.warwick.ac.uk/ fac/ soc/law/elj/jilt/ or http://ejlt.org//issue/archive is published by the Universities of Warwick and Strathclyde in the United Kingdom. JILT covers a wide range of topics relating to IT Law and IT applications in law It contains a diversity of materials including peer reviewed and non-refereed articles, commentaries, work in progress articles, book and IT reviews, and conference reports and papers, as well as information papers, news and UK and global conferences. Issue indexing has been done. Articles are arranged Issue wise. Back of file is Issue 1-3, 1996- Vol.4, 1, 2013 (v .Starts from 2010) and Full text is available in PDF and RTF format. Articles are arranged Issue wise and Articles are arranged Issue wise.

Journal of Information Literacy (JIL)

Journal of Information Literacy (JIL) http://ojs.lboro.ac.uk/ ojs/index.php/JIL/index is published by Chartered Institute of Library and Information Professionals Country: United Kingdom. JIL is an international peer-reviewed academic journal that aims to investigate Information Literacy. The aim of JIL is to investigate and to make generalized observations on how Information Literacy impacts on organizations, systems and the individual. Back of file is Vol. 1, N. 1-3, 2007-Vol. 6, N.2, 2012. Information is given for author, Reader, Librarians. Articles are arranged Volume wise. Current and Archive option has been given and Articles can be browse by Author, Title and Issue. Internal search engine with search tips has been given for searching.

Journal of Information Technology Education (JITE: Research)

Journal of Information Technology Education (JITE: Research) http://www.informingscience.us/icarus/journals/ jiteresearch/publications is published by Informing Science Institute Country: United States. The academically peer refereed Journal of Information Technology Education (JITE) endeavors to improve IT Education around the world. Improve IT education around the world by publishing high quality articles on best practices and other topics of use. Types of articles, including primary, action, and secondary research, provide. JITE is listed in Applied Math and Science Education Repository (AMSER), Cabell's etc. ack of file is Vol.1, 2002-v. 12, 2012 and Full text is available in pdf format. Articles are arranged Volume wise. JITE is printed annually in a single volume and Articles can be browse by simple click. Internal search engine has been given.

Journal of Information, Information Technology, and Organizations

Journal of Information, Information Technology, and Organizations http://jiito.org/ is published by Informing Science Institute, California, Country: United States. JIITO covers a specialized area of information systems research indicated in its title. It focused on empirical studies. Conceptual articles are published just exceptionally. All submissions are blind refereed by three or more peers. Back of file is Vol.1, 2006-v. 8, 2013 (Annual) and fulltext is available in pdf format. Articles are arranged Volume wise and Articles can be browse by simple click.

Journal of Internet Cataloguing

Journal of Internet cataloguing http://www.internetcataloging.com/home.html is published by Published by Haworth, Binghamton, NY. Focus on the Internet Cataloguing. It basically includes on the cataloguing of Internet E-Resources. List of all the issues have been given in one page, which can be Browse. Information can by browse simple click on Volume and then on particular title. Back of file is Vol-1, No1, 1997-v. 5, No1, 2001 and Information if available in HTML format.

Journal of Knowledge Management Practice

Journal of Knowledge Management Practice http://www.tlainc.com/boutjkmp.htm published by Free Press Journals (formerly the Journal of Systemic Knowledge Management under a different publisher). The Journal of Knowledge Management

Practice is devoted to collecting serious research about knowledge management and its practical applications. Authors are invited to read the notes for contributors, and are encouraged to contribute. Issue indexing has been done. JKMP is published in 2006 and onward in Quarterly Issues. Back of file is Vol. 1. 1998-99-Vol.13 N. 4, Dec 2012 and Full text is available in Html. Articles are arranged issue and year wise and can be browse by simple click.

Journal of Library Innovation

Journal of Library Innovation http://www. libraryinnovation. org/about/contact is published by Western New York Library Resources Council, 4455 Genesee St., PO Box 400, Buffalo, New York. It disseminates research and information on innovative practice in libraries of all types. Its main focus is on Original research, reports on innovative practices, literature reviews, case .studies, and book, conference and product reviews. The Journal also welcomes provocative essays that will stimulate thought on the current and future role of libraries in an Internet Age. It is a peer reviewed open access journal. Back of file is V.1 No 1-2, 2010-V3 No 2, 2012. Information is arranged volume wise with pdf format, which can be get by click on Issue Title. Internal search engine has been given.

Journal of Medical Internet Research

Journal of Medical Internet Research http://www.jmir.org/ is published by Gunther Eysenbach Country: Canada. This peer review journal is focus on Medicinepi, Internet. JMIR covers health informatics and all aspects of research, information and communication in the healthcare field using Internet and Intranet-related technologies, which is nowadays called "eHealth". JMIR is indexed in MEDLINE and numerous other databases, and full-text articles are permanently archived in PubMed Central. The new JMIR Impact Factor released in June 2008 is now 3.0. Back of file is Vol. 1, 1-2, - supplement1, 1999-v. 12, 2, 2013and fulltext is available in HTML format. Articles are arranged Volume wise. Author and title search category has been given and can be browse by simple click. Articles can be browse by Author, Title and Issue. Internal search engine with search tips has been given for searching.

Journal of Philippine Librarianship

Journal of Philippine Librarianship http://journals.upd.edu.ph/index.php/jpl/issue/current is published by University of the Philippine. It covers all aspects of Library and information science and includes librarianship, health librarianship, information system, archival studies, children and young adult library services, emerging technology and services, information storage, retrieval, collection management, cataloging, classification, indexing, abstracting, thesaurus construction, reference, access, reader services, preservation and conservation of collections etc. Back of file is Vol. 27, 1-2, 2010- v.31, 1, 2011. Information is arranged by year with pdf format and can be get by click on Issue Title.

Journal of Research and Practice in Information Technology

Journal of Research and Practice in Information Technology http://ws.acs.org.au/jrpit/JRPIT_Volumes.html is published by Australian Computer Society Inc. It includes all aspects of Information Technology deemed to be of interest to part of the readership but not limited to: Computer Science; Information Systems; Computer Systems and Information engineering; Software Engineering. It is indexed by Applied Mechanics Reviews, Applied Mechanics Reviews, Compumath Citation Index etc. Back of file is Vol. 35, 1-4, 2003-v. 43, 1-3, 2011. Information is arranged volume wise with pdf format and Information for Author, Librarian and Readers has been given. Articles can be getting by Simple click on Issue Title and internal search engine has been given.

Journal of Staff Development

Journal of Staff Development http://learningforward.org/publications/jsd#.UUQguzcynUc is published by National Staff Development Council This well-respected, quarterly journal addresses timely issues such as restructuring, the role of principals, program planning, ensuring results with students, and follow-up strategies. Professional magazine on leading and learning published quarterly. It focuses on issues of leadership and learning relevant to all educators involved in professional learning. Primarily practitioners who bring a real world to the challenges of school improvement and organizational change write articles. Issue indexing has been done. Back of file is Vol. 13, N. 3, summer 1992- v. 34. N. 1, 2013. Articles are arranged issue wise. Articles can be browse by simple click.

Journal of Technology Studies

Journal of Technology Studies http://scholar.lib.vt.edu/ejournals/JOTS/ is published by DLA University libraries. Articles are posted online as they are edited and received. As articles are added, the sequence of the articles in the Table of Contents and within the body of this e-journal may be changed to reflect the editor's design of the final print version of the volume. Back of file Vol. XXII, 2, summer /fall 1996- v. XXXVIII, 2, Fall 2012. Information is arranged by issue and Year. Full text is available in PDF and html format. Articles can be browse by simple click.

Journal of the American Medical Informatics Association

Journal of the American Medical Informatics Association http://www.pubmedcentral.nih.gov tocrender.fcgi?action= archive&journal=76 is published by American Medical Informatics Association. JAMIA focus on mainly Desion making, Healt communication, IT, Preservation. Fulltext is available in pdf and html format. Information is arranged by issue and Year. Back of file is Vol 1, 1-6 1994- v. 19, 3, March 2012. Articles can be browse by simple click.

Journal of the Association for History and Computing

Journal of the Association for History and Computing http://mcel.pacificu.edu/jahc/ is sponsored by the American Association for History and Computing. The AHC aspires to promote and develop interest in the use of computers in all types of historical study at every level, in both teaching and research. Goal of journal is to help define useful standards to maximize the utility of computers in historical studies. The Journal is intended for a general audience of teachers, students, and researchers interested in the application of computers in historical studies. Index by Subject , Author, Articles, Coloumns, Editorials, Reviews, Books Reviewed by Title, Books Reviewed by Author, Software Reviewed. Back of file is Vol. 1, N. 1, June 1998-Vol. 11, N.2, August 2008 and full text is available in e-text format. Articles are arranged Volume wise. Option for current and past issue has been given separately. Articles can be browse by Subject, Author, Articles, Coloumns, Editorials, Reviews, Books Reviewed by Title, Books Reviewed by Author, Software Reviewed. Internal search engine has been given.

Journal of the European Association for Health Information and Libraries

Journal of the European Association for Health Information and Libraries http://www.eahil.net/journal/ is published by Medical Library-Univ. of Cambridge, Cambridge. Its aim is Uniting and motivating librarians and information officers working in medical and health science libraries in Europe. It Encourages professional development, improves cooperation and enables exchanges of experience amongst its members. Back of file is Vol.1, 1-4, 2005-v.9, 4, 2013. Information is arranged volume wise with pdf format and can be found by simple click on Issue Title and internal search engine has been given.

Journal of the Medical Library association

Journal of the Medical Library association http://www.ncbi.nlm.nih.gov/pmc/journals/93/ is published by PubMed and from 2002 Medical Library Association, United States. Contribute to the education of health sciences librarians, role of the medical librarian and help to broaden the profession's skill set and has been on continuing work to foster a research mentality among JMLA readers. It covers health sciences, librarianship, education, and information technology. Back of file is Vol1, 1898 - v.101 1, 2013. Archive includes: J Med Libr Assoc: Vols. 90 to 96; 2002 to 2008, Med Library Hist J: Vols. 1 to 5; 1903 to 1907

Bull Assoc Med Libr: Vol. 1; 1902 Med Lib: Vols. 1 to 5; 1898 to 1902.Information is arranged Volume wise at home page. With pdf format and can be found by simple click on the Volume and Internal search engine is available.

Journal of Virtual Worlds Research

Journal of Virtual Worlds Research http://www.jvwresearch.org/index.html Published by TDL electronic Press and hosted by the JVWR Editorial Team. Topics of interest include: Limitations and advantages of educational practices, Development and use of instructional tools, Evaluation and assessment, Innovations in educational assessment methods, Interdisciplinary curriculum and instruction, Educational and research ethics in virtual world. Published peer reviewed research papers. Back of file is Vol. 1, N. 1-3, 2008-Vol. 2, N.1, March 2009. To be published and abstract is available. Full text is available in PDF format. Articles are arranged Volume wise and Articles can be browse by simple click.

LASIE: Library Automated Systems Information Exchange

LASIE: Library Automated Systems Information Exchange http://search.informit.com.au/browseJournalTitle;res=E-LIBRARY;issn=0047-3774 is published by RMIT University. Information can be browse by simple click. The text issues are in Adobe Acrobat PDF format. It includes mainly Library automation and Information Exchange platform. Information is arranged by volume and then Number. Back of file is Vol. 17, No 1-6, 1986-Vol. 33, No1, 2002.

Law Library Journal

Law Library Journal http://www.aallnet.org/ products/pub_journal.asp is published by American Association of Law Libraries. Scholarly articles on law, legal materials, and librarianship are the mainstay of the Journal. Information can be browse by simple click. The text issues are in Adobe Acrobat PDF format. Practice-oriented articles, proceedings of the business sessions of the Annual Meeting, and annual reports of committees, special interest sections, representatives, and chapters are also included.

Information is arranged by Year, Volume and then Number. Vol.92, 1 (Winter 2000)- v.105, 1 (Winter 2013). The Law Library Journal is available on Lexis-Nexis®, WESTLAW, H.W. Wilson and HeinOnline.

Learned Publishing

Learned Publishing http://www.ingentaconnect.com/content/alpsp/lp is published by Association of Learned and Professional Society Publishers. Learned Publishing is the journal of the Association of Learned and Professional Society Publishers, published in collaboration with the Society for Scholarly Publishing. The journal is published quarterly in January/April/July/October. Back of file is Vol.1, 10, 1997-v.26, 1, 2013. Fulltext is available in pdf format. Articles can be browse by simple click. Information is arranged by Volume, Author, and Subject.

LIBER Quarterly Journal of European research libraries

LIBER Quarterly Journal of European research libraries http://liber.library.uu.nl/index.html aim is to assist research libraries in Europe to support a functional network across national boundaries in order to ensure the preservation of the European cultural heritage, to improve access to collections in European research libraries, and to provide more efficient information services in Europe. Vol. 12, 2002-Vol. 18, N.1-2 2008 and Full text is available in e-text, and PDF format. Articles are arranged Volume wise and it represent Interests, needs improvement, standardisation of European research libraries.

Libraries and culture

Libraries and culture http://www.utexas.edu/utpress/journals/jlc.html is Published by UT Press University of Texas, Austin. It explores the significance of libraries; their creation, organization and preservation in the context of cultural and social history. L&CR is an interdisciplinary journal that explores the significance of collections of recorded knowledge and its creation, organization, preservation, and utilization in the context of cultural and social history. All the volumes are not freely available. Free fulltext articles are available from Volume 32 to Volume 35 and Volume 7. Different Indexers index it i.e. EBSCO, ABC, Thomson etc. Vol. 32, N.1 Winter-4 fall, 1997-Vol. 35, N.1 Winter, 2000.Volume 7, N. 3, 1972 and Full text is available in pdf format. Articles are arranged Number wise and Articles can be browse by simple click.

Library Journal

Library Journal http://www.libraryjournal.com is LJ Publisher is Ron Shank and its Editor in chief Francine Fialkoff. Library Journal is the 132nd year oldest and most respected publication covering the library field. LJ is the single-most comprehensive publication for librarians, with groundbreaking features and analytical news reports covering technology, management, policy, and other professional concerns. Over 100,000 library directors, administrators, and staff in public, academic, and special libraries read LJ. Its hefty review sections evaluate nearly 7000 books annually. Back of file is Annual Vol. Dec. 2007- Annual v. June 2012 and Full text is available in e-text format. Articles are arranged in Current Issue and Archive in one page. Free subscription is also available and Articles are arranged in Current Issue and Archive in one page. Free subscription is also available. Internal search engine have been given. Articles can be browse by Issue.

Library Philosophy and Practice

Library Philosophy and Practice http://www.webpages.uidaho.edu/~mbolin/lpp.htm is published by University of Nebraska, Lincoln libraries, United States. LPP is a peer reviewed electronic journal that publishes articles exploring the connection between library practice and the philosophy and theory behind it. It include explorations of current, past, and emerging theories of librarianship and library practice, as well as reports of successful, innovative, or experimental library procedures, methods, or projects in all areas of librarianship, set in the context of applied research. Issue, Author and title indexing has been given. LPP is indexed in LISTA, DOAJ, Library Literature & Information Science, and SCOPUS. Back of file is Annual Annual Vol. Dec. 2007- Annual v. June 2012 and Full text is available in PDF format. Articles are arranged Volume wise. Articles for each issue are accessible from the tables of contents and can be browse by simple click.

Library Resources & Technical Services (LRTS)

Library Resources & Technical Services (LRTS) http://alcts.metapress.com/home/main.mpx is published by the Association for Library Collections & Technical Services, A division of the American Library Association. Its Features library issues related to resources management and technical services. Its purpose is to communicate thoughtful reflection on practice as well as research including collections, Preservation, acquisition, Serials, Cataloguing and classification. LRTS supports the theoretical, intellectual, practical, and scholarly aspects of the profession of collection management and development, acquisitions, cataloging and classification, preservation and reformatting, serials by publishing articles and book reviews. It is primary communication tool of all librarians, information professionals, and educators. Index is available. The general procedures used in compiling the Index Author Title and Subject entries are included. Back of file is Full text from Vol. 40, 1-4, 1996- v. 55, 1-4, 2011 Toc and abstract available till v. 57, 1, 2013 and Full text is available in pdf format. Information is arranged Volume wise at home page. Articles can be browse by clicking on the title.

Library Student Journal

Library student journal http://www.librarystudentjournal.org is published by Buffalo University, Country: United States. This Peer reviewed Journal focus on education, training, career paths, future trends and advance discussion of LIS topics. Issue, Author and title indexing has been given. Back of file is 2006-2012 and Abstract is available and fulltext is available in HTML and pdf format. LSJ is divided into four sections: 1. Articles, Essay, Editorials - opinion pieces of any length, Reviews. Articles are arranged Volume wise. Articles can be browse by Author, Title and Issue. Internal search engine with search tips has been given.

LIBRES: Library and Information Science Research Electronic Journal

LIBRES: Library and Information Science Research Electronic Journal http://libres.curtin.edu.au/ is Published by Published by Curtin University of Technology Country: Australia. LIBRES is an international refereed electronic journal devoted to new research in Library and Information Science. Libres is distributed through a listserver, and an ftp site. ISA, LISA, EBSCO, and SPI index it. Back of file is Vol. 6, 1-2 July 1996-V.22,2 March 2012 (bi-annual) and Fulltext is available in pdf format. Articles are arranged volume wise. Articles can be browse by clicking on particular issue's article. "Library and Information Science Research Electronic Conference is designed to foster library and information science research and support the development of our knowledge base. It shares ideas, solutions, and experiences, and includes discussions of research in progress, reviews of research, queries and responses from participants, and conference announcements."

LIBRI: International Journal of Libraries and Information Services

LIBRI: International Journal of Libraries and Information Services http://www.librijournal.org/ is Published by K. G. Saur Verlag, München, And Country: Germany. LIBRI examine historical and current perspective of LIS, analyze the role of information in cultural, organizational, national and international developments, and report on current trends in LIS. Abstracted or indexed in: Social Sciences Citation Index/Research Alert, Current Contents: Social & Behavioral Sciences, Library & Information Science Abstracts, and Information Science. Back of file is Vol. 49, N.1-4, 1999-Vol. 58, N.1-3, 2008 and Abstract is available and Full text is available in pdf format. Articles are arranged Number wise. Articles can be browse by simple click.

Malaysian Journal of Library & Information Science Malaysian Journal of Library & Information Science

Malaysian Journal of Library & Information Science Malaysian Journal of Library & Information Science http://

ejum.fsktm.um.edu.my/Default.aspx is published by the Faculty of Computer Science & Information Technology, University of Malaya. Higher learning institutions or research and development. Information can be browse by simple click. Fulltext is available in pdf. It is an internet-based management Journal that provides scholarly journal management system for university, higher learning institutions or research and development centers. Information is arranged by volume. Back of file is Vol.1, 1-2, 1996-v. 18, 1, 2013. Author Index has been given.

MC Journal: The Journal of Academic Media Librarianship

MC Journal: The Journal of Academic Media Librarianship http://wings.buffalo.edu/publications/mcjrnl/ is published by The AV Review. It is a peer-reviewed online journal for practical and scholarly information concerning. Back of file is Vol. 1, N1-2, 1993-Vol. 8, N.1-2, 2002 and Full text is available in pdf format. Articles are arranged Volume wise. Articles can be browse by simple click. Internal search has been given for searching.

MELA Notes: The Journal of the Middle East Librarians Association

MELA Notes: The Journal of the Middle East Librarians Association http://www.mela.us/MELANotes/MELANotesIntro.html is published by Middle East Librarians Association. MELA Notes focus mainly on Middle East librarianship. Information can be browse by simple click. The text of the back issues is in Adobe Acrobat PDF format. It discusses mainly university and schools etc. Information is arranged by Number. Back of file is from Number 64 (Spring 1997) to Number 81 (2008) and no. 1- (1973-). MELA NOTES is published twice a year, in spring and fall.

Mississippi Libraries

Mississippi Libraries http://www.misslib.org/index.php/publications/mississippi-libraries/ is published by Mississippi Library Association. The mission of the Mississippi Library Association is to provide professional leadership for the development, promotion, and improvement of library and information services and the profession of librarianship in order to enhance learning and ensure access to information for all. It is indexed in Library Literature. MLA is a chapter of the American Library Association and the Southeastern Library Association. Back of file is V. 64, No. 1 2000- V. 75, No 3, 2012 and Full text is available in pdf format. Articles are arranged Volume wise. Articles can be browse by simple click.

MLA Forum

MLA Forum http://www.mlaforum.org/ is published by Michigan Library Association, United States. MLA Forum, the online Quaterly journal of the Michigan Library Association focuses on all the aspect of Library and education. It is indexed in Library Literature & LISA. In Jan. 2008, it began publishing a single annual volume, Prior to 2008. Back of file is Vol. 1, Issue1-2, 2002- Vol. 5, Issue 1-3, 2007, New Vol. 6 annual 2008 and fulltext is available in e-text format. Articles are arranged Volume wise and Articles can be browse by simple click.

Multimedia Information and Technology Journal (MmIT)

Multimedia Information and Technology Journal (MmIT) http://www.cilip.org.uk/get-involved/special-interest-groups/multimedia/journal/pages/default.aspx is published by chartered Institute of Library and Information Professionals. It includes mainly database, Research and Technology in the field of library and Information Science. Back of file is Vol. 30, 1-4, 2004-v.37, 1, August 2011. Vol. 38 is not open access. Information is arranged by volume and then Number with pdf format and can be found by simple click on Issue Title.

New Knowledge Environments

New Knowledge Environments http://journals.uvic.ca/index.php/INKE is published by University of Victoria. Its main focus is on the implementation of new knowledge in environment, Virtual library and Designing interface. Back of file is Vol.1, 1, 2009. Information is arranged with pdf format and can be found by Simple click on Issue Title. Internal search engine has been given.

North Carolina Libraries

North Carolina Libraries http://www.nclaonline. org/NCL/ is published by North Carolina Library Association, United States. North Carolina Libraries focus on Libraries, librarianship, media centers, and academic libraries. Articles can be browse by simple click and all the volumes are indexed. Fulltext is available in pdf format. Back of file: Vol. 47, 1, 1989-v. 70, 1-2, 2012.

Northwestern Journal of Technology and Intellectual Property

Northwestern Journal of Technology and Intellectual Property http://www.law.northwestern.edu/journals/njtip/issues.htm is published by Northwestern University School of Law. Intellectual property and the intersection of law and technology, copyright, trademark, patents, the Internet, media, telecommunications, health care, antitrust, e-discovery, and trial and litigation technology. It is dedicated to the analysis of the burgeoning body of academic, business, newsworthy and legal issues regarding the rapidly increasing and shifting field of intellectual property and technology law. It provides insightful and timely perspectives on intellectual property and technology law, an important area in the academic, legal and business communities. It is among the top ranked intellectual property and technology journals in the country. Back of file is V. 8, Issue 2 2010-V. 11, Issue 2 2013. Information is arranged Volume wise with pdf and can be found by simple click on Issue Title.

NPO Journal/NPO E-Journal

NPO Journal/NPO E-Journal http://www.bl.uk/blpac/publicationsjournals.html is published by The NPO e-Journal was preceded by the NPO Journal (1998-2003). Its mission is to build a community with the tools and support to actively take part in the preservation of library and archive collections. Information can be browse by simple click. Information is available in simple text format. It believe that preservation is everyone's responsibility. By working together and sharing knowledge and experience users, volunteers and staff working with library and archive collections can embed a culture which ensures that the way collections are managed and used contributes to their long-term accessibility. Information is arranged by Year and then Number No. 1, Feb. 1998- No. 13, Nov 2003 & No.1 May 2004- No.5 March 2007.The NPO Journal was preceded by Library Conservation News (1983-1997).

Partnership: the Canadian Journal of Library and Information Practice and Research

Partnership: the Canadian Journal of Library and Information Practice and Research http://journal.lib. uoguelph.ca/index.php/ perj/index is Published by The Partnership Country: Canada. Feature articles on theory & research and on innovations in practice are in-depth, peer-reviewed articles. Other types of articles include viewpoints, conference presentations, profiles, news& announcements, professional development and reviews. Issue, Author and title indexing has been given. It is ppublished twice a year. Vol. 1, 1, 2006-v. 7 2, 2012 and Abstract is available and full text is available in HTML and PDF format. Articles are arranged Volume wise. Current and archives option has been given. Information is given for author, Reader, Librarians. Articles can be browse by Author, Title and Issue. Internal search engine with search tips has been given.

Progressive Librarian

Progressive Librarian http://libr.org/pl/ is published by Progressive Librarians Guild. Progressive Librarian is a forum for critical perspectives in Librarianship, featuring articles, book reviews, bibliographies, reports and documents that explore progressive perspectives on librarianship and information issues. Back of file is N.1, 1990-N.32, 2009. TOC access till Issue no. 38-39, spring 2012and Full text is available in e-text format. Issue 1, 1990 and Issue 29-30, 2007-2008 is not open access. Articles are arranged Volume wise and can be browse by simple click.

RBM Journal of Rare Books & Manuscripts

RBM Journal of Rare Books & Manuscripts http:// rbm.acrl.org/content/2/2Librarianship http://rbm.acrl. org/

content/2/2 is published by American Library Association. Information can be browse by simple click. The text issues are in Adobe Acrobat PDF format. Disscuss about Books, Mannuals, Manuscripts. Information is arranged by Year and then Number. Back of file is March & Sept 1986- March & Sept 1990 & Vol.1, 1-2, March & Sept 2000- v.13, 2, 2012.

Research Management Review

Research Management Review http://www.ncura.edu/content/news/rmr/archive.php is published by National Council of University Research Administrators. NCURA serves its members and advances the field of research administration through education and professional development programs, the sharing of knowledge and experience, and by fostering a professional, collegial, and respected community. Back of file is V.1, N1, 1987-V.15 N.2 2007. Information is arranged by Volume and year.

Scandinavian Public Library Quarterly

Scandinavian Public Library Quarterly http://www.splq. info/ is published by Scandinavian Public Library Quarterly. It is its strong belief that Nordic public libraries must have a voice in the international library world Its converge is about networking, about establishing good and highly relevant content on the Internet, about bridging the virtual and the real library, about outstanding library architecture, about information policies in some of the strongest democracies in the world. Now that SPLQ is also available electronically, the scene is set for topical discussions, and ideas for possible future articles are always welcome, as are your general comments. Back of file is Vol. 35, 2002- v. 45, 4, 2012 and Full text is available in e-text format. Article indexing has been given. Articles are arranged by year and can be browse by simple click. Internal search engine has been given.

School Libraries in Canada

School Libraries in Canada http://www.clatoolbox.ca/ casl/slic/aboutslic.html is published by Information can be browse by simple click. The text issues are in Adobe Acrobat PDF format. Its mission is to provide national support for the development and maintenance of exellence in Canada's school libraries, media centres, and school library personnel. Information is arranged by volume and then Number. Back of file is Vol. 18 N02, 1998-v. 30 No. 1, 2012.

School Library Journal Online

School Library Journal Online http://www.schoollibraryjournal.com/ is published by Reed Business Information, a division of Reed Elsevier Inc. Online version of the print publication includes Features current news about school libraries and librarians Includes job opportunities. Back of file is Issue 1,3,5,7,9,11, 1996-Issue 1, 2013 and Full text is available in e-text format. Issue indexing has been done. Articles are arranged Volume wise. Articles can be browse by simple click.

School Library Research

School Library Research http://www.ala.org/aasl/slr is American Association of School Librarians, Country: United States, Cahners Business Information. It provides wide range of books and visual media that explore topics as varied as science and history, geography and the arts. Latest issue offers you lots of concrete ways to incorporate the best new books and media into your lesson plans. It's imperative that quality materials, especially those that address neglected subjects, find their way into your libraries and classrooms. Issue indexing has been done. Vol.1, 1998-v.16, 2013 and Full text is available in HTML format. Articles are arranged by Issue. Articles can be browse by simple click.

Simile: Studies in media and information literacy education

Simile: Studies in media and information literacy education http://www.utpjournals.com/simile/simile.html is Published by University of Toronto Press. It is a peer reviewed online journal Features scholarly articles pertaining to bibliographic instruction and information and media literacy. SIMILE is interested in publishing research that advances knowledge about media and information literacy. SIMILE aims to explore the ways in which social and cultural environments impact media production and the methods that could be used to teach the skills needed to "read" these environments. Abstracting and Indexing in Academic Search Premier CBCA Education CEPIEC, EBSCO. Vol. 2, N. 1-4, 2002-Vol. 8, N.1and3, 2008 are not open access. Back of file is Volume 8, N. 2, May 2008 and Full text is available in PDF format. Articles are arranged Volume wise and can be browse by simple click.

South African Journal of Information Management

South African Journal of Information Management http://general.rau.ac.za/infosci/raujournal/ is published by University of Johannesburg Country: South Africa. It presents original research (i.e. not previously published), novel synthesis, or judicious review of current theory, method, policy, or practice in the fields mentioned below. Article submission, review and publication are accomplished entirely electronically. SAJIM) is to publish high quality, peer reviewed articles four times a year in numbered issues. Back of file is Vol.1, No.1-4, 1999-v.15, 1, 2013. Articles are arranged Volume wise. Archives option has been given. Before opening the fulltext User has to fill registration form, which is available, free of cost and Articles can be browse by simple click.

Special Libraries

Special Libraries http://www.sla.org/content/shop/speclibs.cfm#1910 is Special Libraries, the journal produced by the Special Library Association (SLA). SLA offers a wide array of professional development opportunities, including the industries best online education programs, designed to sharpen professional skills throughout your career. Past issue have 4 issue and current have ten issues. Back if file is Vol. 1, 1910-Vol. 87, 1996 and Full text is available in PDF format. Articles are arranged Volume wise. Articles can be browse by simple click.

Studies in Bibliography

Studies in Bibliography http://etext.lib.virginia.edu/ bsuva/sb is published by The bibliographical society of the university of Virginia. It enhances ongoing bibliographical work and encouraging new developments in the field. Its fifty volumes, essential reading when they were published, will continue to be essential reading-not only because they are central to the bibliographical history of the times but also because they contain an extraordinary number of fundamental articles of permanent interest. Information is arranged volume wise. Information can be browse by simple click. Fulltext is available in e-text format. Back of file is Vol. 1, 1948-49-v. 55, 2002. In 2003 the Council published that material as an ebook as well, making Studies the first scholarly journal to be available in that form.

Technological Librarianship: An Online Journal of the American Theological Library Association

Technological Librarianship: An Online Journal of the American Theological Library Association http://journal.atla. com/ojs/index.php/theolib/index is published by American Theological Library Association. It includes professional librarians in colleges, universities, and theological seminaries and others with an interest in theological librarianship in those settings, Professional development of theological librarians, and to contribute to and enrich the profession of theological librarianship. Back of file is Vol.1, 1-2, 2008-v.6, 1, 2013. Information is arranged by Arranged volume wise and Information for Author, Librarian and Readers has been given and can be found Simple click on Issue Title. Internal search engine has been given.

Technology Electronic Reviews (TER)

Technology Electronic Reviews (TER) http://www.ala.org/lita/publications/archive/ter (ISSN: 1533-9165) is a periodical copyright 1995-2007 by the American Library Association. Documents in these issues, subject to copyright by the American Library Association or by the authors of the documents, may be reproduced for noncommercial, educational, or scientific purposes granted by Sections 107 and 108 of the Copyright Revision Act of 1976, provided that the copyright statement and source for that material are clearly acknowledged and that the material is reproduced without alteration. None of these documents may be reproduced or adapted for commercial distribution without the prior written permission of the designated copyright holder for the specific documents. It provides reviews of and pointers to resources, both print and electronic. Resources include books, articles, serials, discussion lists, software, training materials, and bibliographies. Back of file:_Vol. 1, N. 1-3, 1994— Vol. 14, N.2, 2007. Issue indexing has done and Fulltext is available in e-text format.

Texas library journal

Texas library journal http://www.txla.org/TLJ is published by Texas Library Association. It focuses on Academic library, Leadership, Principles, Intellectual freedom, librarians etc. It publishes four Issues Spring, Summar, fall, winter. Back of file is Vol. 84, 1-4, 2008-v. 88, 1-4, 2012. Information is arranged volume wise with pdf format and can be found by click on Issue Title.

The Bone folder: An outgrowth of the Book Arts Web

The Bone folder: An outgrowth of the Book Arts Web http:/ /www.philobiblon.com/bonefolder/index.html is e-journals publisher and editor is The Book Arts Web - Peter D. Verheyen: Bookbinder & Conservator / Special Collections Preservation & Digital Access Librarian, Syracuse University Library, Syracuse, NY. Country: United States. The e-journals publisher and editor is The Book Arts Web - Peter D. Verheyen: Bookbinder & Conservator / Special Collections Preservation & Digital Access Librarian, Syracuse University Library, Syracuse, NY. Country: United States. The Bonefolder is a peer-reviewed "open-access" e-journal for bookbinding and the book arts bookbinding, decorative techniques, education, exhibition reviews, tips & tricks, or book reviews. The Bonefolder publishes significant articles by established and emerging authorities on a variety of book arts topics. These include hand bookbinding, teaching, business practice, the history of the book, the book as art, general tips & tricks, exhibitions, how-to technical articles, and reviews. The

Bonefolder is listed in the Directory of Open Access Journals (DOAJ) and is archived as part of the New York University Library's contribution to LOCKSS (Lots of Copies Keep Stuff Safe). Back of file is Vol. 1, 1, fall 2004-v. 8, 1, 2012 and Full text is available in pdf format.

Code4Lib Journal

Code4Lib Journal http://journal.code4lib.org/ is C4LJ is published by Code4Lib and its editor is Carol Bean, North County Regional Library, Palm Beach County Library System, and United States. C4LJ helps Libraries in computer technology, using computers and the Internet to offer unprecedented access to information and library resources. C4LJ aims to help engender collective understanding and the necessary support for improving library technology and digital services. Issue 1, 2007-Issue 19, 2013 and full text is available in E-text format. Information is Arranged Issue wise. Articles have given previous and current issue and internal search engine have given. Articles can gent by clicking on issue number and then title.

The Idaho Librarian: A Publication of the Idaho Library Association

The Idaho Librarian: A Publication of the Idaho Library Association http://www.idaholibraries.org/idlibrarian/ index.php/ idaho-librarian/index is published by Idaho Library Association. It publishes articles and information relevant to libraries and librarianship in Idaho, though topics need not be unique to the state. Idaho-related articles written by authors not located in Idaho and not members of the Idaho Library Association are within the scope of the journal. Information is given for author, Reader, Librarians and arranged Volume wise with Pdf and Html. Back of file is Vol. 59, 1-2, 2009-v.61, 1, 2011. It is Indexed and peer reviewed.

The International Journal of Database Management Systems

The International Journal of Database Management Systems http://airccse.org/journal/ijdms/ijdms.html is published by

Academy & Industry Research Collaboration Center. Topics of interest include, but are not limited to, the following Digital Libraries, Knowledge Acquisition, discovery & Management, Metadata Management, Knowledge Processing. Back of file is Vol.1, 1, 2009-v.5, 1, 2013. It is indexed in Open Jgate, EBSCO, Inspac, Google etc. Information is arranged Volume wise with pdf and can be found by simple click on Title and Issue. Internal search engine is given.

The International Journal of Managing Information Technology

The International Journal of Managing Information Technology http://airccse.org/journal/ijmit/ijmit.html is published by Academy & Industry Research Collaboration Center. It focuses on innovative ideas and best practices in using IT to advance organizations for-profit, non-profit. It is indexed in Google, EBSCO, Pub Zone, PKP, Scirus etc. Back of file is Vol. 1, 2009- v.5, 1, 2013. Information is arranged Volume wise with pdf format and can be found simple click on Issue Title. Internal search engine is given.

The journal of the Rutgers University Library

The journal of the Rutgers University Library http://jrul.libraries.rutgers.edu/index.php/jrul/index is published Published by Rutgers University, United States. Articles based on the holdings of the Rutgers University Libraries, and in the areas of New Jersey history, Rutgersensia, bibliography, and the history of libraries, books and printing. Issue, Author and title indexing has been given. Back of file is Vol. 1, No. 1, 1937-v. 65, 2012. Articles are arranged Volume wise. Current and archives option has been given. Information is given for author, Reader, Librarians. Articles can be browse by Author, Title and Issue. Internal search engine with search tips Search categories have been given for searching.

The Public Access Computer Systems Review

The Public Access Computer Systems Review http://epress.lib.uh.edu/pr/pacsrev.html is It was established in 1989 by Charles W. Bailey, Jr., who served as Editor-in-Chief for volumes one (1990) to seven (1996). It was published by the University of

Houston Libraries. PACS Review) was an electronic journal about end-user computer systems in libraries. Initially, the journal published scholarly papers (Communications section), columns, and reviews Includes author/ subject index and submission guidelines. Back of file is Vol. 1, N.1-3, 1990-Vol. 9, N.1, 1998 and Full text is available in ASCII text format. Articles are arranged Volume wise. Articles can be browse by simple click. Internal search has been given for searching.

Urban Library Journal

Urban Library Journal http://lacuny.cuny.edu/ulj/ is published by City University of New York Country: United States. Urban Library Journal, formerly known as Urban Academic Librarian is an open access, refereed Journal of research and discussion dealing with all aspects of urban libraries and librarianship, welcomes articles dealing with academic, research, public, school, and special libraries in an urban setting, public higher education, urban studies, multiculturalism, library and educational services to immigrants, preservation of public higher education, and universal access to World Wide Web resources. Back of file is Vol. 9, 2, summer 1995-v.18, 1 spring 2012 and Abstract is available and fulltext is available in HTML and pdf format. Articles are arranged Volume wise. Articles can be browse by simple click.

Virginia Libraries

Virginia Libraries http://scholar.lib.vt.edu/ejournals/ VALib/ is published by Virginia Library Association, United States. This quarterly journal purpose is to promote, and improve library and information services and the profession of librarianship. It is used as a vehicle for members to exchange information, ideas, and solutions to mutual problems in professional articles on current topics in the library and information field in order to advance literacy and learning and to ensure access to information in the Commonwealth of Virginia. Lamp-Post Publicity in Meherrin, Virginia designs the print version of Virginia Libraries. Virginia Tech's

Scholarly Communications Project creates the electronic version. http://scholar.lib.vt.edu/ejournals/VALib. Back of file is Vol. 42, 1, 1996- v. 58, 4, 2012 and fulltext is available in HTML and pdf format.

Webology

Webology http://www.webology.ir/ is published by University of Tehran, Iran. It is an international peer-reviewed journal devoted to the field of the World Wide Web Periodicals, Web science Periodicals, Information science Periodicals, Library science Periodicals. The World Wide Web: Web: information retrieval; Web crawling and indexing; Web cataloging; Web searching; Search engines and directories; Search behavior; Metadata etc. Library and Information Science: Information retrieval systems; Indexing; Abstracting; Information and communication technology; Information Evaluation. It is indexed by LISA, Scopus. The Informed Librarian Online, the Index of Information Systems Journals, DOAJ, EBSCO, Ulrich, Web Citation Index, World Cat etc. Back of file is Vol. 1, 1-2, 2004-v.9, 1-2, 2012 and Full text is available in e-text format. Articles are arranged Volume wise. Information is divided in two parts the World Wide Web and Library and information science. Articles can be browse by simple click.

World Libraries

World Libraries http://www.worlib.org/ is formerly known as Third World Libraries. It is published twice a year by Dominican University Graduate School of Library and Information Science. World Libraries is a unique, free, peer–reviewed library and information science journal focusing on libraries and socio economic development. It is dedicated to librarians and libraries in regions without associations or agencies to encourage scholarly communication and professional development. World Libraries is simply dedicated to the international nature of librarianship, promoting communication and relationships both professionally and personally. Back of file is Vol. 1, 1, 1990-v.20, 1, 2012 and Articles are arranged Volume wise. Articles can be browse by simple click.

5.2. DESCRIPTION OF E-MAGAZINES

AALL Spectrum

AALL Spectrum http://www.aallnet.org/main-menu/ Publications/spectrum/ is published by American Association of Law Libraries. It is an award winning monthly magazine distributed free of charge to members of the American Association of Law Libraries. AALL Spectrum publishes substantive, well-written articles on topics of real interest to law librarians, as well as news about the American Association of Law Libraries - Chapters, Committees, Special Interest Sections, etc. It is now published and distributed nine times a year, monthly with the exception of January and August and with a combined September/October issue.Back of file is Vol.1,9-10, 1997-v.17, July, 2013. Fulltext is available in pdf format. Information is arranged by volume and Issue. Information can be browse by simple click.

Access

Access http://www.aardvarknet.info/access/number46/ index.cfm is published by iGroup. It covers almost all the aspects of Library and Information science. Information can be browse by simple click. Back of file is No-36, March 2001- No-79, Dec 2011. Information is arranged by No. Fulltext is available in pdf format.

American Libraries

American Libraries http://www.ala.org/ala/alonline/ index.cfm is published by the American Library Association. It covers general library science issues. It is open to any individual or organization interested in library service and library and information science. American Libraries is published 10 times a year. A full-text searchable database of issues from 2003 to the present is available online free through Ebrary Back of file is Jan/ Feb 2008- March/April 2013 and Full text is available in e-text format. Articles are arranged Volume wise and can be browse by simple click.

Ariadne

Ariadne http://www.ariadne.ac.uk/ This Web magazine is

published by UKOLN (UK Office for Library Networking), which is funded by MLA, the Museums, Libraries and Archives Council. It covers current digital library initiatives, technological, information service developments and information networking issues, Information Management. Ariadne magazine is targeted principally at information science professionals in academia, and also to interested lay people both in and beyond the Higher Education community. It concentrated originally on reporting in depth to the information community at large on progress and developments within the UK Electronic Libraries Programme (eLib). Issues' indexing with year of publication has been done. All the indexes are offered in the form of text links. Users Can take a hard copy of it. Ariadne is published in January, April, July and October. Back of file is Issue 1, Jan 1996- Issue 70, Nov 2012 and Ariadne presents Information in E-Text format. Users can get text links to all the back issues as well as current issue. The option Full Issue Contents provides Articles of current Issue. Articles of each issue have been divided in to three parts Main article, at the Event, News and Reviews. Current and Back Issues can be browse by simple click on the wanted title. Ariadne has internal search engine to search. It can now be searched using Swish-e. It supports 'AND', 'OR' 'Phrase' and 'Truncation'. "The Ariadne newsletter is aimed initially at subject librarians and other working librarians in academic libraries, though many people in the UK Higher Education and LIS communities will find items of interest within it. The newsletter has two main aims: It describes and evaluates sources and services available on the Internet, and of potential use, to librarians and information professionals. It reports to the library community at large on progress and developments within the Electronic Libraries Programme, and of JISC-funded and other information services, keeping the busy practitioner abreast of current relevant developments."

Book business

Book business http://www.bookbusinessmag.com/ is published by North American Publishing Company. Information is arranged by Year. Information is arranged in five parts Cover Story, Features, Edotor's Note, Coloumns and departments. Back of file is June 2006-Nov 2012. Number of titles published, Digital rights management, everything regarding books. Fulltext is available in html format. Articles can be browse by simple click.

Book Links

Book Links http://www.ala.org/ala/aboutala/hqops/publishing/booklinks/index.cfm is published by American Library Association. Book Links: Connecting Books, Libraries, and Classrooms is a magazine designed for teachers, librarians, library media specialists, booksellers, parents, and other adults interested in connecting children with books. It response to the use of children's trade books in the classroom, the curriculum role of the school library media center, the increased programming in public libraries, and the heavy reliance of child-care centers on children's literature, Book Links publishes bibliographies, essays linking books on a similar theme, retrospective reviews, and other features targeted at those educating young people. The magazine that has been helping librarians, teachers, and parents connect children with high-quality books for more than15 years. Vol. 8, July 1999-Vol. 18, N.1-2, Nov 2008. Nov 2007 sample issue has been given and Full text is available in Html and PDF format. Articles are arranged Volume and year wise and can be browse by simple click. Internal search has been given for searching.

CHOICE

CHOICE http://www.ala.org/ala/mgrps/divs/acrl/publications/choice/previousissues/previousissues.cfm is published by Association of College & Research Libraries. Choice reaches almost every undergraduate college and university library in the United States. Information can be browse by simple click. Fulltext is available in HTM Format. More than 35,000 academic librarians, faculty, and key decision makers rely on the reviews in Choice magazine and Choice Reviews Online for collection development and scholarly research. Information is arranged by

Year, Volume and then Number. Back of file is Vol. 47, 5 Jan 2009-v. 50, 7, March 2013.

Computer in Libraries

Computer in Libraries http://www.infotoday.com/ cilmag/ default.shtml is published by Information Today Inc. Country: USA. Computer in Libraries is a monthly magazine that provides complete coverage of the news and issues in the rapidly evolving field of library information technology. It Focus on the practical application of technology in community, school, academic, and special libraries. CIL include discussions of the impact of emerging computer technologies on library systems and services, and on the library community itself. Back of file is Vol. 20, N. 1-10, 2000-Vol. 24, N.1-10, 2004. VOL. 25, N.1-10, 2005- Vol. 28, N.1- 10, 2008 is not open access. Full text is available in PDF format. Articles are arranged Volume wise and can be browse by simple click.

Cultivate Interactive

Cultivate Interactive http://www.cultivate-int.org/index-2.html is Published by UKLON. It disseminates information on digital cultural heritage. Cultivate Interactive is a Web magazine including articles on the ARCHEOGUIDE, the CIDOC Conceptual Reference Model, LIBECON, MESMUSES, Open Heritage. It is funded under the European Commission's Digital heritage and Cultural Content (DIGICULT) programme. Issue1, July 2000-Issue9, Feb 2003. Full text is available in e-text format. Articles are arranged Issue wise and can be browse by simple click.

D-Lib Magazine

D-Lib Magazine http://www.dlib.org/dlib/september08/ 09contents.html is published by Corporation for National Research Initiatives (CNRI) produces d-Lib Magazine. The magazine is currently supported by the D-Lib Alliance and Its editor is Bonita Wilson. D-Lib Magazine is a solely electronic publication with a primary focus on digital library research and development, including but not limited to new technologies, applications, and contextual social and economic issues. The primary goal of the magazine is timely and efficient information exchange for the digital library community. To meet this goal, both the articles and the shorter pieces are solicited or selected from among unsolicited submissions. The magazine is currently published six times a year. The full contents of the magazine, including all back issues, are available free of charge at the D-Lib web site as well as multiple mirror sites around the world. Author and title index has been done. The Defense Advanced Research Project Agency (DARPA) on behalf of the Digital Libraries and the National Science Foundation (NSF) sponsors it. Back of file is Vol.1, Issue1, 1995-v. 19, Number 1/2, Jan/Feb 2013 and Full text is available in e-text format. The magazine is currently published six times a year. The full contents of the magazine, including all back issues, are available free of charge at the D-Lib web site as well as multiple mirror sites around the world. Author and title index has been done. It has its own search engine ht: // Dig for searching. Quick search tips are also available. Articles can be finding by simple click.

E-Content

E-Content http://www.ecmag.net/ is published by Online, A division of Information Today, Inc. The magazine has a mission to clearly identify and explain emerging digital content trends, strategies, and resources that will help readers navigate the content maze and find a clear path to profits and improved business processes. It delivers essential research, reporting, news, and analysis of content related issues. It is essential reading for executives and professionals involved in content creation, management, acquisition, organization, and distribution in both commercial and enterprise environments. It publishes ten issues in a year. Back of file is May 2002-Jan/Feb 2013 and Full text is available in e-text format. Articles are arranged Year wise and can be browse by simple click.

EDUCAUSE Review

EDUCAUSE Review ttp://www.educause.edu/is the association's award-winning magazine for the higher education IT community. It is published by Universitat Pompeu Fabra bimonthly in print (22,000 distributed copies) and online (over 50,000 visits per month, with 250,000+ monthly page views), the magazine takes a broad look at current developments and trends in information technology, how they may affect the college/university as an institution, and what these mean for higher education and society. In addition to EDUCAUSE members, the magazine's audience consists of presidents/chancellors, senior academic and administrative leaders, non-IT staff, faculty in all disciplines, librarians, and corporate staff/leaders. The magazine has won numerous editorial and design awards including APEX Awards for Publication Excellence, Magnum Opus Awards for Outstanding Achievement in Custom Publishing, Ozzie Awards for Excellence in Magazine Design, and Tabbies Awards, as well as being named Publication of the Year by the Colorado Society of Association Executives. fulltext is available in e-text format and back of File : Vol. 35, 1-6, 2000-v. 48, 1, Jan/Feb 2013.

Ex Libris

Ex Libris http://marylaine.com/exlibris/ is published by Marylaine Block.It is A Weekly e-zine for librarians and information junkies. Ex Libris focus on Computers, Information, It is a free promotional part of business, workshops for librarians and made presentations at several conferences. Past issue indexing has been done. Back of file is March 2002- April 2008 and Full text is available in e-text format. Articles are arranged Issue wise and can be browse by simple click.

Exploit Interactive

Exploit Interactive http://www.exploit-lib.org/ is published by UKOLN with the support of the DBI and the British. Exploit was an accompanying measure designed to promote the results of EU library projects (both FP3 and FP4) and to facilitate their take-up by the market of library and information systems. Exploit Interactive was the Exploit project's Pan-European Web magazine, designed to promote awareness, disseminate and exploit reusable project applications and results. The magazine ran for seven issues and has now finished. The magazine ran for seven issues and has now finished; though the site will remain available for reference from this server for at least another two years. Back of file is Issue1, May 1999-Issue7, oct 2000. Information is arranged by issue and Year. Articles can be browse by simple click. Fulltext is available in html format.

inCite

inCite http://alia.org.au/publishing/incite/archive.html is pub lished by Australian Library and Information Association. Information can be browse by simple click. Fulltext is available in HTML Format. It focus on Research and Education, Special Libraries, IFLA/Engagement etc. Information is arranged by Year, Volume and then Month. Back of file is Vol.17, Jan-Dec.1996-v. 32, Jan-Dec 2011.

Information Today

Information Today http://www.infotoday.com/IT/ nov08/ index.shtml is published by Published by Information Today Inc., USA. The most widely read publication in the information industry, this is the only newspaper designed to meet the needs of the information professional. Information Today delivers total coverage of late-breaking news and long-term trends in the information industry. Accurate, timely news articles inform the reader of the people, products, services, and events that impact the industry, while hard-hitting, topical articles explain significant developments in the field. Back of file is Vol. 17, 1-10, 2000-V. 21, No.1/11, 2004 and V. 22-28, 2005- 2013 is not open access. Issue indexing has been done. Articles are arranged Volume and then Number wise. Full text is available in pdf and HTML format. Articles can be browse by simple click.

Knowledge Management World

Knowledge Management World http://www.kmworld.com/index.cfm is published by Information Today, Inc. Km world provides actionable Information through real world case studies, advice from key practitioners and best practice advice from market leaders. Issue indexing has been done. Back of file is Vol.7 Issue 1-

13, 1998-v. 22 Issue 3 and Full text is available in e-text format. Articles are arranged issue and Volume wise and can be browse by simple click.

Library Juice

Library Juice http://libr.org/juice/ is edited and published by Rory Litwin. It is an irregular, weekly, and then biweekly, then, for a moment, monthly electronic zine for librarians, library and information science students, and other interested people. It included discussions, commentary, announcements, humor, web links and news affecting the library world. Much of the material was about librarianship as the servant and protector of the public sphere - intellectual freedom and social responsibility as central to the profession. The original Library Juice has ceased publication as an electronic zine, and is now a blog and a book. Back of file is March 2006-December 2008. Articles are arranged Issue wise and can be browse by simple click.

Link-Up

Link-Up http://www.infotoday.com/lu/lunew.htm was incorporated into ITI's flagship publication, Information Today. Link-Up Digital is a new, biweekly updated, Available in free Preview/ Abstract format, as well as pay-per-view Full Text, Text+Graphics, or Page Image PDF versions, courtesy of ITI's InfoCentral. Articles can be browse by simple click. Articles are arranged by date. Back of file is 10/1/2002-3/15/2013 and Link-Up: At Home, a new special section of IT packed with news you can use both at home and in your downtime. Link up with Link-Up: At Home and Link-Up Digital. Note: - All articles are not freely available.

Online

Online http://www.infotoday.com/online/default.shtml is published by Information Today Inc, USA. Online is a monthly journal providing articles, product reviews, case studies, and evaluations about selecting, using, and managing electronic resources? ONLINE is written for information professionals and provides articles, product reviews, case studies, evaluation, and informed opinion about selecting, using, and managing electronic information products, plus industry and professional information about online database systems, CD-ROM, and the Internet. This newsletter published six times in a year. Volume 29 to 32 is not open access. Back of file is Vol. 24, 1 Jan- 6 Dec, 2000-V. 28, No. 1-5, 2004 and Volume 29- 36, 2005-2012 is not open access. Articles are arranged Volume wise. Articles can be browse by simple click.

Provenance

Provenance http://www.provenance.ca/about-provenance/index.html the title "Provenance" (first - the electronic magazine, later - the web magazine) came from our managing editor, Guy Robertson. Travel articles in Provenance came around the time of the International Conference of the Special Libraries Association of America, meeting in Seattle, Washington. Literature covering the implementation of Western designed information systems in developing countries. Provenance is maintained and promoted by www.netpac.com developers of "findable" search engine friendly web sites ©2002, 2003, 2004, 2005, 2006 2007 Vancouver-Victoria, BC Canada. Back of file is May-June 2004- Dec/Jan 2013 and Full text is available in e-text format. Article indexing has been given. Articles are arranged by year and can be browse by simple click. Internal search engine has been given.

Research Information

Research Information http://www.researchinformation.info/ is published by Europa Science Ltd. Focus on E-books, Digital, Lis Management etc. Focus on E-books, Digital, Lis Management etc. Back of file is May-June 2004- Dec/Jan 2013. Information is arranged by Volume, Author, and Subject. Fulltext is available in e-text format. Articles can be browse by simple click.

Searcher: The Magazine for Database Professionals

Searcher: The Magazine for Database Professionals http://www.infotoday.com/searcher/default.asp is Published by Information Today Inc. Country: USA. The magazine is targeted to experienced, knowledgeable searchers and combines evaluations of data content with discussions of delivery media. **Searcher** includes evaluated online news, searching tips and techniques; reviews of search aid software and database documentation, revealing interviews with leaders and entrepreneurs of the industry, and trenchant editorials. Issues 2000-Issues 2004. Current Issue Vol. 20 Dec (11) 2012 and 2005- 2012 issues are not open access. Full text is available in e-text format. Articles are arranged Volume wise and can be browse by simple click.

The Bulletin of the American Society for Information Science and Technology

The Bulletin of the American Society for Information Science and Technology http://www.asis.org/bulletin.html is published by the American Society for Information Science and Technology (ASIS&T) and its editor is Irene Travis, Country: United States. It is a bi-monthly news magazine packed with developments and issues affecting the field, pragmatic management reports, opinion, and news of people and events in the info. science community. It is ASIS&T's primary means of maintaining regular contact with its membership regarding ASIS&T activities. This e-magazine is also a vehicle for sharing news and information regarding developments in the field of information science and technology, including political developments. Back of file is Vol. 21, 2-6, 1995-v. 39, 3, Feb/March 2013 and the fulltext is available in HTML and PDF format. Past issues have dealt with such areas as information architecture, technology developments in libraries, , indexing languages, information seeking behavior. Searching is very easy. Information divided in to three parts i.e. special section, feature and other. Articles can be searched by simple click.

The Marginal http://www.gslis.mcgill.ca/marginal/

The Marginal http://www.gslis.mcgill.ca/marginal/ is published by The McGill Library and Information Studies Student Association, known around the school as MLISSA, publish this e-zine. Ezine features articles and opinions from the McGill Library and Information Studies Student Association. Includes links to past issues. The aim of the Marginal is to be a place to publish experiences; not only do we publish articles related to the LIS field, but also those related to other aspects of the lives of library, archives and knowledge management students. Back of file is Volume 4, 3-4, 1997-v. 16, 2, winter 2009 and Full text is available in e-text format. Issue Indexing has been done. Articles are arranged Number wise and can be browse by simple click.

Virginia Tech Magazine

Virginia Tech Magazine http://www.vtmagazine.vt.edu/ is published by Virginia Polytechnic Institute and State University, Blacksburg, Virginia. It does not discriminate against employees, students, or applicants for admission or employment on the basis of race, color, sex, sexual orientation, disability, age, veteran status, national origin, religion, or political affiliation. ISSN 0274-9904) is published quarterly (fall, winter, spring, and summer). Back of file is V.13, N.1, fall, 1990- winter summer, spring, 2009. Fulltext is available in html Format; Articles can be browse by simple click.

5.3. DESCRIPTION OF E- NEWS LETTERS AND OTHER E-RESOURCES

ABAA Newsletter

ABAA Newsletter http://hq.abaa.org/books/antiquarian/abaapages/newsletter is a Publications Committee of The Antiquarian Booksellers. It covers Association of America for members of the organization, libraries and institutions, the antiquarian book community at large and the general public. The ABAA Newsletter (ISSN 1070-7000X) is published quarterly. Back of file is 2005-2008 (winter, Spring, Smmar, Fall). Fulltext is available in pdf format. Information can be browse by simple click. Information is arranged by Issue.

Abbey Newsletter

Abbey Newsletter http://cool.conservation-us.org/byorg/abbey/an/ is published by Abbey Publications, Inc Country: New York. Abbey Newsletter focuses on all the aspects of Library and Information Science including digital library and computers in libraries etc. Author and Title Indexing have been done. Back of file is Vol. 1, N. 1-4, 7, 15, 1978-Vol. 26, N. 1-6, 2002 and Full text is available in e-text format. Articles are arranged Volume wise. Articles can be browse by simple click. Internal search has been given for searching.

Against the grain

Against the grain (News Channel) http://www.against-the-grain.com/d/fulltextarticles (ISSN: 1043-2094) is your key to the latest news about libraries, publishers, book jobbers, and subscription agents. It is a unique collection of reports on the issues, literature, and people that impact the world of books and journals. ATG is published on paper six times a year, in February, April, June, September, and November and December/January. Against the Grain News Channel is primarily intended to be a collaborative resource for subscribers to the journal or attendees to the **Charleston Conference**. In reality, just any book aficionado is welcome to join this community. It is is pleased to offer readers the ability to comment on articles, columns, rumors, etc. However, we expect our readers to engage in lively, yet civil discourse. Full text is available in pdf format and Back of File:_Vol. 1, 1, March 1989 and v. 12, 1-6, 2000-v.21, 1-2, 2009. Its complete volumes are not open access; only some issues are open access.

ALAWON: The ALA Washington Office Electronic Newsline

ALAWON: The ALA Washington Office Electronic Newsline http://www.ala.org/ala/aboutala/offices/wo/washnews/archivea/archive.cfm is ALA. It covers keeping library advocates up to date on major legislative issues in the Nation's Capital. ALAWON stands for ALA Washington Office Newsline. It's a free, irregular e-mail publication of the ALA Washington Office.Back of file is V.1, 1992- V.15, 2006. Information can be browse by simple click. Information is arranged by Volume and Number. Fulltext is available in pdf format.

ALCTS Network News

ALCTS Network News http://bubl.ac.uk/archive/journals/

alctsnn/ is published by Association for Library Collections and Technical Services. It is an electronic publication of the Association for Library Collections and Technical Services. It Carries diversity in libraries to another level and also includes the involvement the members of the community being served. Focus on re-tooling Technical Services staff for the future; changing old habits and concepts. Full text is available in e-text format and Back of File: From Vol. 6, N.20, 1994-v. 19, N. 1-6, 2000. Its Volume 15 Number 14 1998 Not Published. It is an electronic publication of the Association for Library Collections and Technical Services.

ARL: A Bimonthly News Letters for Library Issues and Action

ARL: A Bimonthly News Letters for Library Issues and Action http://www.arl.org/resources/pubs/br/index.shtml is published by ARL, which is a nonprofit organization. ARL is a Bimonthly Report on current issues of interest to academic and research library administrators, staff, library education. ARL is a working tool prepared to assist member leaders to understand, discuss, and engage how the Association deploys its resources. ARL provides some links to Membership Meetings, E-News for ARL Directors. This also can't be loaded locally for home use. Issues archived from Issues 178-183 1995- Issues 256-261, 2008. Fulltext is available in Digital edition, html and pdf format each issue explores a broad range of edition topics of particular importance to research institutes and academic librarians. No search engine/s is available for user to search. Simple crawling procedure has been following for browsing the resources. Users can get text links to all the issues with recent issue

Biblia's Warrior Librarian Weekly

Biblia's Warrior Librarian Weekly http://warriorlibrarian.com/ IS Created and maintained by A B Credaro. It includes Pokes fun at the people who use libraries and the funnier ones who work in them. Library humor index has been done. Back of file is Issue 95, Sep 2001-Issue 261, Dec. 2008. Full text is available in e-text format. Articles are arranged Volume wise and can be browse by simple click.

Biblio-Tech Review

Biblio-Tech Review http://www.ringgold.com/biblio-tech/si_pd.cfm?pid=2 aims to inform and educate all those who wish to keep abreast of the developments within the global library automation industry. Vital to the function of the Review will be the product reviews, comparisons and stories - designed to help the librarian and information worker keep aware of the key issues when automating their libraries. It provides latest news updates from the library automation industry. The Biblio Tech Review is published by Biblio Tech Limited in the UK. The publisher/editor is Peter Evans - an industry consultant involved with library automation for the past 25 years. BTR is currently provided at no cost to the industry as an information resource. Back of file is Jan-Dec 1999-Jan-Dec 2000 and brief articles are available till 2013. Full text is available in e-text format. Articles can be browse by simple click. Internal search has been given for searching.

Business and Finance Division Bulletin

Business & Finance Bulletin http://bf.sla.org/resources/ the-bulletin/ has been an important communication tool and source for the members of the Business & Finance Division of SLA for five decades. It is published by Special Libraries Association (SLA) and full text articles are available in PDF format. The Bulletin conveys information about Division and member activities. It also has developed a reputation for publishing informative and practical articles on the many topics that are of interest to an especially skilled and influential, worldwide readership that currently stands at approximately 2,000 information professionals. The Bulletin is indexed in Library and Information Science Abstracts (LISA), Library Literature, and Information Science Abstracts. The Bulletin offers a peer-review option to article authors while also providing publishing opportunities to those who do not choose this option. The peer-review process is double-blind and draws upon a pool of reviewers offering a broad range of expertise. The peer-review option is available for articles on all relevant topics, including those to appear in the Bulletin's regularly featured columns. Article size can vary as appropriate for topics, and authors should refer to recent issues of the Bulletin for general guidance on style. These many options offer a high degree of freedom and opportunity to authors. Back of file No. 120, spring 2002 -No 149, fall 2012.

Cataloging and Classification Quarterly

Cataloging and Classification Quarterly http://bubl.ac.uk/archive/journals/cacq/ is Held by BUBL Information Service, Andersonian Library, Strathclyde University. Its Topics include her research interests in subject and descriptive cataloging, development of information science and its relationship to librarianship. Articles are arranged Volume wise and can be browse by simple click. Issue indexing has been done. And Full text is available in htm format. Back of file: Vol. 18 N. 1-2, 1993-Vol. 29, N. 1-4, 2000.

CIT Infobits and now TL Infobits

CITInfobits http://its.unc.edu/TeachingAndLearning/Publications/TLInfobits/TL_INFOBITS_2009. In 2006, the title was changed to TL Infobits to reflect its sponsorship by the UNC-Chapel Hill ITS Teaching and Learning division. TL Infobits is an electronic service of the University of North Carolina at Chapel Hill ITS Teaching and Learning division. Each month the ITS-TL's Academic Outreach Consultant monitors and selects from a number of information and instructional technology sources that come to her attention and provides brief notes for electronic dissemination to educators. It began in 1993 by the UNC-Chapel Hill Institute for Academic Technology, titled IAT Infobits. From July 1998 changed to CIT Infobits. Full text is available in e-text format. Articles are arranged by year. Back of file is 1993- 2009 and Articles can be browse by simple click.

Conserline

Conserline http://www.loc.gov/acq/conser/consrlin.htmlPublished by the Library of Congress. CONSERline is a cooperative effort with contributions from program members consisting of news of the CONSER Program and information of interest to the serials cataloging community. CONSERline, the program newsletter, includes news and recent events about the program. Issues for 1994 and 1995 are in ASCII format only; starting in 1996 issues are in HTML format only. Issues for 1994 and 1995 are in ASCII format only; starting in 1996 issues are in HTML format only. Articles can be browse by simple click. N. 1-3, 1994-No 29 Fall 2007.

Free Pint

Free Pint http://www.freepint.com/ is published by Free Pint limited. FreePint is a global network of people who find, use, manage and share work-related information. FreePint publishes a family of resources to help information workers be more effective, raise the value of information in their organizations and contribute to success. Back of file is Issue 1-4, 1997- March, Issue 371, 2013. FreePint publishes newsletters, websites, magazines and resources for the information industry. Full text is available in HTML and Plain Text format. Articles can be browse by simple click. Articles are arranged by year.

Information Today and Tomorrow (ITT)

Information Today and Tomorrow (ITT) http://itt.nissat.tripod.com/ is published by NISSAT.Its Contents include information on new tools and techniques, events concluded and announcements, interesting Internet sites, new database products and services. The format has undergone several revisions in keeping with the changing information scenario. V. 14, 1995-V. 21, 2002. Full text is available in HTML format. It is a quarterly newsletter since the beginning of the programme. With a change in the title, Information Today & Tomorrow, the quarterly periodical is distributed free to 5000 individuals and institutions. Articles are arranged by year. Articles are arranged by year. Articles can be browse by simple click.

Internet on a Disk

Internet on a Disk http://www.samizdat.com/ioad.html is published by Richard Seltzer. Internet-on-a-Disk is free blog-like newsletter to share Richard Seltzer insights and opinions free with all. Internet-on-a-Disk is the newsletter of electronic texts and Internet trends. Back of file is #1 Feb 1994— # 69 April 2009. The full text of all issues is available here for free, with hypertext links to the sites referenced Articles are arranged by date. Full text is available in e-text format and Articles can be browse by simple click.

Internet Resources Newsletter

Internet Resources Newsletter http://www.hw.ac.uk/libwww/irn/irn.html is edited and published by Heriot-Watt University Library staff. The newsletter aims to raise awareness of new sources of information on the Internet, particularly those which are relevant to research interests at Heriot-Watt University, including engineering, science, and Social science. It has sorts of interesting Internet-related Material, new and notable sites, lots of interesting blogs and RSS Elated sites and much more even some Websites. The newsletter is available in the Internet as a free email newsletter to subscribers. An RSS feed is also available. Most of the sources cited in the newsletter were checked at the time of publication; however it is possible that some of the resources are no longer available. Back of file: 1. October 1994 to February 2007. Internet Resources Newsletter is the free, monthly newsletter for academics, students, engineers, scientists and social scientists.

LC Cataloging Newsline

LC Cataloging Newsline http://www.loc.gov/catdir/lccn/ is published by Library of Congress. It is Online Newsletter of the Cataloging Directorate. Information can be browse by simple click. The text issues are in Adobe Acrobat PDF format. The LC Cataloging Newsline is an online newsletter of the Bibliographic Access Directorate of the Library of Congress. Information is arranged by volume and then Number. Back of file is Vol.8, No. 1-12, 2000-Vol. 14, No. 1-5, 2006.

MLS: Marketing Library Services

MLS: Marketing Library Services http://www.infotoday.

com/MLS/default.shtml is published by Information Today Inc, USA. MLS will provide information professionals in all types of libraries with specific ideas for marketing their services. You'll find numerous suggestions for planning programs, making money, increasing business, and proving your value to your administrator. This newsletter published six times in a year. Back of file is Jan-Dec 1998-Jan/Feb 2013. Articles are arranged Volume wise and can be browse by simple click.

NLM Technical Bulletin

NLM Technical Bulletin http://www.nlm.nih.gov/pubs/techbull/current_issue.html is published by U.S. National Library of Medicine. It is created by MEDLARS Management Section, NLM. It covers General Surgery, Primary Health Care, Pulmonary Medicine, Statistics as Topic, Technology, Disaster Medicine, Nanotechnology and Broad Medical Subject Headings are covered. Back of file is Issue 1, 1969-March/April 2013. Article indexing has been given. Articles are arranged by year and can be browse by simple click.

RLG DigiNews

RLG DigiNews http://www.oclc.org/programs/ publications/newsletters/diginews.htm was produced by staff in the Department of Research, Cornell University Library, in consultation with RLG and later, the RLG Programs unit of OCLC Programs & Research. RLG DigiNews focuses on digitization and digital preservation. This bimonthly Web newsletter provided indispensable reports on evolving practices and technology for digitizing materials and digital preservation of research collections, as well as in-depth coverage of notable projects in the field. Author, Issue, Title index has been given. For digitizing research collection this newsletter is indispensable for its articles on evolving practices and technology, events, new projects and publications. Back of file is Vol. 1, N.1, April 15, 1997-Vol.11, N.1, April 15, 2007 Articles are arranged Current Issue and Back Issue wise in one page. Articles can be browse by Issue, Title and Author. Internal search engine has been given for searching.

Serials E-News

Serials E-News http://www.ringgold.com/UKSG/si_pd.cfm is published by UK Serials Group. It is a topical newsletter, Serials-eNews. Serials-eNews is a member benefit of the UK Serials Group. The newsletter and its associated web service provide up-to-the-minute news of current issues and developments within the global serials industry. The current issue is only available via the email alert - this is the demo issue. The full text Information is available from No.33, March 2003-No.291, 8 March 2013. UKSG's electronic newsletter (ISSN 1476-0576) is published every two weeks exclusively for UKSG members and subscribers. Fulltext is available in e-text format. Information can be browse by simple click.

SPARC Open Access Newsletter or Free Online Scholarship Newsletter

Free Online Scholarship Newsletter http://www.earlham.edu/~peters/fos/index.htm is written by Peter Suber. It covers Research topics especially taxpayer-funded research. Open-access (OA) literature is digital, online, and free of charge, Monthly and free of most copyright and licensing restrictions. Back of file is 28 March 2001-2 Issue 167, March, 2013. Full text is available in HTML format. Articles are arranged by Issue. Articles can be browse by simple click.

Sprouts: Working Papers on Information Systems

Sprouts: Working Papers on Information Systems http://sprouts.aisnet.org/home.html is an Open Access publication that provides a fast-turnaround outlet for authentic and original research and work-in-progress carried out by scholars of the information systems field and members of AIS, the Association for Information Systems. Sprouts, is devoted to research about the ways in which information is generated and used in the prevailing complex socio-technical landscape. Sprouts is devoted to publishing research about the ways in which information is generated and used as well as the way related systems are designed, managed and implemented in a complex socio-technical landscapes. Sprouts emphasizes fast-turnaround and quick dissemination of ideas, thereby filling the gap between loose working papers and traditional journals,that are notorious for a long review process at the expense of speed to market. Sprouts is envisioned as a worldwide community-based outlet that can replace or supplement the fractured working papers series of the various IS departments and research groups under one roof, with one access point and a standardized interface. Sprouts is an open access publication that makes all contents available online for instant and free access by academics and scholarly practitioners who are interested in research on information, technology, systems and organizations. Sprouts is managed and published by an alliance of academic institutions that are dedicated to promote the generation and dissemination of information-related scholarly ideas. The Sprouts Alliance is open to any institution that is interested in advancing the mission of Sprouts according to this Charter. Sprouts is geared for any interesting theory driven or theory building work in the context of information environments, systems and organizations, with no limitation of size, genre, or method. It welcomes a broad, theoretically based view of information and systems that encompasses human, social and technical aspects. Innovative and challenging work and research genres are especially encouraged. Back of file: 16, 2001-31, 2008.

The Wired Librarian's Newsletter

The Wired Librarian's Newsletter is published by Micro Libraries. It gives Advice on the implementation of microcomputers in libraries. The Wired Librarians Newsletter has been the unbiased source for news and ideas regarding the implementation of microcomputers in libraries. Back of file is 1983-1985 and Articles are arranged Year wise and can be browse by simple click.

Bibliography

Academic Conferences International Limited. "Electronic Journal of Knowledge Management" EJKM. http://www.ejkm.com/ (accessed September 30, 2009).

Academics Journal. "International Journal of Library and Information Science". Academics Journal http://www.academicjournals.org/ijlis/About.htm (accessed Feb 28, 2011).

Academy & Industry Research Collaboration Center. "International Journal of Computer Science & Information Technology". AIRCC. http://airccse.org/journal/ijcsit.html(accessed May 1, 2011).

Academy & Industry Research Collaboration Center. "International Journal of Managing Public Sector Information and Communication Technologies". International Journal of Managing Public Sector Information and Communication Technologies. http://airccse.org/journal/mpict/ijmpict.html (accessed May 1, 2011).

Academy & Industry Research Collaboration Center. "The International Journal of Managing Information Technology". AIRCC. http://airccse.org/journal/ijmit/ijmit.html (accessed May 1, 2011).

Academy & Industry Research Collaboration Center. "The International Journal of Database Management Systems".

http://airccse.org/journal/ijdms/ijdms.html (accessed May 1, 2011).

Academy & Industry Research Collaboration Center. "International Journal of Multimedia and Its Applications." International Journal of Multimedia and Its Applications . http://airccse.org/journal/ijma_index.html (accessed May 1, 2011).

AI Access Foundation Inc. "Journal of Artificial Intelligence Research." Journal of Artificial Intelligence Research. http://www.jair.org/ (accessed September 22, 2009).

ALCTS Network News. "An Electronic Publication of the Association for Library Collections and Technical Services." BUBL Archive Journals. http://bubl.ac.uk/archive/journals/alctsnn/ (accessed October 30, 2009).

ALIA. "Australian Academic & Research Libraries." Australian library and Information Association. http://www.alia.org.au/publishing/aarl/index.html (accessed November 3, 2009).

ALIA. "Australian Library Journal." Australian Library and Information Association. http://alia.org.au/publishing/alj/ (accessed November 3, 2009).

American Association for History and Computing. "Journal of the Association for History and Computing." American Association for History and Computing. JAHC. http://mcel.pacificu.edu/jahc/ (accessed September 30, 2009).

American Association of Law Libraries. "AALL Spectrum." American Association of Law Libraries. http://www.aallnet.org/ (accessed November 3, 2009).

American Association of Law Libraries. "Law Library Journal." American Association of Law Libraries. http://www.aallnet.org/products/pub_journal.asp (accessed April 2, 2010).

American Association of School Librarians. "School Library Media Research." School Library Media research. http://

www.sajim.co.za/index.php/sajim/issue/current (accessed on 22.12.2008).

American Library Association. "ACRL: Association of College and Research Libraries. ALA. http://www.ala.org/Content/NavigationMenu/ACRL/Publications/College_and_Research_Libraries_News/College_and_Research_Libraries_News.cfm (accessed November 3, 2009).

American Library Association. "American Libraries." American Libraries. http://www.ala.org/ala/alonline/index.cfm (accessed October 30, 2009).

American Library Association. "Book Links." Book Links. http://www.ala.org/ala/aboutala/hqops/publishing/booklinks/index.cfm (accessed November 3, 2009).

American Library Association. *"Library Resources & Technical Services." ALCTS* http://www.ala.org/ala/mgrps/divs/alcts/resources/lrts/index.cfm (accessed September 22, 2009).

American Library Association. "RBM Journal of Rare Books & Manuscripts." RBM. http://rbm.acrl.org/content/2/2Librarianship http://rbm.acrl.org/content/2/2 (accessed March 26, 2010).

American Library Association. "Technology Electronic Reviews." Library and Information Technology Review. http://www.ala.org/ala/mgrps/divs/lita/ter/tertechnology.cfm (accessed October 30, 2009).

American Library Association. "The ALA Washington Office Electronic Newsline (ALAWON)." ALA. http://www.ala.org/ala/aboutala/offices/wo/washnews/archivea/archive.cfm (accessed January 4, 2010).

American Society for Information Science and Technology. "Bulletin of the American Society for Information Science and Technology." asis&t. http://www.asis.org/Bulletin/index.html (accessed November 3, 2009).

American Society for Information Science and Technology. "The Bulletin of the American Society for Information Science and

Technology." Asis&t the Information Society for Information Age. http://www.asis.org/bulletin.html (accessed September 22, 2009).

Arizona State University. *"Current Issues in Educction." CIE.* http://cie.asu.edu/index.php (accessed November 3, 2009).

Ashicroft, Linda., Mclvor, Stephanie. "Electronic Journals: Managing and Changing Culture in Academic Libraries." Online Information Review 25, no. 6 (2001), http://www.mcbup.com/research_registers.

Aslib "Aslib Proceedings." Aslib. http://www.aslib.co.uk/proceedings/index.html (accessed November 3, 2009).

Association for Educational Communications and Technology. "Interpersonal Computing and Technology Journal." Interpersonal Computing and Technology Journal. http://www.helsinki.fi/science/optek/#byissue (accessed November 3, 2009).

Association for Educational Communications and Technology. "Interpersonal Computing and Technology: An Electronic Journal for the 21st Century." Educational Communications and Technology. http://www.helsinki.fi/science/optek/#byissue (accessed July 10, 2009).

Association of College & Research Libraries. "CHOICE." American Library Association. http://www.ala.org/ala/mgrps/divs/acrl/publications/choice/previousissues/previousissues.cfm (accessed April 2, 2010).

Association of College and Research Libraries. "Issues in Science and Technology Librarianship: A Quarterly Publication of Science and Technology Section." Issues in Science and Technology Librarianship. http://www.library.ucsb.edu/istl/ (accessed September 22, 2009).

Association of Indian Universities. "Thesis of the Month: Library and Information Science". University News. (2004-2010): 28-31.

Association of Research Libraries. "A Bimonthly News Letters for Library Issues and Action." ARL. http://www.arl.org/newsltr/ (accessed November 3, 2009).

Athabasca University. "International Review of Research in Open and Distance Learning." International Review of Research in Open and Distance Learning. http://www.irrodl.org/index.php/irrodl (accessed November 3, 2009).

Australian Computer Society Inc. "Journal of Research and Practice in Information Technology." Journal of Research and Practice in Information Technology. http://acs.org.au/jrpit/index.html (accessed May 1, 2011).

Australian Library and Information Association. "inCite." Australian Library and Information Association. http://alia.org.au/publishing/incite/archive.html (accessed April 2, 2010).

Australian Library Association. "Australian Academic and Research Libraries." Australian Academic and Research Libraries. http://www.alia.org.au/publishing/aarl/ (accessed January 24, 2010).

AV Review Database. "MC Journal: The Journal of Academic Media Librarianship." MC Journal. http://wings.buffalo.edu/publications/mcjrnl/ (accessed October 30, 2009).

B&R Samizdat Express. "Internet on a Disk: Free Blog Like Newsletter." Internet on a Disk, Free Blog Like Newsletter. http://www.samizdat.com/ioad.html (accessed November 3, 2009).

Biblia. "Warrior Librarian Weekly." Warrior Librarian. http://warriorlibrarian.com/ (accessed October 30, 2009).

Biblio-Tech Ltd. "Biblio-Tech Review: News Analysis and Comment." Biblio-Tech Review http://www.ringgold.com/biblio-tech/si_pd.cfm?pid=2 (accessed November 3, 2009).

Bisca International Investments Ltd. "Journals." Libdex. http://www.libdex.com/journals.html (accessed September 20, 2009).

Breeding, M, 2001. Providing Virtual Reference Service. Information Today 18: 42-43.

Brown, Christopher C.; Meagher, Elizabeth S. "Cataloging free e resources: Is it worth the investment." Interlending and Document Supply 36, no. 3 (2008): 135-141.

California Digital Library. "Inter-Actions: UCLA Journal of Education and Information Studies." Scholarship. Repository. http://repositories.cdlib.org/gseis/interactions/ (accessed October 30, 2009).

Canadian Association for School Libraries. "School Libraries in Canada." School Libraries in Canada. http://www.clatoolbox.ca/casl/slic/aboutslic.html (accessed March 26, 2010).

Carol Bean. "The Code4Lib Journal." The Code4Lib Journal. http://journal.code4lib.org/ (accessed September 22, 2009).

Casey, D. "Learning from or through the web: Models of web based education." NCIMDiL (1998): 51-54.

Chartered Institute of Library and Information Professionals. "Library and Information Update." Cilip. http://www.cilip.org.uk/publications/updatemagazine/ (accessed October 30, 2009).

Chartered Institute of Library and Information Professionals. "Multimedia Information and Technology." CILIP. http://www.cilip.org.uk/get-Involved/special-interest-groups/multimedia/journal/pages/journalbackissues.aspx (accessed March 26, 2010).

Chauhan (Kaushal) and Mahapatra (R. K.). (2012). Information seeking behavior in digital environment and libraries in enhancing the use of digital information. Encyclopedia of Design, Development, and Management of Resources for Digital Library Services. United States of America:

Information Science Reference p. 289.

Chauhan (Kaushal). (2012). An analysis of facilities and features of free e-journals in library and information science". International Journal of Information Management Science. no.1, p.43. http://www.pageflip-flap.com/read?r=Tw50SABT7FhILMsD7P#/44/view

Chauhan, Kaushal. (2011). A comprehensive evaluation of facilities and features of free e-resources in library and information science. VSRD technical and non technical journal. V.2 (10). (pp.505) Retrieved from http://www.vsrdjournals.com/vsrd/Issue/2011_10_Oct/Web/2_Koushal_Chauhan_491_Research_Article_Oct_2011.html

Chauhan, Kaushal. (2012). Open e-journals in library and information science: An analysis of its Facilities and Features. Journal of Computer Technology & Application. V.3 (2) p.30. http://www.stmjournals.com/index.php?journal=JoCTA&page=issue&op=current

Chauhan, Kaushal. (2012). Selected free e-journals in library and information science in directory of open access journals. DESIDOC Journal of Library & Information Technology, 32 (4), 339-346.

Chauhan, Kaushal. Mahapatra, R.K."Use of Free Online Comprehensive E-Resources in Library and Information Science for Scholarly Communication." Paper presented at the international conference of MDI & IASLIC on Digital Libraries and Knowledge Organization ICDK 2011, MDI, Gurgaon, 14-16 February 2011.

Chauhan, Kaushal., Mahapatra, R.K. "Information Seeking Behavior in Digital Environment and Libraries in Enhancing the use of Digital Information" Paper presented at the international conference of NIFT & IFLA on Convergence of Libraries, Archives and Museums ICLAM 2011, India International Centre, New Delhi, 15-17 February 2011.

Chauhan, Kaushal." E-Resources Characteristics and Free E-

Resources" Paper presented at the Seminar on e resources management and North Zone User Convention of INDEST-AICTE Consortium, Mahatma Gandhi Central Library, Indian Institute of Technology, Roorkee, India, November 18-19, 2010.

Chauhan, Kaushal; Mahapatra R.K. "Use of Directory of Open Access Journals (DOAJ) as an Information Source in Business and Management" Paper presented at the international conference of MALIBNET 2009, in KIIT University, Bhubaneswar, 22-24 January 2009.

City University of Hong Kong. "Electronic Journal on Information Systems in Developing Countries." Electronic Journal on Information Systems in Developing Countries. http://www.ejisdc.org/ojs2/index.php/ejisdc (accessed November 3, 2009).

City University of New York. "Urban Library Journal." ULJ. http://lacuny.cuny.edu/ulj/ (accessed October 30, 2009).

Collection Development Coordinator New Mexico State University Library. "The Good, The Bad & The Ugly: or, Why It's a good Idea to Evaluate Web Sources." Evaluation Criteria. http://lib.nmsu.edu/instruction/eval.html (accessed June 1, 2010).

Cornell Law Library. "International Journal of Legal Information." International Journal of Legal Information. http://scholarship.law.cornell.edu/ijli/vol33/iss1/ (accessed March 2, 2011).

Corporation for National Research Initiatives. "D-Lib Magazine: The Magazine of Digital Library Research." D-Lib Magazine. http://www.dlib.org (accessed September 20, 2009).

Council on East Asian Libraries and the Association for Asian Studies, Inc. "Journal of East Asian Libraries." Harold B. Lee Library. http://www.lib.byu.edu/dlib/spc/jeal/ (accessed April 2, 2010).

Council on Library and Information Resources. "CLIR Issues."

Council on Library and Information Resources. http://www.clir.org/pubs/issues/index.html (accessed November 3, 2009).

Creative Commons Attribution. "Australian Journal of Information Systems". Australian Journal of Information Systems. http://dl.acs.org.au/index.php/ajis/about (accessed on 22.12.2008).

Creative Commons Attribution. "Journal of Technology Studies". Virginia Tech. http://scholar.lib.vt.edu/ejournals/JOTS/ (accessed November 3, 2009).

Creative Commons Attribution. "Journal of the Rutgers University Libraries." The Journal of the Rutgers University Libraries. http://jrul.libraries.rutgers.edu/index.php/jrul/index (accessed November 3, 2009).

Creative Commons License. "Webology." Webology. http://www.webology.ir/ (accessed October 30, 2009).

CSA. "LISA." ILLUMINA. www.csa2.com (accessed June 1, 2010).

Cybermetrics. "International Journal of Scientometrics, Informetrics and Bibliometrics." Cybermetrics. http://www.cindoc.csic.es/cybermetrics/cybermetrics.html (accessed on 22.12.2008).

Dalai, Braja Kishor. "Information Needs of Craft Industries: Special Reference to Applique Craft in Puri District of Orissa." PhD diss.,Berhampur University, 2005.

Das, Debabrata. "State of Collection Development in the CBSE Affiliated Senior Secondary School Libraries of Orissa: An Analytical Study." PhD diss., Berhampur University, 2005.

Department of Information Systems. "Electronic Journal on Information Systems in Developing Countries." City University of Hong Kong. http://www.ejisdc.org/ojs2/index.php/ejisdc/index (accessed July 10, 2009).

Department of Library and Information Science. "Digital Library and E-Scholarship Portal." Vidyanidhi. http://

www.vidyanidhi.org.in/ (accessed June 1, 2009).

DESIDOC and DRDO. "DESIDOC Journal of Library & Information Science". DESIDOC Journal of Library & Information Science. http://publications.drdo.gov.in/ojs/index.php/djlit/index (accessed September 22, 2009).

Devarajan, G, trans. Research in Library and Information Science. New Delhi: Ess Ess Publications, 2002.

DFG. "European Research Libraries Cooperation : ERLC ; the LIBER Quarterly." European Research Libraries Cooperation. http://www.digizeitschriften.de/main/dms/toc/?IDDOC=529251 (accessed January 24, 2010).

Division of Consortium eLearning Network Pvt. Ltd. "Current Trends in Information Technology". Current Trends in Information Technology. http://stmjournals.com/index.php?journal=CTIT (accessed May 1, 2011).

Dominican University Graduate School of Library and Information Science. "World Libraries." World Libraries. http://www.worlib.org/ (accessed November 3, 2009).

Durham University Library. "Online E-Resources: Electronic Resources." Darham University. http://www.dur.ac.uk/library/resources/online/ejournals/?type=ejour&q=all (accessed September 20, 2009).

E R N European Laboratory for Particle Physics. "High Energy Physics Libraries Webzine." High Energy Physics Libraries Webzine. http://library.cern.ch/HEPLW/(accessed on 22.12.2008).

EASI. Information Technology and Disabilities E-Journal." Equal Access to Software and Information. http://people.rit.edu/easi/itd.htm (accessed September 30, 2009).

EDUCAUSE. "EDUCAUSE *Quarterly.*" EDUCAUSE *Quarterly.* http://connect.educause.edu/apps/eq/index.asp (accessed on 22.12.2008).

EDUCAUSE. "*EDUCAUSE* Review." *EDUCAUSE* Review. http://

connect.educause.edu/apps/er/index.asp (accessed on 22.12.2008).

Eduserv. "Journal of Information Literacy." IL. http://www.informationliteracy.org.uk/JIL.aspx (accessed September 30, 2009).

EJUM. "Malaysian Journal of Library & Information Science Malaysian Journal of Library & Information Science." EJUM. http://ejum.fsktm.um.edu.my/Default.aspx (accessed March 26, 2010).

Ellen McCrady. "The Abbey Newsletter Preservation and Archival Material." The Abbey Newsletter. http://cool-palimpsest.stanford.edu/byorg/abbey/an/index.html (accessed November 3, 2009).

Elsevier. "Information Processing & Management: An International Journal." Information Processing & Management. http://www.elsevier.com/wps/find/journaldescription.cws_home/244/description#description (accessed October 30, 2009).

Epractice. Eu community. "European Journal of ePractice." European Journal of ePractice. http://www.epractice journal.eu/ (accessed September 30, 2009).

ETAI Organization. "Electronic Transactions on Artificial Intelligence." ITAI. http://www.ida.liu.se/ext/etai/ (accessed September 20, 2009).

EUROPA Science. "Research Information." Research Information. http://www.researchinformation.info/(accessed November 3, 2009).

Free Pint Ltd. "Free Pint." Free Pint. http://www.freepint.com/ (accessed November 3, 2009).

Ghosh, Rita. "Understanding user needs and building e resources. Information Management in Digital Libraries." NCIMDiL (2006): 671-678.

Google. "List of Free E-Resources in LIS." http://www.google.co.in/

search?hl=en&source=hp&q=List+of+free+E-Resources+in+ LIS&btnG=Google+Search&meta= &aq=f&aqi=&aql=&oq= &rlz=1W1ADFA_en (accessed April 1, 2011).

Google. "Journals: Library and Information Science." Google Directory. http://directory.google.com/Top/Reference/Libraries/Library_and_Information_Science/Journals/ (accessed September 20, 2009).

Griesbaum, J. "Evaluation of Three German Search Engines: Altavista.de, Google.de and Lycos.de." Information Research 9, no. 4 (2004), http://InformationR.net/ir/9-4/paper189.html

Group of Professionals Working in the Area of Library. "Access to Electronic Journals: Newsletters." Infolibrarian. http://www.infolibrarian.com/res.htm#ejournals (accessed August 10, 2009).

Guruprasad, R. "E-Journals and their usage patterns amongst the Indian Aerospace Scientists and Engineers in Bengaluru." DESIDOC Journal of Library and Information Technology 30, no. 6, (2010): 31-38.

H.M. Gladney, HMG Consulting. "Digital Document Quarterly." Digital Document Quarterly. http://home.pacbell.net/hgladney/ddqstart.htm (accessed January 24, 2010).

Haridasan, Sudharma; Khan, Majid. "Impact and use of E-Resources by social scientists in National Social Science Documentation Centre (NASSDOC), India" The Electronic Library, 27, no. 1 (2009): 117-133.

Haridasan, Sudharmna., Khan, Majid. " Impact and Use of E-Resources by Social Scientists in National Social Science Documentation Centre (NASSDOC), India." The Electronic Library 27, no. 1 (2009), http://emeraldinsight.com/Insight/ViewContentsServlet?contentType=Article&Fil.

Hariharan, A. 2007.Customised Web Based Services at SERC library with special reference to Alert Services. DESIDOC Bulletin of Library and Information Science 27, no. 3: 31-38.

HEPLW Team. High Energy Physics Webzine. Libraries Webzine. http://library.web.cern.ch/library/Webzine/index.shtml (accessed June 1, 2011).

Heriot-Watt University. "Internet Resources Newsletter." Internet Resources Newsletter. http://www.hw.ac.uk/libwww/irn/irn.html (accessed January 24, 2010).

Hitchcock, S., Carr, L. & Hall, W. *Web journals publishing : a UK perspective*. http://journals.ecs.soton.ac.uk/uksg.htm (accessed September 30, 2009).

Hochschulverband für Informationswissenschaft. "Review of Information Science." RIS. http://www.inf-wiss.uni-konstanz.de/RIS/ (accessed on 22.12.2008).

Hyldegaard, Jette., Seiden, Piet. "My ejournal Exploring the Usefulness of Personalized Access to Scholarly Articles and Services." Information Research 9, no. 3 (2004), http://InformationR.net/ir/9-3/paper181.html

ICAAP. "E-JASL: The Electronic Journal of Academic and Special Librarianship." E-JASL. http://southernlibrarianship.icaap.org/ (accessed September 20, 2009).

Idaho Library Association. "The Idaho Librarian: A Publication of the Idaho Library Association The Idaho Librarian. http://www.idaholibraries.org/idlibrarian/index.php/idaho-librarian/index (accessed March 20, 2011).

iGroup. "Access." Access. http://www.aardvarknet.info/access/number46/index.cfm (accessed January 2, 2010).

Indian Institute of Science. "Free E-Journals: Newsletters." Some Useful Resources for Library and Information Professionals in India. http://scigate.ncsi.iisc.ernet.in/raja/lib-info-sources.htm#journals (accessed August 10, 2009).

Indian statistical Institute. "Free On-Line Full Text Journals: List of Free On-Line Full Text Journals in Library and Information Science." Indian Statistical Institute Bangalore Centre

Library. http://www.isibang.ac.in/ (accessed July 10, 2009).

Indian Statistical Institute. "Free On-Line Full Text Journals: List of Free On-Line Full Text Journals in Library and Information Science." Indian Statistical Institute Delhi Centre Library. http://www.isid.ac.in/~library/lib.htm (accessed July 10, 2009).

Inflibnet Centre. "Information and Library Network Centre." INFLIBNET. http://www.inflibnet.ac.in/econ/eresource.html/ (accessed November 3, 2009).

INFOREC Association. "Informatica Economica Journal." Informatica Economica Journal. http://revistaie.ase.ro/index.html (accessed September 30, 2009).

Informatics India Limited. "E-Journals Related to Library & Information Science, Electronic Publishing, etc." J-Gate the E-Journal Gateway. http://www.j-gate.informindia.co.in/Misc/librarian.asp#Library%20&%20Information%20Science (accessed August 13, 2009).

Informatics India Ltd. "List of Free E-Resources in LIS." Open Jgate. http://www.openjgate.org/Browse/ByJournal.aspx?alpha=A (accessed April 1, 2011).

Information Centre for Aerospace Science and Technology Organization. "Library Science." ICAST Gateway for Free E-Journals. http://www.icast.org.in/ejournal/ejournalsubject.php?subject=Library+Science&n=0 (accessed August 13, 2009).

Information Science Section of the Department of Political and Social Science of the Pompeu Fabra University. "Hipertext.net." Hipertext.net. http://www.hipertext.net/english/pag100.htm (accessed September 30, 2009).

Information Technology Services for The University of North Carolina at Chapel Hill. "CIT Infobits." UNC Information Tachnology Services.http://its.unc.edu/Teaching And Learning/Publications/TLInfobits/TL_INFOBITS_2009 (accessed November 3, 2009).

Information Today Inc. "Computer in Libraries." Information Today Inc. http://www.infotoday.com/cilmag/default.shtml (accessed October 30, 2009).

Information Today Inc. "Computers in Libraries." Information Today Inc. http://www.infotoday.com/cilmag/default.shtml (accessed November 3, 2009).

Information today Inc. "EContent Digital Content Strategies and Resources." EContent. http://www.ecmag.net/ (accessed November 3, 2009).

Information Today Inc. "Information Today." Information Today, Inc. http://www.infotoday.com/IT/nov08/index.shtml (accessed October 30, 2009).

Information Today Inc. "MLS: Marketing Library Services." Information today Inc. http://www.infotoday.com/MLS/default.shtml (accessed October 30, 2009).

Information Today Inc. "Online." Information Today Inc. http://www.infotoday.com/online/default.shtml (accessed October 30, 2009).

Information Today Inc. "Searcher: The Magazine for Database Professionals." Information Today Inc. http://www.infotoday.com/searcher/default.asp (accessed November 3, 2009).

Informing Science Institute. "Informing Faculty: An International Journal of Higher Education Discussion Cases." IF. http://informingfaculty.org/ (accessed October 30, 2009).

Informing Science Institute. "Interdisciplinary Journal of E-Learning and Learning Objects." Informing Science Institute. http://ijklo.org/ (accessed September 30, 2009).

Informing Science Institute. "Interdisciplinary Journal of Information, Knowledge, and Management." Informing Science Institute. http://www.ijikm.org/ (accessed September 30, 2009).

Informing Science Institute. "International Journal of Doctoral Studies." Informing Sience Institute. http://ijds.org (accessed September 30, 2009).

Informing Science Institute. "Issues in Informing Science and Information Technology." Informing Science Institute. http://iisit.org/ (accessed September 30, 2009).

Informing Science Institute. "Journal of Information Technology Education." Informing Science Institute. http://jite.org/ (accessed October 30, 2009).

Informing Science Institute. "Journal of Information, Information Technology, and Organizations." Informing Science Institute. http://jiito.org/ (accessed September 30, 2009).

Informing Science Institute. "Journal of Medical Internet Research." Informing Science Institute. http://www.jmir.org/ (accessed September 30, 2009).

Informing Science. Informing Science: The International Journal of an Emerging Transdiscipline Informing Science Institute. http://inform.nu/ (accessed September 30, 2009).

Ingenta Connect. "Learned Publishing." Learned Publishing. http://www.ingentaconnect.com/content/alpsp/lp(accessed November 3, 2009).

Inquira. "Knowledge Management World." KM World. http://www.kmworld.com/Archives/ (accessed November 3, 2009).

Institute of Information Technology. "International Journal of Communication Networks and Information Security". International Journal of Communication Networks and Information Security. http://ijcnis.kust.edu.pk/(accessed May 1, 2011).

International Center for Information Ethics. "International Review of Information Ethics." IRIE. http://www.i-r-i-e.net/ (accessed September 30, 2009).

International Council for Science. "Data Science Journal." Data

Science Journal. http://www.datasciencejournal.org/ (accessed January 24, 2010).

International Federation of Library Associations and Institutions. "IFLA Journal." IFLANET. http://www.ifla.org/V/iflaj/index.htm (accessed September 20, 2009).

International Federation of Library Associations and Institutions. "Library & Information Science: General Resources." IFLANET. http://www.ifla.org/II/libdoc.htm#ejca (accessed September 15, 2009).

InterWord Communications. "South African Journal of Information Management." South African Journal. http://general.rau.ac.za/infosci/raujournal/ (accessed October 30, 2009).

ISA. "Indian Science Abstract." NISCAIR. isa@niscair.res.in (accessed June 1, 2010).

ITI Info Central. "Link Up Digital." Link-Up. http://www.infotoday.com/lu/lunew.htm (accessed November 3, 2009).

ITI Research. "EMedia Extra." EMedia Live. http://www.emediapro.net/Newsletters/Default.aspx (accessed November 3, 2009).

Jain, Vivekanand and Saraf, Dr. Sanjiv. 2006. Google search engine and its usefulness to library professionals. DESIDOC Bulletin of Information Technology. 26, no. 5; 23-28.

Janes, Joseph, 2005. Introduction to Reference Work in the Digital Age. New York: Neal-Schuman Publishers Inc.

Jasper, Richard P; Sheble, Laura. "Evolutionary approach to managing e resources." Serials Librarian 4 no. 4 (2005): 55-70.

K. G. Saur Verlag. "LIBRI: International Journal of Libraries and Information Services" LIBRI. http://www.librijournal.org/ (accessed October 30, 2009).

Kacheri, Umeshareddy 2010. Print vs. E-Journals and information seeking patterns of Users: A case study of SPJIMR. DESIDOC

Journal of Library and Information Science 30, no. 1: 22-25.

Katina Strauch. "Against the Grain." Against the Grain. http://www.against-the-grain.com/d/fulltextarticles (accessed October 30, 2009).

Katz, William A. Introduction to Reference Work: Basic Information Sources. New York: McGraw Hill Book Company, 1987.

Katz, William A. Introduction to Reference Work: Reference Services and Reference Processes. Albany: State University of New York, 1992.

Kaur, Baljinder, et al. "Use of Electronic information resources: A case study of Thaper University." DESIDOC Journal of Library and Information Science 29, no. 2 (2009): 67-73.

Kaur, Baljinder; Verma, Rama. "Use and impact of electronic journals in the Indian Institute of Technology, Delhi, India." The Electronic Library, 27, no. 4 (2009): 611-622.

Key2 Information. "Electronic Thesis and Dissertation." Key2 Information. http://key2information.blogspot.com/2008/12/open-access-part-iv electronic-theses.html (accessed July 10, 2009).

Key2 Information. "Library and Information Science E-Journals." Key2 Information. http://key2information.blogspot.com/2008/12/open-access-part-iv-electronic-theses.html (accessed July 10, 2009).

Khode, Subhash; Kumar, Divik. 2004. Free information sources and services on internet for libraries: A selective compilation. DESIDOC Bulletin of Information Technology.24,no.4;13-18.

Kothari, C. R. Research Methodology Methods and Techniques. New Age International: New Delhi, 2004.

Kumar, Anil; Kademani, B. S.; Kumar, Vijai. "Web resources in INSPEC database: A scientometric mapping." SRELS Journal of Information Management 45, no. 2 (2008): 197-208.

Kumar, P.S.G. Library as a Social Institution: Foundation of Library and Information Science. Delhi: B R Publishers, 1998.

Lal, C. Descriptive Questions in library and Information Science for NET (UGC), SLET, SET & Other Competitive Examinations. New Delhi: Ess Ess Publications, 2010.

Lalitha, P. "Demystifying the web for authentic information and morphology of scholarly literature. NCIMDiL (2006): 375-383.

Law and Court Section of the American Political Science Association. "Law and Politics Book Review". Law and Politics Book Review. http://www.bsos.umd.edu/gvpt/lpbr/index.htm (accessed November 3, 2009).

Leigh, S. Estabrook. "On line education and organizational transformation. Sloan c view." Perspectives in Quality Online Education 1, no. 2 (2003).

Library of Congress. "Conserline." Conser. http://www.loc.gov/acq/conser/consrlin.html (accessed November 3, 2009).

Library of Congress. "LC Cataloging Newsline." The Library of Congress. http://www.loc.gov/catdir/lccn/ (accessed March 26, 2010).

Libres Webmaster. "Library and Information Science Research Electronic Journal." LIBRES. http://libres.curtin.edu.au/ (accessed September 22, 2009).

Linberger, Peter; Fielding, Lori Jean; Bove, Frank J. "Developing a web based evaluation tool for purchasing electronic resources: A librarian faculty student partnership." E-JASL: The Electronic Journal of Academic and Special Librarianship 8, no. 3(2007).

Linda, Ashcroft and Stephanie McIvor. Electronic Journals: Managing and Educating for a Changing Culture in Academic Libraries. Online information Review 25, no.6 (March 21, 2001), http://wwwemrald-library.com/ft

LISTA. "Chinese Librarianship: An International Electronic Journal."

Internet Chinese Librarians Club. http://www.iclc.us/cliej/ (accessed September 22, 2009).

Lund University Libraries. "E-Journals in Social Sciences: Library and Information Science." Directory of Open Access Journals. http://www.doaj.org/doaj?func=subject&cpid=129 (accessed August 13, 2009).

Lund University Libraries. "Information Research: An International Electronic Journal." Information Research. http://informationr.net/ir/ (accessed September 20, 2009).

Lund University Libraries. "Information Research: An International Electronic Journal." Information Research. http://informationr.net/ir (accessed September 30, 2009).

Lycos Inc. "Free E-Resources in LIS". Lycos Go Get it. http://search.lycos.com/?tab=web&query=free+E-Resources+in+LIS&diktfc=3334B290B6F49 DDDE7945FD42EE41A0FB6AE02FF2DBA (accessed on 09.12.2008).

Lycos Inc. Lycos Inc. " List of Free E-Resources in LIS." Lycos go get it. http://search.lycos.com/?tab=web&searchForm=true&query=list+of+free+E-Resources+in+LIBRARY+AND+INFORMATION+SCIENCE&x=35&y=20 (accessed April 1, 2011).

MAGERT of the American Library Association. "Coordinates: Online Journal of the Map and Geography Round Table of the American Library Association." MAGERT. http://www.sunysb.edu/libmap/coordinates.htm (accessed September 22, 2009).

Maharana, Bulu, and Nayak, Kalpana. Scholarly Use of Web Resources in LIS Research: A Citation Analysis. Library Review 55, no. 9 (July 21, 2006), www.emerald insight.com/0024-2535.htm

Marcus A. Banks. "Biomedical Digital Libraries". Biomedical Digital Libraries. http://www.bio-diglib.com (accessed January 24, 2010).

Mary Niederlander. "Library, Information Science and Education: Online Journals, Ezine of Interest." Library Support Staff.Com http://www.librarysupportstaff.com/libjourn.html#journals (accessed September 20, 2009).

Marylaine Block. "Ex Libris." Ex Libris. http://marylaine.com/exlibris/ (accessed October 30, 2009).

McGill Library & Information Studies Student Association. "Marginal Librarian." The Marginal. http://www.gslis.mcgill. ca/marginal/ (accessed November 3, 2009).

Medeiros, Norm. "Electronic resources management: An update." OCLC Systems and Services 21 no. 2 (2005): 92-94.

Medical Library Association. *"Journal of Medical Library Association." JMLA.* http://www.pubmedcentral.nih.gov/tocrender.fcgi?journal=93 (accessed September 22, 2009).

Medical Library Univ. of Cambridge. "Journal of the European Association for Health Information and Libraries." EAHIL. http://www.eahil.net/journal/ (accessed March 2, 2011).

MEDLARS. "NLM Technical Bulletin." NLM Technical Bulletin. ftp://nlmpubs.nlm.nih.gov/nlminfo/newsletters/techbull/pdf_tb/novdec97.pdf (accessed November 3, 2009).

Members of the IFLA Division of Special Libraries. "International Journal of Special Libraries." INSPEL. http://forge.fh-potsdam.de/~IFLA/INSPEL/intro.htm (accessed September 22, 2009).

Michigan Library Association. "MLA Forum." MLA Forum. http://www.mlaforum.org/ (accessed October 30, 2009).

Middle East Librarians Association. "MELA Notes: The Journal of the Middle East Librarians Association." MELA Notes. http://www.mela.us/MELANotes /MELANotesIntro.html (accessed March 26, 2010).

Mindspark Interactive Network, Inc. "Free E-Resources in LIS."

Excite. http://msxml.excite.com/excite/ws/results/Web/free%20E-Resources%20in%20LIS/1/0/0/Relevance/iq=true/zoom=off/_iceUrlFlag=7?_IceUrl=true (accessed on 09.12.2008).

MLA. "Mississippi Libraries." Mississippi Library Association. http://www.misslib.org/index.php/publications/ (accessed October 30, 2009).

Moghaddam, Golnessa Galyani. "Why are Scholarly Journals Costly even with Electronic Publishing." Interlending and Document Supply 37, no, 3 (2009), www.emeraldinsight.com/0264-1615.htm.

Monty, V. *Electronic journals : new publishing paradigm*. [http://www.library.yorku.ca/staff2/vmonty/ejournal.htm (accessed September 30, 2009).

Morino Institute. Why Use Electronic Communications. Potomac Knowledge Way. http://knowledgeway.org/ (accessed June 1, 2010).

Mountainside Pblishing Inc. "Library Issues: Briefings for Faculty and Administrators." Library Issues. http://www.libraryissues.com/ (accessed October 30, 2009).

Nandi, Atin. "E books: A source of information for digital libraries." Proceedings of the National Conference on Information Management in E-Libraries (2002): 210-217.

Narayana, Poornima and Goudar I.R.N. "Management of e resources in research and development Centers: A case study of the information center at NAL." International Conference on Information Management in a Knowledge Society (2005): 1070-1071.

National Agricultural Library. "Agricultural Libraries Information Notes." Agricultural Libraries Information Notes (ALIN). http://webharvest.gov/peth04/20041023101316/http://www.nal.usda.gov/NewAlin/ (accessed January 4, 2010).

National Council of University Research Administrators. "Research Management Review." National Council of University

Research Administrators. http://www.ncura.edu/content/news/rmr/archive.php (accessed November 3, 2009).

National Information System for Science and Technology. "DELNET Databases: Thesis and Dissertations." DELNET Developing Library Network. http://164.100.247.21/basisbwdocs/newyear.html (accessed July 1, 2009).

National Library of Australia. "Australian Library Journals." Australian Libraries Gateway. http://www.nla.gov.au/libraries/resource/journal.html (accessed September 20, 2009).

NCTE. "The ALAN Review" ALAN Online. http://scholar.lib.vt.edu/ejournals/ALAN/ (accessed September 15, 2009).

Neelameghan, A. Online Database Searching and Retrieval. Bangalore: Sarada Ranganathan Endowment for Library Science, 1995.

Netscape. "Library and Information Science: Journals." domz open directory project. http://www.dmoz.org/Reference/Libraries/Library_and_Information_Science/Journals/ (accessed March 20, 2011).

NISCAIR. "Annals of Library & Information Studies." NISCAIR online periodical repository. http://nopr.niscair.res.in/ (accessed March 2, 2011).

NISSAT. "Information Today and Tomorrow." Information Today and Tomorrow. http://itt.nissat.tripod.com/ (accessed November 3, 2009).

Nordic Public Library Authorities. "Scandinavian Public Library Quarterly." Scandinavian Public Library Quarterly. http://www.splq.info/ (accessed November 3, 2009).

North American Publishing Company. "Book Business". Book Business. http://www.bookbusinessmag.com/(accessed November 3, 2009).

North Carolina Libraries. "North Carolina Libraries Online Official Publication of the North Carolina Library

Association." North Carolina Libraries.http://www.nclaonline.org/NCL/ (accessed October 30, 2009).

Northwestern University School of Law. "Northwestern Journal of Technology and Intellectual Property." Northwestern Journal of Technology and Intellectual Property. http://www.law.northwestern.edu/journals/njtip/issues.htm (accessed June 1, 2011).

NPO. "NPO E-Journal: Preservation Advisory Centre." British Library. http://www.bl.uk/npo/journaltemp.html (accessed March 26, 2010).

OCLC. "RLG DigiNews." The World Libraries Connecting. http://www.oclc.org/programs/publications/newsletters/diginews.htm (accessed September 22, 2009).

Office of University Relations. "Virginia Tech Magazine." Virginia Tech Invent the Future. http://www.vtmagazine.vt.edu/ (accessed September 15, 2009).

Ohio Board of Regents. "Electronic Theses and Dissertations Center." OhioLINK. http://www.ohiolink.edu/etd/ (accessed August 10, 2009).

Organization of Colleagues. "Journals." Informing Science Institute. http://informingscience.org/ (accessed September 22, 2009).

Overture Services Inc. "List of Free E-Resources in LIS." Altavista. http://in.altavista.com/web/results?fr=altavista&itag=ody&q=list+of+free+E-Resources+in+LIS&kgs=1&kls=0 (accessed April 1, 2011).

Overture Services, Inc. "Free Journals In LIS." AltaVista India. http://in.altavista.com/web/results?q=free+journals+in+las (accessed on 09.12.2008).

Oxford University Press. "Journal." Oxford Journals our Journals. http://www.oxfordjournals.org/our_journals/#A (accessed September 20, 2009).

Pace, Andrew. 2003. Virtual Reference: What's in a Name?.

Computers in Libraries 23: 55-56.

Paper presented at the international conference of NCIMDiL 2006, in IIT Kharagpur, India, 2-4 August 2006.

Parekh, Harsha, Internet in the Scholarly Communication Process. Saroop Shanti: Kolhapur, 2000.

Paul Catherall. "Information for Social Change." Information for Social Change. http://libr.org/isc/journal.html (accessed October 30, 2009).

Peter Suber. "Free Online Scholarship Newsletter." FOS. http://www.earlham.edu/~peters/fos/index.htm (accessed November 3, 2009).

Polish Librarians Association. "Electronic Information Bulletin for Librarians." EBIB. http://www.ebib.info/en/ (accessed September 22, 2009).

Progressive Librarians Guild. "Progressive Librarian." Progressive Librarian.http://libr.org/pl/ (accessed October 30, 2009).

Province Ca. "PROVENANCE: Information Origins, Sources & Destinations Canada and the Web." PROVENANCE. http://www.provenance.ca/about-provenance/index.html (accessed November 3, 2009).

Pub Med Central. "Journal of the American Medical Informatics Association". JAMIA. http://www.pubmedcentral.nih.gov/tocrender.fcgi?action=archive&journal=76 (accessed November 3, 2009).

Publications Committee of The Antiquarian Booksellers. "ABAA Newsletter." Antiquarian Booksellers. http://hq.abaa.org/books/antiquarian/abaapages/newsletter (accessed January 2, 2010).

Ramesh, D. B. Information Technology Applications in Libraries: a Textbook for Beginners. Bhubneswar: Reproprint Pvt. LTd, 2004.

Rath, Pravakar. "Web based education and digital library:

Technologies, issues and challenges." NCIMDiL (2006): 371-374.

Ratnakar, K Venkata 2010. Access and use of E-Resources in science and technology libraries affiliated to Hemchandracharya North Gujarat University. University News. 48, no. 25: 21-27.

Reed Business Information. "Library Journal." Library Journal. http://www.libraryjournal.com (accessed September 22, 2009).

Reed Business Information. "School Library Journal." New world Monkeys. http://www.schoollibraryjournal.com/ (accessed November 3, 2009).

REG-iA. "Journal of Information Architecture." Journal of Information Architecture. http://journalofia.org/archives/ (accessed March 2, 2011).

Regis University. "Collaborative Librarianship." Collaborative Librarianship. http://www.collaborativelibrarianship.org/index.html (accessed January 4, 2010).

Resnick, Taryn., Clark, Dennis T. "Evaluation of Electronic Resources Support: Is Virtual Reference the Answer?." Library Hi Tech 27, no. 3 (2009), www.emeraldinsight.com/0737-8831.htm.

Resnick, Taryn; Ugaz, Ana; Burford, Nancy; Carrigan, Esther. "E resources: Transforming access services for the digital age." Library Hi Tech 26, no. 1 (2008): 141-154.

RMIT University, "LASIE: Library Automated Systems Information Exchange." Informit. http://search.informit.com.au/browseJournalTitle;res=E-LIBRARY;issn=0047-3774 (accessed March 26, 2010).

RMIT University. "Library Automated Systems Information Exchange." RMIT. http://www.slnsw.gov.au/lasie/welcome.htm (accessed on 09.12.2008).

Rocket Theme. "Christian Library Journal." Christian Library Journal. http://www.christianlibraryj.org/pdf/index.htm (accessed October 30, 2009).

Rory Litwin. “Library Juice Concentrate.” Library Juice. http://libr.org/juice/ (accessed October 30, 2009).

Rutgers State University of New Jersey. “Library and Information Science Resources.” Rutgers University Library. http://www.libraries.rutgers.edu/rul/rr_gateway/research_guides/lib_info/lib_info.shtml (accessed March 20, 2011).

Satpathy, Sunil Kumar. 2010. Use of E-Resources by the Faculty Members with Special Reference to CVRCE Bhubneshwar. DESIDOC Journal of Library and Information Science 30, no. 4: 11-16.

Scholarly Communication Center Rutgers University Libraries. “The journal of the Rutgers University Library.” The Journal. http://jrul.libraries.rutgers.edu/index.php/jrul/index (accessed September 30, 2009).

School libraries in Canada Online. “School libraries in Canada (SLIC): A Journal of the Canadian Association for School Libraries.” School libraries in Canada. http://www.clatoolbox.ca/casl/slic/links.html (accessed June 1, 2011).

School of Communication and Journalism. “International Journal of Communication”. IJoC.http://ijoc.org/ojs/index.php/ijoc/about/editorialPolicies#focusAndScope (accessed Feb 28, 2011).

School of Public Health and Health Professions. “International Research Information.” Center for International Rehabilitation Research Information and Exchange. http://cirrie.buffalo.edu/search/journal_list.php (accessed August 13, 2009).

Sharma, C K. “Use of E-Resources in Library and Information Activities and its impact on Information Services.” Journal of Library and Information Technology 5 (2009): 39-40.

Sharma, Sumati, Kumar, Ashok and Singh, Mohinder. 2004. Digital reference service. DESIDOC Bulletin of Information

Technology. 24, no. 6: 11-18.

Shores, Louis. (1954). "Shores' Checkpoints for the evaluation of reference books". Basic Reference Sources. Chicago: American library Association. 134-135. (accessed September 30, 2009).

Shukla, R K. "Social Sciences Information Resources: A Study of Open Access Journals." Paper presented at the national seminar on access to social science information department of LIS Vidhyasagar University, Delhi, India, February 7-8, 2007.

SIOSS Standford University. IT&Society: A Web Journal Studying How Technology Affects Society. IT&Society. http://www.stanford.edu/group/siqss/itandsociety/ (accessed November 3, 2009).

SLA. "Business and Finance Division Bulletin". Special Libraries Association. http://www.slabf.org/bulletin.html (accessed on 22.12.2008).

Society of American Archivists. "American Archivist." SAA. http://archivists.metapress.com/home/main.mpx (accessed January 4, 2010).

Sprouts Alliance. "Sprouts: Working Papers on Information Systems." Sprouts Beta. http://sprouts.aisnet.org/home.html (accessed October 30, 2009).

Stanford University. "Electronic Journals and Newspapers Library and Academic Information Resources." SULAIR. http://www-sul.stanford.edu/ejournals (accessed September 15, 2009).

State University of New York. "Dissertation." Dissertation Dot Com. http://www.dissertation.com/ (accessed August 10, 2009).

State University of West Gorgia. "Journal of Library Services for Distance Education." Journal of Library Services for Distance Education. http://www.westga.edu/~library/jlsde/ (accessed November 3, 2009).

Strathclyde University. "BUBL Journals: Archive Journals." BUBL

Link Catalogue of Internet Resources. http://bubl.ac.uk/archive/journals/ (accessed September 15, 2009).

Susan E. Beck. "The good, the bad and the ugly: Evaluating electronic journals." Computers in Libraries (1997): 34-43.

Syracus University. "The Bonefolder: An Outgrowth of the Book Arts Web." http://www.philobiblon.com/bonefolder/index.html (accessed September 22, 2009).

Tamkang University Press. "Journal of Educational Media & Library Sciences." JOEMLS. http://joemls.tku.edu.tw/index_e.htm (accessed September 30, 2009).

Tenopir and King. *Communication patterns of engineers.* N.J.: Institute of Electrical and Electronics Engineers, fall 2003.

Texas A&M University. "Academic Open Internet Journal." AOI Journal. http://www.acadjournal.com/ (accessed September 20, 2009).

Texas Digital Library. "Journal of Digital Information." JODI. http://jodi.ecs.soton.ac.uk/ (accessed on 22.12.2008).

TLA Inc. Journal of Knowledge Management Practice." JKMP. http://www.tlainc.com/boutjkmp.htm (accessed November 3, 2009).

Tsakonas, G. and Papatheodorou, C. "Analyzing and evaluating usefulness and usability in electronic information services." Journal of Information Science 32, no. 5 (2006): 400-419.

UBC. "Criteria for Evaluating Internet Resources." University of British Columbia. http://www.library.ubc.ca/home/evaluating/Easyprint.html (accessed June 1, 2010).

UCLA CSE. "MIT Lab Priodicals: Periodicals are Aphabetically Aranged by Title." UCLA Information Sudies. http://is.gseis.ucla.edu/lab/collections/periodicals.htm (accessed September 20, 2009).

UK Serials Group. "Serials E-News." Professional Information Gateway to LIS Resources.http://www.ringgold.com/UKSG/

si_pd.cfm (accessed November 3, 2009).

UK University of Kentucky. "Digital Repository 2002-2007: DSpace Software." archive.uky.edu. http://archive.uky.edu/handle/10225/1/simple-search?query=evaluation+in+library+and+Information+science&start=30 (accessed June 1, 2009).

UKLON. "Cultivate Interactive." CULTIVATE. http://www.cultivate-int.org/index-2.html (accessed October 30, 2009).

UKOLN at the University of Bath. "International Journal of Digital Curation." International Journal of Digital Curation. http://www.ijdc.net/./ijdc/issue/current (accessed September 30, 2009).

UKOLN. "Ariadna." Ariadne. http://www.ariadne.ac.uk/ (accessed September 20, 2009).

UKOLN. "Exploit Interactive". EXPLOIT. http://www.exploit-lib.org/ (accessed November 3, 2009).

Uma, V. 2010. The Role of a library in archiving the academic distinctions. University News 28, no. 28: 138-141.

UNC Library. "Electronic Theses and Dissertations 2006-2009: Information and Library Science." UNC University Libraries. http://dc.lib.unc.edu/etd/semester.php?dept=Information+and+Library+ Science%2C+School+of&CISOROOT=/etd (accessed July 10, 2009).

United States. "Library Tools." ProQuest. http://www.proquest.com/en-US/utilities/default.shtml. (accessed August 10, 2009).

University College of Borås. "Human IT: Journal of Information Science Technology Studies as a Human Science." Human IT. http://etjanst.hb.se/bhs/ith//info-eng.htm (accessed September 30, 2009).

University Libraries. "Evaluating Print Sources." Bowling Green State University. http://www.bgsu.edu/colleges/library/assistance/page41013.html (accessed June 1, 2010).

University Library of Virginia Tech. "Electronic Theses and Dissertations at Virginia Tech." dla Special Collections. http:/ /scholar.lib.vt.edu/theses/ (accessed July 10, 2009).

University of Alberta Learning Services. "EBLIP." Evidence Based Library and Information Practice. http://ejournals.library. ualberta.ca/index.php/EBLIP/index (accessed September 30, 2009).

University of Florence. "JLIS.it Italian Journal of Library and Information Science."JLIS.it. http://leo.cilea.it/index.php/ jlis/article/view/4539/4416(accessed March 2, 2011).

University of Glasgow. "Journal of eLiteracy." JLIT. http:// www.jelit.org/index.html (accessed September 30, 2009).

University of Houston. "The Public Access Computer Systems Review." The Public Access Computer Systems Review. http:/ /epress.lib.uh.edu/pr/pacsrev.html (accessed November 3, 2009).

University of Illinois. "First Monday: Peer Reviewed Journal on the Internet." Firstmonday. http://firstmonday.org/ (accessed September 22, 2009).

University of Iowa. "B Sides." Iowa Research Online. http:// ir.uiowa.edu/bsides/(accessed Feb 28, 2011).

University of Iowa. "Electronic journal of Africana Bibliography." EJAB. http://ir.uiowa.edu/ejab/all_issues.html /(accessed March 2, 2011).

University of Michigan Library. "The Journal of Electronic Publishing." JEP. http://www.journalofelectronicpublishing. org/ (accessed September 22, 2009).

University of Mysore. "Open Source Electronic Journals: Library and Information Science." Mysore University Library. http:/ /mul.uni-mysore.ac.in/Pages/online%20journals.htm (accessed August 13, 2009).

University of Nebraska. "Library Philosophy and Practice." Library Philosophy and Practice. http://www.webpages.uidaho.

edu/~mbolin/lpp.htm (accessed October 30, 2009).

University of Nevada. "Electronic Journals: Library and Information Science." Mathewson IGT Knowledge Center. http://www.knowledgecenter.unr.edu/ejournals/subject/subject.aspx?p_subj=56 (accessed August 13, 2009).

University of North Carolina at Chapel Hill School of Information and Library Science. "SILS-ETD." Electronic Thesis and Dissertation SILS. http://etd.ils.unc.edu/dspace/handle/1901/145 (accessed August 10, 2009).

University of Oklahoma. "Communications in Information Literacy." Communications in Information Literacy. http://www.comminfolit.org/index.php/cil/issue/archive (accessed September 22, 2009).

University of the Philippine. "Journal of Philippine librarianship". Journal of Philippine librarianship. http://journals.upd.edu.ph/index.php/jpl/issue/current(accessed May 1, 2011).

University of Toronto Press. "Simile: Studies in Media and Information Literacy Education." SIMILE. http://www.utpjournals.com/simile/simile.html (accessed November 3, 2009).

University of Victoria. "New Knowledge Environments ." New Knowledge Environments (accessed March 2, 2011). http://journals.uvic.ca/index.php/INKE (accessed March 2, 2011).

University of Washington. "Basic Criteria for Evaluating Information." Campus Library Serving University of Washington Bothell and Cascadia Community College.http://library.uwb.edu/guides/eval.html (accessed June 1, 2010).

UOC. "DIGITHUM: The Humanities in Digital Age." DIGITUM. http://www.uoc.edu/digithum/10/eng/index.html (accessed September 22, 2009).

Utrecht Publishing and Archiving Services. "LIBER Quarterly Journal of European Research Libraries." LIBER. http://liber.library.uu.nl/index.html (accessed October 30, 2009).

Vianne Sha. "Library Journals." Internet Library for Librarians. http://www.itcompany.com/inforetriever/index.htm (accessed September 20, 2009).

Vilar, Polona., Zumer, Maja. "Comparison and Evaluation of the User Interfaces of E-Journals. Journal of Documentation." 61, no. 2 (2004): 203-227.

Virginia Tech. "Virginia Libraries." Virginia Libraries .http://scholar.lib.vt.edu/ejournals/VALib/ (accessed March 2, 2011).

Virtual Worlds Research Consortium. "Journal of Virtual Worlds Research." Virtual Worlds Research. http://www.jvwresearch.org/index.html (accessed October 30, 2009).

Vishala, B. K.; Bhandi, M. K. "Advantages and disadvantages of e journals as perceived by the academicians of universities of Karnataka: A survey report." SRELS Journal of Information Management 46, no. 3 (2009): 229-238.

VTLS. "Network Digital Library of Thesis and Dissertations." NDLTD. http://rogers.vtls.com:6080/visualizer/app/Search?sort=_title+asc (accessed July 10, 2009).

Washington State University. "Washington State University Research Exchange: Digital Repository." Washington State University. http://research.wsulibs.wsu.edu:8080/dspace/simple-search?query=reference+service+and+Information+technology (accessed July 10, 2009).

Web Master. "Chinese Librarianship: An International Electronic Journal." The World Wide Web Index. http://www.white-clouds.com/iclc/cliej/indxweb.htm (accessed September 15, 2009).

Western New York Library Resources Council. Journal of Library Innovation. Library Innovation. http://www.

libraryinnovation.org/about/contact (accessed March 2, 2011).

Wiles-Young, Sharon; Landsman, Betty; Terill, Lori J. "e resources e opportunity: Connecting systems, technical services and patrons." The Serials Librarian Serials Librarian 52, no. 3-4(2006): 253-258.

Wiley Inter Science. "Health Information and Libraries Journal." Health Information and Libraries Journal. interscience.wiley.com/journal/120118368/grouphome/home.html (accessed January 24, 2010).

Word Press. "Gateway of LIS E-Resources." Professional Information. http://liprofession.wordpress.com/ (accessed September 15, 2009).

Word Press. "Associates: The Electronic Library Support Staff Journal." ASSOCIATES. http://associates.ucr.edu/journal/ (accessed November 3, 2009).

Wordpress. "Associates: the Electronic Library Support Staff Journal." Associates. http://associates.ucr.edu/journal/ (accessed October 30, 2009).

World Academy of Science. "International Journal of Computer and Information Science and Engineering." International Journal of Computer and Information Science and Engineering. http://www.waset.org/ijcise/(accessed on 22.12.2008).

World Academy of Science. "The Wired Librarian's Newsletter." WASET. http://www.waset.org/ (accessed on 22.12.2008).

Writers Writes. "Internet Writing Journal". Internet Writing Journal. http://www.internetwritingjournal.com/(accessed November 3, 2009).

Zhao, Lisa. "How librarians used e resources: An analysis of citations in CCQ." Cataloging and Classification Quarterly 42, no. 1(2006).

Appendix

APPENDIX-1: LIST OF ONLY SINGLE ISSUE OPEN ACCESS E-RESOURCES

1. Advances in Library Automation and Networking Volume 1 1987
2. Basic and Applied Myology Volume 5 Number 1 1995
3. BookBrag Volume 1 Number 1 1994
4. CNI Newsletter Number 2 1991
5. Data Entries Volume IX Number 1 Fall 1993
6. DECNews for Education and Research Volume 3 Number 1 1994
7. Document World Number 2 1996
8. EBLIDA Newsletter Number 1 1995
9. EdPol-D Volume 1 Number 2 February 1994
10. EFFector Online Volume 9 Number 2 February 1995
11. Electronic ERIC-ECCE Newsletter Volume 5 Number 2 1993
12. Everybody's Internet Update Number 4 July 1994
13. Information Europe Number 1 March 1996
14. Information Week Number 2 April 1997
15. Internet Advertising Review Volume 1 Number 1 1993

16. Journal of Crop Production Volume 1 Number 1 1998
17. Journal of Human Behaviour in the Social Environment Volume 1 Number 1 1998
18. Journal of Knowledge, Education and Libraries Vol. 1 no. 1 February 2002
19. Journal of New Seeds Volume 1 Number 1 1999
20. Journal of Pharmacetical Marketing Practice Volume 1 Number 1 1997
21. Journal of Religion in the Social Services Volume 18 Number 1 1995
22. Journal of Teaching in Social Work Volume 11 Number 1/2 1995
23. Latin American Business Review Volume 1 Number 1 1998
24. Legal Information Service to the Public Newsletter Volume 5 Number 3 Spring 1993
25. LIWOLET Newsletter Volume 4 Number 1 1993
26. MAGnet Newsletter Volume 2 Number 1 1993
27. Middle East Resources Volume 3 Number 1 1993
28. New Books at the Dewey Graduate Library Volume 6 Number 6 1993
29. Public Access Computer Systems News Volume 4 Number 14 1993
30. SCOPE Notes Volume 4 Number 3 1993
31. SIS-EJournal Volume 1 Number 1 1994
32. Slavic and East European Information Resources Volume 1 Number 1 2000
33. Smarter Student (The) Number 11 1993
34. Telelearning Network Synthesizer Number 2 1993
35. UIUCNET Volume 6 Number 3 1993

Glossary

The Glossary defines terms used in the Introduction and throughout the thesis.

1. **ABSTRACT :** A summary of a larger work, such as an article, book, or dissertation, included with citation information in many databases.
2. **ARTICLE DATABASES :** Online tools that index, abstract, or provides electronic access to articles, books, dissertations and other types of content. Many of these databases offer limited full text.
3. **BIBLIOGRAPHY :** A list often with descriptive or critical notes of writings relating to a particular subject, period, or author. The works or a list of the works referred to in a text or consulted by the author in its production, usually given at the end of a work.
4. **BLOG :** a combination of the words "web" and "logs") are an informal but valuable means of communication. Blogs typically include an RSS feed so the blog author can, in effect, push information to interested people. Blog authors could be fellow researchers sharing ideas or librarians alerting readers to new resources or upcoming lectures.
5. **CALL NUMBER :** A unique code assigned to each item in the library. The University Libraries primarily use the Library of

Congress Classification (LCC) System.

6. **CHINOOK :** The University Libraries online catalog and database gateway. Chinook provides access to the millions of holdings in the University Libraries — including all departments in the Norlin Library building and the five external libraries (Business, Earth Sciences, Engineering, Math/Physics, and Music). It includes, but is not limited to, books, periodicals, compact disks, microfilm and microfiche, musical scores, videocassettes and DVDs, electronic databases, and more.

7. **CITATION :** A standardized note documenting the exact title and author of a specific information source, as well as where and when the source was published.

8. **CLIENT :** A *client* is an application or system that accesses a remote service on another computer system, known as a server.

9. **CLOCKSS :** Using LOCKSS concept across a controlled network of institutions and libraries.

10. **COMPUTER HARDWARE :** computer science the mechanical, magnetic, electronic, and electrical components making up a computer system.

11. **COMPUTER LANGUAGE :** programming language designed for use on a specific class of computers. Each and every operation that your *computer* performs has instructions that someone had to write in a programming *language.*

12. **COMPUTER PROGRAM :** A *computer program* (also a software program, or just a program) is a sequence of instructions written to perform a specified task for a computer

13. **COMPUTER SOFTWARE :** computer science written programs or procedures or rules and associated documentation pertaining to the operation of a computer system. Computer *software*, or just *software*, is the collection of computer programs and related data that

provide the instructions telling a computer what to do.

14. **CREATIVE COMMONS LICENSE :** Provide a flexible range of protection and freedoms for author, artists, and Educations. It includes sharing, use, creation, publishing etc.

15. **DATABASE :** A collection of related electronic records in a standardized format, searchable in a variety of ways, such as title, author, subject, and keyword. Common examples of databases are the library catalog and citation indexes.

16. **Directory :** a *directory* service is the software system that stores, organizes and provides access to information in a *directory*.

17. **DOAJ :** It is the Directory from Lund University Libraries for Open access, Free, Full text, Quality control Scientific & Scholarly Journals covering all subjects and many languages.

18. **DTD :** Document Type Definition tells us what tags and attributes are used to describe content in an SGML, XML or HTML document.

19. **FTP :** uses the file transfer protocol to transfer data from one computer to another.

20. **FULL-TEXT :** An electronic resource that provides the entire text of a single work or article, in addition to the citation and (in most cases) an abstract of each work.

21. **INDEX :** A list of citations to journal articles and/or books arranged by subject, author, or title. Indexes may be in print format, electronic format, or both.

22. **INFOLIBRARIAN :** It is group of professionals working in the area of library and computer fields. Objective behind this project is to give maximum Information to working in library and information science Professionals, Teachers, Students at one place.

23. **INTERNET TOPOLOGY :** Voice over Internet Protocol (VoIP) is a general term for a family of transmission technologies

for delivery of voice communications over IP networks such as the Internet or other packet-switched networks. The phenomenon of using the Internet to make telephone calls, regardless of the device used.

24. **KEYWORD :** A significant word or phrase in the title, subject headings, contents notes, abstract, or text of a record in an online catalog or database which can be used as a search term in a free-text search to retrieve all the records containing it.

25. **KEYWORD SEARCHING :** A significant word or phrase in the title, subject headings, contents notes, abstract, or text of a record in an online catalog or database which can be used as a search term in a free-text search to retrieve all the records contains it.

26. **LAN :** local area network: a local computer network for communication between computers; especially a network connecting computers and word processors

27. **LIBRARY CATALOGUE :** A database that organizes materials our library collects and identifies where these material are located. The University Libraries Catalog is named "Chinook".

28. **LITA :** The Library and Information Technology Association is a coalition of members (roster or LITA leaders) and staff (contact LITA) joining together to carry forward LITA's mission and strategic initiatives through internal governance and wide spread representation.

29. **LOCKSS :** Open source software that converts any personal computer into a digital preservation appliance, creatlng low-cost, persistent, accessible copies of e-journal content as it is published.

30. **MAN :** *A metropolitan area network is a network that interconnects users with computer resources in a geographic area or region larger than*

31. **MICROFORMS :** Documents those are reduced in size and

available in either microfiche or microfilm.

32. **MODEM :** from a combination of MOdulate and DEModulate) electronic equipment consisting of a device used to connect computers by a telephone line.

33. **NODE :** In a network, a *node* is a connection point, either a redistribution point or an end point for data transmissions.

34. **ONLINE CATALOGUE :** An online database containing records of the materials owned by the libraries. The University Libraries Online Catalog is called "Chinook".

35. **Open Conference system :** It is a free Web Publishing tool that create complete web presence for scholarly conference.

36. **Open Harvester System :** It is free Metadata Indexing System Developed by Public Knowledge Project.

37. **Open journal System :** It is a Journal Management and publishing system that has been developed by Public Knowledge Project.

38. **PEER REVIEW :** is a generic term that is used to describe a process of self-regulation by a profession or a process of evaluation involving qualified individuals with the related field. Peer review methods are employed to maintain standards, improve performance, and provide credibility.

39. **PERIODICAL :** A magazine, journal, newsletter, or newspaper produced on a regular basis. This term is sometimes used interchangeably with "serial".

40. **PING :** is a computer network administration utility used to test whether a particular host is reachable across an Internet Protocol (IP) network and to measure the round-trip time for packets sent from the local host to a destination computer, including the local host's own interfaces.

41. **POPULAR ARTICLE :** Serials that target general audiences with popular or current news stories. Authors are not usually scholars in a specific disclpline and do not conduct original research. These articles are not peer reviewed.

42. **Portal :** A *web portal*, also known as a links page, presents information from diverse sources in a unified way. Apart from the standard search engine feature, *Web Portal* software from Web Sphere provides a single access point to Web content and applications, personalized to each user's needs.

43. **Public Knowledge Project :** It is dedicated to improving the scholarly and public quality of research. It operates through a partnership among the faculty of education at the university of Berlin Columbia, The Simon Fraser University library, The School of Education Stanford University and The Canadian center for Studies in publish at Simon Fraser University. The partnership brings together Faculty Members, Librarians and Graduate Students dedicated to exploring whether and how new technologies can be used to improve the professional and public value of scholarly research. It continues to provides the leading Open Source Software for Journals and Conference Management and Publishing. All PKP Softwares are available under GNU Public License.

44. **Query Formulation :** The query formulation module transforms the question into a query, which is eventually fed into the retrieval engine to extract answers. The system uses the entity file to recognize the domain specific entities in the question. During initialization, the system reads from default file (which can be set to a particular set of documents by the user) and constructs a hash table of these entities. Individual words in the question are compared from this table to identify the entities. These keywords are considered most important and are given the maximum weight age of 2. Stop words are given the weight age. Rest of the words in the question is given the weight age.

45. **REFERENCE :** The library department which aids patrons in using the library, helps with research problems, and assists in locating information. Materials such as dictionaries,

encyclopedias, and biography guides are found in reference.

46. **RELEVANCE :** The degree to which a source addresses a research topic (some relevant sources may be more broad or more narrow than the specific research topic.)

47. **RSS :** stands for 'Rich Site Summary' or 'Really Simple Syndication'. See Virginia Montecino's definition of RSS in Introduction to Internet Terminology. A Web site can allow other sites to publish content by creating an RSS document or an RSS feed. A web publisher can post a link to the RSS feed so users can read the distributed content on his/her site. Syndicated content can include news feeds, listings of events, new feeds based on research keywords in a Students and faculty need to keep up-to-date with their area of research. Subject specific Blogs and their RSS feeds make it easier than ever to keep up with the latest news, innovations, articles, and groundbreaking research as it is made available. If an electronic journal or a website, offers an RSS feed, it is easy to capture that feed and receive updates from them.

48. **RUN :** *lists other pages on the Web where you can find additional information.*

49. **SCHOLARLY/PROFESSIONAL JOURNAL :** Journals that present in-depth, original research in a specific field. These articles have been reviewed by other scholars in the field for scholastic standards and validity. Professional journals may also contain profession or industry related news.

50. **SEARCH :** The activity of looking thoroughly in order to find something or someone

51. **SERIALS :** A publication that is issued in parts, indefinitely over time. Serials include journals, periodicals, magazines, almanacs, annual reports, numbered monographs, and other materials. This term is sometimes used interchangeably with "periodical."

52. **SERVER :** In computing, a *server* is any combination of

hardware or software designed to provide services to clients.

53. **SMPT :** Simple Mail Transfer Protocol is an Internet standard for electronic mail (e-mail) transmission across Internet Protocol (IP) networks.

54. **STACKS :** The area of the library where books and bound periodicals are shelved. These are items that can be checked out of the library. The Norlin Stacks are located on floors 3A, 3B, and 3C. The departments and branch libraries have their own stacks.

55. **SUBJECTS HEADINGS :** Terms, names, or phrases that are assigned to a publication (book, journal article, video, etc.) and used to describe the contents of that publication. They form a standardized set of terms that are consistently used to group materials together.

56. **SWITCH :** A network *switch* is a small hardware device that join multiple computers together at a low-level network protocol layer. Network.

57. **TCP/IP :** transmission control protocol/internet protocol: a set of protocols (including TCP) developed for the internet in the 1970s to get data from one network device to another

58. **TDL :** Texas Digital Library's is a multi-university consortium dedicated to providing the digital infrastructure to support a fully online scholarly community for institutions of higher education in Texas.

59. **TELNET :** Teletype Network is a network protocol used on the Internet or local area networks to provide a bidirectional interactive communications facility.

60. **UKLON :** UK Office of Library Networking. It is a research organization that aims to inform practice and influence policy in the areas of: digital libraries, information systems, bibliographic management, and web technologies.

61. **VALIDITY :** The quality of research being used to support the argument being made.

62. **WAN :** a wide area network is a geographically dispersed telecommunications network. The term distinguishes a broader telecommunication it is a wide area network is a large network covering cities, countries and continents. A *WAN* is also called an Internet work.

63. **WEB BROUSER :** a web browser is a software application for retrieving, presenting, and traversing information resources on the World Wide Web.

64. **Web Search Engine :** is designed to search for information on the World Wide Web. The search results are usually presented in a list of results and are commonly called hits. The information may consist of web pages, images, information and other types of files.

65. **Website :** A *website* (also spelled *Web site*; officially styled *website* by the AP Stylebook) is a collection of related *web* pages, images, videos or other digital.